ALSO BY JON KUKLA

*Patrick Henry: Voice of the Revolution*
(2001, with Amy Kukla)

*Speakers and Clerks of the Virginia House of Burgesses,*
*1643–1776* (1981)


EDITOR:

*The Bill of Rights: A Lively Heritage* (1987)

*A Key to Survey Reports and Microfilm of the Virginia Colonial*
*Records Project* (1990, with John T. Kneebone)

*A Guide to the Papers of Pierre Clément Laussat,*
*Napoleon's Prefect for the Colony of Louisiana,*
*and of General Claude Perrin Victor* (1993)

# A Wilderness So Immense

*Will republicans, who glory in their sacred regard to the rights of human nature, purchase an immense wilderness for the purpose of cultivating it with the labor of slaves?*

—The Balance and Columbian Repository, September 20, 1803

*Louisiana is ours! If we rightly improve the heaven sent boon, we may be as great, and as happy a nation, as any on which the sun has ever shone. The establishment of independence, and of our present constitution, are prior, both in time and importance; but with these two exceptions, the acquisition of Louisiana, is the greatest political blessing ever conferred on these states.*

—Dr. David Ramsay, May 12, 1804

*No event in all American history—not the Civil War, nor the Declaration of Independence, nor even the signing of the Constitution—was more important.*

—Bernard DeVoto, March 21, 1953

# A Wilderness So Immense

### THE LOUISIANA PURCHASE AND
### THE DESTINY OF AMERICA

## JON KUKLA

ALFRED A. KNOPF

NEW YORK   2003

THIS IS A BORZOI BOOK
PUBLISHED BY ALFRED A. KNOPF

Portions from "Selling a Ship" and "A Various Gabble of Tongues"
previously appeared in *Life* magazine.

Grateful acknowledgment is made to Paul Halsall for permission
to reprint an excerpt from *Ça Ira* translated by Paul Halsall.
Translation copyright © 1998 by Paul Halsall.
Reprinted by permission of the author.

Library of Congress Cataloging-in-Publication Data
Kukla, Jon, [date]
A wilderness so immense : the Louisiana Purchase and
the destiny of America / Jon Kukla — 1st ed.
p.    cm.
Includes bibliographical references and index.
ISBN 0-375-40812-6
1. Louisiana Purchase.    I. Title.
E333 .K85 2003
973.4'6—dc21        2002027395

Manufactured in the United States of America
First Edition

*For Amy,*
*for Jennifer,*
*and for Elizabeth*

L

*Missouri River*

ROCKY MOUNTAINS

Santa Fe •

*Arkansas Ri*

*Red River*

El Paso del Norte •

Nacogdoc

*Rio Grande*

PACIFIC
OCEAN

MEXICO

*Mississippi Valley
and Environs*

Mexico City •

0     MILES     400

0     KILOMETERS     400

# Contents

*Appendixes*

# A Wilderness So Immense

# Tributaries

*The* Mississippi *will be one of the principal channels of future commerce for the country westward of the Alleghaney. From the mouth of this river to where it receives the Ohio, is 1,000 miles by water, but only 500 by land. . . . The Mississippi, below the mouth of the Missouri, is always muddy. . . .*

*The* Missouri *is, in fact, the principal river, contributing more to the common stream than does the Mississippi, even after its junction with the Illinois. It is remarkably cold, muddy, and rapid. . . .*

*The* Ohio *is the most beautiful river on earth. Its current gentle, waters clear, and bosom smooth and unbroken by rocks and rapids, a single instance only excepted . . . three or four miles below Louisville.*

—Thomas Jefferson, *Notes on the State of Virginia,* 1785[1]

IN THE PINE WOODS of northern Minnesota, about one hundred eighty miles inland from Lake Superior and the port of Duluth, the Mississippi River begins its winding journey of 2,552 miles from Lake Itasca to the Gulf of Mexico. As it flows out of the lake to begin a pilgrimage through the heartland of North America, the shallow brook is about a dozen yards wide. Passing tamarack bogs and the burial mounds of the Anishinabe, the river gains width and depth. Fed by scores of glacial ponds and lakes, the Mississippi tumbles over the Falls of St. Anthony, between Minneapolis and St. Paul. Navigable from there to the Gulf, the mighty river swells with the water of tributary creeks and streams that drain more than a million square miles of farmland and forest. As lesser rivers converge into the larger tributaries that join the Mississippi—the St. Croix River at Point Douglas, Minnesota, the Wisconsin at Prairie du

3

Chien, and the Illinois at Grafton—the Mississippi sprawls to half a mile wide or more to greet its peers, the Missouri at St. Louis and the Ohio at Cairo, Illinois. Born of this trinity, the Mississippi River below Cairo rolls omnipotently across the alluvial land that it deposited after the last ice age.[2]

The power and destiny of the Lower Mississippi is scarcely imaginable along the north shore of Lake Itasca, where picnic tables sheltered by tall pines dwarf the tiny stream. Here, fifty years ago, a tow-headed and dimpled midwestern child splashed from rock to rock across the shallow brook, cheerfully ignorant that he was ankle deep in the first tide of a turbulent force of nature and history. Everything impressive about the Mississippi River lay far downstream in his distant future. In time the child who splashed over stepping-stones at Lake Itasca swam against the lazy summer current at Wyalusing State Park. He heard calls for volunteers to pack sandbags against the angry flood near Prairie du Chien. And he stood on the levee at Jackson Square, far below the tributary streams of his childhood, watching the all-powerful and unforgiving river send enormous oceangoing ships skidding through the treacherous bends at New Orleans. As age, distance, and experience revealed the connections between that tiny crystal brook at Lake Itasca and the mighty muddy flood of the Lower Mississippi, the man who long ago played in the clear waters of the Upper Mississippi came to realize that the story of the Louisiana Purchase had its tributaries, too.

At the end of the American Revolution, the Louisiana Purchase lay hidden far beyond the horizon, twenty years downstream into the future. The background stories that comprise its tributaries were as distant from one another as are the easternmost headwaters of the Ohio River—on the Allegheny near Coudersport, Pennsylvania—from the mountain creek near Dillon, Montana, that eventually becomes the Missouri. Like gravity pulling water through a great river system toward the sea, time brought together the stories from Paris, Madrid, New Orleans, New York, Kentucky, and Haiti that finally converged in the monumental events of 1803.

In 1803 the destiny of North America was formally decided by men who never set foot in the Mississippi Valley, who never walked the narrow streets of the Vieux Carré in New Orleans, and who never laid eyes on the rivers that drain an expanse of field and forest slightly larger than Western Europe. Thomas Jefferson never traveled west of the Shenandoah Valley, Robert R. Livingston never got beyond the Catskills, James Monroe never made it west of Erie, Pennsylvania. Napoleon Bonaparte never visited America, and his ministers knew only the Atlantic Coast. François

Barbé-Marbois once visited the Mohawk Valley from his diplomatic post in New York City during the last years of the American Revolution, and Charles Maurice de Talleyrand-Périgord sat out the Reign of Terror in Philadelphia. The key participants in the diplomatic story of the Louisiana Purchase were statesmen in Europe and America who knew the Ohio and Mississippi Rivers only as lines on a map, and the Missouri River only as a legend at third hand. The territory of Louisiana itself was a wilderness so immense that its boundaries remained indefinite for years.

The destiny of America was decided by women and men who crossed the Appalachians into Kentucky and floated their produce to New Orleans on flatboats and bateaux, but their determination was shaped by statesmen with maps and imagination. None of them studied or dreamt more grandly than Thomas Jefferson. No one knew it at the time—least of all Jefferson himself—but elements of the Louisiana Purchase first began to take shape in his map-strewn study near the Champs-Elysées at the edge of Paris in January 1786.

## CHAPTER ONE

# Piece by Piece

*Our confederacy must be viewed as the nest from which all Amer-*
*ica, North and South is to be peopled. We should take care to*
*not . . . press too soon on the Spaniards. Those countries cannot*
*be in better hands. My fear is that they are too feeble to hold them*
*till our population can be sufficiently advanced to gain it from*
*them peice by peice. The navigation of the Mississippi we must*
*have. This is all we are as yet ready to receive.*

—Thomas Jefferson to Archibald Stuart, January 25, 1786[1]

*Mortar never becomes so hard and adhesive to the bricks in a few*
*months but that it may easily be chipped off.*

—Thomas Jefferson to William Buchanan and James Hay,
January 25, 1786[2]

T HE SKIES OVER Paris were cloudy on Wednesday, January 25,
1786, and the early morning temperature was 42 degrees in the
courtyard of the elegant new mansion, the Hôtel de Langeac, at the corner of the Champs-Elysées and rue de Berri just inside the western wall
of the city. Designed by Jean F. T. Chalgrin, who later built the Arc de
Triomphe, the neoclassical townhouse served from 1785 through 1789 as
the office and residence of the forty-two-year-old United States minister
to the court of Louis XVI, Thomas Jefferson.

A decade earlier, on July 1, 1776, Jefferson had started a lifelong practice of recording the temperature every day when he rose and again at
midafternoon. At first he sometimes checked the temperature four times
a day—as he did in Philadelphia on July 4, 1776, perhaps to test the new
thermometer he had purchased on that historic day for three pounds, fifteen shillings from John Sparhawk. Soon he had established a routine:
"My method," he explained,

6

*Thomas Jefferson, about 1787. Despondent over the death of his wife, Jef-*
*ferson found refuge in his appointment as American minister to the court*
*of Louis XVI in 1784. Three years later the artist John Trumbull captured*
*Jefferson in a life portrait for his famous* Declaration of Independence.
*This unsigned watercolor is a copy of Trumbull's original. The artist was*
*a frequent visitor at Jefferson's Hôtel de Langeac starting in 1785, when*
*the two men toured the public buildings of Paris as Jefferson was contem-*
*plating the design of a new capitol for Virginia—as well as the future of*
*North America.* (Courtesy Virginia Historical Society, Richmond)

is to make two observations a day, the one as early as possible in the
morning, the other from 3. to 4. aclock, because I have found 4.
aclock the hottest and day light the coldest point of the 24. hours. I
state them in an ivory pocket book . . . and copy them out once a
week.[3]

Jefferson cluttered his pockets with gadgets. The ivory notebooks in
which he recorded meteorological data looked like small fans—their

pages were wafers the size of business cards joined at one end by a brass rivet. Jefferson jotted his daily notes in pencil on the ivory, and after copying the information into the leather-bound memorandum book at his desk, he wiped the ivory clean for the week ahead.

Eighteenth-century thermometers were large, and Jefferson bought at least twenty of them during his lifetime—along with nearly every other scientific gizmo that caught his eye in Paris or London. He recorded the temperature every morning, with rare exceptions, from the dawn of American independence until shortly before his death at Monticello on July 4, 1826. In the afternoon, other activities occasionally interrupted his daily routine. Nevertheless, over the course of fifty years Thomas Jefferson recorded the morning temperature virtually every day between 5:30 and 8:00 a.m. and the midafternoon temperature, on average, about six days out of seven. He would have loved the Weather Channel.

While in Paris, Jefferson also acquired two kinds of hygrometers to measure relative humidity. Their appeal was irresistible, but if he had felt any hesitation about buying these instruments, the perfect excuse was at hand. He needed them to refute a theory advanced by his new acquaintance, the great French naturalist George-Louis Leclerc de Buffon.

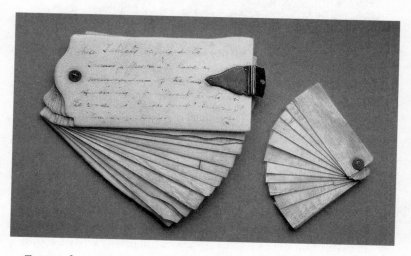

*Twice a day, at dawn and again at midafternoon, Thomas Jefferson recorded the temperature and weather conditions on ivory pocket notebooks. Each week for half a century, from July 1, 1776, to within months of his death on Independence Day 1826, Jefferson transcribed the accumulated meteorological data into a leather-bound folio volume, wiped his pencil notes from the ivory wafers, and started anew.* (Courtesy Monticello—The Thomas Jefferson Memorial Foundation Inc.)

America, the naturalist contended, was more humid than Europe. Moreover, Buffon maintained that high humidity contributed to a universal
degeneracy that he ascribed to *all* the plants, animals, and people of the
New World. Jefferson knew better. Paris itself was damp, and Jefferson
had felt its ill effects for months after his arrival. But the question was a
scientific one, and the patriotic spokesman for the Western Hemisphere
needed proof. The new hygrometers were weapons in Jefferson's battle
against Buffon's theory.[4]

At 42 degrees, the courtyard at Langeac was chilly. On a warmer
morning, after recording the temperature Jefferson might have wandered the curving paths of the garden, planted in the fashionable and
informal "English" style, in Romantic contrast to the classical symmetry
of the great French gardens such as Versailles. In the "hot house" at the
far corner of the property, he might have inquired about seeds or
seedlings imported from America and entrusted to the care of his gar-
dener, a Frenchman whose identity has been lost to history. Or, crossing
the courtyard to the porter's lodge, Jefferson might have said *bonjour!* to
his coachman, Anselen, and glanced into the stables, carriage house, and
harness room.[5]

Save for the papers in his office, nothing in the mansion demanded
Jefferson's attention that morning. His twenty-six-year-old secretary and
protégé, William Short, had rooms at Langeac, but Short and his manser-
vant, Boullié, were away. The kitchen had been without a scullery maid
since December, but the Monticello slave James Hemings, who had
come to France with Jefferson and his eldest daughter, Martha, was in
the kitchen with his culinary mentor, a female chef whose name we do
not know. Hemings had come to Paris for the express purpose of learning
to cook, and Jefferson, who was almost a vegetarian, attached unusual
significance to his gastronomical training. Abigail Adams, wife of his
diplomatic counterpart at the Court of St. James's in London, gleefully
recounted Jefferson's opinion of meat-eating Englishmen to her sister.
"Says he," Abigail reported,

> it must be the quantity of Animal food eaten by the English which
> renders their Character unsusceptible of civilisation. I suspect that it
> is in their kitchens and not in their Churches, that their reformation
> must be worked.

Parisian chefs, Jefferson felt certain, could do more good for the English
than missionaries "endeavor[ing] to tame them by precepts of religion or
philosophy."[6]

Marc, the butler in the main house, had responsibility for five large rooms on the first floor as well as Jefferson's office suite, three main bedrooms, and secondary rooms upstairs. His stewardship was assisted by Sanson, a *valet de chambre* filling in for Adrienne Petit, and the *frotteur* Saget. Painted floors were the fashion of the day, and they required constant attention. Before John and Abigail Adams left Paris for London, Abigail had watched in amazement as her floors had been painted first with pigment and glue and "afterward with melted wax, and then rubbed with a hard Brush; upon which a Man sets his foot and with his Arms a kimbow strip[p]ed to his Shirt, goes driving round your room. This Man is called a Frotteurer, and is a Servant kept on purpose for the Business."[7]

While Saget skated around the Hôtel de Langeac on footbrushes and five or six French employees and James Hemings looked after the house and garden, the labor of the consulate fell entirely to Jefferson himself. Although Jefferson had invited Short to Paris as his personal secretary, Short often traveled on diplomatic business or stayed at the small house in the village of Saint Germain where he had perfected his French. The charming young Virginia bachelor, who now spoke fluent French and moved gracefully in polite society, had become more useful to the nation as an apprentice diplomat than as Jefferson's clerk. And if truth be told, Jefferson really preferred the immediacy, intimacy, and confidentiality of his own pen, even if, when he broke his wrist later that year, it meant learning to scrawl with the quill in his left hand.[8]

In the months since his arrival to succeed Benjamin Franklin as minister to France, the charms of Paris had not yet enthralled the Virginian. He found the climate cold and damp—at least at first. Injury makes us vulnerable, we feel the cold more intensely, and Jefferson had come to Paris profoundly wounded by personal tragedy and the ingratitude of political life. In truth, Thomas Jefferson had fled to Paris and found refuge there in his study and his work.

A chilly morning was no time to dawdle out of doors, and on this particular Wednesday there was much to be done. At long last, Jefferson's final architectural drawings for the new Capitol of Virginia were ready for shipment to Richmond, and a reliable courier was leaving for America the next day. Ezra Bates could be entrusted with all the correspondence that Thomas Jefferson's one-man office could prepare for his Thursday departure. Then the minister could relax with his thirteen-year-old daughter, Martha, a student in residence at the Abbaye Royale de Panthémont, a convent school favored by English families. Panthémont was regarded as the most genteel school in Paris, and Patsy, as she was known to her father—she was "Jeffy" to her schoolmates—had been admitted on the recommendation of a friend of the marquis de Lafayette. She spent Thursdays and Sundays with her father, and they indulged a shared passion for music by playing together on the violin and harpsichord.[9]

Patsy's visits were the bright moments of Jefferson's early years in Paris. As governor of Virginia near the end of the American Revolution, Jefferson and his government had been embarrassed when British cavalry led by Benedict Arnold and Banistre Tarleton raided Richmond, Charlottesville, and Monticello. Like chess players quickly moving their pieces to avoid capture or checkmate, Governor Jefferson had scrambled south to his Bedford County retreat, Poplar Forest, while his councillors and the legislature had scurried over the Blue Ridge Mountains to Staunton. When the danger was long gone—after the American army and French navy engineered the siege and surrender of Cornwallis at Yorktown—a legislative inquiry formally exonerated Jefferson of any hint of misconduct during the emergency. But the inquiry itself still rankled him.

Tall and lanky, Jefferson had the fair and sometimes freckled complexion of a redheaded Englishman. After retiring from the presidency in 1809 he cultivated an air of philosophic serenity, high above the rough and tumble of politics, but as a younger man Governor Jefferson was thin-skinned and easily stung by criticism. By the 1780s he had devoted a dozen years to public service, and the legislative inquest seemed an ungrateful insult. Enough was enough. On the day the legislature of Virginia unanimously voted its gratitude for "his impartial, upright, and attentive administration whilst in office"—on the day the senators and representatives of the Old Dominion voiced their "high opinion . . . of Mr. Jefferson's ability, rectitude, and integrity, as Chief Magistrate of this Commonwealth"—on that very day Jefferson declined election as a delegate to Congress.[10]

"I am fond of quiet," Jefferson confided later to his friend Abigail Adams, "willing to do my duty, but irritable by slander and apt to be forced by it to abandon my post." He was more specific in a letter to James Monroe. "I might have comforted myself under the disapprobation of the well-meaning but uninformed people," he wrote,

> yet that of their representatives was a shock. . . . And I felt that these
> injuries, for such they have been since acknowledged, had inflicted a
> wound on my spirit which will only be cured by the all-healing grave.

Bruised by the public indignities of politics, Jefferson set aside his bitterness to tell Abigail that "Mrs. Jefferson has added another daughter to our family," but "has been ever since and still continues very dangerously ill."[11]

Martha Wayles Jefferson languished in her bed after the birth of Lucy Elizabeth. Jefferson nursed her through the summer, "never out of Calling. When not at her bed side he was writing in a small room at the head of her bed." Ten months after the legislature's clumsy effort "to obviate and remove all unmerited censure" about his actions during Tarleton's raid, private grief compounded Jefferson's public embarrassment.[12]

When Martha Wayles Jefferson died on September 6, 1782, her husband "was led from the room almost in a state of insensibility . . . into his library where he fainted and remained so long insensible that they feared he never would revive." He kept to his room for three weeks, pacing the floor night and day, ignoring the beauty of Monticello in early autumn, as buttery maple leaves floated above the morning fog or gleamed in the afternoon sun.[13]

The legislature convened in Richmond, and his friends dispatched one of their number to Monticello. Jefferson was "inconsolable," cloistered away on his mountain, stricken with a grief "so violent as to justify the circulating report of his swooning away whenever he sees his children."[14]

Outside, on the hills around Monticello in the middle of October, tawny oak leaves diffuse the midday sun until it drifts to the ground without casting a shadow, and the horizontal rays of the setting sun silhouette the trees and light up the ruby foliage of dogwoods and sumac like candlelight through a glass of vintage claret. The beauty of autumn in Virginia escaped his notice. "When at last he left his room," Jefferson "was incessantly on horseback rambling about the mountain."[15]

As the trees went bare, their bony fingers warned of the approaching winter, a landscape suitably bleak for his "melancholy rambles." Young Martha was "a solitary witness to many a violent burst of grief"—until the 25th of October, when a courier arrived at Monticello with a letter from Philadelphia. Congress wanted to send Jefferson to Paris as a peace commissioner to help negotiate the treaty that would end the American Revolution. Perhaps, his friends hoped, the appointment might lure him back into public life and assuage his private grief.[16]

Their ploy worked. Under the cover of duty, he could flee to France. After eleven weeks of virtual silence since Martha's death, Jefferson began "emerging from that stupor of mind which had rendered me as dead to the world as was she whose loss occasioned it." When he had left office at the end of his term as governor, Jefferson had told the marquis d'Chastellux that he had "folded [him]self in the arms of retirement, and rested all prospects of future happiness on domestic and literary objects"—including the composition of his *Notes on the State of Virginia*—but

> a single event wiped away all my plans and left me a blank which I had not the spirits to fill up. In this state of mind an appointment from Congress found [them] requiring me to cross the Atlantic.[17]

He would escape his grief by traveling to France and immersing himself in work.

Jefferson's morning ritual of jotting the temperature into his ivory notebooks had therapeutic as well as scientific value, for his heart was "a blank" and "dead to the world." The pain of Martha's death was still with him, and of their six children, only two survived. Two daughters had died at five months. A son had lived only seventeen days. Most recently, word had come from Virginia to Paris that whooping cough, "most horrible of all disorders," had claimed his two-and-a-half-year-old daughter, Lucy Elizabeth. Jefferson had left Lucy and her sister Mary in the care of his relatives, Elizabeth and Francis Eppes, at Eppington, in Chesterfield County. Arrangements were soon under way to retrieve Mary from the plantation south of Richmond and reunite her in Paris with her father and only surviving sister—a feat that took nearly two years to accomplish.[18]

Mary Jefferson, later known as Maria, reached London in June 1787 and stayed with John and Abigail Adams, who called her Polly. Her companion crossing the Atlantic was not the mature slave woman Isabel, whom Jefferson had requested, but James Hemings's fourteen-year-old sister. "The old Nurse whom you expected," Abigail wrote announcing Polly's safe arrival in London, "was sick and unable to come. She has a Girl about 15 or 16 with her, the Sister of the Servant you have with you."[19]

Their own children were in their teens and twenties, and the Adamses welcomed Jefferson's nine-year-old Polly "and the maid" into their not-quite-empty nest. Abigail did all "such things as I should have done had they been my own." Polly had been "5 weeks at sea, and with men only, so that on the first day of her arrival, she was as rough as a little sailor," but the next day Abigail took her shopping "and purchased her a few articles which she could not well do without"—spending about £12 on clothing for Polly and "the maid." In a few days Polly was "the favorite of every creature in the House"—"She stands by me while I write and asks if I write every day to her pappa?"[20]

Jefferson immediately dispatched Adrienne Petit across the Channel to fetch Polly. He was profoundly grateful for Abigail's "kind attention to my little daughter," and yet fearful (as fathers at heart-wrenching distance often are) that good intentions might be misunderstood. Having "formed an attachment to you," he lamented to Abigail, "she will think I am made only to tear her from her affections. I wish I could have come myself." For her part, having come to know Jefferson's "amiable lovely Child" and "dear little Girl," Abigail Adams could not "but feel Sir, how many pleasures you must lose by committing her to a convent. Yet situated as you are, you cannot keep her with you."[21]

At first glance, Sally Hemings struck Abigail Adams as older than her years: "about 15 or 16." Abigail never mentioned Sally's name in her letters to Jefferson (and John Adams did not mention either of the girls in his correspondence), but that did not matter. There was something that only folks from Monticello knew about "the girl," or "the maid," and her brother. James and Sally Hemings were family.[22]

Jefferson's father-in-law, John Wayles, had outlived three wives and then openly settled his affections on his mulatto slave Elizabeth Hemings. They had six children together. Sally was the youngest, born in 1773, the same year that Wayles's death brought Elizabeth Hemings and her family to Monticello. Sally Hemings was Patsy and Polly Jefferson's aunt. Her brother James, busy mastering French cuisine at the Hôtel de Langeac, was their uncle. Now fourteen but easily mistaken for sixteen, the fair-complected Sally Hemings was said to resemble her half-sister Martha Wayles, the girl Jefferson had married when she was twenty-three and for whom he still grieved. Once Polly Jefferson came to Paris and joined her sister Patsy at the convent school of the Abbaye Royale de Panthémont in 1787, perhaps the only employee lacking in the Jefferson household was a chaperone—although it seems likely that Jefferson's sexual relationship with Sally Hemings began only after they returned to Virginia.

Folding the ivory notebook and slipping it into a pocket, Jefferson carried his thermometer across the burnished floors of the Hôtel de Langeac and retired upstairs to his study. His penknife and goose quill rested near the inkwell and a stack of rag paper. A sheaf of maps were on hand, as were the neatly packaged final architectural drawings of his design for the new Capitol of Virginia. The comfort of busyness awaited him.

First, Jefferson dashed off a confidential note to John Jay, the New York jurist and former diplomat to Paris and Madrid. As secretary for foreign affairs, Jay was the chief diplomatic officer of the United States under the Articles of Confederation, and Jefferson was happy to report that an unnamed "person"—neither of them called him a gentleman—had passed quietly through Paris en route to Warsaw.[23]

The traveler in question was a young Virginia-born soldier of fortune, Lewis Littlepage, who had resided briefly with Jay's family in Paris, forged Jay's signature on bills of credit totaling more than £1,000, challenged Jay to a duel, and, most recently, filled the columns of a New York newspaper with malicious falsehoods before sailing to Europe. Jay had answered the charges in a forthright pamphlet, and the contretemps evaporated as a mere waste of time unworthy of any further notice, then or now, unless for some reason, as some whispered in New York, Littlepage's venture into journalism had been abetted by French officials there. That irksome prospect was dispelled by Jefferson's report that the young scoundrel had passed through Paris entirely unheralded and ridden on toward well-deserved oblivion as a chamberlain to the last king of Poland.

The next item on Jefferson's Wednesday agenda was a short letter to John Banister, a trusted source for transatlantic commercial advice. The Virginia businessman had studied law at the Middle Temple in London, served as a lieutenant colonel of cavalry under Washington during the Yorktown campaign, and helped enact both Virginia's state constitution and the Articles of Confederation. Battersea, his Palladian home near Petersburg, overlooked the Appomattox River and its bateaux carrying tobacco, iron, and other commodities from the Piedmont to the James River and the world beyond. This time Jefferson asked Banister for the eighteenth-century equivalent of a Dun and Bradstreet report about the credit and reputation of a firm doing business in France and America. The letter closed with greetings to Anne Banister and a quick report that Jefferson had seen their son John in good health prior to the boy's departure for Italy and the grand tour.

Jefferson's third letter of the day went to the Philadelphia astronomer, inventor, and mathematician David Rittenhouse along with a copy of the French edition of *Notes on the State of Virginia* (the only book Jefferson ever wrote) and nautical almanacs for 1786 through 1790, "which are as late as they are published." Jefferson was grateful for details of frontier geography that Rittenhouse had sent in September—in a letter that journeyed for four months to Paris and had reached him only "a few days ago"—but the future president of the United States pressed him for facts about "the Western boundary beyond the Meridian of Pittsburgh." Jefferson told Rittenhouse merely that he needed this information "to enable me to trace that boundary in my map." He was more expansive, however, with his thoughts on fossils, shells, and other "curiosities of the Western country" that he had written about in *Notes on the State of Virginia*. He knew that Rittenhouse, the self-taught Quaker genius who designed and built sophisticated instruments for the American Philosophical Society and taught at the University of Pennsylvania, would share his curiosity about a new reflecting telescope developed by the Abbé Rochon using "the metal called Platina," which could be polished to a mirror finish as fine as gold or silver with less chance of tarnishing.

Finally, having attended to the immediate demands of diplomacy, business, and science, Jefferson's thoughts turned to Virginia and a letter that his young protégé Archibald Stuart had posted toward Paris in October. "Nothing is so grateful to me at this distance as details both great and small of what is passing in my own country," he told Stuart. A graduate of William and Mary, member of Phi Beta Kappa, and veteran of the Carolina and Yorktown campaigns of the American Revolution, Stuart had declined the chair in mathematics at his alma mater to read law with Jefferson. With clients throughout the Valley of Virginia, at twenty-five he had won election to the lower house of the Virginia legislature from Botetourt County, across the Blue Ridge some eighty miles southwest of Jefferson's Monticello. While Jefferson was writing to him from Paris, Stuart was attending the legislature in Richmond, where thirty-four-year-old James Madison was engineering the passage of Jefferson's Statute for Religious Freedom—one of the three achievements the author of the Declaration of Independence and founder of the University of Virginia would choose to inscribe on his gravestone.

About three o'clock, Jefferson took his thermometer outside and noted that the skies had cleared and the temperature risen to 51 degrees—but there was no FedEx truck idling at the curb, Ezra Bates was not leaving until tomorrow, and in January 1786 humanity had not yet substituted data for thought and surrendered to the technology of instantaneous miscommunication. Archibald Stuart's news "of what is passing in my own country" had drawn Thomas Jefferson into profound contemplation.

"The quiet of Europe at this moment," Jefferson told Stuart, "furnishes little which can attract your notice, nor will that quiet be soon disturbed, at least for the current year." The current peace in Europe "perhaps . . . hangs on the life of the King of Prussia," the American minister informed his young friend, "and that hangs by a very slender thread." Jefferson was not the only statesmen alert for news from Potsdam, just outside Berlin, where Frederick the Great had retired to spend his last months in the company of his dogs and library at Sans Souci palace. Several times since 1700, the death of a European monarch had brought war as rivals scrambled for territory or advantage. Frederick himself, in the first year of his reign, had attacked Austria on such an occasion, and Jefferson presumed that his death (which finally occurred in August 1786 at the age of seventy-four) might force another violent realignment among the great powers. Europe's other enlightened despots—Catherine the Great in Moscow, Joseph II in Vienna, Gustav III in Stockholm, and Carlos III in Madrid—as well as the constitutional monarch George III in London and the relative royal newcomer, Louis XVI at Versailles, were equally alert for news.

Among these liberal autocrats and philosophe kings, none was more able or eminent (or was now more elderly) than the king who came to the throne of Prussia three years before Jefferson was born. Frederick the Great had transformed Prussia into a world power by his military genius, administrative talent, and political skill. Renowned as a patron of the arts, music, and education, a talented flautist and prolific writer, a longtime friend of Voltaire and an admirer of George Washington, Frederick II had opened his reign in 1740 with the publication of his *Antimachiavell* (in which he denounced statecraft in favor of peaceful and enlightened rule) and the invasion of Austria. By the end of the Seven Years' War in 1763, Frederick's victorious armies in Europe (along with Britain's great navy and its redcoats in North America) had entirely redrawn political boundaries on both sides of the North Atlantic. France had been forced to surrender Canada to England and Louisiana to Spain, while Prussia began to challenge the Austrian Habsburgs for domination of the German states on the Continent.

Thousands of miles from home, surveying the geopolitical prospects of Europe and the Americas in his remarkable letter to Archibald Stuart, Jefferson's gaze quickly focused on Madrid, where Carlos III, king of Spain since 1759, was seventy years old. The realpolitik of Frederick the Great was important for the future peace of Europe, but it was Carlos III who controlled New Orleans and the vast watershed of the Mississippi.

Carlos III's dominions sprawled from the Caribbean past California to the Philippines, north beyond the Missouri River, and south to the tip of Chile. On the map, the empire founded by his predecessors, the Castilian sponsors of Christopher Columbus, had never been larger. All of Mexico, Central America, and South America except the Guianas and Brazil answered to Spain. Of the major Caribbean islands, Spain held Cuba, Puerto Rico, Santo Domingo, and Trinidad. Of the territory that now

*Spanish North America in 1794. Adapted from a plate in Robert Laurie and James Whittle's* Imperial Sheet Atlas *(London, 1799), this map reflects Spain's territorial ambitions on the eve of the Louisiana Purchase. Carlos III and his ministers regarded Louisiana as a borderland defensive buffer zone to keep foreigners away from the lucrative mines of Mexico, which produced half the annual revenue of the entire Spanish empire. An annual subsidy for the support of Louisiana was part of the operating budget of the province of New Spain, or Mexico.* (Courtesy Taqueria Corona, Magazine Street, New Orleans)

comprises the United States, Spain ruled Florida, southern Alabama and Mississippi, and almost everything west of the Mississippi River and south of Canada.

The Spanish empire was impressive on the map, but by the late eighteenth century it was less solid on the ground or when viewed from the royal treasury. In the two centuries since the loss of the great armada of

1588, Britain, France, and even the Netherlands had challenged Spain on the high seas, while France, Austria, and Prussia rivaled her influence on the Continent—but wounded beasts and ailing empires can be more dangerous than healthy ones.

Jefferson was less worried about Spain's claws than her infirmities. Spain's weakening grip on her colonies in North America excited international intrigue and frontier plots in the trans-Appalachian west, as well as commercial rivalries among the thirteen loosely confederated states whose gentle coalition he represented at the court of Versailles. Jefferson was confident that the United States, not Spain, was destined to be "the nest from which all America, North and South is to be peopled," and to that end he advised Archibald Stuart that American frontiersmen

> should take care to not . . . press too soon on the Spaniards. Those countries cannot be in better hands. My fear is that they are too feeble to hold them till our population can be sufficiently advanced to gain it from them peice by peice. The navigation of the Mississippi we must have. This is all we are as yet ready to receive.

Jefferson feared that Spain's weakness in the Mississippi Valley encouraged British expansion from Canada and tempted the French to reenter the continent from the Caribbean—and these fears had substance. The British still held forts around the Great Lakes that they had agreed to surrender after the American Revolution, and British fur traders and merchants plied the rivers of North America with little regard for boundary lines in the forest. And there were Frenchmen who dreamt of regaining Louisiana, and who kept that dream alive in confidential memoranda to Louis XVI and his ministers.

As was often the case for the savvy Virginian, while he did not want American frontiersmen pressing "too soon on the Spaniards," he did not want foreign adventurers pressing on them at all. The United States in 1786 lacked the political, financial, or military capacity for decisive action in the vast interior of the huge continent, and the news from Stuart and others made it clear that the Atlantic states had troubles brewing in the backcountry. Anger was building in western Massachusetts. Hard times, high taxes, and foreclosures for debt would soon ignite an agrarian revolt led by Captain Daniel Shays, a veteran of the Revolution. If Shays's Rebellion put frontier farmers and coastal merchants at each other's throats over east-west differences within a single New England state, what might happen further south where the Appalachian Mountains posed a more formidable obstacle to trade and communication? Where the navigable rivers drained west down the Ohio to the Mississippi? Sectional self-interest, compounded by the ever-increasing distances that separated frontier communities from their eastern capitals, posed a serious threat to the union. "The navigation of the Mississippi we must have," Jefferson said. The survival, independence, and character of the nation depended on it. As Major Isaac B. Dunn, a Revolutionary War veteran from Pennsylvania, wrote from his new mercantile office in New Orleans, "when you have seen the situation of the people, added to the prodegious emigrations pushing to the western side of the Ohio from the eastern part of this continent—you will conclude . . . that nature Designed New Orleans to be the Mart of this country—and this country to be the richest in the World—the Period cannot be very distant."[24]

Jefferson had read Stuart's report that "a separation Betwixt the eastern and western parts of this state will be Proposed in this Assembly" with neither alarm nor surprise. Like most Virginians, he favored eventual statehood for Kentucky, whose residents had carried the Old Dominion's economy and culture far inland from the seat of government at Richmond. The greater danger arose from the divergent "Interests of that country and the Atlantick States," which were, at the moment, working against Kentucky statehood. The danger was not statehood *within* the union, but the specter of western independence and disunion. Stuart knew there was talk in the west of establishing a separate republic "Independent of the Atlantick States"—especially among settlers in the Ohio River Valley who saw their interests stymied in Congress and who worried (not without reason) that the maritime states of New England "are interested in locking up the Mississippi." Stuart had heard Kentucky leaders boast that while Spain's navy "could chastise the Atlantick States with a few vessels," even their "Best appointed Army . . . could never reach the falls of Ohio."[25]

An experienced revolutionary, Jefferson had witnessed plenty of conspiracy and intrigue, and these sentiments alarmed him. "I fear from an expression in your letter," he replied, "that the people of Kentucké think of separating not only from Virginia (in which they are right) but also from the confederacy." That, he believed, would be "a most calamitous event, and such an one as every good citizen on both sides [of the mountains] should set himself against." Jefferson's lifelong commitment to the American union was rooted in his confidence that the expanding republic would eventually look pretty much like rural Virginia. History would run its inscrutable course, Americans would inevitably force Spain to surrender her provinces "peice by peice," and in the meantime Jefferson would quietly do everything in his power to make sure of it. His vision of the future was clear—though not until 1803 with the purchase of Louisiana would he be able at last to safeguard the nation's economic and political future.

On Thursday morning the skies were cloudy again, and the temperature in Paris was 47 degrees as Jefferson prepared to entrust Ezra Bates with his letters to Jay, Banister, Rittenhouse, and Stuart. In addition, draftsmen from the studio of the French architect and antiquarian Charles-Louis Clérisseau had finished the final measured drawings of Jefferson's design for the new capitol of Virginia. Ezra Bates could deliver them as well, along with Jefferson's detailed letter to William Buchanan and James Hay, the supervising directors of the public buildings appointed by the legislature to move the state government from Williamsburg to Richmond in 1780 and arrange for government buildings there.

Even-tempered gentlemen of the Enlightenment were dubious about enthusiasm of any kind, but Thomas Jefferson was a self-described enthusiast about good design. "Architecture is my delight," he told visitors to Monticello, his residential work-in-progress where perpetual renovation was among his "favorite amusements." In public architecture, however, as in government generally, Jefferson was far more frugal than in his private experiments at Monticello, where he alone bore the costs of "putting up, and pulling down." Aesthetics aside, Jefferson knew that well-designed buildings ultimately cost less to build, operate, and maintain than inferior ones—and a wise republic seized "every occasion when public buildings are to be erected" as an opportunity to furnish its citizens with worthy "models for their study and imitation."[26]

Like his letter to Stuart, which mingled exalted geopolitical perspective with political realism, Jefferson's letter to Buchanan and Hay addressed both sublime architecture and backroom politics. The proposed design, he explained, was based on a first-century A.D. Roman temple in the south of France, the Maison Carrée at Nîmes, "erected in the time of the Caesars, and . . . allowed without contradiction to be the most perfect and precious remain of antiquity in existence."[27] From the outset, the legislature had given Buchanan, Hay, and the others virtual autonomy over design and construction, and they gratefully deferred to Jefferson on matters of architecture. Funding depended entirely on legislative appropriations for the new capitol, however, and ripples from the sectional politics that troubled Stuart within Virginia suddenly threatened the whole capitol project as well.

In the last legislative session, delegates from a few tidewater counties of eastern Virginia had come within a few votes of suspending the Richmond work altogether in favor of moving the seat of government back to Williamsburg. At the same time, a rival group of western delegates—"a strong party of the upland"—were clamoring to abandon both Williamsburg and Richmond and move the capital further west. The directors recognized a misadventure in the making—neither group was likely to succeed at anything but delay—and were rushing "to get the building so far advanced before the fall as to put an end to such experiments." In March 1785 they had contracted with Edward Voss, of Culpeper, to lay one and a half million bricks on Shockoe Hill, high above the falls of the James River in Richmond. On August 18, 1785—five months before Jefferson consigned his final plans to Ezra Bates—they had the contractor set a cornerstone into place, hopeful that "the foundation of the capitol will silence the enimies of Richmond in the next October session."[28] The ploy worked. Proponents of relocating the capital did fall silent. Build it and they will stay.

As often happens when sound planning falls victim to stupidity or meddling, however, the ploy that helped keep the capital in Richmond had unforeseen consequences. During the 1785 building season, Voss and his masons laid some four hundred thousand bricks in a foundation that measured 148 by 118 feet. On the final plans that Jefferson consigned to Ezra Bates in January 1786, however, the required foundations measured only 131 by 75 feet. As Jefferson told Buchanan and Hay in his cover letter, "the body of this building covers an area but [three] fifths of that which is . . . begun," and the smaller building "of course . . . will take but about one half the bricks."[29]

Jefferson knew all too well from his endless remodeling at Monticello that "mortar never becomes so hard and adhesive to the bricks in a few months but that it may easily be chipped off." Now that the larger foundation had served its political purpose, the necessary changes could readily be made. In addition to the aesthetic and functional superiority of the final design, he argued (with an eye toward shielding the directors from political criticism), "upon the whole the plan now sent will save a great proportion of . . . expence." Working quickly and quietly in the spring of 1786—careful not to draw too much attention to the deception that had preempted efforts to move the capital somewhere else—Voss and his masons pulled down and rebuilt "one side wall and a few partition walls" to the dimensions of Jefferson's final plans. By October "the pedestal Basement and the principal story were finished," and by autumn 1788 the new capitol was in use.[30] Had they waited for the final plans, the whole project might well have been lost. The great American democrat and his friends were perfectly capable of evading opposition and pushing their projects to completion.


Jefferson and his colleagues had grappled successfully with the political challenge of translating their plan for the new capitol of Virginia into reality. They tracked the changing political situation accurately, finessed conflicting interests, built a sound foundation, and saw Jefferson's vision through to completion, brick by brick. Having assessed the situation of Spain and the west in a letter written to Archibald Stuart from Paris on January 25, 1786, Thomas Jefferson would do the same with his vision for the Mississippi River and the territory of Louisiana, "peice by peice" if necessary.

## CHAPTER TWO

# Carlos III and Spanish Louisiana

*To give you a thorough light into the Spanish system . . . I begin
with the very responsible [character] of the Catholic King, who
has good talents, a happy memory, and an uncommon command
of himself on all occasions. . . . [Carlos III] ever prefers carrying a
point by gentle means, and has the patience to repeat exhorta-
tions, rather than exert his authority even in trifles. Yet, with the
greatest air of gentleness, he keeps his ministers and attendants in
the utmost awe. As a branch of the house of Bourbon, the Catholic
King has an affection for France; but as a Spaniard, and as a powerful prince upon a distinct throne he wishes not to have it
thought that his kingdom, during his reign, is directed by French
counsels, as it was in the time of Philip V.*

—The earl of Bristol to William Pitt, August 31, 1761[1]


CARLOS III hunted nearly every afternoon from one o'clock till
dusk, roaming the countryside in pursuit of wolves and foxes that
preyed on his subjects' farms and livestock. He loved the outdoors and
enjoyed the chase as much as the kill. "I believe there are but three days
in the whole year that he spends without going out a-shooting," an English traveler wrote, and "were they to occur often his health would be in
danger." No less an expert in such matters than Casanova thought that his
passion for the hunt relieved decades of celibacy after the death in 1760
of his beloved queen, Maria Amalia of Saxony, a few months after Carlos
III had ascended the throne of Spain. "No storm, heat, or cold can keep
him at home," the English traveler continued, "and when he hears of a
wolf, distance is counted for nothing." Carlos would traverse "half the
kingdom rather than miss an opportunity of firing upon that favourite
game."[2]

For some of the crowned heads of Europe, hunting meant little more
than revelries conducted on the stand of a deer park. Not so for Carlos,

who had tracked predators through the Spanish countryside and told a foreign diplomat that in nearly three decades he had shot 5,323 foxes and 539 wolves. "You see," he added, "my diversion is not useless to my country."[3]

Up before six, he dressed himself without retainers and prayed until 6:40, when his doctors and chamberlain entered the room. A cup of chocolate at eight, then two hours attending to his papers, interrupted only by visits with his younger children. At eleven he spoke with foreign ambassadors, giving precedence to the representatives of Naples and of France. Carlos dined at noon in public, chatted with guests, and then (unless the heat of summer warranted a brief nap) he was off to hunt until dusk. Between sunset and dinner there was time to consult further with his ministers, or perhaps for a game of cards or billiards. He dined alone, and was always in bed by eleven—alone.

The more popular of Francisco Goya's two portraits of Carlos III shows the king in hunting attire about 1787. Rifle in his left hand, gloves in his right, a hunting dog asleep at his feet, he stands outside Madrid, perhaps at San Lorenzo de El Escorial with its wooded hills and the Guadarrama Mountains rising in the distance. An unruly clump of snow-white hair protrudes beneath his black tricorn hat. He wears black breeches and shoes, lace at his neck, a beige vest, a short sword in his belt, and a coat in the soft blue of worn denim. His only overt symbol of royalty is the Bourbon *cordon bleu*—a sash of blue fabric and gold trim worn across the chest from right shoulder to left hip.[4]

After ruling for half a century—two decades as duke of Parma and king of the Two Sicilies and three decades as king of Spain—Carlos had weathered insurrections as near as the cobblestones of Madrid and as far away as the muddy streets of New Orleans and the mountain passes of Peru. He chose and kept able ministers—Squillaci in Naples, Aranda and Floridablanca in Madrid—and, with some notable lapses, he had also learned whenever possible to avoid war.

His domestic policies promoted learning, manufacturing, and crafts: the tanning of fine leathers at Seville and Córdoba, glass at La Granja, porcelain at Buen Retiro, velvets at Avila, clocks, watches, and optical lenses in Madrid. He curtailed church censorship, eased restrictions on the press, welcomed the practical mind of the Enlightenment, suppressed the Inquisition, and expelled the Jesuits. He built public credit with the national Bank of San Carlos, abolished a tax system that had stifled industry, and revived silver production in Mexico and Peru. His reign brought the people of Spain hospitals and free schools, savings banks and philanthropic institutions, asylums and poorhouses. While in Naples and

Carlos III *by Francisco de Goya y Lucientes, about 1787. Painted within two years of the monarch's death in 1788, Goya's portrait of Carlos III depicts the avid hunter whose dynastic empire extended from Italy to the Philippines. A reformer, patron of the arts and sciences, statesman, and devout Catholic, Carlos III presided over the final glory of the Spanish empire—which began its fatal decline during the reign of his indolent son Carlos IV and his queen, Maria Luisa of Parma.* (Prado Museum, Madrid)

for years thereafter, Carlos was the chief patron of the archaeological discoveries at Pompeii and Herculaneum, and he built the national museum to house the artifacts there as well as his mother's accumulation of art, the Farnese collection. He also embellished the Caserta Palace, founded the San Carlo Opera House, and created the palace of Capodimonte with its porcelain and tapestry works outside Naples. In Madrid Carlos III completed the Royal Palace above the ruins of the Alcázar (the place of his birth on January 20, 1716), and expanded the Prado, the Customhouse, and the Puerta de Alcalá. At the main entrance to the city, the man whom historians recognize as "one of the best, greatest, and most patriotic monarchs that Spain has ever known," erected a statue of Cybele, Roman goddess of nature.[5]

The hunter with his gun and his dog also was a monarch who had learned to wear, and uphold, his authority both firmly and gracefully. In 1786, as Goya began his portrait of Carlos III in hunting garb, that authority reached the far corners of the western world. Spain's empire had never been larger, even in the heyday of Philip II—across the Atlantic to California and on to the Philippines, north beyond the Missouri River, and south to the tip of Chile.

For the three decades that he ruled Spain, Carlos's annual calendar was as predictable as his daily schedule. The yearlong pilgrimage through the circuit of royal residences began each January when Carlos III and his court left the Royal Palace in Madrid and traveled six miles north of the city to El Pardo (the residence of his descendants even today) and its hunting park. For Easter, Carlos went twenty-five miles south of Madrid to enjoy the mild spring weather of Aranjuez, now a museum and park, into July. He spent his summers in the mountains at San Ildefonso, forty miles northwest of Madrid and four thousand feet above sea level. October brought Carlos back to the monumental Escorial, twenty miles west of Madrid—Philip II's equivalent of the pyramids, an imposing palace mausoleum, severely built of granite, slate, and sheet lead, with spartan rooms for living royalty and majestic tombs for the dead. Each December, Carlos and his court returned to the Royal Palace in Madrid, where the circuit began anew. For courtiers and ambassadors—not to mention the king's thirteen children and their various spouses and offspring—the schedule was as regular as the seasons.

Still vigorous at seventy-one in Goya's painting, completed in 1787, Carlos III was unusually conscientious about his final imperial responsibility of providing an able successor to rule an empire that nearly encircled the globe. Like Philip II a century earlier, Carlos III quietly lamented that while God had given him many kingdoms, he had denied him a son fully capable of ruling them. Of his thirteen children with Maria Amalia of Saxony, three were long dead. On the eve of his own accession to the throne of Spain in 1759, he had been compelled by "the notorious imbecility" of their eldest child, Felipe, to exclude him from the succession and place their third son, Ferdinand, on the throne of Naples.

The future Carlos IV, their second child, was now the Prince of Asturias, the customary title of the heir apparent (like the Prince of Wales in the house of Windsor). Carlos knew well, however, that their most talented son was not the Prince of Asturias but Gabriel, his fourth and favorite child, whose marriage to Maria Ana of Portugal was a sign of amity between the two kingdoms of the Iberian Peninsula—one traditionally allied with France and the other with England.

As Carlos pondered the situation of his empire and his dynasty, the rules of succession laid down by his father were never quite as immutable as they seemed to those who lived outside their sway. Courtiers and ambassadors who knew both couples—thirty-nine-year-old Carlos, Prince of Asturias, and his lascivious Maria Luisa of Parma, on the one hand, and thirty-five-year-old Gabriel Antonio and his attractive Maria Ana of Portugal, on the other—had no difficulty supposing that, for the good of all, Carlos III might seriously contemplate altering the succession in favor of his fourth and favorite son.

He never got the chance. In the autumn of 1787—while Americans began pondering the merits of a new constitution to govern five million people along the Atlantic Coast of North America, and while James Wilkinson was returning from his first sojourn among the eight thousand residents of New Orleans—smallpox decided which Bourbon prince would rule the ten and a half million people of Spain and thirteen and a half million residents of an empire that stretched three quarters of the way around the globe.[6]

It was mid-November and the court was at El Escorial when Maria Ana of Portugal and her newborn infant died, followed days later by Gabriel Antonio himself. Carlos III was despondent. "With Gabriel gone," he lamented, "I hardly care to live."[7] A monarch's crown is often said to *descend* from father to son. With Gabriel Antonio dead, the crown of Spain would soon plummet from one of the country's greatest monarchs, Carlos III, to his bumbling heir and namesake. Nevertheless, it was time for the court to move again to the Royal Palace that Carlos III had rebuilt over the ruins of the Alcázar, his birthplace in Madrid.

For thirty years the annual pilgrimage of the royal court had never varied. It seemed part of the natural order of things. And as always, regardless of the weather, Carlos III found solace by hunting most every afternoon. "Rain breaks no bones," he had often said, but now perhaps the sorrow in his heart let the chill and damp take hold.[8]

For the first time since his coronation, Carlos III was sick in bed when his chief minister, José Moñino y Redondo, count of Floridablanca, reminded him that December was near and it was time to go to Madrid.

Carlos suggested he might stay longer at El Escorial. Floridablanca objected. "Have no fear, Moñino," Carlos replied, "isn't it obvious that in a few days I'll be taken on a much longer journey from these four walls?"[9]

On December 9, after the ailing king and his court had returned to the city of his birth, a cold omen came when death summoned his confessor and longtime confidant, Father Joaquín Eleta, as though sending him ahead to open the gates at the next royal residence. Carlos remained lucid and composed in his bed—a great monarch to the last. When advisors and family gathered to witness the reading of his will, grief was visible on Floridablanca's face. "Did you think I was going to live forever?" Carlos asked him gently. Priests brought the reliquary of San Isidore to the palace, administered the last rites of the Church, and read a papal blessing. A bishop asked whether he had pardoned his enemies. "Why should I wait for this pass before forgiving them?" Carlos asked. "They were all forgiven the moment after the offense." Finally, five weeks short of his seventy-third birthday, Carlos III died shortly after midnight in the dark morning hours of Sunday, December 14, 1788.[10]

The body of Carlos III lay in state in Madrid through the day. Sunday evening, royal Spanish and Walloon guards, with arms reversed in mourning, marched by torchlight at either side of his coffin some twenty miles to El Escorial, where the bodies of Queen Maria Amalia of Saxony and his favorite son, Gabriel, lay with his Habsburg and Bourbon predecessors. Chanting the *Miserere,* the monks of San Lorenzo greeted the cortege and carried the body to a temporary tomb. While the great penitential psalm echoed through the monastery—"Have mercy on us, O God, in your goodness"—soldiers fired three salvos in salute and bells rang in mourning at the passing of one of Spain's greatest monarchs. Finally, the captain of the guard approached the vault and called out, "Señor, Señor, Señor." Hearing only silence, the officer broke his baton in accordance with custom, and departed.[11]

Soon after the body of Carlos III had been taken to El Escorial, officials in Madrid began sending edicts to all the provinces of the Spanish empire. On Wednesday, December 24, they signed and sealed the dispatches to Louisiana announcing "the death of our King and Lord Carlos III (may he have Heavenly Glory)" and proclaiming the accession "of our August Monarch Carlos IV (whom God may guard)."[12] These proclamations would cross the Atlantic to Havana, the administrative headquarters for the provinces of Cuba, Louisiana, and the Floridas, and then go by royal packet boat to New Orleans.

New Orleans had been built by military engineers at the southwest end
of the French fur-trading empire that had stretched in a great imperial
arc along the waterways of North America from the Gulf of Mexico to the
mouth of the St. Lawrence River. The walled cities of Quebec and New
Orleans—separated by a canoe trip of thirty-two hundred miles—had
been the citadels of New France.

Quebec, the northern fortress, derived its name from an Algonquian
word meaning "where the river narrows." Samuel de Champlain had
founded the city as a fur-trading post on the site of an abandoned Iro-
quois village at the mouth of the St. Lawrence River in 1608—just a year
after Captain John Smith and a hundred other Englishmen had erected
their wooden palisades at Jamestown and a dozen years before any European had set foot on Plymouth Rock.

From Quebec, New France had expanded ever westward in pursuit of
beaver, whose fur was in high demand as the fiber of choice for the man-
ufacture of felt, especially for hats. By midcentury, French Jesuits and
coureurs de bois (literally "runners of the woods") and their Native American allies had pursued beaver, souls, and glory west through the Great
Lakes to the country of Wisconsin and Illinois.

In the spring of 1673, the explorer Louis Jolliet and the missionary
Jacques Marquette, S.J., had paddled up the Fox River from Lake
Michigan to the site of a village known long since as Portage, Wisconsin.
They had lifted their canoes out of the waters of the Fox River, which
drain to the Atlantic, and carried them a mile and a half over a gentle rise
of land to the Wisconsin River, whose waters ultimately flow past New
Orleans to the Gulf. By summer Marquette and Jolliet had descended
the Mississippi as far as the Arkansas River, twenty-nine hundred miles
from Quebec, where they turned back rather than risk "losing the results
of this voyage . . . if we procedded to fling ourselves into the hands of
the Spaniards who, without doubt, would at least have detained us as
captives."[13]

Finally an expedition led by Robert Cavelier de La Salle pushed
south—through "the most beautiful country in the world, prairies, open
woods of mulberry trees, vines, and fruits that we are not acquainted
with"—to the Gulf of Mexico. On April 7, 1682, they reached the Head
of Passes, where the Mississippi splits into three "very fine, wide, and
deep" channels—the Southwest Pass, Pas à l'Outre, and South Pass—
comprising the bird's-foot delta and the mouths of the Mississippi River.
On the mudflats at the edge of North America's immense green wilder-

ness, La Salle and his men raised a wooden column and a cross painted with the heraldry of Bourbon France. They sang the *Te Deum*—"We praise you, O God, and acknowledge you as the Lord. The whole earth worships You, the eternal Father"—and on April 9, 1682, La Salle claimed the interior of the continent for Louis XIV and named it in his honor. By this little ceremony, in the words of historian Francis Parkman, "the vast basin of the Mississippi . . . passed beneath the scepter of the Sultan of Versailles . . . all by virtue of a feeble human voice, inaudible at half a mile."[14]

New Orleans commanded the single most strategic point between the Appalachians and the Rocky Mountains of North America: the isthmus between the Mississippi River and Lake Pontchartrain known in the eighteenth century as the Isle of Orleans. As always, the Europeans had taken their clue from the Native Americans. Here, on the east bank of the river at a tight bend ninety miles above the bird's-foot delta and the Gulf of Mexico, the isthmus was about four to six miles wide. More significant than the distance, however, was the Indian path on the high ground of the Esplanade Ridge that linked the river with the navigable waters of Bayou St. John and Lake Pontchartrain, a shallow brackish lake half the size of Rhode Island.

Two dozen miles to the east, Lake Pontchartrain drains through the straits of the Rigolets into Lake Borgne and the Gulf of Mexico—a trade route protected by barrier islands and favored by French and Spanish mariners in the age of sail. The French built and the Spanish maintained smaller forts near the mouth of the river and along the Gulf Coast, but New Orleans occupied the uniquely strategic place where two navigable waterways from the Gulf to the Upper Mississippi converged. Adjacent to the Esplanade Ridge, the flat alluvial clay sloped gently back from the natural levee at the river. It lacked anything like the heights of Quebec, but the site yielded gracefully to the symmetrical genius of the eighteenth century. When he founded the city in 1718, the lifelong bachelor Jean Baptiste Lemoyne sieur de Bienville and his engineers laid out New Orleans in a rectangular grid: eleven blocks wide at the river, six blocks deep, giving pride of location to the church and Place d'Armes (now Jackson Square). The name Vieux Carré, as applied to the French Quarter, literally means "the old square."

Far to the north, the seemingly impregnable fortress of Quebec stood on rocky heights high above the St. Lawrence River—a stubborn landscape that dictated the pattern of its cobblestone streets, stone houses, and granite bastions. French engineers found no similar advantages or constraints at the site of New Orleans. Louisiana had no natural stone or gravel, but its alluvial soil offered them cypress, oak, cottonwood, and hickory in abundance. The French built Quebec of stone. They built New Orleans of earth and wood—and after the fortress city of Quebec fell to British major general James Wolfe in 1759, France quickly transferred ownership of Louisiana and its more vulnerable stick-and-mud capital to Spain.

Great Britain and her Prussian allies had been fighting France for five years in the Americas and three in Europe by 1759, when the death of his brother brought Carlos III home to Spain from the kingdom of Naples. If the balance of power in Europe was to hold, France needed Spain's support. Although the war had not gone well for his cousin Louis XV, the turning point of the Great War for Empire and harbinger of French defeat—Wolfe's capture of Quebec—lay six weeks in the future when Carlos III ascended the Spanish throne on August 10, 1759.

Drawn toward France by his Bourbon ancestry and his Roman Catholic faith, Carlos III still resented his humiliation by a British commander who had threatened to shell his palace in Naples in 1744. Now blood, religion, and revenge added their weight, and in August 1761 Carlos III signed the third Family Compact, secretly allying himself with Louis XV just in time for the fortunes of war to turn against the Bourbon partners. Great Britain not only held on to Gibraltar—a thorn under the Spanish saddle since 1704—but trounced the French in both hemispheres. Quebec fell in September 1759, and Britain soon controlled Canada, the French islands of the Caribbean, and all the territory between the Appalachian Mountains and the Mississippi River. And for good measure, before the fighting ended, the British navy seized the Spanish garrisons at Havana and Manila as well.

Against these grim realities, Carlos III accepted Louisiana from France in 1762. A year later, at the bargaining table in Paris, Spain was able to regain Cuba and the Philippines. Nevertheless, proud New Orleanians have long regarded the transfer of their city from France to Spain as though possession of New Orleans was suitable compensation for the Spanish loss of East and West Florida. Louisiana had been expensive for Louis XV and would cost Carlos III no less, but since he was losing the Spanish fortress at St. Augustine as well as control of the Florida coasts from Savannah to the Pearl River (now the coastal boundary between Louisiana and Mississippi), possession of the western half of the Mississippi watershed was now an important strategic burden. Carlos III demanded Louisiana from Louis XV not because he wanted New

Orleans or even the Mississippi River, and certainly not with any dream of making the indigent colony populous or profitable, but simply because it was in his dynastic and national interest to keep Great Britain's aggressive colonists far away from the silver mines of Mexico. After losing Canada to Britain, France had scant reason to spend money on Louisiana, but whether the colony prospered or not, now more than ever its location as a buffer was strategically important to Spain.

In the eighteenth century, the bulk of the world's silver production had shifted from Peru to Mexico. Silver production at Zacatecas in the province of New Spain, with its capital at Mexico City, had doubled under the Spanish Bourbons, and since the American Revolution it had risen steadily from 21.5 million pesos in 1777 to a high of 27 million pesos in 1804. Mexican bullion comprised half of the entire export trade of the entire Spanish empire. One fifth of all this wealth, the *quinta real,* went immediately to the crown. This income was not only essential to the Spanish economy and government; Mexican silver fueled European trade with Asia as well.[15] Carlos III was well aware of these bottom-line realities. Divorced from Canada, Louisiana had lost its critical importance to France. The colony was no prize to compensate for Spanish losses in the Great War for Empire, but in the aftermath of the destruction of New France, the sparsely populated western watershed of the Mississippi River might still serve as a barrier to keep greedy Americans away from the bullion of Mexico—but only if Carlos accepted the nuisance of owning and defending New Orleans and the unexplored wilderness of Louisiana.

By 1788 there were 5,338 people living within the wooden defenses of New Orleans—earthworks surmounted by a palisade of vertical logs with four raised bastions for cannon at the corners, and a fifth battlement in the middle of the north rampart that faced toward Lake Pontchartrain. Within these walls stood a thousand houses and buildings, most of brick-between-post construction and sheathed in wood or stucco. A few boasted roof tiles or slates but most made do with wooden shingles.

According to the eyewitness whose firsthand account of the great fire of March 21, 1788, appeared in a London newspaper, Vicente José Núñez, the twenty-seven-year-old paymaster of the army, was "a zealous Catholic, who, not satisfied with worshipping God in his usual way, had a chapel or altar, erected in his house." At midday he lit "50 or 60 wax tapers" for Good Friday, "as if his prayers could not ascend to heaven without them." By about one-thirty his votive candles, "being left

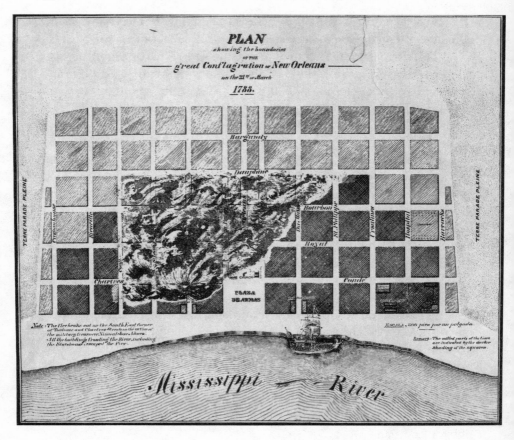

*Fire was a threat to cities everywhere, but New Orleans was particularly unfortunate in the closing years of the eighteenth century. On Good Friday 1788 a great fire consumed 856 of the town's thousand buildings, including the first casa capitular, or Cabildo. No sooner had New Orleans begun to rebuild than a second conflagration on December 8, 1794, destroyed 212 structures. Prominent among the buildings that survived both fires are the Old Ursuline Convent of 1734, on Chartres Street, and the house known as Madame John's Legacy, built about 1726, on Dumaine Street. Along with the Cabildo, completed in 1799, the surviving eighteenth-century structures in the French Quarter of New Orleans exhibit varied mixtures of Spanish, French, and Caribbean architectural influences.* (Courtesy Louisiana State Museum)

neglected at the hour of dinner, set fire to the ceiling, from thence proceeded the destruction of the most regular, well-governed, small city in the western world."[16]

Núñez lived in the heart of New Orleans at 619 Chartres Street, one block upriver from the Place d'Armes and two blocks from the levee. "The south wind was blowing violently," according to another eyewitness, whose account was carried to Vera Cruz on a merchant ship and published in the *Gaceta de Mexico,* and the fire spread with "irresistible fury" from one wooden building to another, from one shingled roof to the next. Flames jumped narrow streets, spreading from the Núñez house in three directions away from the river. "All the prompt and opportune aid and vigilance of the authorities were useless, including the fire apparatus many of which were burnt by the heat of the flames." They moved rapidly down Chartres and across St. Philip Street to engulf the *casa capitular,* or town hall, and the church at the Place d'Armes. Flames consumed tightly built houses along Royal and Bourbon and Dauphine Streets as the fire raced toward the city's northern rampart and the area then known as Place de Nègres and later as Congo Square. The flames blazed steadily upriver, too, destroying houses and businesses as they crossed Toulouse, St. Louis, and Conti Streets. Whenever the fire discovered a cache of gunpowder "which some citizens had cautiously hidden in their houses in violation of government orders and the most strict searches," explosions resounded through the chaos, as though a brigand were daring onlookers to interfere. Residents found it "useless to try to save anything," Governor Esteban Rodríguez Miró reported, "because as soon as they moved things to a place which seemed safe from the flames, the fire would spread there and all would be destroyed."

"In less than five hours," all the eyewitness accounts agree, "eight hundred and fifty-six houses were razed to the ground. Amongst these were all the commercial houses, excepting three." Of the city's thousand structures, scarcely one hundred fifty remained. "The loss of buildings has been estimated at one million and forty thousand pesos," Governor Miró guessed, and "the total loss, which we have grossly considered, will amount to three million pesos."

The human toll was terror and devastation. "If I could only describe with vivid colors what my eyes have seen and my hands touched," Governor Miró wrote in his report to his superiors in Havana,

> it would seem unbelievable. It is a difficult task to decide which has caused the most sorrow, whether the destruction of the city or the pitiful situation of all its inhabitants. Mothers looked for nothing more than a refuge for their children, abandoning the rest of their property to the voracity of the conflagration, running away to the open fields to be mute witnesses of their own misfortune. Fathers and husbands endeavored to save as much as the rapidity of the fire permitted, but as

the fire spread rapidly and there was such confusion, they could hardly find a place of safety for themselves. The darkness of night effaced for a time the picture of horror, but with the dawn the scene appeared more horrible and pitiful, seeing along the road in the most abject misery so many families who, a few hours before, enjoyed large fortunes and more than the average comforts of life. . . . Their tears and sobs, and the ghastliness of their faces told of the ruin of a city which, in less than five hours, had been transformed into an arid and horrible desert—a city which was the product of seventy years of labor.

At first, amazingly, it seemed that no one had died in the great fire of Good Friday 1788. "If . . . there is something capable of mitigating our sorrow," wrote the eyewitness whose letter was published in Mexico, "it is the fact that not a single person perished in the confusion." Governor Miró's report of one fatality was more accurate but still astonishing. "Had this unfortunate event happened in the small hours of the night, it would have caused the loss of many lives," he wrote, "but, thanks to God, the only casualties were some people slightly injured and a sick negress who was killed."

Despite the minimal loss of life or limb, "the dawn of the following day presented the most horrible spectacle. In place of the flourishing city of the day before, one could see nothing more than ruins smoldering and debris."

The official report written by Governor Miró and Intendant Martín Navarro, who was independently responsible to the crown for all the tax revenues of Louisiana, chronicled the destruction of "all the business houses and homes of the principal citizens of the city." Between Chartres Street and the levee, "a few private buildings fronting the river have been saved." Below Dumaine Street the Ursuline Convent, two regimental barracks, the Indian warehouse, and the charity hospital were undamaged. Beyond the walls of the city, a customhouse and tobacco and artillery warehouses were safe along Bayou St. John, where they welcomed ships approaching New Orleans by way of the Rigolets and Lake Pontchartrain. Around the Place d'Armes, however, the *casa capitular,* parish church, presbytere, and Capuchin chapter house were gone—as were the jail, guardhouse, and the arsenal "with all the arms therein contained except for 750 guns." The heart of the city was a wasteland of ash and ruins, and "stupor and silence was the only expression on people's faces, regardless of class and position."

. . .

Governor Miró and Intendant Navarro had witnessed it all. Their offices stood on either side of St. Louis Street, just two blocks upwind of the Núñez house and chapel on Chartres. Their "efforts to save the buildings situated by the river front"—the customhouse, tobacco warehouse, government house, and intendancy—had been largely successful, and they had also rescued the colonial archives and "all His Majesty's money, either in silver or in paper," and "deposited it on the bank of the river." Of the eight thousand residents of New Orleans and its environs, nearly half lived outside the walls of the city, where they now exhibited "the most delicate sentiments of hospitality." Governor Miró distributed biscuits, rice, tents, and small amounts of cash to seven hundred persons whose "extreme want compels them to invoke our aid." He also borrowed 24,000 pesos from the colonial treasury and sent merchant vessels to fetch flour and other commodities from as far away as Philadelphia. The governor and the intendant were proud to report that within twenty-four hours of the disaster, "there was not a person left without shelter," and that "the loss caused to His Majesty by the fire is of slight consideration."

By all accounts, then and since, Esteban Miró and Martín Navarro showed exceptional skill in directing the city's response to the disaster. Eyewitnesses credited their "generous heart and quickness of perception" as deserving of "the greatest applause." Their official report said as much, and for many reasons it may be taken at face value. On the other hand, the Spanish empire was a complex organization replete with all the reports, memoranda, and other paperwork of a mature (some might say antiquated) bureaucracy. Office workers no longer bundle files with crimson ribbons, but the myopic world of red tape is timeless, and Miró and Navarro were, respectively, military and civilian careerists within a huge international bureaucracy.

Had Miró's or Navarro's response to the fire of Good Friday 1788 been inadequate in any respect, posterity would know. Had there been disparaging commentary about Miró or Navarro—in the press, in private letters, or in the gossip of ambassadors and courtiers—word would have reached some eighteenth-century functionary and rival quills would have consigned rumor to paper. Instead, Navarro was honored upon his retirement from New Orleans and welcomed to court at Madrid, and Miró was promoted to brigadier "in testimony of the Royal satisfaction in his zeal."

Notable as well is the fact that two officials, neither subordinate to the other, could act so quickly and harmoniously. Had Miró and Navarro disagreed about what was best for Louisiana or doubted each other's motives, the fire of 1788 would be told as a story of discord as well as disaster. The moment of chaos, when anything can happen, tests a person's wisdom, courage, and morality. Some prove themselves looters—selfishly ready to seize power, spoils, or advantage over a rival. Genuine leaders, on the other hand, build a community response to crisis upon its shared values.

If any ulterior motive can be discerned in Miró's and Navarro's response to the fire, it was a policy objective to which they and others in Louisiana were committed but to which the late Carlos III had been cool: the encouragement of trade and immigration. After chronicling the horrible destruction of New Orleans, the efforts to save lives and property, and the care offered to the hungry and homeless, Miró and Navarro's report anticipated that these measures, "and others that are being taken, using money which has been borrowed from the royal treasury . . . will prevent the total emigration of these [displaced] people by giving them assurance that within a month they will be able to obtain anything they may need." The governor and the intendant also suggested an easing of imperial trade regulations to encourage long-term recovery and prevent the departure of "people who always have bravely battled against hardships and ill fate." None of this was new.

Since the 1760s, Carlos III had valued Louisiana chiefly as a barrier to keep Americans away from the silver mines of New Spain. French ownership of the colony had suited him just fine, but when that was no longer possible, a wilderness inhabited mainly by hostile Native American tribes had sufficed equally well—at least through the end of the American Revolution. In the 1770s Louisiana had witnessed some agricultural experiments with hemp, flax, indigo, and snuff, but Carlos and his ministers were more interested in useful commodities than in making Louisiana self-sufficient. The French crown had thought differently, but it was close to bankruptcy and did not have any silver mines to protect. Within Spanish ministerial circles, Carlos III made no secret of his policies—his accountants tallied the annual costs of administering Louisiana (about 400,000 pesos) as a debit on the books of New Spain. As needed, usually twice a year, the superintendent of the royal mint in Mexico sent a ship full of newly minted pesos to New Orleans via Havana.[17] This subsidy, the *situado*, was regarded as a business expense for the annual convoys that carried tons of Zacatecas silver from Vera Cruz to Cádiz. Late in his reign, Carlos III perhaps sensed a need to reexamine his restrictive policies as Americans ventured into Kentucky and began floating goods down the Ohio—but his death and the subsequent retirement of his chief minister, the count de Floridablanca, prevented the newly created supreme council of state (which might have addressed these issues) from formulating a new and more coherent approach.[18]

From their side of the Atlantic, both Miró and Navarro saw Louisiana's potential for growth and trade. Born in 1738 in Galicia, at the northwest corner of Spain, Navarro was the son of a tavern keeper in the port city of La Coruña, where the invincible Armada found shelter from the weather before sailing toward England in 1588. After ten years' apprenticeship in the treasury office of the poor and densely populated province, he won a promotion of sorts to the new Spanish treasury office in Louisiana. The afternoon of March 5, 1766, was cold and rainy when the twenty-eight-year-old accountant and a handful of civil servants disembarked at New Orleans with the internationally recognized scientist Antonio de Ulloa (a member of the Royal Society of London no less!) and the ninety soldiers with whom he was expected to rule the colony for Spain. Within three years Navarro witnessed the expulsion of the gentle Governor Ulloa by a sullen clique of xenophobic French colonists and the vindication of Spanish rule by General Alexander O'Reilly y McDowell and twenty-one hundred experienced troops in July 1769. Born in Catholic Ireland and drilled in Prussia under Frederick the Great, O'Reilly was a stalwart agent of Carlos III's enlightened despotism. After crushing the rebellion, a thorough investigation identified a dozen ringleaders. He executed five rebel leaders and even they got the final decency of a firing squad, rather than a criminal's death by hanging. Six others went to jail, and O'Reilly offered amnesty to the rank and file in exchange for an oath of allegiance to Spain. The Spanish objective was stability, not revenge. Firmly but fairly, O'Reilly made Louisiana a province of the Spanish empire (and in recognition of his achievement there are drawing rooms in New Orleans where the descendants of those sullen French regard the mention of Alexander O'Reilly's name as unwelcome still).

Six years younger than Navarro, Esteban Rodríguez Miró was a career soldier. Born in Reus, near the ancient Roman seaport of Tarragona on the Mediterranean, Miró had joined the army at sixteen, fought against Portugal in 1762, and risen to the rank of lieutenant during eight years in Mexico. After fighting with O'Reilly in Algiers and a year at the military academy of Avila, Miró arrived in Louisiana in 1778 as a lieutenant colonel. He was second in rank only to the colonial governor, Bernardo de Gálvez, whose talents for administration, diplomacy, and warfare were being challenged by the circumstances of the American Revolution.

*A career soldier and protégé of Bernardo de Gálvez, Esteban Rodríguez Miró governed Louisiana from January 1782 through December 1791— the longest and most effective tenure of the colony's Spanish governors. Returning to Spain as a brigadier general at the age of forty-seven, Miró advised Carlos IV's ministers on colonial affairs in 1792 and 1793. Then, promoted to field marshal and assigned to active duty, he saw action against the French revolutionary armies in the Pyrenees. Miró died at the front, from natural causes, in June 1795.* (Courtesy Library of Virginia)

France and Spain had taken the American side against Great Britain— secretly at first and then openly—and for Louisiana the implications of that alliance were profound.

Miró shared in the glory when Gálvez took Mobile and Pensacola from the British in 1779, and when the crown sent Gálvez to plan a campaign against Jamaica, he appointed Miró acting governor of Louisiana and West Florida in January 1782. During the war, with British seapower a constant threat to Spanish vessels carrying food and supplies to Louisiana, Carlos III eased trade restrictions with the United States as a wartime necessity. Spanish officials in New Orleans not only permitted Americans to bring flour, pork, and other produce down the Mississippi River, they encouraged the American trade, for while the colonists and their slaves produced indigo, lumber, and other commodities for export, they did not raise food sufficient for their needs. Opening the colony to foreign trade was a calculated risk, for it would be difficult to reimpose restrictions when the war ended. And coaxing the genie back into the lamp would be more difficult because, having seen her good works, Governor Miró, Intendant Navarro, and the leading merchants of New Orleans all admired the genie.

Intendant Martín Navarro's treatise, *Political Reflections on the Present Conditions of the Province of Louisiana,* made the case for open trade and population growth. Written late in 1780, after two devastating hurricanes had struck the colony and demoralized its inhabitants, Navarro's treatise blamed Spanish imperial trade restrictions for Louisiana's poverty.[19] Navarro recognized "the indispensable need for forming a barrier to the great and envied continent of Mexico"—the bedrock of Carlos III's North American trade policy since 1762—but he also contended that under "a sovereign whose laws were not opposed to a system of free trade," Louisiana would quickly prove itself "one of the most useful and best established provinces in America." The colony offered "furs, indigo, tobacco, timber, cotton, pitch, tar, rice, maize, and all kinds of vegetables," as well as wheat, barley, hemp, and flax "if they be cultivated with intelligence." Despite its agricultural potential, however, Louisiana's "commerce is poor" because it was conducted "in a manner most harmful and burdensome to the colony as well as to the king." Optimistic about the "advantages that would result from a numerous population and large commerce," Navarro's opinions echoed other critics of mercantilism.

Whether expressed in Spanish, French, English, or Dutch, the free traders' argument was that nations and kings benefited when their colonies thrived, regardless of where the goods went—a viewpoint that Carlos III and his ministers could readily find in Adam Smith's *Inquiry into the Nature and Causes of the Wealth of Nations,* published in 1776. Smith contended that when individuals pursue their own self-interest their actions contribute to the good of all, as if guided by an invisible hand, and that government interference with trade was generally detrimental.[20] Navarro's observations about free trade and laissez-faire economics grew directly out of his experience in Louisiana and his recognition of its strategic importance as a no-man's-land between the United States and Mexico—and for these reasons he had profound influence among Spanish policymakers well into the 1790s.

Reviewing the early economic history of the colony, Navarro blamed both the French and the Spanish for "the decadence of Louisiana." Under the French, royal policies had undermined the currency while local corruption had discouraged credit, "for it was a crime to demand justice for a debt contracted by a member of the council or by any person immediately related to such a member." After the Spanish takeover, trade with France and the French Caribbean was suppressed and Louisiana was forced into a "mercenary trade with Havana," a Spanish port that was unable to supply "articles and things of prime necessity" and where Louisiana products had low market value. "From that time," Navarro concluded,

> the colony experienced the desertion and emigration of various fami-
> lies who went to the French colonies. Property lost three-fourths of its
> value. Houses were not repaired, for the reconstruction cost more
> than the capital investment. The farmer planted no more than he
> could consume . . . preferr[ing] what he might do in another country,
> to the selling for a cheap price of what he had produced in this.

Having described the historic roots of Louisiana's economic decadence, Navarro turned next to the colony's "present state." Martín
Navarro was not Adam Smith, but for a Spanish royal official his arguments were unexpectedly close. Like Smith, Navarro saw the virtue of
"self interest and a bettering of one's fortune." He openly admired the
energy and industry of English and French smugglers "excited by self
interest." Navarro advocated

> a general, free, and common trade with any nation whatsoever . . . by
> permitting the entrance into this river of [ships of] any flag, without
> distinction—the sole and only mode of causing this province to flour-
> ish, populate, and advance.

In this section of his treatise, Navarro referred to "the deity to whom all
the most illustrious nations with just reason present their adoration," but
he was not talking about God. The deity was "commerce"—as he had
seen it practiced by English-speaking interlopers in New Orleans in the
1770s.

New Orleans had been desperate, and "the English were not back-
ward." Smugglers operated with impunity from Natchez and Baton
Rouge on the Mississippi, and from the marshy village at Pass Manchac,
where the Amite River and Lake Maurepas drain into the western end of
Lake Pontchartrain. Between 1770 and 1779 they "established a trade
which was annually worth many millions," and "their audacity c[a]me to
such an extreme that," without permission from Spanish authorities at
New Orleans, "they built a dock on the land in order to facilitate the pas-

sage of the floating warehouses of their vessels"—in short, a place of deposit where cargoes could be transferred from canoes, bateaux, and flatboats to oceangoing vessels.

On one occasion, Navarro recalled, Bernardo de Gálvez attempted to enforce Spanish regulations by confiscating thirteen English vessels in the Mississippi.

> But what happened? From that very moment, the importation of negroes ceased. The colonists ceased to experience that abundance which is produced by the coming of traders, and which alone makes for the happiness and progress of empires.

Navarro admired Bernardo de Gálvez, one of the best governors in the Spanish empire, but in these circumstances even Gálvez "vacillated between extremes, without daring to take other measures than that of conformity—a sad recourse."

Spanish officials had no alternative but to tolerate the contraband trade until Gálvez captured Natchez, Baton Rouge, Manchac, Mobile, and Pensacola in his brilliant campaign of 1779–1780. They stood by, Navarro recalled, "with the pain of not being able to remedy it, although on the other hand, we had the consolation of seeing the inhabitant and the hunter profiting from the fruit of their labors." They knew that Louisiana owed its economic survival "to the illicit trade of the English." Without it, Navarro asked,

> Who was there to furnish these subjects with slaves and tools for the cultivation of their lands? Who would have supplied the things of prime necessity to them? How many ships have come from Spain that would have done it?

"What pain for a watchful governor like Don Bernardo de Gálvez," Navarro wrote. "Although an eyewitness to this forbidden trade," he could not take decisive action without betraying either "the sovereign authority or the happiness of the province." Experiences such as these convinced Navarro of the virtues of free trade, which he advocated in writing and put into personal practice as soon as he could.

In January 1782, Carlos III's ministers wrote new provisional regulations for Louisiana, influenced less by Navarro's study than by a medley of exemptions advanced through the influence of the Gálvez family. On Friday, April 5, 1782, the royal decree was read aloud from the balcony of the *casa capitular.* Artillery units fired a salvo from the Place d'Armes below, answered by a triple salute from decorated ships anchored in the river. The city greeted the new regulations "with such acclamations of joy that there was scarcely time to conclude the meeting with proper formality before attending the High Mass and Te Deum which the King had decreed in gratitude for the success of the Royal Arms over the English." People placed candles in their windows that evening, "indicating how willingly the citizens would have given more appropriate expression to their joy did their circumstances and conditions permit." And finally, French translations were distributed to the citizenry "so that they might know the great benefits His Majesty had bestowed upon them."[21]

The experiment fell short of Navarro's program, but for ten years it opened trade between Louisiana and specified ports in France, opened trade with the French West Indies in case of "urgent necessity," and permitted duty-free importation of slaves. These three provisions took effect in 1783 (with the signing of the treaty that ended the American Revolution) and, together with a special-interest exemption for the export of barrel staves to the sugar islands, they governed Louisiana trade until 1794.

From his long experience enforcing trade regulations, and from the questions asked by puzzled New Orleans merchants, Navarro found many ambiguities in the new rules—who, for example, decided when the colony's necessity was "urgent" enough to permit trade with the French islands? The decree showed signs of haste and the rules lacked the coherence of Navarro's recommendations (so much so that extensive clarifications had to be issued in 1784); nevertheless, they unlocked the door. And in private dealings, the advocate of free trade was not slow to push where the new regulations may have opened doors wider than intended.

Navarro had lived modestly for decades on a salary of 4,000 pesos. Although he never married, he acknowledged his daughter, Adélaïde de Blanco Navarro Demarest, born in 1768, and gave her a dowry of 6,000 pesos for her wedding in 1785. As late as 1781 Navarro had complained that none of his business ventures had ever prospered, but the new regulations included an obscure provision to encourage trade by giving New Orleans merchants two years to buy sailing vessels without paying any duty. Navarro entered a series of partnerships, and between 1782 and 1788 the slave trade, real estate, and money-lending made him one of the richest men in the city.[22]

"A man of talent, active, disinterested, and popular," wrote Governor Miró when he recommended Navarro for appointment as Spanish ambassador to the United States, the intendant was "apt for whatever position [and] possessing ability in the English language." Among the transactions for which records survive, Navarro sold fifteen slaves for 6,400 pesos in 1785, and the next year pocketed 24,455 pesos as his share of the profit on a cargo of slaves imported with Daniel Clark. He invested in rental property in Spain—ten houses, three farms, and two wine shops in partnership with his brother in La Coruña—as well as land and plantations upriver from New Orleans, and rental property on St. Peter Street. He made business loans to a druggist, an indigo planter, and people buying houses or slaves. His largest loan was 14,000 pesos to help a colleague reestablish himself after the fire of 1788. Living elegantly on Royal Street, his own household included his secretary, a housekeeper, apprentices and servants, and a slave trained as a barber and tailor. As he contemplated retiring from the intendancy at fifty, Martín Navarro was worth 3.7 million pesos—living proof that, as he had advised the crown in 1780, "self interest and a bettering of one's fortune overrides all inconveniences."[23]

For all his enthusiasm about free trade, however, Navarro had never lost sight of the strategic importance that Carlos III attached to Louisiana. And despite his lucrative slave-trading partnership with Daniel Clark, an Irish-born, Eton-educated Pennsylvanian who was amassing great wealth as a shipping agent in New Orleans, Navarro regarded Americans as the emerging threat to the Spanish colony. The presence of Americans on the tributaries of the Mississippi, he had warned in 1780,

> gives us motive to reflect very seriously. . . . Although the English posts no longer exist, we must count on new enemies who are regarding our situation and happiness with too great jealousy. The intensity with which [the Americans] are working to form a city and establish posts, and their immediate proximity to our post of the Illinois may be harmful to us some day, unless we shelter ourselves in time by promoting a numerous population in this province in order to observe and even to restrain their intentions. . . . As soon as the population will have reached a respectable number, a barrier to the kingdom of Nueva España [or Mexico] will be fortified and assured. This will be able to oppose any attempt of the Americans already settled on the upper part of the river, and finally may . . . yield a profit in men, reinforcements, and royal duties.[24]

Navarro saw the hard truth that every American who crossed the Appalachian Mountains to settle along the Ohio River and its tributaries weakened the buffer between the Spanish territories and the energetic republican neighbor.

# — CHAPTER THREE —

# Poor Colonel Monroe!

*Poor Col. Monroe! . . . His perfections of person or mind . . . were sum[m]ed up to me this day and amounted to eight which includes every perfection that a female can wish or a man envy. He is a member of Congress, rich, young, sensible, well read, lively, and handsome. I forget the other accomplishment, and will not subscribe to the last unless you prove the dimple on his chin to be what constitutes beauty, and I have a doubt about the sixth unless it is agreed that affording [a] subject for gaiety and liveliness to the company you are in, is the same thing as being gay and lively yourself. . . . At present he is more the object of my diver[s]ion than admiration.*

—Sarah Vaughan, October 10, 1784[1]

THE TWENTY-three-year-old Philadelphia belle Sarah Vaughan only remembered seven of the eight "perfections" that her circle of stylish young women attributed to the tall, shy young Virginian they met aboard a sloop bound for Albany in 1784. Miss Vaughan, whose merchant father helped found the American Philosophical Society, had done her homework. The gossip she was sharing with thirty-three-year-old Kitty Livingston, daughter of the governor of New Jersey, was more accurate than not.[2] James Monroe was a freshman member of Congress, a rising young attorney representing his native Virginia after several years in the state legislature, and on the governor's advisory council. He was not rich, then or later, but at twenty-six he was young and single and had bright prospects.

At seventeen Monroe had abandoned his studies at the College of William and Mary and volunteered for service in the American Revolution. The faculty's dull lectures bore no comparison to the revolutionary ideals voiced in debate near the other end of Duke of Gloucester Street at the Capitol and at Raleigh Tavern. Heading north from Williamsburg

*46*

as a subaltern in the Third Virginia Regiment, Monroe tasted the joy of victory in a skirmish on Manhattan Island in 1775 and again in the surprise attack at Trenton for which Washington's army crossed the Delaware River late on Christmas Day 1776. Wounded in a brave assault against a Hessian artillery position, Monroe nearly bled to death from a severed artery in his shoulder. Promoted to captain and returned to duty after months of convalescence, he soon achieved the rank of major on the staff of Washington's brigade commander William Alexander, known as Lord Stirling in honor of his claim to a Scottish earldom—a title recognized as legitimate by the English law courts but denied to the American-born "Lord" by the House of Lords.

Basking Ridge, Lord Stirling's country house near Elizabeth, New Jersey, offered a gathering place where his aides mingled with fellow officers and polite society. Stirling's wife, Sarah, was a Livingston and her brother William was the governor of New Jersey. The Stirlings and the Livingstons, and their friends and guests, added social distinction to the wartime experiences that widened Monroe's vision of the new nation while shaping his impressions of other American states and their rising leaders. Major Monroe was close at hand when Major James Wilkinson brought news of the victory at Saratoga and then schemed with the Conway Cabal to supplant Washington as commander in chief. Monroe enjoyed the counsel of Mrs. Theodosia Prevost, the future wife of Aaron Burr, as he extricated himself from a sentimental *affaire de coeur* with a young lady he met at the Hermitage, the Prevost mansion in Paramus, New Jersey. As one of the few American staff officers who spoke a little French, Major Monroe became well acquainted with the marquis de Lafayette, who spoke a little English.

When the war moved into the Carolinas, Monroe followed eagerly, bearing a letter of recommendation from Washington "as a brave, active, and sensible officer." Washington's aide Alexander Hamilton offered more exuberant praise: "Monroe is just setting out from Head Quarters," Hamilton advised Henry Laurens, of South Carolina,

> and proposes to go in quest of adventures to the Southward. He seems to be as much of a knight errant as your worship, but as he is an honest fellow, I shall be glad he may find some employment, that will enable him to be knocked in the head in an honorable way. . . . You know him to be a man of honor a sensible man and a soldier. This makes it unnecessary [for] me to say anything to interest your friendship for him. You love your country too and he has the zeal and capacity to serve it.

*Appointed minister to France in 1794 by President George Washington,
James Monroe (opposite page) purchased an elegant house on the rue
de Clichy, near Montmartre. There in 1796 he and Elizabeth Kortright
Monroe (above) sat for watercolor-on-ivory portraits by the Swiss-born
miniaturist Louis Sené. Devotees of French fashion, as were many American republicans, the Monroes resided twice in Europe—in Paris from*

Sarah Vaughan, Kitty Livingston, and their circle sensed that Monroe was
well-read. Perhaps they knew that he had read law with Thomas Jefferson after the war and opened a law office in Fredericksburg, at the falls of
the Rappahannock River, before entering politics. Miss Vaughan had
doubts about Monroe's "gaiety and liveliness" and was undecided about
whether he was handsome. Her friend Kitty Livingston could decide
whether the tall young Virginian's deeply dimpled chin "constitutes
beauty." Clearly, whatever his other merits, James Monroe was sensible.
Sarah Vaughan and Alexander Hamilton were in agreement on that—as
was George Washington, the American paragon of good sense.[3]

Sensible and serious, James Monroe rose quickly in Virginia politics. He
started in 1782 with a seat in the state legislature vacated when his uncle

*1794 to 1797 and in Paris and London from 1803 to 1807—and they brought their taste for elegant French furniture, fashion, and cuisine to the decor of the White House in 1817.* (James Monroe courtesy James Monroe Museum and Memorial Library, Fredericksburg, Virginia. Elizabeth Kortright Monroe courtesy Ash Lawn–Highland, Charlottesville, Virginia.)

and patron, Joseph Jones, went to Congress. He was soon appointed to the executive council along with the future chief justice John Marshall and Jefferson's diplomatic protégé William Short. In an age skeptical of executive power, this council advised the governor and served the commonwealth as a political training ground where promising young men on the way up rubbed elbows with seasoned politicians on their way to retirement. The next summer, Monroe's diligence gained him election to Congress.

As a congressman during the 1780s, Monroe and his colleagues were as much diplomats as legislators, for the Confederation Congress resembled the General Assembly of the United Nations more than its modern congressional namesake. A prominent Massachusetts congressman called his delegation "our Embassy" and hoped its conduct would "merit the Approbation of our Country"—by which he meant his state. Another "mere freshman" from Connecticut described Congress as "a maze, a labyrinth of which I have not yet got hold of the clue. Some business is done in Congress, some in committee and boards. I am labouring to explore these different powers and provinces, but make very slow progress."[4]

Constitutional restrictions, chronic poverty, and habitual absenteeism put the national government in a tight harness. The state legislatures generally chose the members of Congress, and kept them reined in with detailed instructions—all to ensure that political power stayed in the states and localities. Not surprisingly, after independence had been won, many states sent the second string to Congress while their best men stayed at home. "The members of Congress are no longer, generally speaking, men of worth or of distinction," one congressman told a Dutch visitor, "for Congress is not, as formerly, held in respect . . . [and] the government[s] of the States and the foreign missions absorb the men of first rank in the Union." As the largest and most populous state in the Confederation, Virginia generally sent a delegation to Congress that was a cut above the others. Like the state's executive council, the Virginia congressional delegation always included a few seasoned leaders, a couple of promising youngsters sent to test their wings, and some second-stringers to hold down the bench while the others were on the floor or in committee. The fact that Virginia paid its delegates on a per diem basis probably helped, too. Congressmen from some states had fewer incentives for diligence, and they often had difficulty getting paid at all.[5]

Unlike John Francis Mercer, whose outrageous opinions and "great swelling words" prompted a wintry puritan from New Hampshire to give thanks when the "Prince of the South" retired from Congress, Monroe stood out among Virginia's young men (as would James Madison when his turn came).[6] The leaders of his delegation included Monroe's wise old cousin William Grayson, whose intellect and wit enlivened many a debate, the proud aristocratic Richard Henry Lee, and, before Jefferson left for his diplomatic mission to France, the author of the Declaration of Independence. Among the middling talents were Edward Carrington from Cumberland, Samuel Hardy from Isle of Wight, and Richard Henry Lee's irascible younger brother Arthur. The Lee brothers sometimes stood aloof from the rest, but on the whole the Virginians acted together and exercised influence well beyond their numbers.

Fashionable Sarah Vaughan may have doubted the dimpled young bachelor's "gaiety and liveliness," but Congressman Monroe was sensible, attentive, and hardworking. Aboard a sloop in the Hudson River, these character traits may not have swept stylish young ladies off their feet, but when the question of the future of the Mississippi River threw the Confederation Congress into turmoil, Monroe's steady intelligence, keen ear, and diligent attendance proved their worth.

Monroe's second year in Congress ended calmly enough. "There seems in Congress an earnest disposition to wind up our aff[ai]rs as they respect foreign nations," Monroe assured Thomas Jefferson in June 1785. "I have never seen a body of men collected in which there was less party, for there is not the shadow of it here"—a situation that soon changed drastically.[7] That spring Congress had witnessed some disagreements about how to sell land in the Ohio Country. Acting on advice from Massachusetts politician Timothy Pickering, Congressman Rufus King had introduced legislation requiring the sale of western lands in tracts no smaller than thirty thousand acres (a policy that favored land companies and wealthy speculators), while Monroe, Grayson, and others sought to allow the sale of the land in more affordable squares of six hundred forty acres. In the end, "all parties who have advocated particular modes of disposing of this western territory have relinquished some things they wished," said Rufus King, "and the ordinance is a compromise of opinions." The result of that compromise was the Land Ordinance of 1785. "It is not the best in the world," William Grayson declared as he sent a copy to James Madison, but "it is I am confident the best that could be procured for the present."[8]

The Land Ordinance of 1785 gave birth to the straight country roads, right-angle intersections, and rectangular fields that modern travelers take for granted as they fly across the tamed and cultivated expanse of Ohio, Indiana, Illinois, Michigan, and Wisconsin. Upon the ancient forests of the Old Northwest, it branded a grid announcing the arrival of civilization and the Age of Reason. In time these straight lines and right angles, which Thomas Jefferson had first introduced in earlier legislation about western lands, projected American notions of order across the vast unruly landscape of the Louisiana Purchase, too, from the Ohio River to the Rocky Mountains.

While Congress found its way to an amicable compromise over western land policy, Monroe and his colleagues awaited with some trepidation the arrival from Madrid of Carlos III's newly appointed negotiator, forty-nine-year-old Don Diego de Gardoqui. Days after learning that Gardoqui was en route to the new republic, Richard Henry Lee alerted George Washington that he "apprehend[ed] a very firm ostensible demand from him, of the exclusive navigation of the Mississippi." Lee speculated hopefully that Gardoqui's "secret orders touching an ulterior agreement may be another thing," and he concluded that

Time and wise negotiation will unfold this very important matter, and
I hope secure to the U.S. and those Individual states concerned, the
great advantages that will be derived from a free navigation of that
river.[9]

Officially, Congress assured the Spanish court that it would welcome
Gardoqui to New York City with "all the Distinction and Respect which
the Dignity of his Sovereign and the Nature of his Commission may
demand." As to "the great Business he is sent to negociate with the
United States," Congress promised that the negotiations "shall be conducted on their part with the greatest Candor and Frankness."[10] Fair
words—but these congressmen knew that the art of diplomacy is not
always candid or frank. Ambassadors, in the famous remark of an English
diplomat who witnessed his countrymen settling at Jamestown and Plymouth, are honest men sent abroad to lie for their country.


Diego de Gardoqui y Arriquivar was an experienced diplomat. He left a
position as head of Spain's consular service in London to accept the
assignment in New York City, where Congress regularly met at the time.
Born in Bilbao, on the Bay of Biscay in the Basque country north of
Madrid, Gardoqui had studied in London for several years. He spoke
impeccable English and had grown up around British and American
merchants doing business with his father, José Gardoqui. The son had
demonstrated his talents in a series of local appointments when Carlos
III summoned the thirty-one-year-old businessman to court on the eve of
the American Revolution. Within weeks he found himself in the middle
of Spain's effort to help the American colonies without openly offending
Great Britain—a task made more difficult by the appointment of the contentious Arthur Lee as one of America's agents on the Continent. A bull
in the china shop of European diplomacy, Lee was based in Paris and the
Spanish wanted him to stay there. When Lee set out for Madrid, Gardoqui deftly intercepted him—at Pamplona no less—and soon emerged as
Carlos III's expert on all things American. Through his father's firm, Gardoqui and Sons, Spain covertly shipped thousands of dollars' worth of
Spanish goods and matériel to the American army, and the port of Bilbao
became a haven for American privateers.[11]

When Congress sent John Jay to Madrid seeking official Spanish
recognition and a treaty of alliance, Gardoqui was the intermediary
between Jay and José Moñino y Redondo, count of Floridablanca, chief
minister to the king from 1780 to 1792. After the war, Gardoqui was the

natural choice when Carlos decided to send a negotiator to the new American republic. He knew the strengths and situation of the American people. He knew the importance of the Mississippi River, the details of Spanish-American trade, and the predilections of many American leaders—and some of their wives.

Gardoqui had John Jay pegged. "The American," he reported in a confidential letter to Carlos III and his chief minister,

> is generally considered to possess talent and capacity enough to cover in great part a weakness natural to him, [but] appears (by a consistent behaviour) to be a very self-centered man, which passion his wife augments, because, in addition to thinking highly of herself and being rather vain, she likes to be catered to and even more to receive presents. This woman, whom he loves blindly, dominates [Jay] and nothing is done without her consent, so that her opinion prevails, though her husband at first may disagree.

Gardoqui was confident "that a little management in dealing with her and a few timely gifts will secure the friendship of both, because I have reason to believe that they proceed resolved to make a fortune." Nor was Jay "the only one in the country who has the same weakness, for there are many poor persons among the [Congress]," Gardoqui continued, "and I believe a skillful hand which knows how to take advantage of favourable opportunities, and how to give dinners and above all how to entertain with good wine, may profit without appearing to pursue them."[12]

Armed with shrewd advice from their envoy to the United States, Carlos III and his ministers provided Gardoqui ample tools for social diplomacy: a conspicuously handsome residence on Broadway, a salary four times Jay's, and a lavish expense account for dinners, dances, and incidental gifts. These resources came, as requested, with explicit royal instructions to cultivate and entertain the New Yorker and his wife, Sarah Livingston Jay, daughter of the governor of New Jersey.

Jay loved horses. "My inquiries for horses have been frequent and extensive," he confessed to a fellow devotee: "fine, large, and strong, are qualities rarely found" in American horses "since the war." Gardoqui took notice and sent word to Spain. Months later, on March 1, 1786, Jay asked Congress for permission to accept Carlos III's thoughtful gift of an Arabian stallion—fine, large, and strong. The king's favor to the ardent farmer George Washington was selected with similar care: a hardy Spanish jackass, and Washington was delighted. Nor would Gardoqui disappoint the former president of Congress, Richard Henry Lee, who thought "it will be unfortunate for us if Mr. Gardoque should not be a Smoker and so not be provided with Havanna Segars." Gardoqui's unofficial predecessor "used to supply us so copiously," Lee recalled, "that he has occasioned us to loose all appetite for other smoking." Even a congressional nobody from Delaware felt charmed "by Gardoqui the Spanish Ambassador—Who seem'd particular in his Attention to me."[13]

Gardoqui had not crossed the Atlantic to lie for his king and country. He came ready to dine, dance, drink, share his cigars—and listen and learn. For their part, American politicians responded to Gardoqui's hospitality and charm with amazing candor, especially in private conversations. The Americans saved their duplicity for one another.[14]


Spain's wealth dazzled many Americans, as did her potential demand for American fish and agricultural commodities. Even the infirmities of her empire—the seeming lethargy of her colonial populations or the reputed corruption of her customhouse officials—offered opportunities for commerce. From the moment Gardoqui's appointment was announced, Congress put its business with Spain on hold while its members tracked his journey across the Atlantic. In their letters to one another, in their reports home to state governors and legislators, and in their correspondence with influential men around the country and abroad, congressmen revealed their eagerness for Gardoqui's arrival. The buzz escalated with every bit of news: "He was very shortly to sail from Cadiz for Philadelphia in a King's Frigate," South Carolina's delegation reported to their governor in February 1785. "From Spain we expect a Mr. Gardoqui in quality of chargé des aff[ai]rs. All our measures with that court have of course ceased untill his arrival," Monroe advised Jefferson early in April. Soon thereafter a clergyman in Danvers, Massachusetts, learned from Samuel Holten that "the secretary of foreign affairs laid before Congress a letter he had rec[eive]d from Don Diego de Gardoqui informing, that he was arrived at Philadelphia."[15]

Once Gardoqui set foot on American soil, his presence only heightened congressional anticipation and apprehension. Their anxiety derived, in part, because the members of Congress knew that negotiations on several critical matters could easily stalemate. Congressman Holten was eager for Gardoqui to "come forward with his commission and present himself to Congress . . . as we shall soon know the sense of his court upon some important matters." "The Envoy of Spain Mr. Gardoquoie is expected to arrive here in a few Days from Philad[elphi]a," the Connecticut delegation advised its governor on May 27, "when a Negotiation will commence upon the important subject of the Mississippi Navigation and other consequential Topicks." That same afternoon, Samuel Dick, of New Jersey, informed his brother-in-law that "we expect hourly the Arrival of Don Gardoqui." The next day William Grayson told James Madison, "Nothing has happened of any consequence except the passage of the Land Ordinance and the arrival of Don Diego de Gardoqui at Philadelphia." "We expect him soon here," Richard Henry Lee wrote Madison the next day, "so that we shall quickly know whether he can or will do any thing conclusive concerning the Navigation of Mississippi."[16]

The anticipation continued through June: "We look for him here shortly," wrote Pennsylvania congressman David Jackson from his sickbed on June 4. "The navigation, full and free to the United States of the Mississippi must of course become a matter of enquiry, and subject of discussion with his court," Jackson continued, "that is a matter the United States can never give up, otherwise our territory in that quarter would be of little consequence." "The Spanish Plenipotentiary has not yet reach'd this City," Maryland congressman William Hindman reported to his governor on June 24, "but [is] daily expected. I see little Prospect of Congress adjourning in the Course of this Year, being up to their Eyes in Business, and Mr. Gardoqui's Arrival will I expect add considerably thereto."[17]

Once Gardoqui reached New York City, American attention focused more closely on the minister and his mission. "Mr. Gardoqui, chargé des affaires Plenipotentiary from the Court of Spain is at length arrived at this place," Grayson reported to Madison on June 27, "but I believe very few have seen him. I understand he has been bred to the business of a Merch[an]t and is an agreable man; he has resided some short time in Philad[elphi]a and the people from thence represent him in a favorable light." "Mr. Gardoqui has been receiv'd as the Minister of Spain," a Connecticut congressman reported to his governor early in July. "He applied yesterday to know when, and with whom he sho'd enter upon the Objects of his Mission. This shews a good disposition to the dispatch of Business to which he will receive a speedy answer, and the Negotiations may be soon open'd but I will not engage they will be very soon closed. We have much to say to him as well as he to us." Gardoqui "presented a letter of credence from the King and has full powers to treat upon the subject of the disputed boundary etc.," Monroe wrote Madison on July 12, and "is a polite and sensible man."[18]

At last, on July 14, 1786—exactly three years before angry French citizens would storm the Bastille—the polite and sensible representative of His Most Catholic Majesty Carlos III formally presented his diplomatic credentials to the assembled Congress of the young American republic:

"Mr. Gardoqui has had an audience and Mr. Jay will probably be appointed to negotiate with him," Massachusetts congressman Elbridge Gerry reported to John Adams, who was representing the United States in London.[19]

At thirty-nine, John Jay was ten years younger than Diego de Gardoqui. They had first met during Jay's mission to Madrid during the Revolutionary War. Now it was Jay's turn to help Gardoqui adapt to the locale. Together, they adjusted old protocols for the encounter between agents of His Most Catholic Majesty and the world's youngest republic, gracefully side-stepping a few inconvenient details of diplomatic etiquette as the Spanish divine-right monarchy met America's vox populi, vox Dei. "He produc'd a letter from the King with full powers to treat upon the subjects arising between us," Monroe wrote Jefferson in mid-July, "yet his stile is Encargado de negotios. We have had some difficulty in regulating the etiquette respecting him, whether to consider him as a minister or Encargado de Negotios, or chargé des aff[ai]rs," Monroe concluded, "and to avoid giving offence we have us'd the terms us'd by his master. We hope it will have the desir'd effect."[20]

As expected, Congress designated John Jay "to negotiate, treat and sign with Don Diego de Gardoqui . . . whatever Articles, Compacts and Conventions may be necessary for fixing the boundaries between the Territories of the said United States and those of his Catholic Majesty and for promoting the general harmony and Mutual interest of the two Nations"—but Congress also kept the New Yorker on a short leash: "Mr. Jay is authorised to treat with Mr. Gardoqui upon the subjects arising between the two parties," Monroe explained to Jefferson, but "he is to lay every proposition before Congress before he enters into any engagement with him."[21]

The anxiety that American congressmen revealed in their correspondence tracking Gardoqui's advance from Cádiz derived, in part, from the recognition that much was at stake and that negotiations between Jay and Gardoqui could easily stalemate. The requirement that Jay "lay every proposition before Congress before he enters into any engagement" was rooted in a far deeper worry. Of the three matters at issue—western boundaries, international trade, and the navigation of the Mississippi River—the last was likely to cause an impasse.

Spain had not signed the 1783 treaty between the United States and Great Britain that ended the American Revolution, hence Spain had not

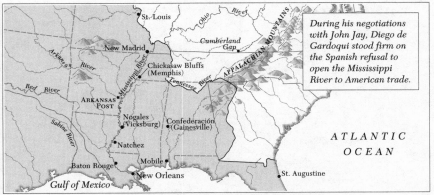

*During his negotiations with John Jay, Diego de Gardoqui stood firm on the Spanish refusal to open the Mississippi River to American trade.*

*Initial boundary proposal in Gardoqui's instructions, 1784*

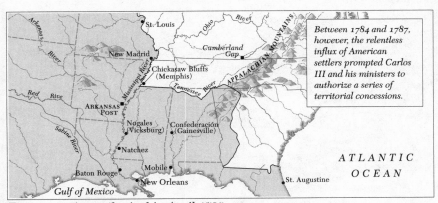

*Between 1784 and 1787, however, the relentless influx of American settlers prompted Carlos III and his ministers to authorize a series of territorial concessions.*

*First concession authorized in April 1785*

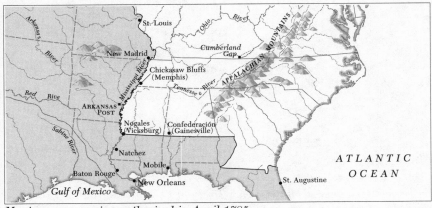

*Maximum concession authorized in April 1785*

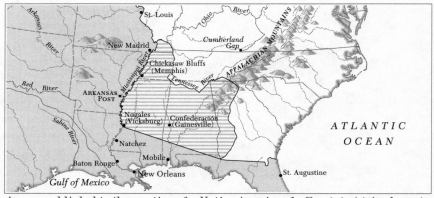

*A proposal linked to the creation of a Native American buffer state (striped area) in September 1787*

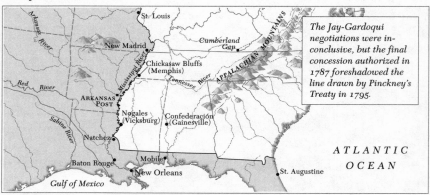

The Jay-Gardoqui negotiations were inconclusive, but the final concession authorized in 1787 foreshadowed the line drawn by Pinckney's Treaty in 1795.

*Final concession sent to Gardoqui in September 1787*

*The boundary established by Pinckney's Treaty in 1795 extended the 1787 line west to the Mississippi River and thereby gave Natchez to the United States.*

agreed to the location of a boundary separating the Gulf Coast of Spanish West Florida from the Tennessee Country. Regardless of where that line might finally be drawn, below it the Spanish claimed control of both sides of the Mississippi River, and on June 26, 1784, they had closed the river to American traders. Carlos III had ordered Gardoqui to deny the Americans use of the Mississippi below Natchez, while Congress had given Jay an equally firm instruction to insist upon free navigation of the Ohio-Mississippi watershed from Pittsburgh to the Gulf of Mexico.

The two men, each fully conversant in the other's language, met and talked week after week through the autumn and the winter and well into the spring of 1786. They were friendly, they made some progress on minor issues, and Gardoqui gracefully entertained the members of Congress and New York society with his personal charm and his monarch's generous hospitality, including "Havanna Segars"—but neither man could yield ground on the question of Mississippi navigation, and both men knew it.

During nearly a year of negotiations, Gardoqui found that the Americans did indeed have much to say to him. Somewhere during the course of his conversations—whether with Jay or with congressmen from the New England states—Gardoqui learned that the American commitment to opening the Mississippi was far from unanimous. He discovered that for the right price, there were men willing to sell the interests of Kentucky frontiersmen and their southern friends down the river. The enticements that he could offer most of these men, Gardoqui quickly recognized, were trading privileges in the ports of the Spanish empire, recognition of American fishing rights in the North Atlantic, and a ready market for New England cod among his Roman Catholic countrymen, especially during Lent. A few might also accept cash.

The problems of Gloucester fishermen, Salem shipowners, and Boston merchants had never elicited strong sympathy west of the Hudson River—or perhaps west of Walden Pond. "The Newfoundland fishery is a source of wealth as valuable to us," exclaimed the *Boston Independent Chronicle* in 1799, "as the hills of Potosi is to the Spaniards." Nevertheless, at the end of the Revolution, during the three-way negotiations among the United States, her ally France, and her former enemy Great Britain, congressional indifference to New England's fishing rights in the North Atlantic drove some Massachusetts politicians to contemplate a separate peace with Great Britain. "Whatever may be our Prospects in every other Respect," complained Bay State congressman Elbridge Gerry in 1782,

they are not favorable as they relate to the Fishery. Should the want of
a thorough knowledge in Congress of the Importance of this Right, to
the United States, or an Inattention in this Point of their Interest, (on
the Part of our [French] allies) deprive Us of the Fishery, the Union
and Alliance so far as they respect this State will no Longer be natural.

Congressional ignorance or neglect of New England's "true Interest,"
Gerry warned, provided Great Britain "with a powerful Means by offering a participation in her Fisheries, to detach this State from the Confederation . . . and make it an Ally of her own."[22] In the end, the British did
admit American participation in the Newfoundland fisheries by the
Peace of Paris signed in 1783, but New England's sensitivity to its maritime interests remained a live coal that Gardoqui could easily fan into
flame.

When James Monroe heard New England congressmen talking
openly of secession in the boardinghouses and taverns of New York as
early as December 1785, perhaps (like subsequent American historians)
he regarded it as hyperbole—the exaggerated tirades of weary legislators
after long hours of debate and a few pints of stout ale. When John Jay
spoke with him privately about the impasse with Gardoqui, however, and
then formally requested a secret committee to manage his negotiations,
Monroe suddenly realized that the talk of a separate New England confederation was real. Although John Jay was probably not yet in league with
the secessionists, the New England congressional delegation embraced
Jay's proposed surrender of the Mississippi as a means to jettison southern
opposition by creating a regional confederacy and signing a separate commercial treaty with Spain.

Who were these separatists in the spring and summer of 1786? The
ringleaders were Massachusetts congressmen associated in Bay State
politics with Salem and Boston mercantile conservatives known as the
Essex Junto. Boston merchant and judge Nathaniel Gorham, forty-eight,
was president of Congress. Attorney Nathan Dane, thirty-four, graduated from Harvard in 1778 and practiced law in Beverly, across the harbor from Salem in Essex County. "The Southern States have much to fear
from a dissolution of the present Confederacy," Dane advised Essex
attorney Edward Pulling: "They surely must be alarmed even at the suggestion of a confederacy of the States north of the Potomac or even the
Delaware." Years later, Dane would also participate in the separatist
Hartford Convention of 1814.[23]

The rising genius of the New England separatists of 1786 was thirty-one-year-old Rufus King, who lived to carry the banner of Federalism into the second quarter of the nineteenth century. Born a hundred miles up the coast from Boston into a Tory mercantile family, King had graduated at the head of his Harvard class of 1777, read law in Salem with Theophilus Parsons, a senior member of the junto known to his students as "Theawfullest Parsons," and begun his legal practice in the Essex County courts.

Congressman Rufus King's flirtation with separatism began in November 1785, when he was working with Caleb Davis, a Boston merchant and shipowner who was also speaker of the Massachusetts House of Representatives, to circumvent the obvious weaknesses of the confederation government and find alternative ways to strengthen American trade (and the New England economy) in the face of aggressive foreign rivals. British merchants enjoyed both unrestricted access to markets in America and the continued protection of their Navigation Acts at home. Their American counterparts were suffering, so much so that Massachusetts and New Hampshire had recently retaliated with restrictions on foreign merchants, even though their policy had no chance of success unless it extended to *all* American ports of entry. The best way to achieve a level playing field would be for Congress to tear a page from the British playbook and restrict all of America's trade "to her own ships and Mariners." If only Congress could do that, Rufus King and his Bay State allies agreed, America would promptly benefit from "the great number of ships, which would be built, and the multitudes of men who would become mariners."[24]

As in all debates over protectionism and free trade, however, self-interest gave other Americans—in this instance the farmers and planters of the south and west—incentives to uphold the status quo. Congress, King told the speaker of the Massachusetts legislature, would be unable to act because "the Southern and Eastern states cannot and will not soon agree in vesting powers in Congress to regulate external and internal commerce"—and even if Congress was given the authority to regulate commerce, passage of the kind of legislation they sought was not assured.[25]

Casting about for another way to make something happen, King looked to the states. Since each of them could, in theory at least, pass laws on subjects that were denied to Congress, a coordinated policy of retaliation against the British merchants might be enacted through the state legislatures. The challenge, in practice, was to get all thirteen clocks to strike at the same time, as they had in July 1776, in the face of the same diverging economic interests that frustrated Congress (not to mention the mercantile rivalries between New England and New York ports of entry and their respective customs services). All in all, Rufus King and the maritime interests of Massachusetts could not be optimistic about getting "uniform Acts passed by the several States." With this realization—that they were stymied in and out of Congress—the maritime interests of Massachusetts took a creative first step toward separatism.[26]

"The Confederation admits of Alliances between two or more States," King wrote,

> provided the purpose and duration thereof are previously communicated to, and approved by, Congress. The seven Eastern states have common commercial interests . . . and are competent to give the Approbation of Congress to such sub-confederation, as they might agree upon . . . which would not only remedy all their Difficulties, but raise them to a degree of power and Opulence which would surprize and astonish.

In short, as Rufus King read the Articles of Confederation, with seven out of thirteen votes in Congress, the eastern and commercial states had the power to give constitutional sanction to a sub-confederation composed of the very same seven eastern and commercial states.[27]

The more Rufus King thought about a sub-confederacy the more he liked the idea, for even "if Congress had the power to regulate Trade," King feared that "they would be without the Disposition to do it." He doubted that "the Southern States will relinquish their partial [i.e., one-sided], and unfederal, policy concerning commerce, until they find a decided disposition in the Eastern States to combine for their own security." Only if the northern states banded together to form a commercial sub-confederation, he concluded, would "the southern states . . . sensibly feel their weakness, and accede to such measures as may be adopted by the majority of the Confederacy."[28]

In his November 1785 correspondence with the speaker of the Massachusetts House of Representatives, Rufus King planted the seeds of the first New England separatist movement. The months ahead only confirmed his forecasts and his calculations of sectional voting patterns in Congress. Although by February 1786 ten states did agree to expand the commercial regulatory powers of the whole Congress, without the consent of Delaware, Georgia, and South Carolina that reform died on the vine—as did a parallel plan for a requisition system to address the national government's chronic poverty. With the failures of these measures in the spring of 1786, Massachusetts politicians could "easily see . . . a dissolution of the federal Government and with that an end to all our National importance and happiness."[29]

As things stood in the spring of 1786, the country seemed to have four options: the continued decline of the existing government, the creation of a limited sub-confederation for commercial purposes, the creation of a separate confederation of like-minded northern commercial states, or the vague prospect that something useful might come out of Virginia governor Patrick Henry's invitation to discuss the nation's commercial problems at Annapolis, Maryland, on the first Monday in September.[30] Of these four policy options, the congressmen from New England had favored the second and had worked hard to strengthen the Confederation, but as prospects for success grew slim in the spring and summer of 1786, it was not difficult for the skillful Spanish diplomat Diego de Gardoqui, a man with twenty years of experience in transatlantic commerce, to entice the New Englanders toward the third option: a separate northern confederacy and a commercial treaty with Spain.[31]

In politics, Rufus King was a protégé of the dour puritan Timothy Pickering, whose Salem ancestors included a "hanging judge" in the Salem witchcraft trials. Pickering, forty-one, had spent his political career scheming to protect puritan virtue and high Federalism—one and the same in his constricted mind—from a variety of enemies, foreign and domestic. From 1786 through 1814, except when his party held sway in national affairs, Pickering was the inveterate New England separatist. After President John Adams dismissed him from his cabinet for undermining American foreign policy on the brink of war in 1799, Pickering's friends in the Essex Junto arranged the former secretary of state's election to the Senate. There he became the leading voice of New England separatism from the Louisiana Purchase of 1803 to the Hartford Convention of 1814, until his thirty-year obsession died along with Lieutenant General Sir Edward Michael Pakenham in the middle of a muddy battlefield below New Orleans on the afternoon of January 8, 1815.

Geographically, Theodore Sedgwick, forty, was the odd man out among the congressional separatists of 1786. Born in West Hartford, Connecticut, Sedgwick had studied theology and law at Yale and hung out his shingle in the Berkshire mountain towns of Great Barrington and Sheffield. Rising through the state legislature to a seat in the Confederation Congress, Sedgwick would preside as speaker of the House of Representatives during the Sixth Congress (the last ever to see a Federalist majority).

Seeking support from other northern states, Gorham, Dane, King, and Sedgwick talked openly of separating New England from the southern states and the prospective southwestern states of the Ohio River Valley. Thus "in conversations at which I have been present," James Monroe heard hopes for "a dismemberment so as to include Pen[nsylvani]a." Occasionally they also hoped for Delaware, and perhaps even Maryland. "Sometimes," Monroe said, they talked of gathering into a northern confederation "all the states south to the Potowmack."[32]

Savvy men did not entrust sensitive matters to the common mail, and because they saw each other almost every day in Congress, Gorham, Dane, King, and Sedgwick had little call to write to one another about their scheme—except if one of them went out of town. When Nathan Dane went home for a visit, he wrote guardedly to assure Rufus King that "all the men I have conversed with appear to have adopted ideas similar to ours." King replied with equal discretion that he was "happy to lea[r]n that prudent and discreet men concur with us in Opinion concerning the Spanish negotiation," adding that "it would appear strange to me if a contrary Opinion was entertained by any sensible man North of the Potomack."[33]

Theodore Sedgwick was less circumspect in a letter home to conservative state senator Caleb Strong, of Hampshire County in the Connecticut River Valley of central Massachusetts. "It well becomes the eastern and middle States . . . seriously to consider what advantages result to them from their connection with the Southern States," Sedgwick wrote in August 1786. "They can give us nothing," he thought, and

> even the appearance of a union cannot . . . long be preserved. It becomes us seriously to contemplate a substitute; for if we do not controul events we shall be miserably controuled by them. No other substitute can be devised than that of contracting the limits of the confederacy to such as are natural and reasonable.[34]

"Controul" or "be miserably controuled"—that was the question. Whether t'was better for New England to suffer the slings and arrows of outrageous fortune within the union, or to adopt separatist measures against its sea of troubles.

From December 1785 (when James Monroe first heard the New Englanders talking of separation) until late August 1786, congressional rules about the secrecy of its deliberations, rules intended to protect freedom of debate, created a greenhouse environment for political intrigue. Nevertheless, the conflict between New England and the southern states over the Jay-Gardoqui negotiations did not escape notice by the French chargé d'affaires, Louis-Guillaume Otto—in part because he had been approached as a possible mediator. "The negotiations relating to the treaty of commerce with Spain," Otto reported to French authorities, "have . . . been the constant subject of the deliberations of congress." The southern states were attempting to dissuade Pennsylvania and New Jersey from joining "the league of the North" and join their insistence on opening the port of New Orleans "as a commercial entrepôt for all the commodities of the interior." Their efforts, however, encountered "serious opposition from the states of the North." Northern congressmen felt that "the navigation of the Mississippi [was] . . . far from being advantageous to the confederation." Opening the Mississippi, the New Englanders believed, would sever the "interior country" from its dependence upon the Atlantic states. "The inhabitants of Kentucky," Otto explained, would no longer feel the need for commercial connections with the maritime states, and "would only think of rendering themselves wholly independent of Congress as of a sovereign body from which they could derive no benefit." Not that these New England congressmen were terribly concerned about the fate of settlers in the Ohio River Valley. What did concern them was a prospective exodus of Yankee farmers and sailors to the fertile lands along the Ohio River—an exodus "of the most industrious inhabitants of the northern states" that would cripple the fleets, send land values plummeting, and consign New England to a minority role in national affairs. "Who would not hesitate an instant," Otto reflected, "to exchange the arid rocks of Massachusetts and of New Hampshire for the smiling plains of the Ohio and the Mississippi"?[35]

As the representative of the court of Versailles, Louis-Guillaume Otto was no republican. Still, as a man of the Enlightenment he knew his Montesquieu as well as any of the Americans, for whom the great Frenchman and John Locke were demigods of republicanism. "It is natural for a republic to have only a small territory, otherwise it cannot long subsist," wrote Montesquieu:

> In an extensive republic the public good is sacrificed to a thousand private views. . . . In a small one, the interest of the public is more obvious, better understood, and more within the reach of every citizen.[36]

Sprawling from Maine to Georgia, the United States was "already of too great extent," the New Englanders contended, "and . . . their territory ought to be reduced rather than augmented beyond all proportion." Hence it was necessary "to recall the ultimatum which proposed the opening of the Mississippi as a condition sine qua non" for a commercial treaty with Spain.

"Mr. Gardoqui," Otto continued, "affects the greatest indifference about these negotiations. . . . He has often said to me that . . . it would be impossible to prevent contraband trade and other disorders which the Americans would not fail to cause." Carlos III's main objective was simply to discourage "establishments on the Mississippi which might one day become neighbors so much the more dangerous for the Spanish possessions."

Montesquieu's maxim was accepted wisdom in the age of the Enlightenment. Classical history proved that republics were naturally suited to small territories. Sparta had endured by maintaining the "same extent of territory after all her wars," while Athens and Rome demonstrated the dangers of imperial expansion: decadence, despotism, and eventual collapse. Even as they invoked his theory about the dangers of an extensive republic, however, American congressmen were engaged in exactly the kind of self-interested politics Montesquieu had warned about, when "the public good is sacrificed to a thousand private views."

The depth of sectional division did not escape Louis-Guillaume Otto's notice, either. "I have had the honor thus far of explaining to you merely the ostensible arguments of the two parties," Otto reported to Louis XVI and his ministers, "but a long acquaintance with the affairs of this country authorizes me, perhaps, to divine the secret motives of the heat with which each state supports its opinion." The southern states were "not in earnest" when they contended that closing the Mississippi would force the western frontiersmen to "seek an outlet by way of the [Great] lakes, and . . . throw themselves into the arms of England." American patriotism, born of the Revolution, ran deeper in Kentucky than the New Englanders knew. And the rivers that lead to Canada looked more inviting to easterners studying their maps than to farmers loading heavy barrels of flour, salt pork, beef, and other bulky commodities aboard makeshift rafts that floated better downstream than up.

"The true motive" of the vigorous contention between the northern and southern states, Otto believed, was rooted in calculations of sectional political and economic self-interest within a union that was at best only a dozen years old (counting from the First Continental Congress of 1774). The northern states, Otto knew, were "eager to incline the balance toward their side," while the southern states "neglect no opportunity of increasing the population and importance of the western territory, and of drawing thither by degrees the inhabitants of New England, whose ungrateful soil only too much favors emigration." This westward movement of population was a two-fisted blow to New England, Otto observed,

> since on the one hand it deprives her of industrious citizens, and on the other it adds to the population of the southern states. These new [western] territories will gradually form themselves into separate [state] governments; they will have their representatives in congress, and will augment greatly the mass of the southern states.

Otto's analysis did not miss much. Southerners insisted upon access to the Mississippi and New Orleans for the good of themselves and "their establishments in the West." A treaty containing "only stipulations in favor of the northern fisheries" threatened to increase the prosperity, commerce, and "preponderance of the northern states" in national politics. The French diplomat did not expect the congressmen from either region to give ground, and he knew that Gardoqui would stand firm. Grateful that this diplomatic mess was not in his portfolio, Otto noted that "the conduct of this thorny negotiation is in the hands of Mr. Jay."

As far as it went, the French diplomat's assessment of the regional conflict over the Jay-Gardoqui negotiations was accurate. But neither Otto nor the American populace knew just how close the nation came to fragmentation. Between January and August 1786, very few men in and around Congress witnessed the full progress of the secret Massachusetts separatist movement. One who did was the attentive and sensible James Monroe.

The nation's first separatist movement occurred on Monroe's watch. It began quietly in November 1785, festered for nine months, and then erupted in August. With his ear cocked to the diplomatic stalemate over the Mississippi River, Monroe caught the first hints of the New Englanders' scheme in January, and witnessed its development during subsequent months. When their talk turned to action, a secret ploy to surrender the Mississippi to Spain, it was James Monroe who sounded the alarm—first in May and then in August 1786.

Soon after John Jay and Diego de Gardoqui began their conversations, Congress had directed Jay "particularly to stipulate the right of the United States to . . . free Navigation of the Mississippi, from the source to the Ocean." On this point, Gardoqui had his own explicit instructions to deny the Americans use of the Mississippi where Spain controlled both banks of the river. Jay and Gardoqui quickly recognized their dilemma and reported the impasse to their superiors. Jay spoke informally with Monroe and other influential members of Congress and Gardoqui sent written reports to Spain. There could be no progress on the Mississippi question (or much else) unless either Congress or Carlos III gave ground, but in the meantime Jay and Gardoqui met weekly and talked cordially.

Whether directly from Jay or perhaps in whispered conversations with New York merchants or New England congressmen, Gardoqui discovered that many influential Americans thought that closing the Mississippi River was just fine. By January, his discussions with Jay were focused on what seemed an attractive compromise. In exchange for guaranteeing fishing rights off Newfoundland and trade privileges in Spanish ports (the equivalent of most favored nation status), Spain asked the United States to surrender navigation of the Mississippi for a period of twenty-five or thirty years. While Gardoqui waited for further guidance from Spain, Jay tested the waters with selected members of Congress. He even spoke to Monroe, who "was appriz'd [of Jay's thinking] upon my first arrival here in the winter"—around Christmas 1785—but probably not in great detail. The conversation put Monroe on alert for any threats to the Mississippi, and he monitored what he came to regard as "all the previous arrangements [that] those in fav[o]r of [relaxing Jay's instructions] found necessary to make, to prepare for its reception" in Congress.[37] Nevertheless, until early summer, Monroe found no reason to link John Jay with the talk he was hearing from Massachusetts congressmen about creating a separate New England confederacy.

The next development in the Jay-Gardoqui negotiations occurred during the last week of May. On May 25, 1786, bolstered with fresh advice from Carlos III and his ministers, Gardoqui increased the pressure on Jay with a letter explaining not only that his king regarded the navigation of the Mississippi River as nonnegotiable, but that Spain claimed the territory east of the Mississippi as theirs by conquest. As instructed, Gardoqui urged the United States to concede these rights.

Four days later, on May 29, Jay reported to Congress that difficulties had arisen in his negotiations with Gardoqui—and then he dropped the other shoe. Jay asked Congress to appoint a special secret committee with full authority to direct and control his negotiations with Gardoqui. The ploy was clever enough: a secret committee could quietly rescind the insistence upon American rights to navigate the Mississippi River. If negotiations led to an attractive treaty, everyone might be happy. If not, no harm was done. And if a controversy arose, those responsible for the reversal could hide behind parliamentary procedure. The only hitch was James Monroe, who "immediately perciev'd that the object was to relieve [Jay] from the instruction respecting the Mississippi and to get a committee to cover the measure."[38]

Rufus King greeted Jay's letter about the Spanish negotiations with a long smoke-and-mirrors speech, but his rhetorical diversion failed. The Virginians pegged him as "associated in this business" with Jay, but the votes simply were not there—for either side.[39] For reasons that soon became fully apparent to Monroe (and that will soon be clear to the reader, too), Jay's ploy to create a secret committee could work only if the measure slipped quickly and quietly through Congress. Jay's friends did not have the votes to reverse his instructions, but if the southerners who cared about the Mississippi had been looking the other way, the trick might have worked.

Three years of careful attention to business, however, had taught Monroe a few tricks of his own. He had learned that few things were easier than to persuade Congress to duck an issue by consigning it to further study. Instead of appointing the committee Jay wanted—one with power to direct his negotiations and alter his instructions—Congress appointed three men to consider Jay's request and report back later. They met the next day, came to an immediate and permanent deadlock, and two months later recommended that Congress summon Jay to the floor and take up the issue in a full congressional debate. And so it happened that in August 1786 the fate of the Mississippi River forced Congress into the most divisive sectional conflict of the Confederation period while the New England separatists tried one last time to make their scheme work.

## CHAPTER FOUR

# A Long Train of Intrigue

*The Southern States have much to fear from a dissolution of the present Confederacy. Enervated, disposed over a large territory but little inured to constraint, they are capable of making . . . but little resistance to a foreign enemy or one near home. Nor are their best men totally unacquainted with these circumstances. These considerations must press them into Federal measures— they surely must be alarmed even at the suggestion of a confederacy of the States north of the Potomac or even the Delaware and give up their opposition to avoid such a measure.*

—Nathan Dane to Edward Pulling, January 8, 1786[1]

*This is one of the most extraordinary transactions I have ever known, a minister negotiating expressly for the purpose of defeating the object of his instructions, and by a long train of intrigue and management seducing the representatives of the States to concur in it. . . . Certain it is that Committees are held in this town of Eastern men and others of this State upon the subject of a dismemberment of the States East of the Hudson from the Union and the erection of them into a separate gov[ernmen]t.*

—James Monroe to Patrick Henry, August 12, 1786[2]

"THERE ARE OBJECTIONS to New York," a lawyer visiting the seat of Congress with his wife admitted in the summer of 1786. "The water for Example is execrable. There are more flies than in most places; nor is there a scarcity of muskettoes." Manhattan's "houses are ill constructed; the rooms often very small. They have not an inch of garden, nay, hardly of yard. In most parts of Town, the Streets in general are very narrow—illy paved, and crooked. Their Butter and Meats are far inferior to Phil[adelphi]a." Despite these and other shortcomings, however, the rising Virginia jurist St. George Tucker liked New York. "Under all these Circumstances," he admitted, "if my fortune would permit it I would live on the Island of New York in preference to any spot I have ever seen"[3]— a sentiment that countless other visitors mixing business and pleasure in Manhattan have echoed through the decades.

His extended family's legal affairs had brought Tucker to New York from Virginia, where today his restored house stands a few doors from the Governor's Palace in Williamsburg. He also hoped the northern excursion might help his wife recover from the miscarriage of what would have been her ninth child. Frances Bland Randolph Tucker was regarded "as a woman not only of superior personal attractions, but [one] who excelled all others of her day in strength of intellect." Married in 1778, the Tuckers had five young children together, but his chatty diary of their trip to New York was something that St. George Tucker intended for the benefit and amusement of his three teenage stepsons. Jack, the youngest of the Randolph boys, would serve in Congress almost thirty years into the next century—the brilliant and eccentric John Randolph of Roanoke[4]—but by ancestry and upbringing all the boys in the household were destined for careers in politics and public life.

While the Tuckers visited New York City in August 1786, the members of Congress with whom they dined and partied were engaged—entirely in secret—in the most divisive arguments about the future of the country since the Declaration of Independence ten years earlier. Their debates were so cloaked in official secrecy that even as astute and well placed a visitor as St. George Tucker, writing entirely for the private edification of three aspiring young politicians, heard nothing about schemes that many participants (and their descendants and biographers) preferred to forget.

The deliberations of Congress were secret. A dozen years earlier, at its first meetings in 1774, Congress had resolved that its doors "be kept shut during the debates And that every Member be obligd under the strongest obligation of Honor to keep secret the proceedings of the Congress until they shall be ordered to be publishd"—a fact that delegates quickly learned to explain to their friends. "I am obliged to be very reserved," a typical congressman wrote, "by the Injunction of Secrecy laid on all the Members of the Congress, and tho I am aware of the Confidence I might repose in your Prudence, I must nevertheless submit to the Controul of Honour."[5]

Despite the constraints of house rules, honor, and prudence that had kept St. George Tucker in the dark about the goings-on in Congress, there were practical political limits to the secrecy of congressional debates. It is true, as *Poor Richard's Almanack* put it, that "three may keep a secret, if two of them are dead," but absolute secrecy was neither possible nor desirable for congressmen of the Confederation period. Congressmen were accountable to the state legislatures and governors who had sent them to Philadelphia or New York, and who wanted to know, at least in summary, what their agents (and the other states' agents) were up to. Term limits enforced this primary allegiance, for a man could serve no more than three one-year terms within any six-year period in Congress. Owing their seats not to independent citizen voters but to the state legislatures, congressmen had few incentives to go public with the details of congressional deliberations. Poor Richard might have professed surprise at how well American congressmen kept their deliberations secret (especially in wartime), but the real Benjamin Franklin and his colleagues spent a sweltering Philadelphia summer behind the closed doors of the Pennsylvania State House—from May to September—with the windows nailed shut to protect the secrecy of the deliberations that created the United States Constitution. This eighteenth-century predilection for keeping public debates out of the public eye offered a secure field upon which statesmen and scoundrels might play for good or ill— shielded even from the gaze of astute and well-connected political observers like St. George Tucker.

Settling into their "intollerably hot" rooms on Maiden Lane, the Tuckers initially regarded New York City in mid-July 1786 as "a very hot disagreeable situation." Despite the heat, however, their spirits soon were lifted by an evening at the theater. Then came an invitation to dinner with one of Mrs. Tucker's cousins, Virginia congressman Henry ("Light-Horse Harry") Lee, who "very politely traversed half the town to aid [them] in search of a good house." Within a few days the couple were happily immersed in "the hurly burly of paying and receiving visits," and socializing with members of the Virginia congressional delegation. Colonel Edward Carrington "looks wretchedly," they thought, but they found James Monroe "much improved by matrimony."[6]

The Tuckers ate well, too. Breakfast was "always a scene of the highest good humour and Entertainment," Tucker wrote, but "dinners are no less a Scene of unrestrained Gayety and lively conversation." The Tuckers dined several times with Boston merchant Nathaniel Gorham, president of Congress and a leader of the Massachusetts delegation, and feasted with Baron von Steuben and General Henry Knox, secretary of the War Department, as frequent dinner guests of New York City mayor James Duane.

One afternoon while savoring "the hurly burly and bustle of a large town" (New York was home to about thirty thousand people), they stepped out of a fashionable shop and nearly stumbled over a congressman whose girth had "given rise to a waggish observation. That the State he represents has more weight in Congress than any other in the Union." A few days later Tucker tagged along on a hunting expedition near von Steuben's summer retreat along the East River overlooking Long Island. Finally, the Tuckers accepted an invitation to reside with Virginia congressmen Edward Carrington and William Grayson, who had rented a large house "about an hundred yards out of the city . . . commanding a fine view of the north river," where St. George Tucker hoped the "fine, pure, refreshing air" of suburban New York might improve his wife's health.[7]

During their entire visit, however, nothing in or around New York City pleased St. George Tucker more than the company of Diego de Gardoqui. The Tuckers first met the Spanish envoy to the United States during the first week of August while visiting Anthony Walton White at his country estate north of the city. Gardoqui and the Dutch minister Pieter Johann Van Berckel, along with Gardoqui's secretary Francisco Rendón and several Americans, had spent the afternoon shooting waterfowl near the Harlem River, where "the heat of the day had occasioned them to drink rather more than usual." At dinner that evening, Tucker noted in his diary,

> The Dutchman preserved his phlegm but the Spaniard [Rendón] had no longer any pretensions to his national Gravity. He sung, laugh'd, danc'd and play'd as many tricks as [a] West-Indian or Frenchman. I have since observed that neither himself, nor Don Gardoqui have any of that solemnity about them which characterizes the spanish nation. In the case of the latter . . . he is a Biscayan, the natives of which province are celebrated for the vivacity as well as Versatility of their parts and Genius. I dined with Don Gardoqui this week, in company with a number of members of Congress. He is an extremely polite well bred man, and is allowed . . . in particular to excel the whole Diplomatic Corps.[8]

Three weeks later, the Tuckers boarded a stagecoach for Philadelphia and headed home to regale the Randolph boys with stories of congressmen, diplomats, the mayor, and nearly everyone who was anyone around Congress—with some notable exceptions. They had not, of course, pene-

trated the Knickerbocker aristocracy of old New York. Nor had they
dined with John Jay or the young Rufus King, who had married into that
exalted society. And if Tucker's otherwise chatty diary can be held
accountable for its silences, the debate raging in Congress over Jay's
negotiations with Diego de Gardoqui was kept from their ears.

On August 6, 1786, Diego de Gardoqui dictated a confidential report to
Madrid on the status of his negotiations with Secretary for Foreign
Affairs John Jay. Every word of his report was translated into code. The
original message was dispatched to Spain by way of Boston, while copies,
also in code, went by other routes and other ships. The codes and copies
were standard operating procedure in the Spanish administration of a
New World empire that dated back to Columbus. The first of these
reports to reach the Spanish court was promptly deciphered and presented to Carlos III and his chief minister (and the duplicates remain to
this day undeciphered in the Spanish archives).

The procedures were familiar, but Gardoqui's news from New York
was unexpected. Despite a year of weekly meetings, despite the lavish
dinners to impress Jay's wife, despite all the cigars and fine wines for the
members of Congress, and despite the gift of a Spanish stallion for Jay
himself, the talks between the Spanish envoy and the American secretary
remained at an impasse. Gardoqui had demonstrated surprising flexibil-
ity on the question of drawing a western boundary line between America's trans-Appalachian territories and the Spanish colonies of Louisiana
and the Floridas (see maps on pp. 57–58).[9] He was offering an attractive
package of trading privileges in Spanish ports in Europe, the Caribbean,
and the Philippines, Spanish support for American access to the rich cod
fisheries of the North Atlantic, and the Spanish market as a new outlet for
the catch. Jay and many congressmen, especially from New England,
were eager to say yes.

The only remaining obstacle to a treaty that could benefit the farmers,
merchants, and fisherman of the northern and middle states was Carlos
III's insistence that the Mississippi River remain closed to American
boats and traders. Carlos knew (though his able negotiator did not let on)
that the silver mines of Mexico accounted for half the export trade of the
entire Spanish empire. No wonder Carlos III assigned all the expenses of
Gardoqui's mission (generously budgeted at 50,000 pesos a year!) to the
viceroy of Mexico.[10] Louisiana was the buffer between those mines and a
boisterous adolescent republic. The Mississippi River was the key to
Louisiana, and Carlos III was not inclined to loosen his grip.

John Jay had been over this ground before, and at heart he cared little about the Mississippi River. He was, of course, bound by his instructions—but he had made no secret of his personal opinion that the United States had plenty of land and opportunity for its citizens east of the Appalachian Mountains. As early as 1779, when Jay was president of Congress, the New Yorker had persuaded himself that if Spain were to close the Mississippi to American trade for a period of years, the interruption would somehow encourage backcountry families to establish farms, develop "an attachment to property and industry," and stop "living in a half-savage condition." "Would it not be wiser," Jay wondered privately,

> gradually to extend our Settlements than to pitch our Tents through the Wilderness in a great Variety of Places, far distant from each other, and from those Advantages of Education, Civilization, Law, and Government which compact Settlements and Neighbourhood afford?[11]

Anyway, a diplomat's instructions could change with changes in circumstances. As the American minister to Spain from 1780 to 1782—at a time when America's desperate need for money to fight the war overshadowed any hopes of future navigation on the Ohio and Mississippi Rivers—Congress (with Virginia's explicit blessing) had reluctantly authorized Jay to surrender all American claims to the use of the Mississippi in exchange for Spanish support in the war against Great Britain. As Carlos III's rising expert on all things North American, Diego de Gardoqui had been party to Jay's negotiations in Madrid. He knew how Jay and many East Coast Americans felt, and with that knowledge he played them like a violin throughout the spring and summer of 1786. In Gardoqui's own figure of speech, he squeezed them like an orange.

"For nearly a month," Gardoqui reported in the encoded confidential dispatch of August 6, 1786, to José Moñino y Redondo, count of Floridablanca, "the Congress has worked with vigor concerning our affairs. Never has it had greater nor more acrimonious debates because those of the North argue in accord with us and those of the South oppose bitterly." The northern congressmen, he told Carlos III's chief minister, "have gone as far as to threaten secession and that they will make a treaty with His Majesty." The result was that John Jay would be called before Congress to report on the Spanish negotiations. Jay "resisted giving his verbal opinion," Gardoqui knew, "and he gave it in writing. I believe it is not bad."[12]

Gardoqui knew that Jay was seeking permission to surrender navigation of the Mississippi for a period of twenty-five or thirty years in
exchange for the attractive commercial treaty Spain was offering. The
Spanish negotiator may not have known exactly how Jay hoped to evade
the constraints of his instructions. He did know that within a few days, on
August 10, "Congress must meet in a great assembly." He expected "very
bitter debates," but he was uncertain of their outcome. "I don't have full
confidence" of success, he admitted, but in the hope that Jay and the
northern congressmen might pull it off, "I do not cease working day and
night. A deep secrecy is kept and it seems strange to everyone."

The Spanish envoy was too worldly to indulge in paranoia, but his
closing remarks reveal just how tense things were—with the future of the
American union at stake. Even though his letter was written entirely in
secret code, Gardoqui was circumspect. He "had much to say but there is
no safe conduit and as a contingency I write this via Boston. They ought
to decide soon; I will take care to inform your excellency."

Having dictated his report to the clerk who would translate it into
code—probably his able secretary, predecessor, and hunting companion
Francisco Rendón—Gardoqui continued to work day and night toward
his goal, and apparently with success. Before dispatching his report to
Madrid, Gardoqui was able to add a momentous postscript, also in code:

> I have just finished putting together a secret meeting with those of the
> North for tomorrow.

While Congress was busy trying to remedy its chronic poverty and lack of
authority, James Monroe had been closely monitoring the Jay-Gardoqui
negotiations. In letters to influential Virginians such as George Washington, James Madison, and Governor Patrick Henry, Monroe consistently
reported that he had caught wind of the northern stratagem "upon my
first arrival here in the winter, and [had] been acquainted with all the previous arrangements, those in favor of it found necessary to make, to prepare for its reception." Their "plan," as Monroe saw it, was "to enter into
engagements" with Gardoqui that would close the river "at least for a certain term . . . and further to enter into a reciprocal guarantee [between
Spain and the United States] of their respective possessions in America."
In exchange for surrendering the use of the Mississippi for twenty-five or
thirty years, Jay and his northern supporters expected a commercial
treaty with Spain in which "we are to be admitted reciprocally, they into
our ports here and we into theirs in Europe, upon an equal footing."

The northern scheme had begun to unfold (and unravel) on May 29, 1786, when Secretary Jay informed Congress of the difficulties in his negotiation with Gardoqui and asked Congress for a special committee with full power to direct his negotiations. "It was immediately perciev'd," Monroe told Madison, "that the object was to relieve him from the instruction respecting the Mississippi and to get a committee to cover the measure." The plan, in short, was to sidestep a straightforward debate in Congress about giving up the use of the Mississippi—which Jay and the New Englanders knew they could not openly win. By asking Congress to establish a special committee "to instruct and direct him on every point and subject relative to the proposed treaty with Spain," Jay, King, and their collaborators sought to evade the congressional stipulation insisting upon "the free Navigation of the Mississippi, from the source to the Ocean, as established in their Treaties with Great Britain."[13]

When Jay's letter reached the floor of Congress on May 31, Monroe continued, Rufus King ("who is associated in this business") rose to distract the delegates' attention from their hidden agenda with "a long speech in which he took a view of the insidious designs of France" in its recent negotiations about the Newfoundland fisheries. King's real objective, Monroe believed, was to make "a tryal of the pulse of the house on the subject" of lifting the Mississippi restriction in Jay's instructions. Congress failed to take the bait. Instead it referred Jay's request to a committee composed of Charles Pettit, the former assistant quartermaster general from Pennsylvania; Rufus King, who was in on the scheme; and James Monroe, who was on to him. They immediately arranged to meet with Jay the next day, June 1, 1786.

King was enthusiastic and Pettit was perhaps willing to evade the Mississippi restriction, but Monroe's presence kept them from acting. Their impasse, Monroe knew, was more important than it seemed. The separatists' "plan failed," he wrote Jefferson, "in not carrying a committee in the first instance for the purpose" of evading Jay's instructions.[14] After enduring their hopeless deadlock for two months, on Tuesday evening, August 1, the three congressmen agreed to refer the matter back to the full Congress. Their recommendation was accepted, their committee disbanded on Wednesday, and Congress called Jay to report on the state of his negotiations on Thursday, August 3, 1786.[15]

"From the best investigation that I have been able to give the subject," Monroe reminded Madison, "I am of opinion that it will be for the benefit of the U. S. that the river sho[ul]d be opend." Monroe recognized that America might be too weak to mount a military challenge if Spain unilaterally closed the river—"nor even think of it for the present"—but he reasoned that "if we enter'd into engagements to the contrary, we [would] seperate those people I mean all those westward of the mountains from the federal government and perhaps throw them into the hands eventually of a foreign power."

None was willing openly to admit it—except in private conversations and occasional correspondence—but Rufus King, Nathan Dane, Nathaniel Gorham, Timothy Pickering, and Theodore Sedgwick had reached exactly the same conclusion. By forcing the west and the south out of the union, they were, as Sedgwick put it, merely "contracting the limits of the confederacy to such as are natural and reasonable."[16]

The letter that Charles Thomson, secretary to Congress, wrote to John Jay, secretary for foreign affairs, on August 1, 1786, was politely succinct. Known to some at the beginning of the Revolution as the "Sam Adams of Philadelphia" and the "Life of the Cause of Liberty," Charles Thomson had been named secretary twelve years earlier at the first meeting of Congress. He was fair, and everyone knew it. "With respect to the taking the Minutes," Thomson later recalled, "what congress adopted, I committed to writing; with what they rejected, I had nothing farther to do; and even this method led to some squabbles with the members, who were desirious of having their speeches and resolutions, however put to rest by the majority, still preserved upon the Minutes." After a dozen years, Thomson surely had forgotten that upon his nomination as secretary of Congress back in August 1774, "Mr. Duane and Mr. Jay discovered [i.e., revealed] at first an Inclination to seek further."[17] Thomson was a neutral in the debate over the Mississippi, but the tone of his letter to a man known for his personal vanity was as polite and succinct as an arrest warrant:

Sir
I have the honor to inform you that the United States in Congress assembled require your attendance in Congress on Thursday next at 12 oClock on the subject of your letter of the 29th of May.

With great Respect, I am, Sr, Your obedt humble Servt,
Cha Thomson[18]

"The position of Mr. Jay becomes very embarrassing," wrote the French chargé d'affaires Louis-Guillaume Otto, who was monitoring congressional deliberations and Gardoqui's negotiations as closely as he could. "He cannot conclude his treaty without encountering bitter reproaches from the five southern states, who loudly accuse him of . . . all sorts of intrigues," while, "on the other hand, this minister cannot refuse to execute the orders of a party of which he is himself the most zealous partisan"—the northern congressmen—"without losing his popularity and influence. Whatever Mr. Jay's conduct may be," Otto concluded, "it is to be feared that this discussion . . . may be the germ of a future separation of the southern states."[19]

Shielded from public scrutiny by the confidentiality of congressional debates, Jay testified in favor of relinquishing navigation of the Mississippi for twenty-five or thirty years. He regarded that concession as a small price to pay for the commercial advantages with which Gardoqui had been dazzling the northern commercial and maritime states.

At last the contentious issue had reached the floor of Congress for open debate, although the debate itself indicated that Jay and the northern separatist congressmen had already failed. Their best shot at success had been to cloak the intended surrender of the Mississippi in the appointment of Jay's special advisory committee—thereby forcing the south and west either to accept a fait accompli or leave the union. Stymied by the failure of their covert strategy, the schemers lacked the nine-state majority they needed for an overt success. Then, as news of the first rumblings of what became Shays's Rebellion in western Massachusetts shook their confidence in their ability to control New England itself, the secret separatists tried to bury the whole episode. With Congress about to embark upon the most divisive debate since its arguments over independence, however, the damage had already been done. Congress was deadlocked—and sectional distrust would quickly spread to the south and west.

The southern delegates chose thirty-four-year-old Charles Pinckney as their champion to answer Jay point for point. Born in Charleston into a preeminent planter family, Pinckney was one of South Carolina's most eligible bachelors, with seven low-country plantations and a fine townhouse on lower Meeting Street. He had read law at home when the Revolution disrupted his enrollment at the Middle Temple in London, entered the state legislature at twenty-two, served as an officer in the state militia, and spent time in a British prison ship and a year on parole for his part in defending the city during the siege of Charleston. Pinckney was destined to leadership in the Philadelphia Convention of 1787, four terms as governor, a seat in the United States Senate, and marriage to his social equal, Mary Eleanor Laurens, daughter of the patriot, planter, and former president of Congress Henry Laurens. Given a week to prepare his speech, Pinckney came to the floor of Congress on Thursday, August 10, with a written text that disputed Jay's testimony, disparaged the value of Spain's offers, and vindicated America's claim to the Mississippi.[20]

Jay's testimony on August 3 and Pinckney's reply a week later framed the most divisive debate in the nation's short history—a debate about the future that was too vital to remain entirely secret forever. The South Carolinian's speech was so important that in response to requests from "many of the southern members to furnish them with copies, I had a few printed." For this Pinckney turned to Francis Childs, who published both the *New York Daily Advertiser,* the city's oldest daily paper, and the weekly *New-York Price-Current.* Childs's office at Water and King Streets was discreetly convenient, but Pinckney's choice of his printer in New York probably had more to do with his kinship to Nathan Childs, publisher of the *South-Carolina Weekly Gazette* and the *Charleston Morning Post,* than to convenience.[21]

*Mr. Charles Pinckney's Speech, in Answer to Mr. Jay* is an odd-looking thing: four long columns of small type on two sides of a fourteen-by-sixteen-inch foolscap sheet of paper. The press run was small, perhaps only a few dozen copies. Neither Pinckney nor his compositor, perhaps one of the shop's apprentices, wasted time on fancy presswork or careful proofreading. Typographical errors abound, even for an age in which spelling was still a creative art. The substitution of a six for a zero in the date of the speech has bred confusion (and footnotes) for generations of historians.

In essence, Francis Childs's print shop struck off copies of *Mr. Charles Pinckney's Speech, in Answer to Mr. Jay* that were little more than galley proofs, corrected hastily if at all, and rushed them to Pinckney, who had most of them "confidentially delivered to some of my friends." Three years later Pinckney sent President Washington "one of the few copies I have left," and fifteen years apparently passed before James Madison got his own copy—even though he visited Monroe in New York that August and replaced Monroe in Congress that November. The copy of *Mr. Charles Pinckney's Speech, in Answer to Mr. Jay* preserved in Madison's papers at the Library of Congress is likely one that Pinckney sent him in July 1801, when Madison was secretary of state and Pinckney was President Jefferson's nominee for ambassador to Spain. Another extant copy, also at the Library of Congress, may have belonged to Charles Thomson, secretary of Congress.[22]

One reason so many of his colleagues wanted copies of Pinckney's speech is that it was long on facts and short on rhetoric (good news for modern readers accustomed to politicians who think in fifteen-second sound bites). Another reason is that although Charles Pinckney disagreed with John Jay at every point, he answered Jay's arguments without distorting them, thus conveniently summarizing both sides of the debate as it eventually went public. The third reason is that everyone in Congress assigned grave importance to the implications of the debate, and Pinckney's speech, for the future of the union.[23]

Congress assembled on Thursday, August 10, 1786, and immediately "resolved" itself into a committee of the whole—a routine procedure that made formal debate easier. The president of Congress, Boston merchant Nathaniel Gorham, whom Gardoqui believed "behaves well and will hold firm," vacated the chair for South Carolina delegate John Bull, who chaired the committee of the whole during the debate.[24] Ten years Pinckney's senior, John Bull lived near Beaufort and had come to Congress with Pinckney two years earlier. Now he was the presiding officer to whom, in the tradition of English-speaking legislatures everywhere, the younger South Carolinian addressed arguments meant for all. At the end of the afternoon, as was then customary, the minutes of Congress would say only that "after some time" Mr. Gorham "resumed the chair, and Mr. Bull reported, that the committee . . . having come to no determination, desire leave to sit to-morrow."[25]

"Mr. President," Pinckney began dispassionately, "the Secretary for Foreign Affairs has reported, that, in consequence of the commission and instructions he had received from Congress for the purpose of negotiating with Mr. Gardoqui, he has had several conferences with him," and that he had discussed "an offer from Mr. Gardoqui to enter into a commercial treaty upon certain principles," provided "that Spain and the United States should fix the boundaries of their respective territories" and that Americans relinquish "their right to navigate the river for twenty-five or thirty years."[26] Pinckney thought the terms were ill-advised, and he set out to explain why.

First, despite her great wealth and vast empire, it seemed clear that Spain was weaker than Jay and his friends were willing to admit. Already wary of the example of American independence, Spain "views with a jealous eye the emancipation of these States, and dreads [our proximity] to her rich and extensive, tho' feeble colonies of South-America." The "deranged state" of American finance and the weakness of the Confederation, Pinckney admitted to his colleagues, gave Carlos III hope that "your distress will force you into a compliance." Nevertheless, Pinckney was confident that America's difficulties were only temporary, while "the Spanish Monarchy carries in its bosom the seeds of its dissolution." America's situation, he said, "though unpleasant, is not yet sufficiently desperate to force us into measures derogatory to our national honor. Spain has more to risque, and more to dread . . . than we can fear."

Secondly, although Gardoqui claimed to offer "principles of perfect reciprocity," his promise was a sham. Spanish ports in the West Indies and South America would remain closed to American trade, tobacco would remain "prohibited in her European ports," and import duties would remain unfair. Americans trading into Spanish ports "will pay four, and in some instances six times as much as their merchants will in our ports." Spanish products would pay duties of 2 or 2.5 percent as they entered the United States (5 percent only if the states approved a proposed impost, which they did not). Conversely, American grain could enter the port of Cádiz with a 10 percent duty, while the tariff on merchandise entering other ports in Spain was "generally estimated at 25 per cent"—and for South American ports "not less than 25 per cent, ever, and in many cases much higher."

Next Pinckney reviewed Spain's interest in specific American commodities. The offer to purchase masts and spars was of "no consequence," he declared. "If you have masts and spars of equal size and fitness with those imported from the Baltic, you will always find purchasers." As to grain, every few years dry weather forced Spain to import wheat from Sicily and Poland, so Spain bought "American wheat when it is as good and as cheap." This fact demonstrated, Pinckney contended, that Spain's idea of reciprocity was to open their ports when it served their interests, "but in the lucrative and truly important trade of their islands and other dominions, or wherever they are afraid of a rivalship, there you are to be prevented."

"It is said," Pinckney laughed, "that Mr. Gardoqui is not personally averse to our going to the Philippines." But he also admits that the "invariable maxim of Spanish politics [is] to exclude all mankind from trading with their colonies and islands." Trade to the distant Philippines was a fantasy, Pinckney warned, "a ministerial finesse . . . to which his instructions do not, nor ever will reach." Commerce with Spain's nearby Caribbean islands was denied.

The American states had varied trading interests. The European trade of Connecticut, New Hampshire, New Jersey, and Rhode Island was "inconsiderable." New England enjoyed "a beneficial trade with Spain, in the export of their fish, lumber, and other articles," but since "Spain in her treaty proposes no advantages that we do not now enjoy," Pinckney could not see "any particular benefit that will result even to the New-England States." New York and Pennsylvania exported wheat, barrel staves, and some other articles that Spain valued "in proportion to the scarcity, and failure of [her] crops, and . . . under the treaty nothing more is proposed to them." As to his own state's export commodities, the Spanish had indigo from their islands and colonies "in much greater quantities than they can consume, and of a superior quality," and Pinckney knew that South Carolina's rice was "in such demand in Europe, that it wants not the aid of a treaty." Maryland, Virginia, the Carolinas, and Georgia exported some wheat and lumber to Spain, but "their great staple tobacco is expressly prohibited." Virginia, Pinckney said, stood to "be more injured than any State in the union" by the cession of the Mississippi and of all the states "the least benefitted under the treaty." In every instance, Pinckney contended, Spain's commercial proposals offered "nothing more than she will always be willing to grant you without a treaty, and nothing which can be termed an equivalent for the forbearance she demands."

And what of the Mississippi? Jay's argument had three parts. First, "that the navigation is unimportant, and that a forbearance will be no sacrifice." Second, that while it was "disgraceful" to assert a legal claim without enforcing it, war was "inexpedient." Third, therefore, the best way to prove America's claim was by inference, by "consent[ing] to suspend the claim for a certain time." This was an argument only a lawyer could love, Pinckney said, for "the right of the United States to navigate the Mississippi has been so often asserted, and so fully stated by Congress."

Pinckney implored his colleagues to look forward in time. The western settlers "must either be the future friends or enemies of the Atlantic states." If Congress surrendered the Mississippi to Spain, "can they be blamed for immediately throwing themselves into her arms for that protection and support which you have denied them"? By dividing "the inhabitants of the western country entirely from us," Spain would render them "subservient to her own purposes."

Finally, what of the existing union? "Our government is so feeble and unoperative that unless a new portion of strength is infused it must in all probability soon dissolve," he admitted—but reform of the Articles of Confederation required the unanimous consent of all thirteen states. The proposed treaty was "calculated to promote the interests of one part of the union at the expence of the other" and dash all hopes for national reform. Thoughtful men everywhere, Pinckney warned, would recognize "the impropriety of vesting [Congress] with farther powers" when it has "so recently abused those they already possess." Adopt Jay's course,

Pinckney warned, and the sovereign states will refuse "to grant us those additional powers of government, without which we cannot exist as a nation"—all for a treaty that offered "no real advantage that we do not at present enjoy." "Let me hope," Pinckney concluded, that "the general welfare of the United States will be suffered to prevail, and that the house will on no account consent to alter Mr. Jay's instructions."

While it clearly articulated the southern critique of the Jay-Gardoqui negotiations, Charles Pinckney's speech did not change anyone's mind. President Gorham had scarcely settled back into his chair when William Grayson, of Virginia, took the floor. Seconded by Timothy Bloodworth, of North Carolina, Grayson demanded that John Jay immediately supply Congress with documentation "respecting the sentiments of the court of France touching our right of Navigating the Mississippi," and "that he state to Congress the territorial claims of Spain on the east side of the Mississippi." The New Englanders were nearly as quick and more to the point. Massachusetts delegate Rufus King bluntly moved to lift the restrictions in Jay's instructions. Theodore Sedgwick seconded King's motion. When the resolution passed a few weeks later, the stipulation that Jay insist upon "the free navigation of the Mississippi, from the Source to the Ocean" in his negotiations with Spain was "repealed and made void" by a seven-to-five vote of the twelve states (Rhode Island being habitually absent).[27]

As he listened to Charles Pinckney's speech in August 1786, after almost three years in Congress, James Monroe's personal stake in the future of the republic was greater than it had been when Sarah Vaughan wondered whether the dimple on his chin constituted beauty. In February, two weeks shy of his twenty-eighth birthday, Monroe had married Elizabeth Kortright, the seventeen-year-old daughter of New York merchant Lawrence Kortright, and the "next morning decamp[e]d for Long Island with the little smiling Venus in his Arms, where they have taken house, to avoid fulsome Complements during the first Transports."[28] Their daughter, Eliza, was born that December.

The Monroes were not the year's only congressional newlyweds. A colleague compared Congress in 1786 to "Calypso's Island," with the charming daughters of New York City merchants in the role of Calypso, the sea nymph who seduced Odysseus. At Trinity Episcopal Church in January, Monroe had stood as best man for Massachusetts congressman

Elbridge Gerry, forty-one, when he married twenty-year-old Ann Thompson, regarded by some as "the most beautiful woman in the United States" and known to all as the daughter of wealthy New York merchant James Thompson. The Monroes exchanged their vows in February, and March brought the marriage of thirty-one-year-old Rufus King to sixteen-year-old Mary Alsop, the only daughter of the wealthy merchant and former New York congressman John Alsop. Finally, in May, treasury commissioner and former Massachusetts congressman Samuel Osgood, a widower of thirty-eight, married the wealthy New York City widow Maria Bowne Franklin.[29]

In five months, the stylish daughters of Gotham had vanquished three Bay State delegates and a Virginian—and gossip in and around Congress held that "other conjunctions copulative are talked of." These New York City "intermarriages" delighted John Jay because "they tend to assimilate the States, and promote . . . the people of America [as] one nation in every respect." Lest anyone at home worry that matrimony might weaken his ties to the Old Dominion, however, Monroe quickly assured his friends that Bitzy "will be adopted a citizen of Virg[ini]a." Similarly, Rufus King declared his "increasing love for our particular country" and pledged that "Mrs. King will not detach me from Massachusetts." The need for these reassurances reflected a heightened sense of regional difference and alienation in 1786—as did Elbridge Gerry's earthy banter in a letter to Monroe (weeks after Ann Thompson Gerry apparently had suffered a miscarriage). "How are your matrimonial prospects?" Gerry smirked,

> *fertile,* I presume for southern soil is almost spontaneous. Mine are not yet promising for after the loss of one harvest a little time is requisite to prepare another. Does brother King make disposition for a summer crop? or does he propose to put in winter grain: as to Friend Osgood's field, I somewhat expect it is run out, unless by being unimproved, it is become enriched.[30]

Those privy to the raging debate in Congress had no doubt about either James Monroe's allegiance to Virginia or Rufus King's love for his *"particular country."*[31] Monroe spent Saturday, August 12, describing the crisis and reviewing its origins in a long letter to Governor Patrick Henry. Unable to encode his letter because someone in the delegation had misplaced the key to the Virginia cipher, Monroe sent his letter to Henry unenciphered, for the crisis was "of such high importance to the U.S. and

ours in particular" that it warranted the "risque [of] communication without that cover." Monroe's three years in Congress were nearly over, and
he urged Governor Henry to convene the legislature "sufficiently early"
so that Virginia's new congressmen were on hand to take their seats "precisely on the day that those of the present delegation expire. Aff[ai]rs
are in too critical a situation for the State to be unrepresented a day—
eminent disadvantage may result from it."[32]

By way of explanation, Monroe reviewed the whole intrigue for Governor Henry (whose formidable opposition to the Constitution two years
later is rooted in these discoveries). Back in December, Monroe recalled,
he had spoken with John Jay and learned that Jay was talking with Gardoqui about a commercial treaty based on "a forbearance of the use of the
Mississippi for 25 or 30 years." The New Yorker "was desirous of occlud-
ing the Mississippi," Monroe wrote, "and of making what he term'd advantageous terms in the treaty of Commerce the means of effecting it."

Monroe had been frankly puzzled by Jay's candor. "Whether he suppos'd I was of his opinion . . . or was endeavoring to prevail on me to be
so I cannot tell." Several prominent Virginians envisaged the Potomac,
not the Mississippi, as gateway to the west, and perhaps Jay thought
Monroe was one of them. Monroe said nothing and kept listening as Jay
worried aloud that if he brought his plan "to the view of Congress they
wo[ul]d most probably disagree to it . . . or conduct themselves so indis-
creetly as to suffer it to become known to the French and Engl[is]h residents here and thus defeat it." Jay also told Monroe—months ahead of
time—that he was thinking of asking Congress to delegate its authority to
a special committee "to controul him in the negotiation [and] to stand to
him in the room of Congress." At this point in their conversation Monroe
reminded Jay "of the instructions from our state respecting the Mississippi and of the impossibility of their concuring in any measures of the
kind." Jay immediately realized he had let the rat out of the bag, and his
conversations with Monroe "on this subject ended from that time."

In February, Monroe continued, when William Grayson returned to
Congress after the holidays, the two Virginians had discussed "all these
circumstances with my opinions on them." From that moment on, Monroe and Grayson kept their eyes on Secretary Jay, and saw him "intriguing with the members to carry the point." On the fateful 29th of
May—Governor Henry's fiftieth birthday—when Jay asked Congress for
the special committee, Monroe and Grayson immediately "knew the
object was to extricate himself from the instruction respecting the Mississippi." Monroe assured Henry that "we of course oppos'd it"—and it
was soon thereafter that he and Grayson learned that Jay was "engag'd"

with the congressmen from "the eastern States in the intrigue especially Mass[achusetts]," and "that New York, Jersey and Pen[nsylvani]a were in favor of it."

"This is one of the most extraordinary transactions I have ever known," Monroe exclaimed, "a minister negotiating expressly for the purpose of defeating the object of his instructions, and by a long train of intrigue and management seducing the representatives of the States to concur in it." And there was more. Monroe was certain "that Committees are held in this town of Eastern men and others of this State upon the subject of a dismemberment of the States East the Hudson from the Union and the erection of them into a seperate gov[ernmen]t." The separatist scheme, Monroe reported, "is talk'd of in Mass[achusetts] familiarly and is suppos'd to have originated there." Closing the Mississippi and creating a northern commercial confederacy were linked. Congressmen Nathaniel Gorham, Rufus King, and Theodore Sedgwick were using Jay's idea of closing the Mississippi "as a step toward" the creation of a separate northern confederacy, and Monroe believed their plan was also "connected with other objects—and perhaps with that upon which the Convention will sit at Annapolis."

"The object in the occlusion of the Mississippi on the part of these people," Monroe warned Henry,

> is to break up . . . the settlements on the western waters, prevent any in future, and thereby keep the States southw[ar]d as they now are— or . . . make it the interest of the [western] people to seperate from the confederacy, so as . . . to throw the weight of population eastward and keep it there, to appreciate the vacant lands of New York and Massachusetts. In short it is a system of policy which has for its object the keeping the weight of gov[ernmen]t and population in this quarter.

Monroe was appalled at the scheme being "purssued by a sett of men so flagitious, unprincipled and determind in their pursuits, as to satisfy me beyond a doubt they have extended their views to the dismemberment of the gov[ernmen]t." Finally, to emphasize that his warnings rested on more than inference, Monroe presented Henry with the most damning firsthand evidence for the truth of these serious allegations: "In conversations at which I have been present," Monroe wrote, "the Eastern people talk of a dismemberment so as to include Pen[nsylvani]a . . . and sometimes all the states south to the Potowmack."

. . .

On August 20, 1786—two weeks after his first secret meeting with a group of northern congressmen—Diego de Gardoqui sent a follow-up report across the Atlantic in a French diplomatic pouch to Floridablanca and Carlos III. This remarkable document (which has never been published or consulted by American historians) confirms Monroe's suspicions. "Not finding a better occasion," Gardoqui wrote, "I take advantage of the French mail to tell you that we are in a critical time. Never in Congress has there been a controversy more combated than that of our Mississippi."[33]

Gardoqui tried to be modest about his accomplishments. "Shy and timid of appearing to show the least self esteem," he wrote with the self-deprecating pride of an accomplished diplomat,

> [my nature] obliges me to keep secret what I have done and reduces me to say that it has even been [asked of] me . . . whether I have come to disunite the Confederation. It has come to such an extreme that a general fast is observed . . . for the preservation of the union.

While the final outcome of the acrimonious debate in Congress was still uncertain as he wrote, Gardoqui was pleased that men from both north and south "talk with the greatest respect of His Majesty and with approbation of my conduct."[34]

Gardoqui admitted that the prospect of signing a commercial treaty with anyone in America was now bleak. "The opposition is insurmountable, even though they flatter me that I have spoiled more of it than I believe." More significantly, however, he knew that the success or failure of his commercial negotiations would no longer really matter to Carlos III. (Pinckney, after all, was quite right about Spain's willingness to buy what it wanted from America, treaty or no.)

During thirteen months of conversation with John Jay and many other American leaders, Diego de Gardoqui had found his way to a stratagem older than Caesar: divide and conquer. With cigars and promises for the members of Congress, fine wine and lavish dinners for New York society, a stallion for John Jay, presents for Sarah, a strong Spanish jackass for Washington, and gilded visions of prosperity for the merchants of Boston and Salem—Diego de Gardoqui had probed the weak points in the American union, and he had exploited them. Perhaps nothing had changed along the banks of the mighty river during those thirteen months, but Spain's grip on the Mississippi and Louisiana was stronger in 1786 than it had been before because Congress was deadlocked five states to seven along sectional lines. Spain had gotten "as much as could be hoped," Gardoqui assured Carlos III and Floridablanca on August 20, 1786, "because I believe without vanity to have squeezed this orange to the last drop."[35] And so he had, leaving John Jay with an empty rind and Congress with a mess of worthless pulp.

## CHAPTER FIVE

# The Touch of a Feather

*The Western settlers, (I speak now from my own observation)
stand as it were upon a pivot—the touch of a feather, would turn
them any way—They have look'd down the Mississippi, until the
Spaniards (very impoliticly I think, for themselves) threw difficulties in their way; and they looked that way for no other reason,
than because they could glide gently down the stream; without
considering perhaps, the fatigues of the voyage back again.*

—George Washington, October 10, 1784[1]

BY CONJURING UP visions of maritime prosperity for the merchants and fisherman of the eastern states, Gardoqui had led Rufus
King and his New England friends to the brink of separatism during
the summer of 1786. Once the question of revoking Jay's instruction
reached the floor of Congress, however, Gardoqui knew that the real
prospect of a treaty was over—and that Spain's best interests required
him to act as though everything were still possible. He quietly probed for
southern congressmen who might be amenable to persuasion, or cash,
and he continued to entice Rufus King and the New Englanders with
details about Spanish commercial regulations. Gardoqui did all he could
to bolster their conviction that "a Treaty with Spain is at this time a desirable Event," and to pump up their dream that it would "not be long
delayed."[2]

While the August 29 revocation of the Mississippi clause in Jay's
instructions was a victory for the eastern states, the Virginia delegation
contested it immediately on the grounds that the Articles of Confederation required the vote of *nine* states to ratify any treaty. On this procedural question the Virginians were outvoted again, seven to five, but the
matter quickly became a moot point. As long as the Congress remained
in a seven-to-five deadlock, no treaty could hope to win the required support of nine states. Gardoqui really had squeezed the last drop from this

orange, leaving Congress bitterly divided over the future of the Mississippi River and the west.

Antagonism bred by the Jay-Gardoqui negotiations festered in Congress for two full years. The Spanish treaty was dead in the water, but both sides were on their guard just in case. An air of suspicion permeated national politics. Distrust made routine business more difficult, aborted a promising congressional reform movement to strengthen the union, and inflamed regional friction both in the Philadelphia Convention of 1787 and in the state conventions that ratified the new federal Constitution. Eventually, on September 16, 1788, three weeks before adjourning for the last time, the Confederation Congress resolved "that no further progress be made in the negotiations with Spain . . . but that the subject to which they related be referred to the federal government which is to assemble in March next."[3] The underlying issues of national and regional self-interest were not about to disappear. The Jay-Gardoqui negotiations revealed attitudes toward the Mississippi River and the west that shaped the events of the next decade and the subsequent history of North America—jealous hostility from New England, competitive neglect from the middle states, expansive hopes from the south, and impatient frustration in Kentucky and the Ohio Country.[4]

The empire founded by the Castilian sponsors of Christopher Columbus had never been larger than it was in 1786. The New World dominions of His Most Catholic Majesty Carlos III embraced all of Mexico, Central America, and South America except the Guianas and Brazil. Of the major Caribbean islands, he held Cuba, Puerto Rico, Santo Domingo, and Trinidad. Of the territory that now comprises the United States, he ruled Florida, coastal Alabama and Mississippi, the east bank of the Mississippi River from Natchez to the Gulf of Mexico, and virtually everything west of the river and south of Canada.

The vast Spanish empire looked formidable on a world map, but more precarious in ledgers of the royal treasury. Silver production at Zacatecas in the province of New Spain, with its capital at Mexico City, had doubled under the Spanish Bourbons. By 1786 Mexican bullion comprised 49.5 percent of the annual export trade of the entire Spanish empire. Carlos III and his chief minister, José Moñino y Redondo, count of Floridablanca, were keenly aware that this wealth comprised about a third of the royal income, and that it was essential to the survival of the Spanish economy and government.[5]

With half the wealth of its world empire at stake, Spain's imperial objective was to maintain the watershed of the Mississippi River as a protective barrier against its nearest and most aggressive rival. For this reason—after opening the river during the American Revolution as a covert slap at Great Britain—Floridablanca had slammed the door on American traders in 1784. That official policy did not drastically change until Carlos III joined his beloved queen, Maria Amalia of Saxony, in the royal crypts of El Escorial. Diego de Gardoqui reflected this sentiment in a private conversation with James Madison, when he "betrayed strongly the anxiety of Spain to retard the population of the Western Country; observing that when ever a sufficient [American] force should arise therein, it w[oul]d be impossible for it to be controuled."[6]

During the Jay-Gardoqui negotiations of 1785–1786 and the ongoing debate into 1788, two distinct groups of Americans—New Englanders and middle state advocates of rival streams—favored closing the Mississippi River to American trade for twenty or thirty years. "Every Citizen of the Atlantic States, who emigrates to the westward of the Allegany is a total Loss to our confederacy," Rufus King and his friends believed. "Nature has severed the two countries by a vast and extensive chain of mountains" and "interest will keep them separate," King wrote.

> The feeble policy of our disjointed Government will not be able to unite them. For these reasons I have ever been opposed to encouragements of western immigrants—the States situated on the Atlantic are not sufficiently populous, and loosing our men, is loosing our greatest Source of Wealth.

Boston merchant Nathaniel Gorham, president of Congress, was blunt: "Mr. Ghorum avowed his opinion that . . . shutting the Mississippi would be advantageous to the Atlantic States, and wished to see it shut." In a private fit of exasperation, John Jay was even more blunt. "Would that the world had no Mississippi!" he exclaimed during a frustrating moment of his negotiations with Diego de Gardoqui.[7]

The "rage for emigrating to our western country" astounded Jay. "Thousands have already fixed their habitations in that wilderness," he wrote a friend, "and the seeds of a great people are daily planting beyond the mountains." Would they be friend or foe? "That western country will one day give us trouble," Jay feared. "To govern them will not be easy, and whether after two or three generations they will be fit to govern themselves is a question that merits consideration."[8]

When John Jay worried that the United States was already too big for a single republic, his opinion was bolstered by the best of eighteenth-century political science. On this point, Americans looked to Montesquieu's *Spirit of the Laws,* a book of applied political theory published in 1748, widely translated and reprinted, and highly regarded by statesmen of the revolutionary generation. Montesquieu's book was ideally suited to men of a practical American temperament: its short chapters and numbered paragraphs were filled with pithy maxims about monarchies, aristocracies, and republics—an eighteenth-century *Cliffs Notes on Classical Government.* Educated men read Montesquieu firsthand (skimming lightly over familiar citations to Aristotle and Plato, Plutarch and Livy, Cicero and the rest), and they repeated his basic ideas in newspaper essays, pamphlets, and political oratory. Montesquieu's writings readily explained the fall of the Roman republic, the inequities of the Stamp Act, and the recent decline of the Confederation Congress.[9]

With nods to "the great Montesquieu" and "the experience of all ages," James Monroe's neighbor and law partner, John Dawson, proclaimed "that no government, formed on the principles of freedom, can pervade all North America." The very idea of a single republic "one thousand miles in length, and eight hundred in breadth, and containing six millions of white inhabitants all reduced to the same standard of morals, of habits, and of laws," wrote the former librarian of Harvard College, James Winthrop, in the *Massachusetts Gazette,* "is in itself an absurdity, and contrary to the whole experience of mankind."[10]

For several months in 1786, as we have seen, the Massachusetts congressional delegation and their friends in New England had drawn a parallel lesson from Montesquieu as they flirted with separatism. Having reconsidered the merits of "their connection with the Southern States" and convinced themselves that "even the appearance of a union cannot . . . long be preserved," men like Rufus King and Theodore Sedgwick had conspired to "contract . . . the limits of the confederacy to such as are *natural* and *reasonable.*" In the smaller northern republic of their dreams, the needs of merchants and fishermen and the value of a commercial treaty with Spain would be obvious, understood, and beyond the reach of savage frontiersmen and slaveholding "Southern Nabobs [who] behave as though they viewed themselves a Superior order of animals when Compared with those of the other end of the Confederacy."[11]


Chilling news from the western counties of Massachusetts rapidly cooled the impulse toward New England separatism in the autumn of 1786.

Squeezed by postwar recession, overextended credit, and outrageously high taxes payable only in hard currency, the farmers of western Massachusetts rose up against the courts, lawyers, creditors, and tax collectors who threatened to foreclose on their farms and imprison them for debt. In August and September 1786, armed groups of farmers forced the closing of courts in five Massachusetts counties.

By Christmas the movement found its nominal leader in Captain Daniel Shays, an impoverished Revolutionary War veteran from the Connecticut River Valley town of Pelham, Massachusetts, thirty miles north of the government arsenal at Springfield. Late in January, eleven hundred angry men and boys attacked the arsenal and were repulsed by a single volley of cannon fire. By spring Shays's Rebellion was over. Four men had died in skirmishes (three rebels and a militiamen), four were wounded, two rebel leaders were hanged, and the rest fined, whipped, or briefly imprisoned. Daniel Shays himself faded into obscurity, drink, and poverty, dying in 1825 at the age of eighty-four.[12]

When the first news of frontier unrest reached New York City late in August 1786, the Massachusetts delegation was, simultaneously, working to win Congress more authority for the proper regulation of American trade while also flirting with ideas of separation or a commercial sub-confederation. Despite the apparent contradiction, either path might move New England toward prosperity, and what other options did they have? The status quo was hopeless. Congress needed a transfusion of energy and money for the union to survive, but the plan of a convention to revise the Articles of Confederation seemed dangerous—a cure worse than the disease, and all the more suspicious because it was so popular among the wealthy planters of Virginia and Maryland. Massachusetts chose not to be represented at the Annapolis convention, a meeting that Theodore Sedgwick believed masked "an intention of defeating the enlargement of the powers of Congress."[13] How could slaveholding planters and southern nabobs sympathize with the real problems of commerce? "The proposition for the Annapolis convention, which originated in the Assembly of Virginia," warned Rufus King, "did not come from the persons favorable to a commercial System common to all the states." The Chesapeake grandees pushing for a convention seemed just hapless tools of Philadelphia financier Robert Morris and his ilk. Surely their intended convention would summon "thro out the Union an Exertion of the Friends of an Aristocracy" and degenerate into "a plan of foederal Government essentially different from the republican Form now administered."[14]

Coupled with the rejection of measures to strengthen the Confederation Congress, the grim news from the frontier counties of Massachusetts undermined all the political calculations of Rufus King, Nathaniel Gorham, Theodore Sedgwick, and their friends. Compared to Daniel Shays and the angry plowboys of Massachusetts, those superior animals, the southern nabobs, and their proposed convention looked better than it had. Agrarian unrest at home made a stronger alliance with men of property increasingly attractive, even if their property included slaves.

"The affair of the Mississippi hangs at present in suspence," William Grayson reported with relief in November 1786 to James Monroe, who was heading home after three years in Congress, and to his successor, James Madison. "The M[assachusetts] Bay delegation have been more on the conciliatory plan, since the late insurrections in that State," Grayson added. "They of course depend greatly on the foederal aid," Grayson reminded Madison, and were now wishing "not only for a continuance of the confederation, but that it may be made more adequate to the purposes of government." For the past year Grayson and Monroe had seen the New Englanders in their more provincial and selfish moments—but Shays had changed their mood. "The Massachusetts delegation have been much more friendly . . . since the late insurrection in their State," Grayson smiled to Monroe, and now "they look upon the foederal assistance as a matter of the greatest importance [and] of course they wish for a continuance of the Confederation."[15] Of course.


The Massachusetts delegation of 1786 couldn't have cared less about America's future claim to the Mississippi River, but many politicians and merchants from the middle Atlantic states (and several prominent Virginians) quietly agreed with John Jay about a *temporary* closing of navigation on the river. These were men who assumed (along with other southerners and westerners) "that all North America must at length be annexed to us," but who were committed to other rivers as trade routes into Kentucky and the west.[16] If fate kept the Mississippi closed for a few years, they were not averse to developing a variety of dreams and schemes for waterways and canals connecting their favored streams to the lands beyond the Appalachians.

Gazing across the lawns of Mount Vernon toward the Potomac River, George Washington wrote that "our clearest interest is to open a wide door, and make a smooth way for the produce of that Country to pass to *our Markets* before the trade may get into another channel."[17] In subsequent decades, how many thousands of American enthusiasts for *our* canal and *our* turnpike, *our* railroad and *our* interstate highway, *our* airport and *our* information technology corridor have echoed Washington's sentiment?

In Richmond, men dreamt of connecting the James River (which pierces the Blue Ridge Mountains) with the Kanawha, a tributary of the Ohio. They began work in 1784 but fell behind their rivals in New York. Eventually their canal system was interrupted and damaged by the Civil War, and later its surviving towpaths supported the railroad line named for the connection they dreamt of: the Norfolk and Western.[18]

George Washington supported the James River project, but he and his neighbors were more enthusiastic about linking the Potomac River with any of the tributaries of the Ohio that converge near Pittsburgh. Toward this end, at the great falls of the Potomac, Washington started a canal that opened in 1800, only to be superseded by the Chesapeake and Ohio Canal in 1825, which in turn blazed the trail for Peter Cooper's steam-powered *Tom Thumb* and the Baltimore and Ohio Railroad.[19]

Washington's favorite river had more northern rivals, as well. From the headwaters of Chesapeake Bay, Pennsylvanians dreamt of reaching inland to Pittsburgh via the Susquehanna River, with a portage of eleven miles to the Allegheny (a major tributary of the Ohio) and another portage of only seven miles to Lake Erie. It was plain, Pennsylvania's William Maclay bragged in the *New York Daily Advertiser*, that the Susquehanna had better connections to the west than the Potomac, "and is besides intimately connected with the northern waters, and great lakes; advantages which the Potowmac cannot pretend to."[20]

Regardless of Washington's and Maclay's grand claims for the Potomac and the Susquehanna, their mid-Atlantic rivalry for the western trade was mild compared to the ancient contest between the Hudson and the St. Lawrence Rivers. Pioneered by the *coureurs de bois* of New France, the great commercial empire of the St. Lawrence followed the beaver along waterways stretching westward from Quebec and Montreal through the Great Lakes into the Canadian Rockies. Canada dominated the North American fur trade through most of the eighteenth century, despite the fact that the St. Lawrence freezes over every winter. The Canadians lost their advantage in the Great Lakes when America won its independence. In the new century they would finish second to their New York rivals in the race to build canals to carry inland produce from the Great Lakes to the sea.[21]

In this commercial competition between the major rivers of the Atlantic Coast, first place went eventually to the ice-free port at the mouth of the Hudson. Forty years after John Jay's protective measures to close the Mississippi and stifle western expansion had failed, a more visionary generation of New Yorkers led by De Witt Clinton started a 363-mile canal between Albany and Buffalo. Completed in 1825, the Erie Canal would reduce the cost of shipping freight from Lake Erie to Manhattan from $100 a ton to $6 a ton and crown New York City as the great storehouse and emporium of the East Coast.[22]

George Washington began his love affair with the west at sixteen, riding along the Shenandoah River "through the most beautiful Groves of Sugar Trees" on a bright Saturday in March 1748—the same year that Montesquieu warned that extended republics cannot long subsist. The young Virginian had crossed the Blue Ridge with a surveying party "and Spent the best part of the Day in admiring the Trees and Richness of the Land." By twenty he owned two thousand fertile acres on the Virginia frontier, by 1767 he had acquired land west of the Alleghenies, and by his death in 1799 the squire of Mount Vernon owned forty-five thousand choice acres of western land scattered through the Shenandoah Valley and the modern states of Kentucky, Ohio, West Virginia, and Pennsylvania.

In the west, Washington believed, "an enterprizing Man with very little Money may lay the foundation of a Noble Estate . . . for himself and posterity." After all, "the greatest Estates we have in this Colony were made . . . by taking up and purchasing at very low rates the rich back Lands which were thought nothing of in those days, but are now the most valuable Lands we possess." As a surveyor, planter, and speculator, Washington had felt the lure of western lands as intensely as any colonial Virginian. As a statesman and strategist whose military career began with the first shots of the French and Indian War near Fort Duquesne, however, Washington had learned in the American forest what Harvard librarians found in Montesquieu, that distance and self-interest could disrupt empires and republics.[23]

At the end of the Revolution, Washington warned that Americans would move across the mountains "faster than any other ever did, or any one would imagine." And he knew that their political allegiance would tend toward the nation that provided them access to markets. Opening the Potomac River was "of great political importance," Washington wrote in 1784, "to prevent the trade of the Western territory from settling in the hands either of the Spanish or British." If "the trade of that Country should flow through the Mississippi or St Lawrence . . . they would in a few years be as unconnected with us [as] we are with South America."

For Virginia's well-being, he believed that extending the "inland navi-gation of the rivers Potomac and James" was essential. If America's west-ern settlers "cannot, by an easy communication be drawn this way," Washington warned, "they will become a distinct people from us—have different views—different interests, and instead of adding strength to the Union, may in case of a rupture with either [Spain or Britain] be a formi-dable and dangerous neighbour."[24]

Aside from his obvious attachment to the river that washed Mount Vernon, Washington was indifferent to the Mississippi River chiefly because it belonged to Spain and emptied into the Gulf of Mexico. "The more communications are opened" between east and west, he advised a friend in Maryland, "the closer we bind that rising world (for indeed it may be so called) to our interests; and the greater strength we acquire by it . . . not only as it respects our commerce, but our political interest, and the well being and strength of the Union also."[25]

"The Western settlers," Washington said, speaking "from [his] own observation," stood "as it were upon a pivot—the touch of a feather, would turn them any way." During the Revolution they

> look'd down the Mississippi, until the Spaniards . . . threw difficulties in their way; and they looked that way for no other reason, than because they could glide gently down the stream; without considering perhaps, the fatigues of the voyage back again . . . and because they have no other means of coming to us but by a long Land transporta-tion and unimproved roads. . . . But smooth the road once, and make easy the way for them, and then see what an influx of articles will be poured in upon us—how amazingly our exports will be encreased by them, and how amply we shall be compensated for any trouble and expence we may encounter.[26]

Other Potomac planters shared Washington's indifference to the Missis-sippi. From George Mason's silence "upon this subject," James Monroe concluded that Washington's neighbor, the influential master of Gunston Hall and principal author of the Virginia constitution and Declaration of Rights, was "not with us."[27] Monroe also suspected that Congressman Richard Henry Lee and his cousin Light-Horse Harry Lee, while voting dutifully with the Virginia delegation to uphold the stipulation about the Mississippi in Jay's instructions, privately "held the opposite sentiment."[28]

An active patriot since the Stamp Act and a Virginian who had often

allied with the radicalism of Samuel Adams in national affairs, the aging
and gout-ridden Richard Henry Lee, now fifty-four, was more concerned
with European than with western affairs. Opening the Mississippi, he
suggested in a letter to George Washington, was "an Object unattainable
for many years, and probably Never without War not only with Spain, but
most likely with the Bourbon Alliance." European hostility seemed a
greater danger than "an Alliance of Kentuckians with the British," for
"after all, if this navigation could be opened and the benefits be such as
are chimerically supposed, it must in its consequences depopulate and
ruin the Old States."[29]

More interesting than his cousin's intermittent correspondence with
the influential squire of Mount Vernon, however, was the full-court press
that Light-Horse Harry Lee mounted on the subject of the Mississippi
between April and October 1786. In no fewer than six letters to Washington, Lee urged a temporary closing of the river in exchange for the commercial treaty. Lee's arguments were familiar. "Rather than defer longer
the benefits of a free liberal system of trade with Spain," he asked during
the secret congressional debates in July, "why not agree to the occlusion
of the Mississippi"? If America accepted Gardoqui's terms, Lee reiterated a week prior to Charles Pinckney's speech, "we give in fact nothing,
for the moment our western country become populous and capable, they
will seize by force what may have be[en] yielded by treaty."

Sweetening his pitch in September, Lee alluded to current talk of
improving Washington's favorite river. "If the Potomac navigation proceeds in the manner these gentlemen mention," Lee said, "it . . . will be a
strong argument among the politicians, [in] favor of the Spanish treaty
and the occlusion of the Mississippi." The final and most lengthy letter in
the series, early in October, summarized Jay's arguments on behalf of the
treaty and "confess[ed]" Lee's "hope that the state of Virginia will consider a treaty with Spain on the principles of the project"—that is, with
restrictions on navigation of the Mississippi—"essentially necessary to
her political happiness, and to her commercial aggrandizement."

Light-Horse Harry Lee's persistent appeals to Washington are interesting less for what he said than for his motive for pressing the matter.
Through Gardoqui's good offices, Washington had already accepted the
gift of a fine Spanish jackass from Carlos III, and along with one of Lee's
letters came a "small box given to me by Mr. Gardoqui for you." The contents of that small box are unknown, and no one (least of all Gardoqui)
would imagine that General Washington could be bribed. So, with Congress deadlocked seven to five, Gardoqui recruited Henry Lee to culti-

vate Washington's support for the proposed commercial treaty on the long-shot chance that he might induce Virginia to reverse its position on the navigation of the Mississippi. Gardoqui's expense accounts and confidential reports, however, prove that Light-Horse Harry Lee—a man remembered mainly as the father of Robert E. Lee and the eulogist who proclaimed George Washington to be "first in war, first in peace, and first in the hearts of his countrymen"—was a hired mule. For his services in smuggling pro-Spanish arguments to Washington, Gardoqui secretly gave Lee a total of $5,000 in loans, which Lee never repaid.[30]

About the time of Light-Horse Harry Lee's last letter to Washington in October, his "heterodoxy" on the issue of the Mississippi aroused deep suspicions back in Virginia, where the legislature was "full of consternation and complaint" about Jay's "project for bartering the Mississippi to Spain." Lee was eligible for reelection and had always voted in accord with his instructions (regardless of his private opinion) but on November 7, 1786, the legislature summarily "dropt" him when it reelected the other eligible members of the Virginia congressional delegation. Lee regarded his "disgrace" as "cruel and ungrateful," and his friends were pained by "the mortification in which it must involve a man of sensibility." It was an embarrassing snub to any man of honor. "I feel as you do for our acquaintance Colo[nel] Lee," Washington wrote with greater empathy than grammatical precision: "Better never have delegated, than left him out." Happily for Lee's political reputation, he was reelected to a vacancy in the Virginia congressional delegation a few weeks later—and the Spanish bribe remained a secret until discovered in the archive of Gardoqui's confidential reports and expense accounts by diplomatic historian Samuel Flagg Bemis in the twentieth century.[31]

Even Thomas Jefferson's commitment to the Mississippi was a recent development. Trade with the west, Thomas Jefferson had written to Washington in October 1784, was "under a competition between the Hudson, the Patomac and the Mississippi." The Mississippi had the advantage for heavy commodities, but with navigation in the Gulf of Mexico "so dangerous, and that up the Mississippi so difficult and tedious," it was unlikely "that European merchandize will return through that channel." The Mississippi and its tributaries invited "flour, lumber and other heavy articles . . . floated on rafts which will be themselves an article of sale . . . the navigators returning by land or [upstream] in light batteaux."

For imported goods, Jefferson foresaw "a rivalship between the Hudson and Patowmac." Poring over his maps, Jefferson calculated that the navigable tributaries of the Ohio were closer to Alexandria, Virginia, than to New York "by 730 miles, and . . . interrupted by one portage only." Nature, Jefferson solemnly decreed, "has declared in favour of the Patowmac."

Like Fortune, however, Nature is profligate with her charms. "Unfortunately," Jefferson lamented, "the Hudson is already open and known in practice," while "ours is still to be opened." Washington, he hoped, would inspire Virginia to open the Potomac River and seize "the moment in which the trade of the West will begin to get into motion and to take its direction." Avowing that he personally did not own "nor ever hav[e] a prospect of owning one inch of land on any water either of the Patowmac or Ohio," Jefferson regarded his own "zeal in this business [a]s public and pure"—civic virtues presumably transferable to any gentleman who helped enforce Nature's verdict, even if he happened to own land along the chosen river.[32]

Washington's enthusiasm for the Potomac and Jefferson's verdict in its favor as Nature's preferred artery to the west occasionally blinded both men to the inconvenient fact that water runs downhill. Not so the intrepid Pennsylvania democrat William Maclay. "During all the time of the high price of wheat, flour, etc. in the Atlantic states," Maclay asked, has "a single boat been loaded with these articles at Fort Pitt, and *ascended* the Monongohela or any other stream, so that these same articles reached the mouth of the Potowmack? The answer must be, no."[33] Would not the farmers of the west rather "take their chance of the Mississippi market at 2000 miles distance? the answer must be yes." To clear a profit, Maclay knew, boats laden with country produce

> must be heavily loaded, [and] such cannot ascend streams with ease if the water is high. . . . If shallow, they cannot proceed for want of water . . . and even then the labor of the boatmen is extreme. Hence country produce will always descend the full stream, be the prospect of the market ever so distant.

"Thus it is plain," Maclay concluded, "that the Atlantic rivers never can supply any town on their banks with provisions or any heavy articles, but those which are produced on their own lands."[34] Despite William Maclay's affection for the Susquehanna, his critique of the Potomac applied equally to the Pennsylvania river. For impatient western families and clear-eyed southerners, it was the Mississippi that ultimately mattered. Until their countrymen got over their regional infatuations with lesser streams on the Atlantic Coast, however, American sentiment remained divided—and that division gave Spain room for diplomatic manuevering and frontier intrigue.

## CHAPTER SIX

# Bourbons on the Rocks

*Carlos, Carlos, ¡qué tonto tú eres! [How foolish you are!]*

—Carlos III to the future Carlos IV, ca. 1788[1]

*This Federal Republic is born, so to speak, small; and before it could establish its independence it had to have the support of nations as powerful as France and Spain. The day, however, will come when it will be gigantic, and a formidable colossus in these regions; then it will forget the benefits which it has received from both Powers, and will think of nothing but its own aggrandizement.*

—Pedro Pablo Abarca de Bolea, count of Aranda, 1783[2]

A SIDE FROM THE OLD Ursuline Convent and a few other struc-tures that survived the disastrous fire of 1788, the oldest buildings in New Orleans stand near Bayou St. John. Along Moss Street the West Indian rooflines and pencil-post columns of plantation-style houses built in the second half of the eighteenth century compete for the soul of the neighborhood with nineteenth-century shotgun doubles and spacious 1930s bungalows. Formerly navigable to Lake Pontchartrain, Bayou St. John was the preferred gateway to Spanish New Orleans. By entering Lake Pontchartrain through Lake Borgne and the straits of the Rigolets, thirty miles east of the city, Spanish sailing vessels avoided the shoals near the crow's-foot delta of the Mississippi and the slow drudgery of tacking and jibing against the current through ninety miles of winding river. Bayou St. John is now severed from the lake by the modern city's protec-tive levees, but a small bronze plaque outside the West Indian plantation-style house at 1300 Moss Street, built about 1784, marks Grand Route St. John. Then a simple dirt road, despite its magnificent name, Grand Route St. John followed an old Indian path along a slight ridge between the river and the bayou that connected Spanish New Orleans with its international port of entry. It was here that the royal packet boat from Havana moored late on Friday afternoon, April 3, 1789.

That morning at their regular weekly meeting Governor Esteban Rodríguez Miró and members of the Cabildo had honored their retiring colleague, Intendant Martín Navarro, who was returning to Spain. Now the Havana packet boat was discharging an unwelcome messenger. As the afternoon sun cast shadows of moss-laden oaks across tile roofs and stucco walls, a royal courier rushed along Grand Route St. John toward the city with sealed proclamations announcing "the death of our King and Lord Don Carlos III (may he have Heavenly Glory)" and the accession of his eldest son, the former Prince of Asturias, now Carlos IV.[3]

As soon as the information reached him, Governor Miró sent messengers to summon the members of the Cabildo to meet in "extraordinary session" early Saturday morning. Gathering at nine o'clock in the "chambers of the Capitol" (the provincial government house that served as Miró's residence and office near the river on St. Louis Street), they learned of "the grievous occurrence . . . of the death of our King and Lord Don Carlos III . . . at 15 minutes to one on the 14th of December." Miró outlined the funeral rites that would be conducted "in accordance with the Royal orders of His Majesty the actual King" and "with the greatest possible solemnity and propriety in the small church of the Hospital, which was not destroyed by the flames of the late disastrous fire."[4]

On Monday, two members of the Cabildo, "wearing mourning, and preceded by the two mace-bearers of the City with their maces, also in mourning," would announce the king's death to the populace of the city. At nine o'clock on Tuesday, April 22, the mace-bearers, once again "dressed in strict mourning, and accompanied by the officers of the Military Corps," would lead Governor Miró, the members of the Cabildo, and other dignitaries in a solemn procession "from the government buildings (which serve for the meetings of the Cabildo, due to the burning of the casa capitular in the fire of the 21st of March last year) to the Church at Charity Hospital" on Rampart between Toulouse and St. Peter Streets "(instead of the parochial church which was likewise destroyed in the said fire)."[5]

In the center of the church stood a "majestic sepulchral bier." At the top were the ceremonial funeral urn covered with a royal mantle in bright red velvet and "a scepter and gilt crown with bright beautiful enamel, which resembled precious stones" resting on a red velvet pillow decorated with gold braid—all of it sheltered beneath "a beautiful canopy which . . . descended in four arched festoons" bearing insignias of the king and medallions of the royal orders. Sixty royal coats of arms graced the altar, the pulpit, and the walls of the chapel, "all illuminated by a large number of torches and candles . . . giving splendor to the mournful display." As the city gathered in "a spectacle equally respectful and demonstrative" of their veneration for the late Carlos III, the Reverend Father Antonio de Sedella, a Capuchin friar known also as Père Antoine, offered an eloquent eulogy. Tears and prayers for absolution were punctuated by a volley of artillery fired in salute to the passing of one of Spain's greatest monarchs. Finally, about midday, the governor and members of the Cabildo "returned in the same order . . . to the Government Buildings where courteous leave-taking took place among those present, and all retired to their respective homes."[6]

A great monarch was dead and his able intendant, Martín Navarro, was leaving New Orleans. For twenty-five years, Carlos III had been willing to subsidize Louisiana as a borderland barrier protecting the silver mines of Mexico from foreigners. More recently, his intendant had advocated free trade and population growth as a better means to the same end. Without these two men guiding Spanish policy in Madrid and New Orleans, however, their successors wavered in the face of American westward expansion. The death of Carlos III and the ineptitude of his Bourbon cousins in France and of his son Carlos IV set in motion a sequence of world events that enabled the United States to pluck territories from Spain more aggressively (and in much larger pieces) than Thomas Jefferson had anticipated while Carlos III was still alive.

Conflict between governors and intendants, each of whom answered independently to a different set of imperial officials, was commonplace throughout the Spanish empire. When Esteban Rodríguez Miró and Martín Navarro responded so promptly and cooperatively to the great fire of 1788, that moment may well have marked the pinnacle of executive efficiency for the Spanish regime in Louisiana. The able partnership of able men was rooted in their shared perception of the colony's needs, and in their shared commitment to the benefits of free trade and increased immigration. Devastating as it had been, Louisiana had survived the fire of 1788. New Orleans would rebuild (as it would rebuild yet again after another major fire in 1794), but the province would never recover from the death of Carlos III or the retirement of Martín Navarro. Their departures made the year 1788 an unmarked turning point for the future of North America.

For all his enthusiasm about free trade and his emulation of Anglo-

American entrepreneurial values, Martín Navarro had never lost sight of the strategic importance that Carlos III attached to Louisiana. The king and his intendant agreed that colony was, first and foremost, a buffer zone to keep foreigners away from the silver mines of New Spain. Englishmen had once been the main threat, but the situation had changed after the American Revolution. The English still held Canada, but in his *Political Reflections on the Present Conditions of the Province of Louisiana,* Navarro had warned that American settlements in the Ohio and Illinois Country now gave Spanish statesmen "motive to reflect very seriously." He minced no words. American frontiersmen were "new enemies who are regarding our situation and happiness with too great jealousy." With this formidable threat in mind, Navarro had recommended that Carlos III ease restrictions on Louisiana trade to encourage "a numerous population in this province . . . [as] a barrier for the kingdom of Nueva España" capable of "oppos[ing] any attempt of the Americans already settled on the upper part of the river."[7]

As Navarro and his partners demonstrated before the intendant retired with a fortune of 3.7 million pesos, expanding the trade of New Orleans was easy. The great river channeled commodities and money past Spanish officials who controlled the port of New Orleans. Regulating immigration and defending a border that stretched sixteen hundred miles from St. Augustine west to Natchez and north along the Mississippi past modern Rock Island, Illinois, was far more complicated. Navarro had warned that the American presence in the upper reaches of the Mississippi Valley was cause for Spanish statesmen "to reflect very seriously." With the accession of forty-year-old Carlos IV, however, the crowned head of the Spanish empire was no longer capable of thoughtful reflections upon policy—indeed the new king was incapable of distinguishing between a serious statesman and a sycophant who was sleeping with his queen.

The new king inherited his father's passion for shooting, but little of his father's energy or self-discipline. Trim and athletic, Carlos III had loved to stalk wolves through the countryside, matching his wits against a wily predator that threatened his subjects' livestock. His sluggish son preferred blasting away from a platform as retainers drove captive deer and wild boar into range for the slaughter, or on one occasion, according to a dyspeptic Englishman, firing six small cannon into a herd of "two thousand deer cooped up in an enclosure." Carlos III promoted the applied sciences by founding the Royal Clock-Making School in 1771 and a royal clock factory in 1788. His successor collected thousands of pocket watches and hundreds of mantel clocks and spent the better part of rainy days repairing them, tinkering with carpentry and plumbing, or wrestling with stable hands. On evenings when Carlos IV indulged his love of music by playing with a string quartet, a successful concert depended on the other players' ability to anticipate the erratic tempo of the royal violinist. One musician who pointed out that their sheet music called for three bars of rest was informed that "Kings never wait." More frequently Carlos IV closed his day with a huge evening meal and "a game of cards in which he invariably fell asleep."[8]

All too aware of his father's disappointment in him, and cursed with "just enough intelligence to realize his mediocrity," according to biographer Sir Charles Petrie, Carlos IV sought "refuge in a state of mental inactivity." Personal tranquillity became his sole objective, "and anyone who would relieve him of the necessity of taking a decision was his friend." In exchange for his repose, Carlos IV eventually sacrificed "his authority as a prince, his dignity as a husband, the interests of his country, and, finally, his crown."[9]

Maria Luisa of Parma, the new queen of Spain, had been beautiful as a girl and was always decisive if not headstrong. Married to her first cousin on her fourteenth birthday in December 1765, the young Princess of Asturias at first impressed the French ambassador as a girl of "courtesy, wit, and graces . . . [who] spends her whole time in her suite of rooms, her only pleasures being conversation and music." Soon enough, however, her father-in-law and the Spanish court learned that a third pleasure frequented Maria Luisa's suite of rooms. The princess was "a woman of excessive temperament," wrote one courtier, "whose appetites were not satisfied by her lovers, and whose ardor was not slaked by the passage of years." She was born "with special aptitudes and robust appetites, which marriage aroused but could not satisfy because . . . her veins demanded more than the conjugal duty of a gentle husband."[10]

While her father-in-law was still alive, a pattern developed in Maria Luisa's dalliances with aristocrats and courtiers. Her first lover was a marquis who, when discovered, found himself appointed by Carlos III to a post in the Canary Islands and ordered to leave Madrid within twenty-four hours. Her second, the count of Lancaster, was also sent to the Canaries. Next came the count Pignatelli, promptly dispatched to the Spanish legation in Paris, and then a courtier named Ortíz, who was banished to a far corner of Spain. Maria Luisa's husband remained oblivious to it all. On one occasion he astonished his father by observing that princes were more fortunate than other men because their wives would never be unfaithful with a man of lower rank. "Carlos, Carlos," replied the king wearily, "¡qué tonto tú eres!"—How foolish you are![11]

After the banishment of Ortíz, the princess preyed on the easier ranks of the royal guard—whether to evade her father-in-law's watchful eye, or to exploit her husband's pomposity, or perhaps, more cruelly, as her physical beauty faded. "Many confinements [and] several illnesses," the Russian ambassador wrote, "have completely wrecked her. Her skin is greenish and the loss of several teeth, replaced by false ones, has given the coup de grace to her outward appearance." The radiant young lady gazing out of Anton Rafael Mengs's 1765 engagement portrait was gone. Francisco Goya's portraits after 1789 depict a woman ridden hard by life. "Maria Luisa has her past and her character written on her face," Napoleon would soon remark. "It surpasses anything you can imagine."[12]

Luis Godoy, a sturdy captain from the rugged province of Extremadura on the Portuguese border—birthplace of the conquistadors Cortés, Pizarro, and Balboa—was the first member of the royal guard who attracted Maria Luisa's attention. Inevitably, however, Carlos III learned of the affair and had the guardsman transferred to a distant province so quickly that Godoy had no chance to say good-bye to the princess. Entrusting a note of farewell to his younger brother and hand-some comrade, Manuel Godoy, the departing guardsman thereby intro-duced Maria Luisa to her next lover, who ruled Spain as *privado,* or royal favorite, until 1808.[13]

At seventeen, Manuel Godoy had followed his brother into the first brigade of the royal guards in 1784, and at twenty-one into the bedroom of Maria Luisa. After Carlos III died and Maria Luisa was queen, his rise was meteoric: colonel and knight of the Order of Santiago in 1789 at twenty-two, field marshal at twenty-four, duke of Alcudia, grandee of Spain, and first secretary of state at twenty-five. Despite Godoy's provin-cial education, the English ambassador Lord Holland found his conver-sation "elegant, and equally exempt from vulgarity and affectation," and his disposition "somewhat indolent, or as the French term it nonchalant." More than any other "untravelled Spaniard," Holland thought, Manuel Godoy displayed

> a mixture of dignity and politeness, of propriety and ease. He seemed born for a high station. Without effort he would have passed in any mixed society for the first man in it.[14]

Lady Holland described Godoy as a "large, coarse, ruddy-complexioned" man "with a heavy sleepy voluptuous look." His countrymen were less charitable. The nickname Choricero (sausage-maker, a sneer at the staple in the diet of his native Extremadura) was one of their gentler insults. As an upstart and a favorite, wrote one Spanish observer, "the noblemen hated him for his improvisations [and] the people because they preferred to suffer under a deified lord rather than under one of their own number raised to the nobility."[15]

To Spaniards and foreigner alike, however, Godoy's influence at the court of Carlos IV and Maria Luisa was astonishing and offensive. "It is hardly conceivable that a young man without experience . . . could be appointed to the most important ministry," the French ambassador, Jean-François Bourgoing, reported, "a man, moreover, whose attentiveness toward the queen leaves him so little free time." Despite Godoy's accumulation of "lofty titles, unbounded wealth, solid power, and dazzling magnificence," one English visitor wrote, he was "treated by the first class with silent contempt." Another English traveler described Godoy as "a foul beast of prey," and a third Englishman translated the common gossip of Spain into English literature. "How carols now the lusty muleteer?" asked Lord Byron in the first canto of *Childe Harold* (written after Napoleon had sent Godoy and his royal patrons into exile),

> As he speeds, he chants "Viva el Rey!"
> And checks his song to execrate Godoy,
> The royal wittol° Charles, and curse the day
> When first Spain's queen beheld the black-eyed boy
> And gore-faced treason sprung from her adulterous joy.[16]

"The thing that must strike those most who watch Charles IV in the bosom of his Court is his blindness where the conduct of the Queen is concerned," the next French ambassador reported.

> He knows nothing, sees nothing, suspects nothing of the irregularities . . . going on all around him . . . nor the attentions which violate all usage and decency, nor even the existence of two children who bear, as is obvious to all, a striking resemblance to the Prince of the Peace [Godoy's title after 1795].[17]

Carlos IV's passions for hunting and tranquillity (and his utter dependence upon Godoy and Maria Luisa) made this possible—as did the fact that Manuel Godoy maintained an office and bedroom directly below the

---

°*Wittol:* a cuckold who knows of his wife's infidelity and submits to it.

royal apartments, in addition to his own sumptuous house in Madrid. "Every day, wet or fine, winter or summer," the imprudent king confided to Napoleon of all people, "I would go out after breakfast, and after hearing mass, go hunting up to one o'clock." Then, immediately after the midday meal,

> I would return to the hunting field and stay there until dusk. In the evening Manuel would never fail to tell me whether things were going well or ill, and I would go to bed to start again the next day.

As a gentleman of the household, Godoy attended Carlos and Maria Luisa at their one o'clock dinner, and then retired to his apartments for his own meal. Here, each afternoon, he was "joined by the Queen, who, once the King has gone off hunting, arrives by a secret stair," explained the Russian ambassador. "It is in the course of these secret talks"—and whatever else might have gone on—"that the Queen and Godoy decide what proposals to lay before the King."[18]

Soon after the death of Carlos III, the queen described the emerging new regime with a phrase that offended Spanish Catholics as badly as the near blasphemy of her favorite's eventual title, Prince of the Peace. Ménage à trois might have been more accurate, but the queen suggested that she and her husband and Manuel Godoy comprised *"la santa trinidade en la tierra"*—a holy trinity on earth. The royal couple, Godoy wrote in his *Memoirs*, "needed a vigilant, active, and self-sacrificing person, who, without making it obvious, would lead them by the hand in their actions." Dismissing both of Carlos III's capable ministers in 1792 — the master bureaucrat José Moñino y Redondo, count of Floridablanca, and the Aragonese nobleman Pedro Pablo Abarca de Bolea, count of Aranda—the new king and queen "found the right man in the lowly guardsman, whom they placed in the necessary surroundings, so that he could provide them the services they needed."[19]

In less perilous times the world's largest empire might have survived the rule of another *privado*. In less dangerous times the dirty linen of these Spanish Bourbons might have stayed within their palaces to fuel malicious gossip and petty intrigue and add a few salacious footnotes to Iberian history. With the fall of the Bastille on July 14, 1789, however, and with thousands of Americans moving past the Appalachian Mountains into the valley of the Ohio River and clamoring for access to the Mississippi River and New Orleans, the times demanded statesmanship far beyond the capacity of a sluggish monarch, his promiscuous queen, and their sleepy voluptuous favorite.

· · ·

In December 1783, a few months after Great Britain acknowledged American independence in the Treaty of Paris, which ended the Revolution, Elizabeth House Trist, of Carlisle, Pennsylvania, set out toward Natchez, where she intended to meet her husband, a former British officer and naturalized American citizen who had bought a plantation along Bayou Manchac, between Baton Rouge and New Orleans. Riding on horseback to Pittsburgh, she spent the winter with friends and waited for the spring thaw. In May, when the Upper Ohio was clear of ice, Mrs. Trist and her traveling companion, Polly, joined the procession of American families boarding flatboats for the trip downriver. "People seem to have caught the infection of the country," she noted in her travel diary: "a desire for the Kentucki."[20]

Another traveler on the Ohio River, the French-born essayist known as "An American Farmer," put the dreams of his adopted compatriots into eloquent words. "Never before had I felt so disposed to meditation and revery," wrote Hector St. John de Crèvecoeur as he gazed at the passing banks of the Ohio River in 1789. "My imagination darted into the future," and

I saw in fancy these beautiful shores ornamented with handsome houses, covered with crops, the fields well cultivated. . . . What an immense chain of plantations! What a great career of activity, of industry, of culture and commerce is offered to the Americans.

Crèvecoeur regarded the settling of the Ohio River Valley as "one of the greatest enterprises ever presented to man," and thought the region itself was "destined to become the foundation of the power, wealth and future glory of the United States." These dreams of the American Farmer were contagious, and every new inhabitant of Kentucky helped spread "the infection of the country."[21]

The pastoral dreams of an American Farmer represented a looming imperial nightmare for the Spanish monarchy and its officials in Pensacola, New Orleans, and Natchez. The first shadows were hunters and explorers like Daniel Boone, men enthralled with "the diversity and beauties of nature" and comfortable in the solitude of the great American forest. Spain was not immediately threatened by a man in buckskin who, according to his contemporary Timothy Flint, "saw the country only with the eye of a hunter, with very little forecast of its future value and destiny." Spanish interests were not at risk when Boone climbed to "the summit of a commanding ridge, and, looking round with astonishing delight, beheld . . . the famous river Ohio that rolled in silent dignity, marking the western boundary of Kentucke with inconceivable grandeur"—and then "kindled a fire near a fountain of sweet water, and feasted on the loin of a buck, which a few hours before I had killed." The danger arose from American men and women who did recognize "its future value and destiny"—settlers who gazed at the riverbanks with the American Farmer and readily imagined "these beautiful shores ornamented with handsome houses, covered with crops . . . [and] an immense chain of plantations!"[22]

Virginians like Daniel Boone had been wandering in and out of Kentucky since 1750, when a group of explorers led by Jefferson's Albemarle County neighbor Dr. Thomas Walker followed the migratory trail of bear, deer, and buffalo over a relatively low gap in the Cumberland Mountains—seventeen hundred feet above sea level—on the Virginia–North Carolina line about four hundred thirty miles inland from the Atlantic Ocean. By 1775 James Harrod had established the first English settlement in Kentucky, and a North Carolina entrepreneur had engaged Boone to blaze the Wilderness Road from the Holston River, in southwestern Virginia, through the Cumberland Gap to the bluegrass country of the Elkhorn and Kentucky Rivers—but in that year the total English population of Kentucky was only a hundred fifty settlers. As the Revolution ended, however, American settlements grew rapidly. From about eight thousand inhabitants in 1783, Kentucky jumped to thirty thousand in 1784 and then to 73,677 according to the first federal census of 1790 (which recorded another 35,691 settlers in Tennessee, mostly along the Cumberland River). Then, in the 1790s, the population of Kentucky tripled again to reach 220,955—one fifth of them slaves—in the census of 1800. From the perspective of Spanish New Orleans, the shadow of Daniel Boone had grown into the nightmare of the American Farmer.[23]

An American farmer with a gun. Official notices in the *Kentucky Gazette* reminded all men between the ages of eighteen and forty-five that

> every non commissioned officer and private is by law directed, to furnish himself with a good clean musket, containing an ounce ball, three feet eight inches long in the barrel, with a good Bayonet and iron ramrod, well fitted thereto, a cartridge box, properly made, to contain and secure twenty cartridges fitted to his musket . . . and to have at every [quarterly] muster one pound of good powder, and four ounces of

lead, including twenty blind cartridges; and every serjeant to have a pair of moulds fit to cast balls, in their respective companies.[24]

Even if the actual ownership of guns fell short of Kentucky's legislated requirements, newspaper items like this one scared the hell out Spanish authorities in New Orleans.[25]

Off and on, soon after those earliest 1775 settlements in Kentucky, a few American flatboats began floating down the Ohio and Mississippi Rivers. They opened a mutually advantageous riverborne trade during America's war against Catholic Spain's recurrent adversary in the centuries since the Reformation and the Armada. Early in the Revolution, Spain used New Orleans as a conduit for covert shipments of money and military supplies to the American patriots. In turn, as the British navy clamped down on French and Spanish shipping through the Gulf of Mexico, the population of New Orleans became utterly dependent on upriver farmers for flour, beef, and other commodities.

Perhaps, had the populations of Louisiana and Kentucky increased at equal rates after the American Revolution, Spanish officials would have found less reason for worry. When they did the numbers, however, there was no comfort. In 1785 the non-Indian population of the entire Spanish territory from Natchitoches to the Arkansas River to Pensacola was 30,471 persons. Of every ten Spanish subjects living along the Lower Mississippi and Gulf Coast, five resided in or near New Orleans and six were slaves or free people of color.[26] In 1784 Kentucky's thirty thousand inhabitants already matched the entire population of the Lower Mississippi, and the gap was spreading at a frightening rate. By 1800 the Spanish colonial population in the Lower Mississippi had grown to fifty thousand, "including more Frenchmen, Englishmen, Americans, and Germans than Spaniards." That same year, the population of Kentucky and Tennessee was 326,000. Starting with approximately equal populations in 1785, in fifteen years the population of the Ohio River Valley grew seven times faster than that of the Lower Mississippi—not counting the additional thousands of Americans settling the future states of Ohio, Indiana, and Illinois.[27]

Either from the fort at Natchez or from the upper windows of his residence and office on St. Louis Street near the levee, Governor Miró and his colleagues watched with increasing resignation as the ceaseless current of the Mississippi River carried Kentucky flatboats and country produce into the heart of their capital city. Officially, by an order from imperial authorities in Havana in 1784, the river had been declared closed to English and American commerce. On March 18, 1785, however, Miró reported the arrival in Natchez of a flatboat laden with flour from Pittsburgh owned by one Benet Truly and several prospective settlers, and asked what he should do. Five weeks later, the captain-general in Havana waffled. "As regards the first matter," he replied, "there is the insurmountable objection on our part that to allow these people . . . to settle there would be to multiply the enemies within our territory"—so he advised Miró to write "directly to the ministry [in Spain] in order that [a] decision may be handed down by His Majesty." As to the flour, the captain-general was equally unhelpful, advising Miró to let Intendant Martín Navarro (an advocate of open trading on the river) "determine what he considers most conformable to the instructions of the King."[28]

The final disposition of Benet Truly's cargo and company are unknown, but when Thomas Ormis (or Amis) appeared with two flatboats and a pirogue laden with ninety barrels of flour and other country produce in June 1786, Navarro confiscated the flour for the garrison at Natchez. The intendant sold the remaining goods at auction in New Orleans on August 3, while Ormis escaped upriver, denouncing the Spaniards to anyone who would listen.

When Ormis's complaints came to the attention of George Rogers Clark, who was leading a Kentucky expedition against the Wabash Indians, Clark responded by capturing three Spanish traders at Vincennes and confiscating their goods—a cautionary show of force that sent a clear message to officials in New Orleans. Thereafter, so long as Americans kept a civil tongue and a generous hand in their dealings with minor Spanish officials, many flatboats and their cargoes slid past the official restrictions with ease. Between February and July 1790, for example, 41 flatboats brought 4,904 barrels of flour, 916 hogsheads of tobacco, 261 barrels and 34,000 pounds of meat, 47 barrels and 100 gallons of whiskey, 35 barrels and 500 pounds of butter, 11 tons of iron, and 7 tons of hemp to New Orleans.[29]

Smuggling and corruption had become rampant. Estimates vary, but Spanish officials may have neglected to record between one quarter and two thirds of the American produce that came downriver between 1785 and 1803. Merchant Phineas Bond declared, for example, that in 1786 Philadelphia's contraband trade with the Spanish colonies was worth $500,000, while Governor Miró estimated that the illegal exports of gold and silver to pay for these goods totaled 400,000 pesos annually.[30]

From Fort Harmar, at the confluence of the Muskingum and Ohio Rivers near Marietta, General Henry Knox monitored the traffic downriver between 1786 and 1789. According to Knox, 598 wagons and 1,109 boats came down from Pittsburgh and Wheeling carrying 18,761 people, 8,487 horses, 2,199 cattle, and 1,833 sheep—but only 33 hogs.[31] Pigs usually traveled the Ohio and Mississippi in barrels, as did those arriving in Natchez on April 11, 1790: 44 barrels of meat, 1,100 pounds of pork, 280 pounds of lard, 3 barrels of tallow, and 40 pounds of candles—along with 101 hogsheads of tobacco on three flatboats from Kentucky.[32]

"The river is at present defenseless," Governor Miró reported in January 1788. Then, with self-assurance born of desperation, he justified opening New Orleans to American trade as a defensive measure. "It is very easy," he reminded his superiors in Havana, for the American settlers west of the Appalachian Mountains "to form an expedition against this province without our being able to notify [anyone] in time." In the event of an invasion, Miró wrote, it was most probable that the Americans "will inform us by starting hostilities." As Miró and Intendent Navarro had "informed the court, a long time ago," the Americans were aggressive because they "had no other means of shipping their produce than the navigation of the Mississippi," and "because they would be obliged by any other way to cross the summits of the [Appalachian] Mountains," in which case "the cost of transportation would absorb the value of [their produce]."[33]

"Who can tell if this day they may be in Tennessee," Miró warned,

> constructing flatboats, which we call *chalanas* here, in order to come down after the snow melts. And how could I obtain news in time, since it takes three months to make a voyage from here, and it only would take them fifteen days . . . to go to Natchez, which is the first of our possessions that might see them? Your Lordship will be surprised . . . that the said settlements have one hundred and fifty thousand men capable of carrying arms: this is certain.[34]

Twenty months later, living confirmation of Governor Miró's warning strolled into his office in New Orleans.

"There has just arrived from Quebec," Miró exclaimed on October 30, 1789, "Lord Edward Fitzgerald, Sergeant-Major of the British Infantry Regiment," bearing a passport from Guy Carleton. Knighted after successfully defending Canada from the American invasion of 1775–1776, Sir Guy Carleton was now Lord Dorchester, governor-general of

Canada.[35] One can only imagine his amusement as he signed the papers to indulge a high-spirited young nobleman's impulse for a joyride up the Great Lakes and down the Mississippi to the Gulf of Mexico.

Twenty-year-old Fitzgerald impressed Miró with "the education and manners of his rank" (not his military rank but his social position as brother of the duke of Leinster and nephew of the duke of Richmond). "His object does not seem to be anything but the noble ambition to see new countries and obtain knowledge," Miró wrote, hoping that it was true. "With this praiseworthy object . . . he undertook the journey in a birchbark canoe," departing from Quebec on April 27 with Lieutenant Thomas Brisbane and six "oarsmen." Fitzgerald and his party canoed from Quebec up the Great Lakes and either followed the familiar waterways of the *coureurs de bois* across Wisconsin or paddled through Lake Superior and down the Mississippi through Minnesota. Miró was unclear about the northernmost details of their route, but he knew they had paddled downstream to New Orleans as fast as any messenger could carry a warning from the Spanish outposts they passed en route.

Miró was in shock. Fitzgerald arrived "without my being aware of this until he, in person, brought me the news as soon as he landed in this city." The young sergeant major's ramble from Quebec demonstrated the vulnerability of the entire colony of Louisiana. "This example," Miró lamented, "shows how this province is exposed." Utterly without warning, Louisiana could be overrun from the north at any moment. If it happened, Miró shuddered, the invaders themselves would "give us the first news with their presence."[36]

Miró faced a military crisis of profound historic dimensions. For centuries Spain had relied on a flexible network of religious missions and small garrisons, or presidios, as a distant early warning line that wandered across North America from St. Augustine to San Francisco. Some were permanent outposts, others were temporary responses to immediate threats. Together they defined the northernmost defensive salient of the Spanish borderlands—the sparsely settled zone protecting the riches of Mexico. Seen from an imperial perspective, these borderlands were ultimately expandable.[37] Deep down, as Governor Esteban Rodríguez Miró prepared to return to Spain in December 1791, he knew that his successors faced one of the most difficult of all military assignments: an orderly retreat.

"A new and vigorous people, hostile to all subjection [were] advancing and multiplying," Governor Miró's successor wrote in 1794, "with a prodigious rapidity." Sweeping the Indians aside as they moved west, Miró's successor continued, the Americans were

> attempting to get possession of all the vast continent which those nations are occupying between the Ohio and Mississippi Rivers and the Gulf of Mexico and the Appalachian Mountains . . . at the same

*François-Louis Hector, fourteenth baron de Carondelet et Noyelles, brought a military career and two years of administrative experience to the post of governor of Louisiana in December 1791. Under Carlos IV, family patronage connections were allowed a greater role in Carondelet's appointment than had been apparent during the previous reign. Carondelet's modest achievements in New Orleans, his canal linking the city with Bayou St. John and the introduction of oil-burning streetlights, were overshadowed by serious failures. His vacillations toward planters, slaves, Indians, and free people of color, for example, contributed to the abortive Pointe Coupée slave uprising of 1795. The creation of the Natchez district in 1789, with Manuel Gayoso de Lemos as governor, put Louisiana's frontier affairs into the hands of an abler man. By 1797 Gayoso had so demonstrated his superior diplomatic skills that Carondelet was dispatched to Quito, Ecuador, where he died in 1807, while Gayoso moved to New Orleans and became governor-general of Louisiana.* (Courtesy Library of Virginia)

time that they are demanding with threats the free navigation of the Mississippi.[38]

As governor of Louisiana, Miró's successor, François-Louis Hector, baron de Carondelet et Noyelles, enjoyed a reputation based as much on a stylish French surname and facile pen as his actual administrative skills.

Born in 1747 in Cambrai, on the Schelde River near Flanders in the north of France, Carondelet was a captain of the Walloon Royal Guards at fifteen and subsequently joined the Spanish army. After recovering from severe wounds received in the invasion of Algiers in 1775, he fought valiantly in the 1781 siege of Pensacola and was promoted to lieutenant colonel. After two years as governor of San Salvador, then a part of Guatemala, Carondelet succeeded Miró on December 30, 1791. The new governor was energetic but quick-tempered, gullible, and inclined to rash decisions based on inadequate information. "He has always shown a great predilection for new projects, formations of thousands of militiamen, and other variations," an official in the ministry of war sneered, "without ever thinking of the funds or expenditures that such Projects naturally will cost."[39] He was perhaps an odd choice to govern Louisiana at such a critical moment—but he wrote well, he had married well, and perhaps he looked good on paper to Manuel Godoy.

Carondelet knew that the "writings, public papers, and speeches" of the frontiersmen "all have as their object the navigation to the Gulf . . . and the rich fur trade of the Missouri." In time, he warned, "they will demand the possession of the rich mines of the interior provinces of the very kingdom of Mexico," and "their method of spreading themselves and their policy are [as] much to be feared by Spain as are their arms."

A carbine and a little maize in a sack are enough for an American to wander about in the forests alone for a whole month. . . . With some tree trunks crossed one above another, in the shape of a square, he raises a house, and even a fort that is impregnable to the savages by crossing a story above the ground floor.

If these Americans and their log cabins "succeed in occupying the shores of the Mississippi or of the Missouri," Carondelet warned, "there is, beyond doubt, nothing that can prevent them from crossing those rivers and penetrating into our provinces."[40]

The danger was clear: "A general revolution," Carondelet concluded, "threatens Spain in America, unless it applies a powerful and speedy remedy." His plan of defense—one of several eloquent proposals he offered Godoy—involved building and improving twenty-two Spanish forts all over North America, as far north as Minnesota, at a cost of 607,000 pesos. All this despite the fact that Carondelet could count on only 840 troops in his garrison at New Orleans (one sixth of whom were sick in hospital) and 5,440 militiamen spread from Illinois to Mobile and capable of sending "3000 men to a point on the Mississippi in 15 days when necessary." Far too little, far too late—as the joy ride of Sergeant-Major Lord Edward Fitzgerald demonstrated—in the event of a surprise attack from the north.[41]

Carondelet's deficiencies as governor of Louisiana were offset, during the last years of Miró's administration, by the creation at Natchez of a new administrative district in the borderlands with an able new governor, Manuel Gayoso de Lemos. In effect, upon Miró's retirement, Carlos III sent two men to replace him and gave the forward position to the more capable man.

"This officer served four years with me in the Lisbon Regiment from 1773," Miró wrote proudly, "and even then he had distinguished himself through his talent, knowledge of various languages, and excellent conduct." Gayoso was exactly Carondelet's age, and in every respect the better man. Any doubt on that score can be settled by comparing Gayoso's clearheaded 1792 report on the "Political Condition of the Province of Louisiana" with Carondelet's visionary 1794 "Military Report on Louisiana and West Florida."[42]

Born in 1747 in Oporto, Portugal, the wine-exporting coastal town where his father was Spanish consul-general, Gayoso always identified himself as a native of Pontevedra, site of his family's estate in Galicia. Educated at Westminster College in England, Gayoso retained, according to his American neighbors in Natchez, "the manners and customs of that nation . . . especially in his style of living." A career soldier with a flair for diplomacy and a good understanding of languages, law, economics, and politics, Gayoso advanced rapidly under Carlos III. His was the kind of talent that senior officials coveted. While serving as an officer on the warship *La España* during the Spanish siege of Gibraltar of 1779–1783, General Alexander O'Reilly (whose many accomplishments included the imposition of Spanish rule in Louisiana in 1768) recognized his linguistic and diplomatic skills and recruited him as an aide-de-camp.[43]

Promoted to captain, Gayoso learned the art of civilian administration at O'Reilly's side during his tenure as governor of Cádiz from 1779 to 1786—except when he was polishing his diplomatic talents in Lisbon, where the Spanish ambassador "borrowed" him for months at a time (and where he also met and married the beautiful Theresa Margarita Hopman y Pereira). Not surprisingly, when the minister of the Indies cast about for the right officer to command the new district at Natchez, he found "that all the necessary qualities for this task are combined in the person of Lieutenant-colonel and Adjutant of the Plaza of Cadiz, Don Manuel Gayoso de Lemos." Gayoso spent October and November 1787 in Madrid, studying Miró's reports and correspondence from Louisiana and conferring with Floridablanca and Carlos III's senior ministers.[44]

Prompted in part by Diego de Gardoqui's inability to achieve a treaty that closed the Mississippi to American traders, in part by the pressure of American settlements west of the Appalachians, in part by the advice of New Orleans officials such as Martín Navarro and Esteban Miró, and in part by the vacillation that accompanied the death of Carlos III, Spain was lurching toward new defensive policies for the Lower Mississippi. As early as May 1788, Floridablanca had floated a trial balloon to Gardoqui. If Spain could no longer keep the Americans from using the river, Floridablanca wondered, why not

> attract to our side the inhabitants of the Ohio and Mississippi, be it by alliance, by placing them under the protection of the King, or through union with his dominions under treaties which will insure their liberty, thus allowing them to export their products to New Orleans and to provide themselves at that town with goods they need from other countries.[45]

Gayoso was fully briefed by Floridablanca before the death of Carlos III and encouraged to communicate directly to the ministry in Spain.

After many delays—including the birth of Manuel and Theresa Gayoso's first child, a difficult passage across the Atlantic, storms in the Gulf of Mexico, and a lengthy stop at Havana so that Gayoso could explain the nature of his mission and the evolving defensive policy to the captain-general of Cuba (Miró's and Carondelet's superior in the imperial chain of command)—the small brig *La Industria* moored near Grand Route St. John. On April 12, 1789, the new governor of Natchez stepped ashore to greet his old friend and comrade, Esteban Miró. The governor of Louisiana would soon return to Spain, and his successor, Carondelet, would come and go—dispatched after his six-year tenure in New Orleans to Quito, Ecuador, where he died in 1807.[46] As governor of Natchez until 1797 and then governor of Louisiana until he succumbed to yellow fever in July 1799, Manuel Gayoso de Lemos represented Spain's best hope of controlling the Mississippi River for a few more years.

## CHAPTER SEVEN

# Questions of Loyalty

*I hope that no one can say of me with justice that I break any law of nature or of nations, of conscience or of honor, in transferring my allegiance, from the United States to his Catholic Majesty.*

—James Wilkinson, August 22, 1787[1]

*He has compromised himself entirely, so that should he not succeed in severing Kentucky from the United States, he will not be able to stay there, unless he has suppressed those articles which might be injurious to him—a possible procedure.*

—Governor Esteban Rodríguez Miró, April 17, 1789[2]

*That I have ever, in all my correspondence and intercourse with the Spanish government, conceded a tittle of the honour or interests of my own country, I most solemnly deny, in the face of God and man.*

—James Wilkinson, *Memoirs of My Own Time,* 1816[3]

T HE ROBUST American officer who came downriver to meet Governor Esteban Rodríguez Miró in New Orleans on July 2, 1787, was a perfect chameleon. Born in 1757 at Hunting Creek, near the tidal waters of the Patuxent River on Maryland's western shore, James Wilkinson had begun studying medicine with a local physician at fourteen. By 1774 he was enrolled at the College of Philadelphia, America's best medical school, and was practicing at the Pennsylvania Hospital. A few blocks away, the buzz of revolutionary politics at the First Continental Congress in Carpenter's Hall and the flash of bright uniforms in the city's patriot encampments caught the young physician's fancy. "Arms," James Wilkinson decided, would be "his profession and politics his hobby"—and thereafter he managed both with amazing dexterity.[4]

By December 1783, when Brigadier-General Wilkinson arrived in Kentucky as the accredited mercantile representative of Barclay, Moylan & Co., of Philadelphia, his career had already demonstrated a bent for intrigue. "Some men are sordid, some vain, some ambitious," he once told Diego de Gardoqui. "To detect the predominant passion, to lay hold of it, is the profound part of political science." Wilkinson knew whereof he spoke. He had served closely with Benedict Arnold in the invasion of Quebec and with Horatio Gates when Burgoyne surrendered at Saratoga, and he was deeply involved in the so-called Conway Cabal of 1777, a purported scheme to replace Washington with Gates as commander in chief. Most recently he had resigned as clothier-general of the army in 1781 amid charges of irregularities in his accounts.[5]

"Not quite tall enough to be perfectly elegant," a hostile contemporary thought, but "compensated by symmetry and [the] appearance of health and strength," Wilkinson exhibited a face "beaming with intelligence." His manners were "gracious and polite," he spoke persuasively and wrote with florid eloquence and superb penmanship, and "by these fair terms he conciliated; by these he captivated."[6] Relying on his knack for persuading someone to hear more than he actually said and, equally important, on a good memory for the prodigious array of targeted exaggeration, omission, partial truth, and insinuation that comprised his vocabulary of intrigue, James Wilkinson positioned himself as frontier Kentucky's man of the hour.

When Wilkinson arrived in Lexington, the two major issues in the rapidly growing Kentucky district were access to markets down the Mississippi and the prospect of statehood. (The latter, in part, offered better frontier defense against the Indians than state officials in the Virginia capital at Richmond, five hundred miles to the east, were able to provide.) Vaguely authorized by a series of enabling acts passed by the General Assembly of Virginia, Kentuckians held nine or ten statehood conventions between November 1784 and the state's eventual admission to the union in 1792. Wilkinson arrived in time to witness the third convention, in May 1785, and to win a seat in the fourth that August, which, as had become customary, petitioned the legislature of Virginia for an act "declaring and acknowledging the independence of the District of Kentucky."[7] Or so it seemed.

In May, the third convention had linked its call for separation from Virginia with the expectation of acceptance into the union as a fourteenth state. The August petition and address to the people of Kentucky and

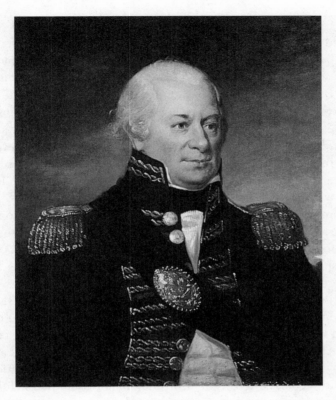

*Beaming from the canvas of this 1813 oil portrait by John Wesley Jarvis, the robust face of General James Wilkinson offers no hint of the shadows in his remarkable career. Implicated in the Conway Cabal against General Washington during the Revolution, the Maryland-born Wilkinson moved to Kentucky after the war, negotiated a lucrative Spanish pension and trade privileges down the Mississippi, and schemed to separate Kentucky from the union in the 1780s. Soon after helping to secure the transfer of Louisiana to the United States in December 1803, Wilkinson began plotting with Vice President Aaron Burr to bring an expedition down-river to New Orleans, ransack the city's banks, and thereby finance their conquest of Mexico. Participants were "as greedy after plunder as ever the old Romans were"—"Mexico glitters in our Eyes." The plot gained momentum after Burr killed Alexander Hamilton in 1804 but eventually collapsed after Wilkinson reported it to President Jefferson and then became the principal witness at Burr's trial in 1807. Wilkinson was summoned before a court of inquiry in 1815 on a range of charges, including neglect of duty along the Canadian border during the War of 1812. Acquitted and honorably discharged from the army, he died penniless in Mexico City on December 28, 1825. (Courtesy Historic New Orleans Collection, acc. no. 1991.3)*

Virginia, written by none other than James Wilkinson in what he described as the "plain, manly, and unadorned language of independence" (actually the rococo eloquence he customarily employed for intrigue), called for Kentucky independence but *not* for admission to the union.[8] By Wilkinson's design and the convention's inadvertence, the Kentucky resolution ignited an imperceptible spark that unforeseen events helped Wilkinson fan into the famous "Spanish Conspiracy."

Entirely ignoring the omitted clauses in the Kentucky petition, on January 6, 1786, the legislature of Virginia passed another enabling act for Kentucky statehood, with a clear twenty-month schedule. A fifth convention was to meet at Danville, Kentucky, in September 1786. If that convention endorsed statehood, then Kentucky needed to adopt a suitable constitution and by June 1787 obtain consent from Congress to join the Confederation. Once these steps were taken, Virginia was willing to relinquish its authority over the Kentucky district as early as September 1, 1787.[9]

The timetable could not have been more ill-fated. The Massachusetts delegation was using the Jay-Gardoqui negotiations secretly to push the southern states out of the Confederation, and when everything came to a head in August 1786 the sectional deadlock in Congress killed any hope of approval for Kentucky statehood. Later, as the Confederation Congress continued its drift toward insolvency, major issues like statehood for Kentucky were deferred until the Philadelphia convention drafted and nine states ratified the new Constitution.

Early in 1787, the two-year-old spark from James Wilkinson's petition began to glow. That January a letter from Richmond was carried down the Ohio and Kentucky Rivers to Buck Pond, the home of fifty-seven-year-old Thomas Marshall, who had come to Fayette County as a surveyor in 1781. Marshall's son John, then a member of the General Assembly of Virginia (and later chief justice of the United States), alarmed his father with news out of Congress that the seven northern states were threatening to barter away American navigation rights to the Mississippi River. Soon thereafter, the Scots-born and Virginia-trained chief justice of the Kentucky district court, George Muter, opened a letter from Congressman James Madison asking, "Would Kentucky purchase a free use of the Mississippi at the price of its occlusion for any term, however short?" From these and countless other sources, the dire news spread, and it provoked exactly the kind of anger that Rufus King and the Massachusetts separatists had expected. A resident of Louisville exclaimed that news of "the late commercial treaty with Spain has given the western Country an universal shock, and struck its Inhabitants with an amazement."[10]

"I have not mett with one man," Judge Muter hastily replied to Madison, "who would be willing to give the navigation up, for ever so short a time, on any terms whatever." Kentucky attorney general Harry Innes, a transplanted Virginian who had attended the College of New Jersey with James Madison, read law with George Wythe, and practiced in the Old Dominion for ten years before moving to Kentucky, warned the governor of Virginia that "this western country will, in a few years, Revolt from the Union and endeavor to erect an Independent Government." The Reverend Caleb Wallace, another of Madison's classmates at Princeton, who was formerly affiliated with the Hanover Presbytery in Virginia and was now a judge of the district court, predicted that Kentucky would declare "absolute independence" if Congress failed to offer statehood. "Freedom from State and Federal obligations would enable us to govern and defend ourselves to advantage," he continued, because "we should no longer be in subjection to those who have an interest different from us." These were the voices of reasonable and responsible elected leaders who gathered in conventions to chart the district's future. When Kentuckians gathered at court days and church services, at militia musters and squirrel hunts, however, impatient voices could also be heard echoing Wilkinson's boast that "the People of Kentucky alone, unaided by Congress in any particular whatever, could dislodge every Garrison the Spaniards have on or in the neighborhood of the Mississippi . . . with ease and certainty."[11]

Although Wilkinson proclaimed that "a Free Trade out of the Mississippi" was the "inestimable prize [for which] we are all unanimously ready to wade . . . through Blood,"[12] attacking New Orleans at the head of an army of Kentucky militiamen was not his plan. Flatboat diplomacy was. Late in 1786, with help from John Marshall, Wilkinson sought a passport from the governor of Virginia for a journey down the Mississippi—and about the same time he attempted, through Baron von Steuben, to get a passport from Diego de Gardoqui. Formal authorization to travel into Louisiana might have been convenient, but neither request was successful, so before leaving Kentucky on December 20, 1786, Wilkinson dispatched a personal letter written in French to the Spanish commandant at St. Louis, Francisco Cruzat.[13]

Why French? Perhaps the lingua franca of European court diplomacy was intended to make a good impression, or perhaps to shield the letter's contents from curious eyes. Or both. If Cruzat or his superiors wondered about the identity of this new informant, Wilkinson's letter did not expressly claim any authority beyond that of a private citizen. Surely Cruzat could be counted upon to draw his own conclusions when Wilkinson's letter happened to arrive with the same courier, "a brother in arms," who brought Cruzat a separate note from a man in Louisville who chanced to describe himself as a friend of "General Wilkinson's."[14]

"I venture to assure you that the outrage recently committed against the property of a Spanish merchant at the post of Vincennes," Wilkinson purred, "is generally disavowed here, and is the work of only a small number of unprincipled men under the command of General [George Rogers] Clark"—who had captured three Spanish boats in retaliation for the Spanish seizure of Thomas Ormis's boats at Natchez in June 1786. "At this very moment," Wilkinson volunteered, "a certain Colonel Green and other desperate adventurers are meditating an attack on the posts of his most Catholic Majesty at Natchez." If the Spanish commander at St. Louis got the impression that Wilkinson's promise to "do everything in our power here to foil this band" came from a Kentucky officeholder, that was just fine. If Wilkinson's warning gave Cruzat "time to inform his Excellency, Don Miró, of [Green's] projected plan" and of Wilkinson's help in thwarting it, so much the better.[15]

Lacking formal passports from Virginia or from Gardoqui, in April Wilkinson set off for Louisiana on a tide of bravado, with a cargo of hams, butter, and tobacco (all contributed for the purpose without any investment by Wilkinson) and a pair of fine horses. "Loudly exclaiming in the mean time against restraints on the rights of navigation and free trade," according to an eyewitness, Wilkinson left "his countrymen enraptured with his spirit of free enterprise and liberality, no less than his unbounded patriotism."[16]

On June 16, 1787, the glib American arrived at Natchez in a canoe, accompanied by Captain Carberry (the "Gentleman of the late American Army" who had carried Wilkinson's first letters to St. Louis), one slave, and an *enganchado,* or boatman. Carlos de Grand-Pré, the Spanish commander of Fort Panmure, at Natchez, duly advised Governor Miró that he had given Wilkinson "a room in this fort, entertaining him to the best of my ability, since this officer is a very worthy person in every respect." Wilkinson was "awaiting here a big barge, which should arrive today," Grand-Pré continued, "in order to continue with it his voyage to [New Orleans], where he is to embark for Philadelphia." The commander saw no need to mention Wilkinson's friendly gift of the two fine horses.[17]

At Natchez Wilkinson apparently transferred his remaining cargo onto flatboats, perhaps as many as five of them, before going on to New Orleans. While the evidence about some details of Wilkinson's journey is contradictory, it is certain that the general reached New Orleans on July 2, 1787—as did Grand-Pré's letter warning Miró of his imminent arrival. Escorted directly to the governor's office by a Spanish corporal, Wilkinson quickly impressed Miró and Intendant Navarro as "a person endowed with high talents" whose influence in Kentucky might prove useful for the defense of Louisiana. Portraying himself as the man "in whom the [Kentucky] settlements have placed their hope of future happiness," Wilkinson "informed the governor and myself," Navarro wrote, "that it was the[ir] intention . . . to put themselves under the protection or vassalage of his Catholic Majesty."[18] On the chance that Wilkinson might be able to deliver on this promise, Miró and Navarro allowed him to sell his cargo and began a series of secret conversations, lasting into September, that launched the Spanish Conspiracy.

Two months into their negotiations, on August 22, 1787, James Wilkinson wrote and signed a formal document "transferring [his] allegiance, from the United States to his Catholic Majesty." "Born and educated in America," Wilkinson wrote,

I embraced her cause in the recent revolution, and steadfastly I adhered to her interests until she triumphed over her enemy. This event, having rendered my services no longer needful, released me from my engagements . . . and left me at liberty, having fought for her welfare, to seek my own. Since the circumstances and policy of the United States have rendered it impossible for me to attain this desired object under her government, I am resolved, without wishing them any harm, to seek it [with] Spain.[19]

During the course of his secret talks at the government house on St. Louis Street, Wilkinson also wrote a lengthy essay describing the western situation and his plan for Kentucky's separation from the United States and subordination to Spain.

New Orleans can be a gossipy village, but Miró and Navarro protected Wilkinson and their negotiations about Kentucky separatism with a cover story to dispel "the excessive curiosity of the prominent men of this capital." They "insinuated that Wilkinson came as a commissioner of the settlements to solicit a general permission to send down their produce." The disinformation spread quickly, "the good effect of which is that nobody has imagined anything else."[20]

Ostensibly, Wilkinson's *Memorial* (as the document has come to be known) recommended to Miró and Navarro "what ought to be the policy of the Spanish Court at this critical juncture." In fact, with their help, the

*Memorial* was written so that they could forward it to Spain. It opened with a review of the rapid growth of the western settlements, their dependence on the Mississippi River to counterbalance "those commercial advantages which their Brethren on the Atlantic enjoy," and the American Confederation's inability to protect western interests. Kentucky independence was inevitable, Wilkinson contended. When it came, Spain would have two options. On the one hand, "an accommodating deportment" could entice Kentucky to become "subservient to the interest of Spain." On the other, "hostile restraints" would surely "drive them into the arms of Great Britain."[21]

"If Spain drives the Americans into the arms of Great Britain," Wilkinson warned, "she immediately endangers her Louisianian territories, and eventually her Mexican provinces," but "if she attaches the Americans to her interests," Kentucky would serve as "a permanent barrier against Great Britain and the United States." As things stood, it was essential that Diego de Gardoqui "absolutely refuse to Congress the Navigation of the Mississippi," Wilkinson advised, "for should this Gentleman form a treaty by which the Americans may become intitled to the independent enjoyment of this Navigation, he will destroy the power which Spain now enjoys over the American settlements, and entirely defeat our principal" objective. It was "an absolute Fact that these Settlements will . . . look up for protection to that power which secures them this most precious privilege." Therefore, let Spain "carefully preserve this right to herself, until she can employ it in exchange for such concessions as she may think proper to demand from the western settlers of America."

Opening the river *"generally"* to American trade—Wilkinson underlined the word—was contrary to Spain's best interests, and his own: "The prohibition of intercourse by the Mississippi . . . should be still supported, generally, with as much rigor as ever," he advised, but with one or two carefully chosen exceptions. "In order to conciliate and prepare the Minds of the western Americans for the grand object of these speculations," he wrote, "it may be politic . . . to offer indulgence to men of real influence." If Miró and Navarro could grant special trading privileges to one or two prominent Kentuckians (men like Brigadier General James Wilkinson leapt to mind) surely that valuable "indulgence" (*monopoly* is such an ugly word!) "would attach the leading characters in that Country to the interest of Spain." What's more, the benefits of trading privileges would surely trickle down from the favorites, "cheer the People with the hope of a free and friendly intercourse," dissuade them from "outrage and hostility," and pave the way for a "transition from the renouncement of the federal Government of America to a Negociation with the Court of Spain" that would be "natural and immediate."[22]

"Know then," Wilkinson's *Memorial* asserted, "that the leading characters of Kentucky . . . urged and intreated my voyage hither, in order to . . . discover . . . whether [Spain] would be willing to open a negociation for our admission *to her protection as subjects*" (Wilkinson's emphasis). Accordingly, if Miró and Navarro agreed to the propositions they had helped him write, Wilkinson promised to return to Kentucky and "exert my political weight and influence to familiarize and recommend to the Body of the People among whom I live those views which constitute the design of my present voyage, and which have already fixed the attention of the discerning part of that Community." His final request was for "the most inviolable secrecy" in all that he proposed.[23]

"Gentlemen," he reminded Miró and Navarro, "I have committed secrets of an important nature, such as would, were they divulged destroy my Fame and Fortune forever. . . . If the plan should eventually be rejected by the Court, I must rely on the candor and high honor of a dignified Minister to bury these communications in eternal oblivion."[24]

How rare and pleasant are the moments when national and personal interests honestly mesh. How generously Wilkinson offered to send down from Kentucky cargoes comprising

> Negroes, live Stock, tobacco, Flour, Bacon, Lard, Butter, Cheese, tallow, [and] Apples [in] the amount of fifty or sixty thousand Dollars . . . which articles may be sold for my account, and the proceeds held by his Excellency the Governor, as a pledge for my good conduct until the issue of our plans is known, or I have fixed my residence in Louisiana.

How intelligently—the very next day—Miró and Navarro encouraged their undercover agent by accepting his trade proposal, "though not to exceed half of the sum he had suggested." How shrewdly the governor and intendant protected the crown by investing their own money, as silent partners, in the cover operation of buying tobacco at $2 per hundredweight in Kentucky and selling it for $10 in New Orleans. And later, when Wilkinson's first shipment arrived and he asked for immediate payment rather than leaving his money on account, how sensibly Miró "determined to gratify him on this occasion." Compared to "the mischief that might arise from vexing him" or the "impediments that a lack of money would doubtless put in the way of his operations," how wise of Governor Miró to forgo "the greater security we might have in keeping his money in the treasury."[25]

On Monday, September 17, 1787, thirty-nine members of the Constitutional Convention in Philadelphia signed their newly drafted plan of government and recommended it to Congress and the states. By replacing the Confederation Congress with a more vigorous national government, their handiwork eventually contributed to the opening of the Mississippi and the demise of Wilkinson's Spanish Conspiracy. Two days later, in New Orleans, General James Wilkinson bade farewell to Miró and Navarro and boarded a ship for Charleston. Among his papers was the key to one of Spain's "most incomprehensible ciphers" so that he could communicate with Miró when he got back to Kentucky. The chosen code happened to be Number 13 in the series of Spanish ciphers, which led to Wilkinson's designation as Agent 13 in his continued dealings with Spain during the next fifteen years.[26]

In forwarding Wilkinson's lengthy *Memorial* to the ministry in Spain, Miró and Navarro asked permission to support Wilkinson's plans to separate Kentucky from the United States and to encourage Americans to settle in Louisiana as subjects of His Most Catholic Majesty. It suited Wilkinson's purposes to regard both aspects as integral to his plans, but the governor and the intendant had equally good reasons to see them as distinct alternatives. Wilkinson, after all, was not alone in his ability to detect a predominant passion and lay hold of it. He had given Miró and Navarro plenty of reason to suspect that his grand promises cloaked a more selfish and less ambitious short-term interest in monopolizing the riverborne trade out of Kentucky—they suspected that his "grandiose undertakings" were meant to disguise "a means of realizing a profitable commercial speculation."[27]

In letters both to Miró and to Gardoqui, Wilkinson vigorously urged the Spanish to keep the river closed to American trade—despite the outrage that he had expressed and fomented in Kentucky on the eve of his first visit to New Orleans. Ostensibly his goal was "to alienate and eradicate american principles and connexions" among his Kentucky neighbors, but Miró and Navarro were not blind to the fact that by keeping the river closed to others, the value of Wilkinson's special trading privileges increased. Only time would tell which goal figured more prominently in Wilkinson's heart. The Spaniards watched him closely, and they soon concluded that Wilkinson was a better informant than agent provocateur.[28]

.  .  .

Faced with the continued influx of Americans into Kentucky and a suspension of negotiations with John Jay until the new American government was in place, Spanish policy toward the Mississippi River was beginning a slow change that culminated in Pinckney's Treaty of 1795—a change that also made Wilkinson's information more useful than his grandiose undertakings. As early as May 24, 1788, José Moñino y Redondo, count of Floridablanca, had informed Diego de Gardoqui that Spain now wished

> to attract to our side the inhabitants of the Ohio and Mississippi, be it by alliance, by placing them under the protection of the King, or through Union with his dominions under treaties which will insure their liberty, thus allowing them to export their products to New Orleans and provide themselves at that town with goods they need from other countries.

Then on November 20, 1788, the Council of State met to consider Miró's and Navarro's recommendations about Wilkinson's *Memorial*. The council rejected outright Wilkinson's request for support of a separatist revolution in Kentucky, and it sidestepped his proposed trading privileges on the Mississippi.[29]

Spain simply had too much to lose by venturing into any scheme that might excite a military response from the United States. Until Kentucky established its complete independence, no Spanish official was to advance any promise or payment to aspiring frontier revolutionaries. Nor did the Council of State see any advantage in Wilkinson's proposals for trade and immigration. Rather than give Wilkinson and his friends control of trade down the Mississippi, Spain decided to open the river to all Americans subject only to a 15 percent export duty that Miró could lower at his discretion to 6 percent in particular cases. In addition, rather than promoting immigration through Wilkinson (or any of a dozen other Americans who had approached Gardoqui or Miró about establishing settlements in Louisiana[30]) Spain would offer land grants, commercial privileges, and religious toleration to any genuine immigrant willing to settle in Louisiana and swear an oath of loyalty to Carlos IV.[31]

The new trade and immigration policies had two principal objectives—both rooted in Louisiana's strategic role as the northern buffer for Spanish America. First, Spain wanted to placate Americans in the Ohio Valley before angry militiamen decided to challenge the feeble defenses of New Orleans. Second, the council sought to encourage immigration and settlement in Spanish territory to balance the rapid growth of population in the American west. They hoped that the 15 percent export duty would be low enough to appease American farmers, but high enough to encourage them to settle in Spanish territory.[32]

In February 1789 the crown's response to Wilkinson's *Memorial* reached Governor Miró. In March he communicated its provisions to a crestfallen James Wilkinson, and on April 20, 1789, Miró proclaimed Spain's new policy to the inhabitants of the American west.

1. It will be permitted to every good Inhabitant to come down and settle in the Province of Louisiana either at Natchés or any other place of both Mississippi's shores. They will not be molested on religious matters, although no other publick worship will be permitted to be publickly exercised than that of [the] Roman Catholic Church. Land shall be granted gratis to them at their arrival in proportion of the hands, or facultys each Family should have . . . under the condition they shall at the same time take the due oath of allegiance and bound themselves only to take up arms in defense of this Province against Whatsoever enemy who could attempt to invade it.

2. His most gracious Majesty generously grants the inhabitants of these Districts the trade with this town, and so they will be able to bring down Pelletry, tobbacco, flower, provisions, and every other produce of their own country. . . . This trade carried on by those who should not choose to settle in this Province can not be permitted but under the duty of fifteen percent which is in my power to diminish in favor of men of influence, who should apply to obtain this favor. . . .

3. Upon the proposal . . . respecting the wishes of those Districts in order to make a connexion with the Court of Spain, after disevering themselves from the United States it is not in my power to stipulate anything, nor to promote the scheme: because the good understanding subsistent between his most catholic Majesty and the United States prevents it . . . [but] should it happen that they could obtain their absolute independence from the United States then his Majesty will grant them the favor, succours and other advantages consistent with his royal bounty and agreeable to the situation wherein they should find themselves.[33]

In Kentucky things had not gone well for James Wilkinson. From the floor of the most recent of Kentucky's statehood conventions, the general had read most of his *Memorial* in a lengthy speech, but the convention had utterly rejected its arguments for independence linked to a Spanish alliance. With considerable reluctance and skepticism, Kentucky leaders resolved to give the new national government a chance. Never one to accept failure as his own, however, Wilkinson fastened upon Spain's new trade policy and its 15 percent duty as the explanation for the collapse of his separatist plans. Then, with amazing cheek, the general offered Miró an elaborate and expensive plan to promote immigration into Louisiana, for which he would need about $18,000 to send his agents throughout the western settlements. He also asked Miró to buy another two hundred hogsheads of tobacco on the crown's account. By August Wilkinson was conjuring up visions of a British attack on Louisiana from Canada, for which he needed $500 from Miró to support a sentinel at the Straits of Mackinac to monitor any movement of troops from Lake Huron to Lake Michigan—and another $140 in reimbursement for the messenger and two oarsmen who had carried these offers to New Orleans.[34]

The pattern of Wilkinson's activities had become abundantly clear. He had failed to bring Kentucky out of the union, and he had little to show for his efforts to promote American immigration into Louisiana. Nevertheless, his incriminating oath of allegiance to Spain was tucked safely in Miró's strongbox, and the general was about $7,000 in debt to Miró's administration. An ineffectual friend is better than a meddlesome adversary, and for all his limitations as an agent provocateur Wilkinson remained a well-placed informant. "He is always useful even when he does not achieve his object," Governor Miró told Luis de Las Casas, the captain-general at Havana, "since he serves as well to block those enterprises planned against the Province as to give notice of others he cannot stop." The charming schemer who once aspired to be the "Washington of the West" had finally proved his real worth. For a pension of just $2,000 a year (applied at first to pay down his debt to Miró's treasury), Spain bought General James Wilkinson as a stool pigeon and a spoiler. In the years ahead their investment paid for itself many times over.[35]

The one risk in the new policy of encouraging American immigration into the borderland buffer of Louisiana—as Governor Miró's superior in Havana, Captain-General Luis de Las Casas, warned Carlos IV and his ministers—was that the immigrants would retain their native language, customs, religion, and affinity to the United States. By offering farm-sized land grants to individual settlers, instead of large tracts for promoters and speculators, Miró wisely precluded the creation of dangerously independent "republics" within Spanish territory. Nevertheless, oaths of allegiance to Spain were a slender reed on which to base the security of the colony and the empire below it. Las Casas recommended sending immigrants directly from Spain to dilute American strength within the population of the territory, but nothing ever came of his suggestion.[36]

In matters of religion, the encouragement of American immigration into Louisiana required a measure of toleration unknown elsewhere in the empire of His Most Catholic Majesty Carlos IV. Protestants were allowed freedom of worship in their homes, and they were exempt from financial support for the established Roman Catholic Church. Catholic mass was the only public worship permitted in the colony, however, and priests were required to officiate at marriage and baptismal ceremonies of Protestants and Catholics alike. Both to accommodate the American-born population and to entice converts to Catholicism, Governor Miró worked with Bishop Andrés of Salamanca to recruit English-speaking Irish priests, educated at the Irish College of the University of Salamanca, for missionary service in Louisiana. The crown gave them $375 for clothing, books, and other supplies, and an annual salary of $480. In addition to preaching and administering the sacraments, like their Protestant counterparts in many areas of the United States, the clergymen of Louisiana also offered classes for youngsters to learn Spanish.[37]

The first four Irish priests arrived from Cádiz in 1787, six more priests came from La Coruña in 1792, and two Carmelite friars arrived in 1795. Of the twelve, five were dispatched to the settlements around Natchez, one to Nogales (near Vicksburg), a sixth to Sainte Genevieve and Kaskaskia in the Illinois Country, and a seventh to the Tensaw River settlement above Mobile Bay—the others filled vacancies around New Orleans. Most of these missionaries dispatched by His Most Catholic Majesty into the valley of the Mississippi were able men of good heart, but only four occasioned unusual comment by their contemporaries. The amiable Father Gregorio White, in the Natchez district, became a serious drunk. The Carmelite John Brady, in the same area, was said to be "the best shot, the best rider, and the best judge of horses in the district."[38]

Father William Savage, former vice rector of the University of Salamanca, became renowned for his preaching—filling his new Church of Our Savior of the World in Natchez with Protestants and Catholics alike and astonishing the urbane and genial Governor Manuel Gayoso de Lemos with the number of Protestants who converted to his faith. When death ended his exemplary ministry in April 1793, Father Savage's successor undid everything he had accomplished. A Capuchin zealot supported by Governor Miró's successor, Father Francis Lennan never set foot in the pulpit during his first two years in Natchez. He devoted his energies to complaining about the area's Protestants, and spreading rumors that disturbed the public tranquillity. Gayoso lamented that Lennan "hope[d] to drive from the Province all the Protestants, who are the wealthiest and most numerous class of settlers, and to keep here only a sprinkling of Catholics, who are mainly Irish and not the best people of their nation because almost all of them are turbulent and intriguing spirits." The stark contrast between the tolerant appeal of Father William Savage and the coercive bigotry of his successor is instructive. Similar things happened at the Government House on St. Louis Street in New Orleans when Esteban Miró returned to Spain on December 30, 1791.[39]

## CHAPTER EIGHT

# Banners of Blood

*The weakness of the [French] government seems to allow any-*
*thing. . . . People speak openly in the Palais-Royal of massacring*
*us, our houses are marked out for this murder and my door was*
*marked. . . . The Court expected, at any minute, to see itself*
*attacked by forty thousand armed brigands who, it was said, were*
*on their way from Paris. . . . The defection of troops is general and*
*everything announces a great revolution. . . . The Estates-General*
*of 1789 will be celebrated but by a banner of blood that will be*
*carried to all parts of Europe.*

—Marquis de Ferrières to Madame de Medel, June 28, 1789[1]

*Let's string up the aristocrats on the lampposts!*
*We will win, we will win, we will win.*
*We'll string up the aristocrats!*
*Despotism will die, Liberty will triumph*
*We will win, we will win, we will win. . . .*
*Equality will reign throughout the world. . . .*
*We will win, we will win, we will win.*

—"Ça Ira," 1790[2]

SOON AFTER the citizens of New Orleans finished mourning the
death of Carlos III and celebrating the accession of his son to the
throne of Spain, Governor Esteban Rodríguez Miró received a troubling
visit from an often troublesome Capuchin monk. The Reverend Father
Francisco Antonio Ildefonso de Sedella—Père Antoine as he was known
with some affection long after the Louisiana Purchase—was born in the
Spanish province of Granada. Conquered by the Saracens in the eighth
century, the area was ruled by the Moors into the fifteenth century, and
the young man who grew up in the shadow of their Alhambra had fer-
vently embraced the religion of the Crusaders. At twenty-three Sedella

had joined the Capuchin order in Canada, and a decade later he had come to Louisiana in 1781. Père Antoine affiliated himself with the priests of St. Louis Church (now Cathedral) on the Place d'Armes in the heart of New Orleans and always wore the *cappuccio,* or hooded robe, of the Capuchin order.

At nine o'clock on April 28, 1790, Father Sedella rushed into Governor Miró's office with all the impatient self-righteousness that fueled his life of recurrent conflict with civil and religious authorities. The Capuchin

*Deported by Governor Miró in 1790 after he attempted to bring the Inquisition into Louisiana, the Spanish Capuchin Francisco Antonio Ildefonso de Sedella returned to New Orleans and was elected pastor of St. Louis Cathedral on March 14, 1804. Although he was popular with many New Orleanians, Père Antoine clashed with religious authorities appointed by the new American bishop, Charles Carroll of Baltimore, and caused a schism in the Louisiana Church. Sedella outlived most of his rivals, however, and was widely mourned after his death on January 22, 1829.* (Courtesy Louisiana State Museum)

presented the weary governor with a letter newly arrived from the inquisitor general of Spain reviving his appointment as Louisiana's commissary of the Holy Office (the official name of the infamous Inquisition) and directing Father Sedella to suppress and confiscate subversive literature in the colony. The Capuchins had begun as a fervent reform movement within the Franciscan order, and their man in New Orleans was ready to embrace his inquisitorial authority with "exact fidelity and zeal."[3]

Father Sedella promised Miró the "utmost secrecy and precaution" in his pursuit of New Orleanians who were sure to possess writings condemned by the Church. By 1790 Church censors had compiled a lengthy list of authors and titles they regarded as dangerous. The *Index Librorum Prohibitorum* had been updated two dozen times since its first publication in 1559, and its definition of immoral and heretical works was sweeping. Theology presented the usual suspects, including liberal Catholics such as Abelard and Erasmus and Protestants from Calvin to Zwingli, but Father Sedella's new credentials also empowered him to expunge the European Enlightenment from the bookshelves of Louisiana. The *Index* condemned the political writings of Montesquieu, Voltaire, and Jean-Jacques Rousseau along with Michel de Montaigne's *Essays,* Denis Diderot's *Encyclopedia,* and the philosophical works of René Descartes. Prominent English authors were seen as equally sinister. The puritan poet John Milton's *State Papers* were prohibited along with John Locke's *Essay Concerning Human Understanding,* the satire and journalism of Jonathan Swift and Daniel Defoe, Edward Gibbon's *Decline and Fall of the Roman Empire,* and everything from the materialist pen of Thomas Hobbes. Until the moment that Père Antoine entered Governor Miró's office in April 1790, however, the Inquisition had not ventured onto the North American mainland, preferring to apprehend errant residents of Louisiana only when they traveled to Mexico, Cuba, or Spain. The zealous Capuchin was eager to set things right in the colony, and he advised the governor that his mission would require "recourse at any hour of the night to the Corps de Garde from which I may draw the necessary troops to . . . carry on my operations."[4]

Before Miró could finish reading the documents Father Sedella had given him, the monk had rushed from the governor's office as quickly as he had arrived. The next day, ablaze with the urgency of his holy assignment, the Capuchin grew impatient as the hours passed without word from Governor Miró. At six o'clock, from his spartan room near the Place d'Armes, Father Sedella sent Governor Miró a formal order complaining that the success of his assignment for the Inquisition was imperiled by Miró's "tardy measures." He demanded that Miró "inform me without further delay what steps you intend to take so that I may proceed promptly to accomplish my task."[5]

That night the newly appointed representative of the Inquisition was roused from his bed by heavy knocking. As yet unaware of the parallel between his midnight visitors and Carlos III's midnight expulsion of the Jesuits from Spain for their complicity in an assassination plot and growing support of the Inquisition in 1767, the Capuchin monk greeted Governor Miró's officer and the platoon of royal grenadiers who stood at his door.

"My friends, I thank you and his Excellency for the readiness of his compliance with my request," Father Sedella said, "but I have now no use for your services. You shall be warned in time when you are wanted," he promised as he prepared to return to his sleep. "Retire then with the blessing of God."[6]

Instead, the captain placed Father Sedella under arrest. "What!" exclaimed the monk, "will you dare lay your hands on a Commissary of the Holy Inquisition?"[7]

"I dare obey orders," the officer replied, as he ushered Father Sedella aboard a vessel that sailed the next day—April 30, 1790—for the Spanish port of Cádiz.[8]

"When I read the communication of that Capuchin," Governor Miró reported to the ministry in Spain, "I shuddered." The emerging policy of strengthening the Spanish borderlands through population growth—a policy Miró fully supported—depended upon "the pledge that the new colonists should not be molested in matters of religions, provided there should be no other public mode of worship than the Catholic." Miró knew that "the mere name of the Inquisition uttered in New Orleans would be sufficient, not only to check immigration . . . but would also be capable of driving away those who have recently come."[9]

As it was, Miró feared that his prompt deportation of Father Sedella might still have "fatal consequences" arising from "the mere suspicion of the cause of his dismissal."[10] The success of Spain's new defensive policies in the borderlands depended not on the fidelity and zeal of the Spanish Inquisition but on winning the loyalty of new settlers, most of them American Protestants, during a cataclysmic decade that challenged loyalties of every kind in Europe and the Americas.

The revival of Père Antoine's appointment as Louisiana commissary of the Inquisition and his specific assignment to root out subversive literature were direct reflections of Spain's initial reaction to the French Revolution—an event that shocked the Atlantic world, played havoc with Spanish efforts to maintain control of the Mississippi River Valley, and in many ways set the stage for the Louisiana Purchase. Already vulnerable to attack from the north, Louisiana was now exposed both to the imperial wars unleashed by the French Revolution and to the example of a successful slave revolt, fueled by revolutionary propaganda, in the Caribbean colony of St. Domingue.

"Spanish by its government," New Orleans merchant James Pitot wrote, Louisiana's population was "still generally French in its tastes, customs, habits, religion, and language." At a distance of three thousand miles from the Parisian crowds and their pikes, the early patriotic appeal of the French Revolution—"Arise ye children of the fatherland, the day of glory has arrived!"—melted thirty years of disenchantment with a nation that had abandoned Louisiana to the Spanish in 1761. The residents' nostalgia for *la Patrie* gave the colony's governors—Miró, who returned to Spain at forty-seven in 1791, and his forty-four-year-old successors, Governor François-Louis Hector, baron de Carondelet et Noyelles, in New Orleans, and Governor Manuel Gayoso de Lemos in Natchez—new reasons for worry. "In our very midst in this province," Gayoso wrote in July 1792, "there is one disadvantage which must be watched with as great care as those offered by our enemies." Louisiana "is inhabited by people of French extraction," he warned, and "although many of them are pacifically inclined, the majority are fond of novelty, have communication with France and with [French] posessions in America, and hear with the greatest pleasure of the revolution in that kingdom." Gayoso feared that "if war were declared on France, we should find but few inhabitants of Lower Louisiana who would sincerely defend the country."[11]

Slave conspiracies in 1791 and 1795 at Pointe Coupée, halfway between Natchez and New Orleans, compounded the problems facing the Spanish governors—as did the vacillating imperial policies of Carlos IV and his ministers, especially Manuel Godoy, as they reacted to the ramifications of tumultuous events in Europe. At the same time, Carondelet's trade and Indian policies undercut the promising intrigues with James Wilkinson and other Kentucky separatists, while the continued growth of the American western settlements and the establishment of a stronger federal government under the new Constitution posed a greater threat from the north. Governor Miró's prompt deportation of Father Antonio Sedella on a vessel to Cádiz averted one minor tempest in the colony, but in the years between the fall of the Bastille on July 14, 1789, and the Treaty of Basle on July 22, 1795, Louisiana itself was like a tiny sloop caught in a hurricane of world events.

. . .

By itself, bad weather does not topple governments, not even the crippled monarchy of Louis XVI, who had ascended the throne of France at twenty on the eve of the American Revolution. Like his Bourbon cousin in Madrid, who was six years older, Louis XVI was a devotee of hunting who liked to tinker with clocks. On the eve of the French Revolution both men were comfortable in their mediocrity, chronically indecisive, and easily manipulated by their wives and courtiers. In an age of reason, neither man inspired confidence in the antique verities that supported absolute monarchy. It did not help that foreign wars and the expenses of the court at Versailles had rendered the monarchy bankrupt, forcing Louis XVI to summon for the first time since 1614 a meeting of representatives of the clergy, aristocracy, and people (roughly analogous to the British Parliament) known as the Estates-General.[12]

On July 13, 1788, violent hailstorms swept across most of France. Huge pellets of ice ripped branches from trees, leveled crops, and killed birds and wildlife in a four-hundred-mile swath from Normandy, near the English Channel, to as far south as Toulouse and Languedoc, near the Mediterranean. The hail ruined grapevines from the Loire Valley east through Burgundy to Alsace. The storm wiped out apples, oranges, and olives in the Calvados and the Midi. South of Paris the hail destroyed fruits and vegetables in the Ile-de-France, flattened wheat fields around Orléans, and devastated cereal crops to the west in Beauce. "A countryside, erstwhile ravishing," farmers complained, "has been reduced to an arid desert."[13]

As though some biblical curse had been unleashed upon the ancien régime, drought followed the hailstorm. The autumn harvest was meager, and a cruel winter, the worst since 1709, came hard on the heels of the drought. Grain grew scarce and flour even more dear, as ice froze the waterwheels of mills throughout the country and deep snow impeded shipments of emergency supplies. "Everywhere I have found men dead of cold and hunger," a visitor reported from Provence in January 1789, "and that in the midst of wheat for lack of flour, all the mills being frozen."[14]

In normal times, bread was the dietary staple for three quarters of the French population, and in normal times the standard four-pound loaf cost about 8 sous. With average daily wages of 20 to 30 sous for a manual laborer, most families normally spent half their income on bread. After the devastating hail, drought, and winter of 1788–1789, however, prices of firewood and bread soared—by February a four-pound loaf of bread cost 15 sous. The failed harvest of 1788 drove day laborers into the cities in desperate hordes. As discretionary spending plummeted and markets for manufactured goods collapsed, urban artisans joined the ranks of the unemployed, soon followed by construction workers as economic depression brought building projects to a halt. By the summer of 1789 displaced laborers comprised between one third and three quarters of the French rural population, while in every major city tens of thousands of artisans and their hungry families were idle. Outside the mirrored halls and soothing gardens of Versailles, where the Sun King, Louis XIV, had relocated the royal court at a safe distance from Paris in 1682, starving French men and women grew increasingly fearful and angry, armed and organized.[15]

Events moved quickly in the year following the hailstorm of July 13, 1788, as anger spread in the streets of Paris and along the roads of rural France. Censorship was suspended during the election campaigns for seats in the Estates-General, and a flood of pamphlets expressing Enlightenment ideas circulated throughout the country. In May and June 1789 the meeting of the Estates-General gave voice to pent-up grievances—then fell into interminable squabbles between the elected representatives of the Third Estate and the privileged clergy and aristocracy. While the king dithered between conciliation and force—never altogether certain that he could count on the loyalty of his army—orators and journalists called for liberty, equality, and fraternity (and retribution against the enemies of the people) while rioters helped themselves to bread, food, and weapons. One gunsmith reported that Parisians raided his shop thirty times, arming themselves with a total of 150 swords, 576 unfinished blades, 58 hunting knives, 20 pistols, and 8 muskets.[16]

On June 12, a company of royal dragoons found itself outnumbered when sent to disperse an angry crowd at the Place Vendôme. A disorderly skirmish ensued, and by morning the king's troops had retreated across the Seine, effectively abandoning the old city. Crowds of Parisians began dismantling the ten-foot wall around Paris built by the Farmers-General to enforce its high taxes on salt, flour, and other commodities. They destroyed forty of its fifty-four customhouses, then sacked the monastery of Saint-Lazare, carrying off grain, wine, vinegar, oil, and twenty-five Gruyère cheeses. With royal authority collapsing around them, city officials took charge, expanding their urban militia as a hedge against anarchy and a defense against royalist counterattack. Proper uniforms were an impossibility on short notice, so the militiamen decorated their hats and coats with a red and blue cockade, the colors of Paris. Days later, when he accepted command of the new national guard, the marquis de

Lafayette interposed a band of white, the king's color, in a gesture toward national unity.

Armed at first only with kitchen knives, weaponry stolen from city gunsmiths, and antique halberds and pikes expropriated from a guard-house near the Tuileries, Lafayette's militia soon gained thirty thousand muskets and some cannon from the barracks at the Hôtel des Invalides. They needed gunpowder—and regardless of General Lafayette's moderation, they knew where it was stored.[17]

On July 14—one year after the hailstorm—a crowd gathered at the fortress and arsenal of the Bastille. Built in the fourteenth century with walls five feet thick, a seventy-foot moat and drawbridge, and eight stone towers, the Bastille was a notorious symbol of Bourbon absolutism, the dungeon for political prisoners arrested in secret and held without trial, sometimes for months (as with Voltaire) and often for life. By nightfall, after ineffectual negotiations gave way to violence, the Bastille was taken. While the militia confiscated 246 barrels of gunpowder from the arsenal of the Bastille, unruly crowds murdered the commandant and paraded his severed head on a pike through the streets of Paris.[18]

The next day at Versailles, the duc de La Rochefoucauld-Liancourt informed Louis XVI of the fall of the Bastille.

"Is it a revolt?" the king asked.

"No, Sire," Liancourt replied, "it is a revolution."

At first, circumstances allowed Liancourt and responsible moderates like Lafayette and Honoré-Gabriel Riqueti, comte de Mirabeau, some hope of a peaceful resolution to the nation's political crisis—replacing Bourbon absolutism with a constitutional monarchy on the English model admired by philosophes like Voltaire and Montesquieu. At every critical moment, however, the revolution seemed to grow more violent and more radical. The freshly severed head of the commandant of the Bastille, bobbing on a pike high above the crowd that carried it triumphantly through the streets of Paris, inaugurated a gory ritual of blood lust—butchery only sanitized by the ruthless efficiency of an ingenious mechanical device invented by Dr. Joseph-Ignace Guillotin.[19]

Two days after the fall of the Bastille, Louis XVI donned a simple morning coat and left Versailles for Paris in a plain coach drawn by eight black horses. The marquis de Lafayette and the National Guard, awash with red, white, and blue cockades, greeted the king at the edge of the city and escorted him to the Hôtel de Ville, where Louis XVI spoke a few inaudible words of conciliation, accepted a tricolor cockade from the mayor, and pinned it to his hat. Throngs shouted *"Vive le roi"* and *"Vive la nation"* at the auspicious ceremony, and many who were present honestly hoped for constitutional reform and the rights of man and citizens. The revolution, however, marched to the cadence of a more violent crowd, hearkening to legislators who believed they must "destroy everything; yes, destroy everything; then everything is to be recreated." The revolution spoke of constitutional reform, the rights of man and citizen, and ideals of equality and fraternity, but it followed the crowds who carried bloody heads on pikes, cheered each time the blade of the guillotine fell, and sang "Ça Ira":

> Lafayette says, "Let he who will, follow me!"
> And patriotism will respond,
> Without fear of fire or flame.
> The French will always conquer,
> We will win, we will win, we will win. . . .
> Let's string up the aristocrats on the lampposts!
> We will win, we will win, we will win. . . .
> And we will no longer have nobles or priests,
> We will win, we will win, we will win.
> Equality will reign throughout the world. . . .
> We will win, we will win, we will win.

As the marquis de Ferrières feared it would, the French Revolution offered "a banner of blood . . . to all parts of Europe."[20]

Few events in modern history unleashed as many strong passions as the French Revolution. "Considering that we are divided from [France] but by a slender dyke of about twenty-four miles," the British statesman Edmund Burke (an admirer of the American Revolution a decade earlier) gave thanks in his *Reflections on the Revolution in France* (November 1790) that his countrymen were "not the converts of Rousseau" and "not the disciples of Voltaire," and especially that "atheists are not our preachers; madmen are not our lawgivers." Safe on the far side of the Atlantic, Americans from Maine to Georgia were initially united in joy at the creation of a sister republic—happy for the citizens of France who had sent them Lafayette, the king's legions, and a fleet to help win American independence.[21]

Then came shocking news of the execution of Louis XVI on January 21, 1793, and the mad efficiency of Dr. Guillotin's invention in the hands of Maximilien de Robespierre and the Jacobin party. Forty thousand people were executed during their Reign of Terror, when Robespierre headed the bloodthirsty Committee of Public Safety from April 1793 through July 1794. Whether the crime was treason, petty theft, or insufficient enthusiasm for Jacobin opinions, practice made perfect. In October 1793 Paris executioners beheaded twenty-two Girondin leaders (former allies of the Jacobin party) in thirty-six minutes. Two months later, executioners in Lyon lopped off thirty-two heads in twenty-five minutes. A week after that residents of rue Lafont complained that blood from the scaffold at Place des Terreaux, where the executioners dispatched twelve heads in five minutes, was flooding the drainage ditches near their homes.[22]

After 1793 the French Revolution became an equal-opportunity calamity, more divisive than any domestic issue in American politics. For twenty-five years—from the Bastille to Waterloo—its wild oscillations offered everyone something to fear: violence, repression, and cowardice, tyranny and anarchy, mobs and dictators, atheists and demagogues, imperialism, civil war, and world war. Like the reflection in a fun-house mirror, the French Revolution distorted the beauties and blemishes that Americans saw in one another, polarizing Federalists and Republicans, who voiced their opinions in blindingly passionate rhetoric. "Behold France," warned a Massachusetts Federalist, "an open hell, still ringing with agonies and blasphemies, still smoking with sufferings and crimes, in which we see . . . perhaps our future state." Look at England, came the Jeffersonian reply, the corrupt tyrant of the seas, driven into perpetual debt by its war machine, trampling the liberties of citizens and neighbors alike. At issue in the French Revolution, Jefferson proclaimed from the safety of his study, was nothing less than "the liberty of the whole earth . . . but rather than it should have failed, I would have seen half the earth devastated."[23]

The French hailstorm of July 1788 may have dissipated in the foothills of the Pyrenees, but seen from Madrid those rugged mountains offered scant defense against the tempest of revolution. Carlos III's trusted minister, José Moñino y Redondo, count of Floridablanca, who had devoted his career to enlightened administrative, economic, and cultural reform, recoiled in horror at the first news of revolution to the north. Reform programs were shelved and he slammed the door on revolutionary ideas with ironclad censorship. His measures established a cordon sanitaire at the Pyrenees that kept revolutionary tracts and pamphlets out of Spain, but no diplomatic tools could reverse the tide of revolution.[24]

Carlos IV next called in his father's ambassador to France, Pedro

Pablo Abarca de Bolea, count of Aranda, who was known for his sympathy for French rationalism. A friend to Voltaire and d'Alembert, a grand master of the Spanish Freemasons, and a prime mover in the expulsion of the Jesuits, Aranda did all he could to mitigate the circumstances of Louis XVI—but the new republican government paid no heed to counsels of moderation from the Spanish Bourbons. Aranda's young successor, the queen's favorite and lover, Manuel Godoy, tried the machinery of negotiation one more time, greased by generous bribes to members of the French legislature, but again to no avail. In 1792 the Republic of France had declared war on Austria, and now a collision with Bourbon Spain had become inevitable.[25]

On February 1 and March 7, 1793, France declared war against Great Britain and Spain respectively. Spain responded with a counter-declaration of war against France on March 23. Within two weeks "their Britannic and Most Catholic Majesties," traditional enemies since 1585, were negotiating a military alliance against France, signed on May 25. At first the war went well for Godoy. Spanish armies drove far into France, while Austria advanced from the north. Then the tide turned. By the spring of 1795 French armies had punished the Spanish in a series of resounding victories, captured Bilbao and Vitoria in the Basque country, and were marching into Castille. Godoy sued for peace.[26]

"We need peace," Godoy whispered to his chief negotiator, "whatever the price." Ignoring Spain's treaty obligations to Great Britain, Godoy signed the Treaty of Basle in the nick of time on July 22, 1795. "The French armies," said one Spanish observer, "would soon have paid a visit to Carlos at Madrid if his favorite minister, with more address than he ever discovered in his subsequent management of political affairs, had not concluded and ratified the peace of Basle." Spain, for the moment, was safe. Graced by his thankful patrons with the title of Prince of the Peace, Godoy boasted that his "glorious treaty did not cost Spain a single tree of her soil." Godoy gave some thought to bartering away Louisiana in exchange for peace, but he held back, and in the end Spain lost only its brief alliance with Great Britain and the Caribbean colony of Santo Domingo (the eastern part of Hispaniola, now the Dominican Republic) in exchange for the return of territory captured by France south of the Pyrenees.[27]

As a result of the Treaty of Basle, France in 1795 gained nominal possession of the entire island of Hispaniola. An island the size of Ireland, about fifty miles east of Cuba, Hispaniola was divided by a nearly impassable range of mountains into the tropical plantation colony of St. Domingue (now Haiti) and the arid colony of Santo Domingo, where cattle ranchers and subsistence farmers predominated. Visited by Columbus in 1492, the native Arawak tribe of Hispaniola had been quickly exterminated by European diseases and exploitation, and equally quickly replaced with African slaves. "I do not know if coffee and sugar are essential to the happiness of Europe," a Frenchman wrote in 1773,

> but I know well that these two products have accounted for the unhappiness of two great regions of the world: America has been depopulated so as to have land on which to plant them; Africa has been depopulated so as to have the people to cultivate them.[28]

French sugar planters regarded St. Domingue as the finest colony in the world. When the Bastille fell in Paris, trade with St. Domingue engaged seven hundred fifty French ships, employed twenty-four thousand sailors, and was valued at £11 million a year. France consumed one third of the island's exports, and the rest were processed in France and shipped abroad by a workforce estimated at several million Frenchmen.[29]

As an economic entity, St. Domingue thrived by importing slaves from Africa and working them to death in order to supply Europe's insatiable demand for sugar, coffee, and cocoa. St. Domingue imported thirty thousand African slaves a year, expendable replacement parts for the grim machinery of its sugar plantations. Each year, French merchants invested about 8.5 million livres to organize an average of three hundred African slaving expeditions. Nearly half of the French slaving fleet sailed from Nantes, "the City of Slavers." Most of the rest sailed from Bordeaux, La Rochelle, or Le Havre—but British and American traders smuggled slaves into St. Domingue as well.[30]

So lucrative were the island's exports that, in addition to clothing and manufactured goods, St. Domingue's large plantation owners found it cost-effective to import such basic necessities as food, firewood, and barrel staves rather than divert land or labor from the production of sugar, coffee, and cocoa. As a society, St. Domingue presented a grim caricature of eighteenth-century America: half a million slaves (two thirds of them African-born), thirty thousand mulattoes (including some of the island's wealthiest plantation owners and slaveholders), and thirty thousand whites, either very rich (the *grands blancs*) or very poor (the *petit blancs*)—all inclined to hate and fear one another.[31]

Liberty, equality, and fraternity were inherently hostile to the institution of slavery, and in 1791 the revolutionary banner of blood brought the world's most perfect plantation economy a great slave revolt that lasted a dozen years. "In its spectacle of disintegration," the Haitian Revolution pitted "grand blanc against petit blanc, white against mulatto, mulatto against black." The Haitian Revolution was more vicious and bloody— and more frightening to its American neighbors, especially to slaveholders in Louisiana and the American south—than the Reign of Terror in France. Refugees scrambled with their slaves to Baltimore, Charleston, New Orleans, Cuba, or Jamaica at the beginning of the Haitian Revolution, bearing tales of incredible horror: men and women hacked to death with cane knives, pregnant mulatto women cut open and their unborn children thrown into fires, and severed heads mounted on pikes at every burned plantation.[32]

The extraordinary violence of the Haitian Revolution was rooted in the gruesome history of what once had been the perfect French colony. "I have reached the stage of believing firmly," a French colonial governor had informed the minister of marine and colonies, "that one must treat the Negroes as one treats beasts." The governor's standard would have seemed progressive on St. Domingue, where domestic animals were never subjected to the punishments routinely inflicted on human beings. Long before the revolution, barbarity and sadism were commonplace on the island (as was often the case where vastly outnumbered slaveholders lived in constant fear, sleeping with loaded pistols under their pillows while gangs of hopeless slaves were crushed by the relentless demands of tropical agriculture).[33]

As regulated by the French Code Noir, a disciplinary whipping was not to exceed thirty-nine lashes (or later, fifty) with a whip of woven cord. But planters of St. Domingue who preferred the cowhide *rigoise* or the *lianes* (made of stiff island reeds supple as whalebone) seldom kept count. Slaves were whipped to death, and the everyday vocabulary of plantation discipline on St. Domingue described a brutal range of punishments: "The four post," in which the slave's hands and feet were tied to posts on the ground; "the hammock," in which the slave was suspended by four limbs; and "the torture of the ladder." Mutilations were common, and other outrageous punishments seemed torn from the pages of medieval martyrologies. Slaves were burned alive, roasted to death on grills over slow coals, scalded with wax or boiling cane sugar, or stuffed with gunpowder and ignited—a practice common enough to have its own vicious phrase: "to burn a little powder in the arse of a nigger."[34]

Notices for runaway slaves from the *Gazette Générale de Saint-Domingue* and the *Moniteur Colonial* bear candid testimony to the horrors of the slave regime:

*Louis,* 35 years old, who has scars all over his face and whose body is covered with welts from whippings.

*Mathieu,* 14 or 16 years of age, whose left hand is missing and whose right hand is crippled as a result of burns.

*Joseph,* a Negro from the Congo, who has been branded with the Jesuit cross on his chest.

*Désiré,* the slave from Fort Dauphine, who can be recognized easily from the chain that ties his left arm to his left leg.

*John Baptiste,* whose body is covered with recent wounds and whose nails are all missing.[35]

The grisly realities behind these advertisements for runaways were not forgotten when the revolution came to St. Domingue. The slaves who fought for their freedom sang "Ça Ira" and "La Marseillaise," but they still remembered the words of an ancient voodoo song invoking the Congolese rainbow serpent, Mbumba, for protection against European slave traders and the coastal African tribe, Ba Fioti, who did business with them and were dreaded for their witchcraft:

> *Eh! Eh! Bomba! Hen! Hen!*
> *Canga bafio té!*
> *Canga moun de lé!*
> *Canga do ki la!*
> *Canga li!*

Eh! Eh! Rainbow spirit serpent / Tie up the Ba Fioti / Tie up the whites / Tie up the witches / Tie them.[36]

When Governor Carondelet landed at New Orleans in December 1791, he found local Jacobin clubs distributing revolutionary pamphlets throughout the capital and he heard French residents singing "Ça Ira" and later "La Marseillaise." In the theaters, taverns, and coffeehouses of New Orleans, rowdy punsters dubbed the new governor *"cochon du lait"* (suckling pig) in their adapted version of the "Carmagnole":

> When we will be republicans,
> When we will be republicans,
> We will hang all the rascals,
> We will hang all the rascals.
> Quachondelait will be the first,
> Will be the first to be guillotined.

Clearly, the situation terrified Carondelet. He quietly packed up his baroness, María de la Concepción Castaños y Aragorri, and their two small children, Luis Angel and María Felipa Cayetana, and shipped them off to the safety of Havana. Then he turned his attention to the presumed Jacobins of New Orleans, many of whom seem to have been newly arrived "businessmen," including two that he described as "talented men, very astute, and the wealthiest men in the capital."[37]

Never one to underestimate the dangers at hand, the new governor was suspicious but also gullible, and he was temperamentally inclined toward dramatic, expensive, and contradictory measures. When it came to handling a crisis, the contrast between Carondelet and Miró could not have been more stark.

In June 1791, for example, the summer before Carondelet arrived, five fires were started deliberately in various parts of New Orleans (two of them "on the fence of the very same house") and a sixth at the suburban home of Lorenzo Sigur. Having witnessed the great conflagration of 1788, Miró was all too familiar with the threat of fire, but his response was measured and effective. Without indulging in alarmist rhetoric about the possibility of Jacobin saboteurs, Miró increased the number of nightly patrols as a precautionary measure, and then (like a Neighborhood Watch program) he appealed for assistance to the city's merchants and traders, asking them to "keep watch with their friends . . . either walking or on horseback." Each evening, Miró gathered a group of municipal and colonial officials to ride with him "in the night on horseback with [the] dragoons," visibly reassuring the populace while also raising the morale of his patrols. The culprits were believed to be three prison escapees, "among whom is a real bad one . . . seen in the woods nearby," so Miró sent search parties into the woods, initiated random patrols outside the city after dark, and offered "two prisoners of good faith who had never committed a serious crime"—trusties, in modern parlance—"their freedom if they should catch the main one."[38]

While Miró calmly monitored the danger, he described the situation to Luis de Las Casas, the captain-general at Havana, "so that Your Excellency may not have any extra worries . . . because things are always exaggerated as they travel from one to another." By the end of August Miró could report "the apprehension of the suspected negro, whose trial is now being prepared," and assure his superior that "fears that the city might be set on fire are gradually ceasing."[39]

A year later, Governor Carondelet reacted very differently to reports of "seditious people" in the colony. He deported Jean Dupuy, a French trader, "for having made remarks suggestive of a revolution in this province," as he did a man named Bujeac, "one of the most fanatical of all the partisans of the revolution." Carondelet complained that Bujeac, despite his warnings and threats of banishment, was "always on the lookout for dangerous news which he was spreading with the greatest effrontery in the most public places against the monarchical government." On another occasion Carondelet banished a free black tailor, newly arrived from St. Domingue, because he was "a native of that part of Santo Domingo that belongs to the French and is mixed up in all the intrigues and harassments of the French colony, besides being ungovernable and audacious. Having such a character around under the present circumstances," Carondelet explained, "might produce bad results."[40]

Oblivious to the fact that deportations were as likely to arouse as to curb seditious talk, Carondelet eventually banished sixty-eight men to Cuba. Some of them were heads of families, and all of them were people whom the governor regarded as having "no respect for anyone, nor any law nor duty." The captain-general of Havana, Luis de Las Casas (who was Carondelet's brother-in-law), was not so sure. "Real traitors," Las Casas cautioned Carondelet in June 1795, were more likely to be "adventurers" than merchants, "since men of property are not going to risk their investments with this nonsense. After all, by reuniting with France"— where slavery had been abolished in 1794—"they automatically forfeit their slaves." The greater danger, Las Casas warned his impulsive brother-in-law (with an eye toward the situation in St. Domingue), was "that the free men of colour and the slaves will allow themselves to be tempted by the corruption of French government . . . with the desire which they so much value—to possess liberty."[41]

The revolutionary ideals that especially appealed to free people of color in Louisiana, as in St. Domingue, were equality and fraternity.

Many of them accepted the existence of slavery, and Louisiana's more successful free men of color (none of whom achieved the grandeur of St. Domingue's wealthy mulatto class) commonly owned slaves themselves. What they wanted was respect. Respect from their white property-owning neighbors, and respect from the officers of government.[42]

Among the more vocal of Louisiana's ambitious free men of color was Pedro Bailly, a mulatto lieutenant in the free-colored militia. Bailly had an instinct for business. Starting as a blacksmith, carter, and wood dealer after his manumission in 1776, Bailly had become a comfortable self-made entrepreneur trading in slaves and real estate. He had purchased his mother's freedom in 1781, kept at least five slaves for his household, and acquired hundreds of pesos to lend at interest. As was often the case in Spanish society, his good fortune accompanied a steady rise in the ranks of the militia, which also excited jealousy among those who owed Bailly substantial amounts of money. Playing to Carondelet's paranoia with exaggerated or fabricated testimony, two fellow officers testified, falsely, that Bailly shirked his responsibilities as an officer. They also claimed, probably truthfully, that when the militia was sent to repair cracks in the levee, Bailly sent a slave in his place—a common practice among wealthy white militiamen that caused deep resentment among the colored militia, even when the man who could afford it was one of their own.[43]

In March 1794 Governor Carondelet deported Lieutenant Bailly to Cuba for his "diabolical ideas of freedom and equality" and for "having made remarks against the Spanish government . . . showing himself to be inclined to the principles of the French rebels." Bailly was basically guilty of advocating social equality between whites and free men of color, both in Louisiana society and in the colony's militia—opinions that only made the example of St. Domingue loom larger in the governor's mind. The testimony of Luis Declouet, a white militia lieutenant and tobacco merchant, offers a clear glimpse of Bailly's expressed sentiments—opinions quite beyond the reach of men of color in Virginia and other American slave states.[44]

In November 1793, anticipating a French invasion from the Gulf of Mexico during the short-lived Spanish-English alliance, the two men had accompanied their militia unit to Fort St. Phillip, in Plaquemines Parish on the Mississippi River below New Orleans. In a conversation while waiting for an attack that never came, Lieutenant Declouet described the French as enemies of the state and of religion and foes to all humanity.

"Humanity! Humanity!" Bailly replied. "I am going to speak frankly to you, sure that you are a man of honor. . . . It is true that they have done wrong by murdering their king, but sir, the French are just; they have conceded men their rights."[45]

Declouet asked Bailly which rights he referred to. "A universal equality among men, us, people of color," Bailly replied.

We have on the Island of Saint-Domingue and other French islands the title *ciudadano activo* [i.e., participatory citizen]; we can speak openly, like any white person and hold the same rank as they. Under our [Louisiana] rule do we have this? No, sir, and it is unjust. All of us being men [rather than slaves] there should be no difference. Only their method of thinking—not color—should differentiate men. Under these circumstances of war . . . Senor Maxant politely received us here at Fort Placaminos, telling us that on this occasion there would be no difference between us and the whites, implying at other times there are distinctions. Every day Senor Maxant invites officers of the white militia to eat at his table. And why are we not paid the same attention? Are we not officers just as they are?[46]

Whether Bailly's actions deserved two years' imprisonment in Cuba may be doubted, but Carondelet (like Miró before him) had reason to be concerned about the opinions Bailly so eloquently expressed. They and everyone else knew that from 1791 through 1793 the Haitian Revolution had begun not as a slave uprising but as a conflict between propertied, slaveholding whites and propertied, slaveholding mulattoes. For decades, in St. Domingue, in Louisiana, and in other Caribbean colonies, French and Spanish royal officials had nurtured the three-tiered societies of whites, free mulattoes, and slaves, playing each group off the others as a strategy to strengthen their own imperial authority.

In 1791, when a slave conspiracy was discovered in Pointe Coupée Parish, in the rich bottomland between the Atchafalaya and Mississippi Rivers about a hundred miles upriver from New Orleans, none other than Pedro Bailly had been hauled into court for talking about "strik[ing] a blow like at the Cap"—a geographical reference to Cap Français (now Cap-Haïtien) on the north coast of St. Domingue and a rhetorical allusion to the limited goals of the mulatto party, who sought only equality with whites as citizens and not the abolition of slavery. With Governor Miró presiding, the court had acquitted Bailly in 1791, in part because the evidence against him was all hearsay, in part because he may have done nothing but talk, and in part because the mood of the colony was still calm, for in 1791 the news from St. Domingue was only of discord between elite whites and mulattoes.[47]

With a full-fledged slave revolt raging in St. Domingue, however, the mood in Louisiana was more apprehensive in 1795, when a second and more serious slave conspiracy was discovered at Pointe Coupée. "If our information is correct," a Pointe Coupée planter wrote to authorities in New Orleans, "the Saint-Domingue insurrection did not have a more violent beginning." Although not as severely outnumbered by their slaves as the planters of the sugar islands, Pointe Coupée's two thousand white residents did live on large isolated plantations stretching for twenty miles along the west bank of the Mississippi River and were outnumbered by their seven thousand slaves. While the Code Noir forbade possession of weapons by slaves, enforcement in Pointe Coupée was lax and many of the area's slaves had guns. Finally, while there had been no credible evidence of outside agitation in 1791, this time Jacobin provocateurs probably were at work up and down the Mississippi, circulating radical literature, denouncing slavery, and distributing and proclaiming the French National Convention's declaration of February 4, 1794, "that all men, without distinction of color living in the colonies are French citizens enjoying all rights assured by the Constitution."[48]

With France and Spain at war, a French victory could bring a general emancipation, thought Joseph Bouyavel, a French-born teacher who lived on the Goudeau estate at Pointe Coupée. Bouyavel was accustomed to reading revolutionary literature to the slaves, including antislavery passages from the Declaration of the Rights of Man from his copy of *Théorie de l'Impôt*. Bouyavel counseled the slaves "to be patient because slavery would not last very long," but other whites, including a German-born tailor from Philadelphia and an agitator from the Republic of Raguse, a revolutionary state established in Yugoslavia at the height of the French Revolution, spread a more insidious rumor, fraught with implications of double-dealing on the part of slaveholders.[49]

Jean Baptiste, one of the principal leaders of the conspiracy, heard the story from a slave from Curaçao, near Venezuela, who recounted that "they are awaiting at the Capital an Order of the King which declares all the slaves free." Soon thereafter Antoine Sarrasin, the other chief leader of the Pointe Coupée plot, told Jean Baptiste that although "this order of freedom" had been sent to the commandant of a neighboring parish, an overseer at the Poydras estate (where both leaders were slaves) had convinced the commandant not to publish it. Instead, this overseer, named Duffief, had drawn up "a petition for the slaves to sign," renouncing their freedom, "without telling them what the petition said." As another slave heard the rumor, "the King had given us our freedom, but the masters made a petition to prevent it" and were forcing their slaves to sign a petition "renouncing their freedom and saying that they wanted to end their days with their masters." A foolhardy planter's wife gave further credence to the rumor when she taunted her slaves for their refusal to plant corn with a threat to send for the petition that Duffief had tricked them into signing so that "when all the nègres will be free, you will never be free here." "If all this was true," Jean Baptiste reasoned, the slaves of Pointe Coupée "must oppose it and kill the whites."[50]

"We are free," a planter overheard one of his slaves say, "but the settlers do not want to give us our freedom. We must wipe them all out. We have enough axes and sticks to kill them. We missed once, but I do not think this coup will miss." At a secret meeting of conspirators in Antoine Sarrasin's cabin on the Poydras plantation at Pointe Coupée, the German tailor and the Yugoslav firebrand asked the obvious question: If the rumor was true, "would [it] not be better for you to do like the nègres du Cap"? If the planters of Louisiana were the only obstacle to their freedom, the slaves of Pointe Coupée "could do the same here as at Le Cap." The logic was lethally indisputable. "I would go to bed [armed to the teeth] with the most sinister thoughts creeping into my mind," a militia officer wrote, "taking heed of the dreadful calamities of Saint-Domingue, and of the germ of revolt only too widespread among our own slaves. I often thought, on my going to bed, of the means I would use to save [my wife] and my son."[51]

Perhaps inevitably, since the conspirators' main lines of communication extended at least a hundred miles along the banks of the Mississippi River and perhaps as far north as Natchez, the uprising planned for the night of April 12–13 was discovered or betrayed on April 9. The local Spanish commander, Captain Guillermo Duparc, quickly arrested the suspected ringleaders. Subsequent arrests culminated on April 30, when Governor Carondelet ordered a simultaneous raid of Negro quarters on plantations throughout Louisiana at 5:00 a.m. to round up any remaining weapons or strangers. Eleven days of formal hearings and trials began at Pointe Coupée on May 8, and more than fifty slaves and three whites were found guilty of conspiracy. Five days of sentencing and executions began on May 29. By June 2 three white conspirators were bound for prison in Havana, thirty-one slaves were flogged and sent to hard labor at Spanish presidios in Mexico, Florida, Puerto Rico, and Cuba, and between twenty-three and twenty-six slaves were hanged. Their severed heads were nailed to posts along the levee road from Pointe Coupée past Baton Rouge to New Orleans—grisly evidence that in the name of liberty, equality, and fraternity, a banner of blood had been carried from the Bastille into the Caribbean and up the Mississippi River.[52]

## CHAPTER NINE

# A New Era in World History

*I am arming the Canadians to throw off the yoke of England. I am arming the Kentuckians, and I am preparing an expedition by sea to support their descent on New Orleans.*

—Citizen Edmond Charles Genet, June 19, 1793[1]

*Why should not I have the luck of that fanatic priest . . . who preached in France and the other States of Europe for the Conquest of the Holy Land. Louisiana and its wretched inhabitants are assuredly more interesting than that barren Country: The Spaniards who defend the Mississippi are more worthy of Contempt than The Ottoman; and the French . . . burn with the Divine fire and sacred enthusiasm which Liberty inspires. Subscriptions will be opened and immediately filled up, and Thousands of brave patriots will present themselves for that superb and truly Holy Expedition.*

—Citizen August Lachaise, May 9, 1794[2]

WHILE THE National Convention was preparing to abolish the French monarchy and begin "Year I of the Republic," in September 1792 the German poet Johann Wolfgang von Goethe was traveling with a regiment commanded by his literary patron, Duke Karl-August of Weimar, as they advanced through Alsace and Lorraine toward Paris. The imprisonment of Louis XVI had shocked the crowned heads of Europe, momentarily joining Bourbons, Hanoverians, Habsburgs, Hohenzollerns, and Romanovs in sympathy with their beleaguered cousin. Emperor Leopold II of Austria, Marie-Antoinette's brother, led the reaction, dispatching an Austrian force and some Prussian troops to save the king of France from the wrath of his subjects and force the genie of revolution back into its bottle.

Goethe was working on theories of optics and color at the time and had gone along for the ride, curious to observe what he called the color of war. "A kind of brown-red tint," he decided while watching French artillery halt the Prussian advance at Valmy on September 20, 1792, "which makes the situation as well as the surrounding objects more impressive." The color of war, as any soldier from any war could have told him, was the color of mud and blood.

Late that evening, in the rainy forest of the Argonne, a hundred twenty miles east of Paris, the author of *Faust* huddled near a campfire with a group of despondent Prussian soldiers. Throughout the campaign Goethe "had been in the habit of enlivening and amusing the troops with short sayings," but when asked for his impressions of the day's events, he stared into the fire and spoke a few words as chilling as the night: "From this place and this time forth commences a new era in world history," Goethe replied, "and you can all say you were present at its birth."[3]

Emboldened by the success of its army, the French National Convention embraced and confirmed Goethe's prophecy. No longer satisfied with defending its borders and its revolution against invasion by coalitions of kings and despots, on November 19, 1792, the convention offered its assistance to "all those wishing to recover their liberty," and embarked on an aggressive policy of foreign liberation. "We cannot rest," Jacques Pierre Brissot de Warville proclaimed to the convention, "until all Europe is ablaze." The dynastic and imperial wars of Europe were "puny projects," Brissot declared, "compared with the worldwide risings, the gigantic revolutions, that we are called upon to achieve." On that same day in November, the convention confirmed the appointment of a new minister to the United States, twenty-nine-year-old Edmond Charles Genet.[4]

Born at Versailles in 1763, Edmond Genet was something of a child prodigy, having learned English, Swedish, Italian, and Latin by the age of twelve and having accepted at fourteen a gold medal from the king of Sweden for his translation of Olof Celsius's *History of Eric XIV of Sweden,* published in 1776. Through his father, a gifted linguist and career civil servant specializing in Franco-American relations, young Genet met Benjamin Franklin, John Adams, John Paul Jones, and other American patriots as they visited his father's office. His father arranged for Genet to experience the capitals of Europe in a series of temporary postings at Frankfort, Berlin, Vienna, and Moscow—a virtual diplomatic grand tour. After his father's death in 1781, Genet was named chief of the Bureau of

Interpretation at nineteen, and then secretary of the French legation in St. Petersburg, and, at twenty-six, chargé d'affaires at the court of Catherine the Great. Polished in manners, witty in conversation, adept at the harpsichord and in song, Genet was attractive and energetic but also, perhaps owing to his youth and his "very ardent mind," prone to superficial and impulsive decisions.[5]

An enthusiastic convert to the revolution, Genet busied himself writing grandiloquent reports about Russian commerce and gossipy letters about the schemes of royalist émigrés at the Romanov court. Catherine the Great was more interested in annexing Poland than in rescuing Louis XVI—but until the moment that she seized Poland, openly denounced the revolution, and sent the French *"demagogue enragé"* packing in July 1792, Genet believed that his own efforts helped dissuade the empress of Russia from intervening in French affairs. Arriving back in Paris in September, just as the French turned back the Austrians and Prussians at Valmy and declared themselves a republic, Genet found himself immediately welcomed by Brissot de Warville and the Girondin leadership. They shared his admiration for America and its republican institutions, and they regarded Genet's ouster as the venom of a Russian tyrant directed against the only person in the entire French diplomatic corps "who had dared act like a free man."[6]

After he completed two brief diplomatic missions to The Hague and to Switzerland, the National Convention appointed Genet minister to the United States on November 19. By mid-December the instructions for his mission were complete. Genet was to propose a pact by which the two republics "would amalgamate their commercial and political interests . . . promote the extension of the Empire of liberty, guarantee the sovereignty of all peoples, and punish the powers still retaining colonial systems"—particularly Spain and Great Britain—"by refusing to admit their ships to the harbors of the two contracting nations." In addition to commercial ties, the proposed alliance was aimed at the "liberation of Spanish America" by "open[ing] the Mississippi to the inhabitants of Kentucky, deliver[ing] our brothers in Louisiana from the tyrannical yoke of Spain, and perhaps add[ing] the glorious star of Canada to the American constellation."[7]

In addition to the republic's grand objectives, Genet had three specific assignments, two of which stemmed from the 1778 Franco-American treaty of alliance during the American Revolution. First, Genet was instructed to negotiate advance payments on America's debt and use the money to purchase grain and supplies for France and its Caribbean possessions. Second, he was to insist upon strict enforcement of Articles

17, 21, and 22 of the treaty, by which France and the United States allowed each other to outfit privateers in one another's ports while excluding the ships of their enemies. Third, Genet was authorized to recruit and commission officers for military expeditions against Louisiana, Florida, and Canada and to commission French privateers based in American ports.[8]

Departing from Paris on January 21, 1793—the very day that Louis XVI's head dropped into the basket below the guillotine—Genet and his entourage (two secretaries of legation, a private secretary, and two personal servants) were delayed at Rochefort by foul weather in the Bay of Biscay. Genet's baggage included his carriage, a bidet, and two hundred fifty blank military commissions—an indication of the magnitude of the expeditions he hoped to send against Louisiana, Florida, and Canada. At last on February 20 the forty-gun warship *Embuscade* cleared the harbor and set sail for Charleston, South Carolina. By then Genet knew that France and Great Britain were formally at war, that within weeks the republic would soon declare war on Spain, and probably that George Rogers Clark had offered to mount an expedition against New Orleans.[9]

After a long and difficult voyage, the *Embuscade* moored in Charleston on April 8, 1793, and Citizen Genet stepped ashore amid the cheers of a large and enthusiastic crowd. Sending the legation secretaries and their baggage by sea to Philadelphia, Genet unloaded his carriage, bought four strong horses from General Thomas Pinckney, and on April 18 commenced a leisurely journey overland to Philadelphia. Buoyed by friendly receptions at towns and cities along the way, the young minister charmed his way north. Genet "appears to be a man possessed of much information, added to the most engaging and agreeable manners that I ever saw," James Monroe's law partner informed James Madison when the minister reached Fredericksburg, Virginia. "He is very easy, communicative and dignified and will precisely suit the taste of our countrymen—all who have seen him are delighted."[10]

In Philadelphia, a somewhat cooler reception was being prepared. Upon learning of the outbreak of war between France and Great Britain, President George Washington had interrupted his vacation at Mount Vernon, summoned his cabinet, and hurried back to Philadelphia. Regardless of personal sympathies, neutrality came easily to Americans so long as the news was only of French, Austrian, and Prussian armies clashing on distant battlefields. A century of experience, however, had taught Americans that when England and France went to war the fighting inevitably went to sea and found its way to American shores and American shipping. Within Washington's cabinet, Treasury Secretary

Alexander Hamilton favored the British and their substantial trade with America, while Secretary of State Thomas Jefferson admired republican France.

The two secretaries had already faced off on domestic issues, especially Hamilton's programs to fund the national debt and encourage manufacturing and trade. Now they clashed on foreign policy as well, and their adherents were beginning to throw partisan epithets at one another. Hamilton and the conservatives (who would eventually organize the Federalist party) regarded the "democratic element" as mobs and Jacobins, while Jefferson's "republican interest" (as they were beginning to identify themselves) saw their rivals as aristocrats, monarchists, Tories, monocrats, and Anglocrats. "Parties seem to have taken a very well defined form in this quarter," Jefferson advised Congressman James Monroe in the spring of 1793. "The old tories, joined by our merchants who trade on British capital . . . and the idle rich of the great commercial towns are with the kings. All other descriptions [are] with the French. The war has kindled and brought forward the two parties with an ardour which our [domestic] interests . . . could never excite."[11]

Despite the growing animosity between his chief lieutenants, Washington and his cabinet were united in their determination to maintain American neutrality and keep the nation out of war. Washington issued a formal proclamation of American neutrality on April 22, and as Citizen Genet rambled toward Philadelphia the president instructed his secretary of state to receive the French minister but "not with too much warmth or cordiality." When at last he met with President Washington on May 18, Genet was "affectionate" and "magnanimous."[12]

On the difficult issue of whether to allow French and British privateers to operate from American ports, however, Jefferson and Hamilton were closer to basic agreement about American neutrality than they were inclined to admit. By Article 22 of the Franco-American treaty of 1778, Jefferson reported to the cabinet, "we cannot permit enemies of France to fit out privateers in our ports." Since the treaty prohibited British privateering from American ports, Jefferson continued, "we ought not therefore to permit France to do it, the treaty leaving us free to refuse, and the refusal being necessary to preserve a fair and secure neutrality." Jefferson feared, however, that by accommodating Great Britain "under pretence of avoiding war on the one side," Hamilton and other Anglophiles in Washington's cabinet had "no great antipathy to run foul of [war] on the other" by offending France and joining "the confederacy of princes against human liberty."[13]

At this delicate juncture, despite Jefferson's initial friendship and best efforts to help the young French minister achieve his goals, the worst effects of Edmond Charles Genet's temperament began to show. "Never in my opinion was so calamitous an appointment made," Jefferson complained privately to Madison in July 1793,

> as that of the present Minister of F[rance] here. Hot headed, all imagination, no judgment, passionate, disrespectful and even indecent toward the P[resident] in his written as well as verbal communications, talking of appeals from him to Congress, from them to the people, urging the most unreasonable and groundless propositions, and in the most dictatorial style etc. etc. etc. . . . He renders my position immensely difficult. He does me justice personally, and, giving him time to vent himself and then cool, I am on a footing to advise him freely . . . but he breaks out again on the very first occasion, so as to shew that he is incapable of correcting himself.

As secretary of state, Jefferson knew that the conflict with the Washington administration over French privateering was likely to bring about Genet's recall, as it eventually did. Privately, Jefferson also knew that France and its minister were engaged in western intrigues, although he withheld much of this information from the cabinet.[14]

Weeks before Genet arrived in Philadelphia, Jefferson (with Washington's tacit concurrence) had advised his protégé William Short, who was then stationed in Madrid, "that France means to send a strong force early this spring to offer independence to the Spanish American colonies, beginning with those of the Mississippi." Hence, in any negotiations with Spain, Short "should keep ourselves free to act in this case according to circumstances, and . . . should not, by any clause of treaty, bind us to guarantee any of the Spanish colonies against their own independence." Jefferson, as Sir Guy Carleton, now Lord Dorchester, observed, "has a degree of finesse about him, which at first is not discernable."[15]

"I am arming the Canadians to throw off the yoke of England," Genet had reported home in June. "I am arming the Kentuckians, and I am preparing an expedition by sea to support their descent on New Orleans." On July 5, Genet had met secretly with Jefferson to inform him, off the record, of these plans. "He communicated these things to me," the Virginian confided to his diary with discernable finesse, "not as Secy. of state, but as Mr. Jeff." Genet had drafted proclamations encouraging insurrection by the French inhabitants of Louisiana and Canada, Jefferson noted, and "he speaks of two generals at Kentucky"— Revolutionary War heroes George Rogers Clark and Benjamin Logan (although Jefferson finessed their names, too)—"who have proposed to . . . take N[ew] Orleans if he will furnish the exp[edition] about £3,000 sterl[ing]."[16]

Their private conversation left no misunderstandings about the nature of Genet's project. "Officers shall be commissioned by [Genet] in Kentuckey and Louisiana, [and] they shall rendezvous *out of the territories of the US*" (Jefferson's emphasis). After gathering "a battalion . . . of inhabitants of Louisiana and Kentuckey and getting what Ind[ia]ns they could," Jefferson wrote, Genet planned "to undertake the expedition against N[ew] Orleans, and then Louisiana [was] to be established into an independent state connected in commerce with France and the US."

Innocent of Lord Dorchester's insight into the character of "Mr. Jeff." and impatient about such technicalities anyway, Citizen Genet was blind to the secretary of state's emphasis on the convenient presumption that Clark would rendezvous his forces outside American territory. Nor did he much care for Jefferson's warning that by "enticing officers and souldiers from Kentuckey to go against Spain, [he] was really putting a halter about their necks, for . . . they would assuredly be hung, if they comm[ence]d hostilities against a nation at peace with the US." More to Genet's liking was Jefferson's remark "that leaving out that article I did not care what insurrections should be excited in Louisiana."[17]

The ostensible purpose of Genet's off-the-record conversation with his friend "Mr. Jeff." was to ask for a slight revision in a letter of introduction that the secretary of state had written to the governor of Kentucky for the French botanist André Michaux. Jefferson agreed to add a seemingly innocuous reference to Genet and his "esteem for" and "good opinion of" Michaux—phrases intended to support Michaux's covert assignment as the agent carrying Genet's commission and instructions to George Rogers Clark.

Formerly employed by Louis XVI to gather botanical specimens for the royal Jardin des Plantes, Michaux had traveled extensively throughout the American west since 1786 and had sent home some sixty thousand trees. Now he was headed west on a scientific mission endorsed by Jefferson and the American Philosophical Society "to explore the interior country of North America from the Mississippi along the Missouri, and Westwardly to the Pacific ocean." Upon his return Michaux was "to communicate to the said society the information he shall have acquired of the geography of the said country, its inhabitants, soil, climate, animals, vegetables, minerals and other circumstances of note." In its combination of overt scientific objectives and covert geopolitical goals, Michaux's mission was a precursor of the Lewis and Clark expedition a decade later. "Mr.

Jeff." was playing with fire, and the secretary of state knew it. Still, the combined lure of western scientific and geographic exploration—coupled with the possibility of an insurrection in Spanish Louisiana and an expedition led by an old boyhood friend from Albemarle County—was tempting.[18]

By reputation, forty-one-year-old George Rogers Clark was the "Conqueror of the West" who had pushed the British out of the Ohio River Valley during the American Revolution. "I don't suppose," he once admitted, "there is a person living that knows the Geography and Natural History of the back Cuntrey better if so well as I do myself. . . . It has been my study for many years." Born in King and Queen County, near the York River in tidewater Virginia, Clark had moved with his family to Albemarle County, about a mile from Jefferson's Monticello, and then to Caroline County before his father settled near Louisville, at the falls of the Ohio, as the American Revolution ended.[19]

The legendary Conqueror of the West with whom Genet was dealing, however, was a profoundly bitter man, unfairly hounded by creditors, prone to drink, and shabbily treated by the governments he had served. For six years during the American Revolution, Clark had signed countless drafts (the eighteenth-century equivalent of checks) for the Commonwealth of Virginia, and he had also extended his personal credit to provide his frontier forces with food, clothing, and other supplies. Clark had never paused to ask for reimbursement (or for his own military pay) until the spring of 1781, when he traveled east to confer with Governor Jefferson about attacking the British at Detroit. Clark's timing was ill-fated. Along with other paperwork then in the hands of the state auditors' office, Clark's expense vouchers were lost on January 5, 1782, when a British fleet dashed up the James River and unleashed the turncoat Brigadier General Benedict Arnold and eight hundred troops in a surprise raid on Richmond.[20]

Soon thereafter, when George Rogers Clark presented the auditors with expenses totaling $20,500—for which they now had no original documentation—the bean counters in Richmond began dragging their feet. Virginia owed Clark about $3,500 a year for capturing and defending the Ohio River Valley—about a penny per square mile—but Arnold's raid had destroyed the paperwork. The auditors quibbled for a few years about the prices Clark had paid in wartime on the frontier for goods that were now several times cheaper in peacetime on the East Coast. Then they ducked responsibility altogether on the grounds that when Virginia ceded its western lands to Congress in 1784, Clark's reimbursement became a national matter, too.

At the end of the Revolution, Congress had greeted Clark with a standing ovation. "Young man," Benjamin Franklin declared, "you have given an empire to the Republic." Yet governments and institutions often turn stingy and forgetful when proper gratitude demands more than rhetoric. In 1792 the Commonwealth of Virginia rejected Clark's accounts. In lieu of his reimbursement and back pay, Jefferson did help secure Clark a tract of Indiana land, but by then, fearful that assets held in his own name would only be seized by creditors, the Conqueror of the West was signing property over to his younger brothers. "I have rode for Bro. Geo in the course of this past year upwards of 3000 miles," William Clark (who would later explore the continent with Meriwether Lewis) wrote his brother Edmund, "attempting to save him" from his "disagreeable situation [and] three or four heavy suits pending."[21]

Surrounded by Kentuckians talking of separation and clamoring for decisive action to open the Mississippi River for the export of their produce, George Rogers Clark was desperate and disgusted when he learned in November 1792 of Virginia's refusal to reimburse his expenses for supplies purchased during the Revolutionary War. While French authorities were preparing to send Citizen Genet as minister to the United States with instructions to move against Louisiana, Clark and his feisty Irish-born brother-in-law, Dr. James O'Fallon, were developing a parallel plan in Kentucky. Shortly before Christmas, Clark wrote to the French consul at Philadelphia offering to mount an expedition of fifteen hundred men to attack New Orleans and capture Spanish Louisiana. O'Fallon, a former associate of James Wilkinson, friend of Thomas Paine, and agent for one of the Yazoo land companies seeking title to thousands of acres on the Georgia frontier, wrote a similar letter to Paine, then in Paris as a member of the National Convention. Between November 1792 and February 1793 these two plans—concocted independently on either side of the Atlantic—came together.[22]

Early in the new year, an executive council of the French republic had "the General's offers and propositions" under consideration. Paine was confident that "every, or the greater part of [Clark's] terms will be complied with" as soon as France declared war on Spain. "You may, therefore," he told O'Fallon, "expect very soon to hear of the General's nomination to the post and command solicited by him." Clark's military prowess had been confirmed by "Mr. Jefferson's private sentiments respecting him" (an off-the-record recommendation that Jefferson apparently whispered to the French consul in Philadelphia). Paine also informed O'Fallon that "the principal characters among the French inhabitants of Louisiana, have already petitioned this convention, for the reduction of that country from the vile servitude under which it actually groans." Prospects for the invasion were bright. "All we fear," Paine wrote, was "that the intrigues of certain personages in the American cabinet, who are the friends of Britain and votaries of Kings, may obstruct the General, in his plans of raising men, and procuring officers."[23]

Because the letters written by Clark and O'Fallon late in 1792 have been lost, we cannot be certain that they reached Paris in time for Citizen Genet to see them. Three bits of evidence strongly suggest, however, that Genet knew about General Clark's proposal before he sailed for America on February 20, 1793. First, in his reply to O'Fallon, Paine described Genet as "my sincere friend" and assured O'Fallon that "your name is already made known to him by me." Second, Paine and Genet clearly were in close contact in the months between Genet's appointment and his departure, for in December Paine had introduced Genet to the American minister to France, the patrician Gouverneur Morris of Pennsylvania, who despised them both. Finally, there is a curious ambiguity in the wording of Paine's comment that Genet "is to set out for America speedily."

Genet had left Paris on January 21, but Paine's reply to O'Fallon was dated February 13, seven days before Genet's ship sailed from Rochefort, two hundred fifty miles southwest of Paris. Either Paine wrote his letter earlier than he dated and sealed it, or he knew that Genet had been delayed in the harbor. Either way, it seems likely that Clark's and O'Fallon's proposals reached the French minister before his ship left port.

Talk of attacking Louisiana was an open secret on both sides of the Atlantic. Details of the French plan to attack Louisiana reached Jefferson in February 1793, and Paine's letter suggests that Jefferson had prior knowledge of Clark's intentions as well. In light of these circumstances, Genet's apparent failure to contact Clark immediately upon his arrival in America remains puzzling.[24]

Regardless of what the new minister may have known when he left France, however, Paine's letter to O'Fallon prompted Clark to begin planning his expedition while Genet made his way across the ocean to Philadelphia. First he would overrun the forty-man Spanish garrison at New Madrid with a swarm of Kentucky frontiersmen and a few brass cannon. Then he would carry its cannon downriver and capture Nogales, near modern Vicksburg. From there Clark could move against Natchez, where the garrison of fifty Spanish soldiers was completely surrounded by American settlers. Finally, with a French fleet blockading the Mississippi to prevent reinforcement by sea, he would capture New Orleans.[25]

In the spring of 1793, all George Rogers Clark really needed was a green light and about £3,000. "The possession of New Orleans will secure to France the whole Fur, Tobacco and Flour trade of this western world," Clark assured Genet in February, "and a great consumption of her manufactures. . . . All we immediately want is money to procure provisions and ammunition for the conquest."[26]

To avoid entangling the United States in a war with Spain, Clark wrote, "we must first expatriate our selves, and become French citizens. This is our intention. My country has proved notoriously ungrateful, for my Services." Had Citizen Genet sent immediate encouragement to Clark when he arrived in Charleston on April 8, 1793, or even when he reached Philadelphia on May 16, Spain might well have lost Louisiana ten years earlier, by conquest.[27]

On July 15, three full months after Citizen Genet arrived in Philadelphia, André Michaux and two companions left Philadelphia bearing Genet's commission to George Rogers Clark as major general of the "Independent and Revolutionary Legion of the Mississippi" and about $750 toward his expenses. Ever the scientist, Michaux moved slowly, even by eighteenth-century standards.[28] Traveling at first "by moonlight" to avoid the summer heat, he took notes and collected botanical specimens as he wandered through the Appalachians and into Kentucky. On August 29, instead of hurrying to Louisville by river with his companions, Michaux rambled overland into the lush rolling countryside of the bluegrass district.[29]

On September 11 Michaux visited General Benjamin Logan near Harrodsburg, site of the 1774 settlement thirty miles south of Frankfort and Lexington near the Kentucky River. "A large, raw-boned man," six feet tall and two hundred pounds, Logan was one of Kentucky's earliest settlers, and his son William the first white male born there. Although he would have been "delighted to take part in the enterprise," General Logan informed Michaux, his situation had changed. A recent letter from Kentucky senator John Brown affirmed that the United States was opening negotiations with Spain about the Mississippi. An invasion, General Logan calculated, might now spoil the chance of diplomatic success, so he was no longer inclined to join Genet's expedition.[30]

Michaux rambled on toward the falls of the Ohio. Overland travel was slow in the eighteenth century, but his final seventy-mile jaunt through the bluegrass district took Michaux six days. When Genet's emissary finally reached George Rogers Clark on September 17, 1793, he found that Clark, having heard nothing from Genet during the long months of summer, had also given up on the expedition, at least temporarily. More desperate than General Logan and far more disenchanted with East Coast politicians and international diplomacy, Clark had also come to blows with his brother-in-law, James O'Fallon. Nevertheless, with a major general's commission from Genet in hand and the prospect of financial support, Clark was ready to resume planning the expedition by himself. Accordingly, André Michaux abandoned his trek toward the Pacific for the American Philosophical Society and headed east to bring Genet details of Clark's plans and his request for money.

During the summer, O'Fallon's abusive treatment of his wife, Clark's sister Fanny, drove an angry wedge between the doctor and his in-laws. While O'Fallon was in Lexington tending to his medical practice and political career, Fanny had stayed with her parents, John and Ann Rogers Clark, at Mulberry Hill, just south of Louisville. There she began seeing apparitions, pacing the floor at night, and suffering violent fits. She was "so fearfull that she will not be by hir self," her father wrote. "Hir mother [is] obliged to lay with hir every night." At first the Clarks attributed Fanny's depression or nervous breakdown to the prospect of moving to Lexington, where O'Fallon anticipated a more profitable medical practice. "Hearing you ware to settle in Lexington—I expe[c]t it sunk hir sperets," her father explained. "She agread you might get more money in Lexington then hear but not Live so happy," and she said "She had a grate deal Ruther go to hir Grave then to Lexington . . . [and] much Rither die near hir frends then far off." As many battered spouses do, Fanny Clark O'Fallon hid the fact of her husband's abuse from her family and friends, worrying that "she would be Blam[e]d" if she failed to accompany him to Lexington, and saying only that "no one knew what she suf[fere]d." Fanny had "kept hir Complant in hir own Breast," her father wrote, but "hir Heart was Brock . . . [and] it was not in our powr to Releave her."[31]

Fanny's parents discovered the real nature of their daughter's plight late one night when Fanny was pacing the floor while O'Fallon slept. "Your father coming up stairs, into our room," O'Fallon recalled in a peculiarly self-serving attempt to coax his wife back, "said, Fanny come away, you shall never sleep with the Rascal again, and so, instantly, turned me out of doors." O'Fallon denied that he "frequently bit her with his teeth," or "so pinched you at times, as to compell you to leave my bed, into which I refused to suffer your return"—but the rumors circulating in the neighborhood could well have originated with family members who saw bruises.[32]

"Your Brother George," O'Fallon complained in his peculiar letter to Fanny, "is said by 20 witnesses to have asserted in various places . . . that I was a Rogue, Rascal and Villain; . . . that I attempted to poison my son, Johnny; that I would poison . . . any family if they took my medicines . . . that the house and bed stunck where I lived or slept . . . and that I had murdered my former wife."[33]

O'Fallon's list of Clark's accusations also reflects the rivalries of frontier leaders in the young republic. Clark, O'Fallon believed, was telling people that the doctor had "forged Gen[eral Anthony] Wayne's letters" inviting him to serve as physician on an Indian campaign north of the Ohio River. Wayne's 1794 defeat of a confederation of Delaware, Miami, Shawnee, and Wyandotte tribes at the Battle of Fallen Timbers (near present-day Toledo) led to the Treaty of Fort Greenville (northwest of modern Dayton) in 1795, which opened the present state of Ohio to American settlement.[34]

The final episode in this domestic drama, an angry brawl between George Rogers Clark and James O'Fallon, had an international audience. General Clark "provoked me without cause," O'Fallon complained to his estranged wife, "and he suffered for it." "He attempted to strike me," the defiant Irishman bragged, "but before his blow could reach, he lay sprawling on the floor, from blows which heavily reached him." From Natchez, where he was monitoring developments in Kentucky as best he could, Governor Manuel Gayoso passed along a different version of the fight in a letter to Governor Carondelet in New Orleans. "O'Fallon has parted from his wife," Gayoso reported, "who has withdrawn to the house of Clark, her brother, and he, in resentment of this offense has maltreated O'Fallon, even going so far as to break his stick over his head, inflicting injuries from which he had not yet recovered."[35]

Hard times may have been forced upon George Rogers Clark, but he was a Virginian, an officer, and a gentleman—and O'Fallon was "a Rogue, Rascal and Villain," and an Irishman to boot. Gentlemen settled their differences on the field of honor, but a caning—a thorough beating about the head and shoulders with a stout hickory stick often resulting in serious injury and utter humiliation—was the way gentlemen chastised men of inferior status. James O'Fallon was dead at forty-five within months of his encounter with the cane of George Rogers Clark.[36] What damage, Gayoso and Carondelet must have wondered, might Clark be capable of inflicting if he donned a tricolor cockade and marched thousands of men against Louisiana?

Throughout the United States, forty Democratic-Republican societies loosely modeled on the Jacobin clubs of France were clamoring for "the free and undisturbed use and navigation of the Mississippi River [a]s the natural right of the inhabitants of the countries bordering on the waters communicating with the river." Such was the language of an October 1793 resolution written in Lexington, Kentucky, and endorsed by Democratic-Republican clubs from Vermont to South Carolina.[37] The moment was ripe for George Rogers Clark to mount a successful expedition against New Orleans in the autumn of 1793, and his military preparations put real teeth behind the Democratic-Republican societies' angry rhetoric.

"The feeble attempts which have been made by the executive under the present government, and the total silence of Congress on this important subject" infuriated the influential Democratic-Republican Society of Lexington. Presidential inaction and congressional silence were "strong proofs that most of our brethren in the eastern part of America, are totally regardless whether this our just right is kept from us or not." Near Pittsburgh, the Democratic-Republican club of Washington County, Pennsylvania, warned that "patriotism, like every other thing, has its bounds," and that "attachment[s] to governments cease to be natural, when they cease to be mutual." Free navigation of the Mississippi was "a right which must be obtained," the Washington County society declared. "If the general government will not procure it for us, we shall hold ourselves not answerable for any consequences that may result from our own procurement of it." Frontier Americans "are strong enough to obtain that right by force," the Lexington club warned, although "we hope . . . we shall not be driven to use those means to effect it with which we have been furnished by the God of nature."[38]

Clark's main obstacle was money. Genet had sent him only $750, and his personal finances were a mess. But with Michaux en route to Philadelphia with Clark's request for funds, neighbors and supporters of the Conqueror of the West could make a few things happen. "This kind of Warefare is my Ellement," Clark assured Genet in October, and "had you fortunately have got my Letter in time . . . I could have before this time in all probability Executed my first Project that of getting compleat Possession of the Mississippi . . . but at present the season being far advanced and I find an impossibility of keeping it a secret I of course shall in some Instance deviate from my first plan and act agreeable to Circumstance." Preparing for an attack in the spring of 1794, Clark's associates at Louisville assembled two boats, five hundred pounds of powder, and a ton of cannonballs. More boats were being built at Cincinnati, and Kentucky's Democratic-Republican clubs at Georgetown, Lexington, and Paris were gathering food, military equipment, boats, ammunition, and "all the encouragement in their power."[39]

In the middle of all this activity, with Clark's urgent pleas for money tucked into his baggage along with seeds and bark samples, André Michaux spent the last week of September and the entire month of October visiting prominent Kentuckians and collecting botanical notes and specimens. By November 10 Michaux had only reached Danville, eighty miles east of Clark's home, were he began in earnest the seven-hundred-fifty-mile trek toward Philadelphia by way of the Cumberland Gap and Wilderness Road. This southern route through Tennessee and Virginia was only forty miles longer than Michaux's alternative through Pittsburgh and western Pennsylvania. With winter approaching it was the wiser choice, and for once Michaux traveled at the pace of a courier rather than botanist. Averaging nearly twenty-five miles a day, he reached Philadelphia on December 12, reported to Genet on the 13th, and met with Jefferson and David Rittenhouse, president of the American Philosophical Society, on the 14th.[40]

George Rogers Clark's best opportunity to attack Louisiana had already slipped away in the accumulated delays on the part of Genet and Michaux, and the failures were political, not military. The French minister not only lacked money for Clark, but on December 5 President Washington had informed Congress that he had asked France to recall Citizen Genet. Washington and his cabinet had made the decision in August, and Secretary of State Jefferson had scarcely finished his lengthy letter to the American minister in Paris chronicling Genet's "gross usurpations and outrages of the laws and authority of our country," when he had opened an urgent message from the Spanish commissioners in Philadelphia.[41]

In their letter, Josef Ignacio de Viar and Josef de Jaudenes, Diego de Gardoqui's successors, informed Jefferson that since mid-July they had been investigating rumors of an expedition against Louisiana and had "managed to get our hands on one of the printed circulars," which they enclosed. Not surprisingly, since there are three additional copies in his papers, Jefferson recognized the pamphlet as Genet's address to the citizens of Louisiana, printed in Philadelphia as *Les Français Libres à leurs frères de la LOUISIANE.* The Spanish consuls were especially troubled by the passage "in which the author promises that the inhabitants of the western part of these States will assist and protect the people of Louisiana whenever they start the revolution." The author, they felt, was guilty "of plotting, fomenting, and printing in a country that is both neutral and a friend of Spain, projects that quite openly have as their object the stirring up of one of her possessions and separating it from the [Spanish] government." They asked Jefferson "to tell us whether such an offer has been made with the knowledge of your government." If not, they hoped the American "government will properly take measures to punish the daring of the man who has proposed, without any authority, to involve the United States" in events that could lead to war. That autumn, Governor Carondelet sent a translation of the printed circular back to Spain, vowing to prevent its dissemination in Louisiana, "since its diffusion in this province, inhabited in great part by French settlers, might have the most fatal consequences not only here but also in the old, inland provinces of the kingdom of New Spain."[42]

Viar and Jaudenes also warned Governor Carondelet, in New Orleans, that Genet was "engaged in secretly seducing and recruiting . . . to form an expedition against Louisiana," supported by "two ships of seventy-four [guns], and six or eight frigates" from a French fleet that had carried refugees from St. Domingue to the United States. The fleet, they thought, correctly, "will meet with endless obstacles." Its sailors were on the verge of mutiny and insisted on returning to France, as they eventually did. The danger, Viar and Jaudenes warned Carondelet, was attack by land, "since the perversity of the French, scattered through the whole continent, gives much ground for apprehension."[43]

Jefferson's immediate response, on August 29, signaled a change in attitude toward Genet and Clark that would eclipse the military expedition and open the way for a diplomatic resolution in Pinckney's Treaty. Jefferson, of course, knew much more than he let on when he promised the Spanish consuls that "the President will use all the powers with which he is invested to prevent any enterprize of the kind proposed." He also informed them that he was forwarding the printed circular to the governor of Kentucky—the same Isaac Shelby to whom "Mr. Jeff." had recommended Genet's emissary, André Michaux, only two months earlier—"with instructions to pay strict attention to any endeavors . . . among the citizens of that state to excite them to join in the enterprize therein proposed or any other, and to use all the means in his power to prevent it." Just how much authority the president or the governor actually had, remained an open question, and surely "Mr. Jeff." knew that.[44]

Written the same day as his letter to the Spanish consuls in Philadelphia, Jefferson's letter to Isaac Shelby described the Spanish consul's complaint and enclosed Genet's printed address. On behalf of President Washington, who reviewed and approved the letter, Jefferson asked Shelby "to be particularly attentive to any attempts of this kind among the citizens of Kentucky." Jefferson urged Shelby to "take those legal measures which shall be necessary to prevent any such enterprize." As if to explain his own change of heart, Jefferson pointed out that both "the peace of the general Union" and "the special interest of the State of Kentucky" would now suffer if Clark marched against Louisiana. "Nothing could be more inauspicious," he wrote, "than such a movement at the very moment when those interests"—the navigation of the Mississippi—"are under negotiation between Spain and the United States."[45]

An early immigrant from the mountains of Virginia, forty-five-year-old Isaac Shelby was nobody's fool and nobody's tool. Deliberate and clear in his thinking, slow to anger, Shelby was the first elected governor of Kentucky. Upon learning of his nearly unanimous election in 1792, however, Shelby kept everyone waiting for several days as he pondered whether "his walk through life . . . quallified him to fill [the office] with real advantage to his country or honour to himself."[46]

The rivers of Lincoln County, where Shelby lived about fifty miles south of Lexington, flow into the Kentucky and the Cumberland Rivers, and the governor was as resolute as any Kentuckian about opening the Mississippi. A few years earlier, his friend John Brown, now one of Kentucky's first United States senators at the age of thirty-six, had worked closely with Gardoqui and Wilkinson in the so-called Spanish Conspiracy. Born in Staunton and educated at Washington College, the College of New Jersey, and William and Mary, Senator Brown had read law with Jefferson and opened his law office in Frankfort, Kentucky, in 1782. "Competent people," a foreign visitor wrote, "tell me that in Virginia he is inferior only to Mr. Madison," who shared the same congressional boardinghouse in Philadelphia. The senator's brother, James Brown, was Governor Shelby's attorney general and a founder and officer in Lexington's Democratic-Republican Society.[47] No one knows how far Shelby's personal sympathies extended toward Wilkinson's separatism or Clark's expedition, but the Browns helped Governor Shelby make the most of that uncertainty.

Nothing in Jefferson's letter escaped Shelby's notice, and on October 5, only weeks after he had met with André Michaux while Genet's emissary was in Kentucky, Shelby wrote Jefferson a short note of reassurance saying exactly what the Spanish wanted to hear. Thanking Jefferson for his warning about "an interprize against the Spanish Dominions on the Mississippi," Governor Shelby pretended to be "well perswaded at present none such is in Contemplation in this State. The Citizens of Kentucky possess too just a Sence of the Obligations they owe the General Government, to embark in any interprize that would be so injurious to the United States." As expected, Jefferson sent a copy of the note to the Spanish commissioners Viar and Jaudenes. Shelby, meanwhile, passed along Jefferson's warning to the French agent Charles Depauw with a diffident comment that "to this charge I must pay that attention which my present situation oblidges me."[48]

*"Tempora mutantur et nos mutamur in illis,"* Gouverneur Morris commented in a letter briefing Jefferson about the situation in Europe— "The times change and we change with them"—and the adage was no less true along the Mississippi. "I find that we can get as many men as we pleace," Clark wrote, "but it will be out of our power to keep our design a secret. It is gen[eral]ly known already."[49]

Two men who were very attentive to news of Clark's plans were François-Louis Hector, baron de Carondelet et Noyelles, in New Orleans and Manuel Gayoso de Lemos in Natchez. Their military situation was desperate. "If the project planned by the enemies is carried into effect," Governor Carondelet advised the Spanish minister Manuel Godoy in a top-secret letter, "the whole of upper Louisiana" from St. Louis to the Walnut Hills (now Vicksburg) "will fall into the hands of the enemy in Spring, since the forces that can be collected for the defense of the[se] forts . . . do not amount to 90 men of regular troops and 200 militia; and even these can be but little trusted." Once those forts were taken, Carondelet believed, "it is evident that all Louisiana will fall into their hands with the greatest rapidity and facility, since . . . few of the American inhabitants will side against an army composed of their countrymen, and as the French inhabitants will still less offer to take arms in our favor." Once Clark took Natchez and moved south against New Orleans, Carondelet lamented, "I shall have no other resource than an honorable surrender, or to perish."[50]

Gayoso drew darker but more accurately nuanced conclusions in a report that Carondelet forwarded to Godoy on January 1, 1794: "The capital destined for this expedition is a million dollars," Gayoso wrote, and Clark's army was "composed of 5,000 men." The attack would "start next spring," and Clark's aim was "to invade Louisiana and Mexico." Grasping at straws, Gayoso could only hope that "the transportation of artillery" might not work, or the money not "be realized," or the differences between Clark and O'Fallon might be disruptive, or, finally, "that the measures of the American Government" might prove "sufficient to obstruct this enterprise."[51]

With no prospect of timely reinforcements from Cuba, Carondelet offered "no further hope than in the [errors] the enemy may commit and in accidents which may perhaps favor us." Clark committed no errors, and even the "impossibility of keeping it a secret" from the Spanish was not fatal. If anything, the intelligence from Kentucky that reached Carondelet, Gayoso, and their garrisons was demoralizing. Clark's expedition was poised to move "on or before the 20th of February,"[52] and Carondelet and Gayoso knew that St. Louis, New Madrid, and Natchez would fall in succession. Unless some "accident" or "measure" intervened, they expected to surrender Louisiana in the spring of 1794.

By January 1, 1794, the high visibility of George Rogers Clark's impending military expedition, regardless of its ultimate fate, had created a diplomatic opportunity that Kentucky governor Isaac Shelby was quick to exploit. Early in November Secretary of State Jefferson and Secretary of War Henry Knox had warned Shelby that Genet had dispatched four French agents—Citizens August Lachaise, Charles Depauw, Pis Gignoux, and a carpenter named Mathurin—"with money . . . and with blank commissions" for an expedition "to descend the Ohio and Mississippi and attack New Orleans." The next day General Arthur St. Clair dispatched a letter from Marietta, Ohio, on the Ohio River a hundred and forty miles below Pittsburgh, warning Shelby "that General Clark has received a commission from the government of France, and is about to raise a body of men in Kentucky to attack the Spanish settlements upon the Mississippi"—and that "a large sum of money, a paymaster, and a number of French officers, are arrived at the Falls of Ohio; and a number of boats for the expedition laid down." To round things out, on November 25, the French agents August Lachaise and Charles Depauw wrote Shelby directly. They were puzzled about "strange reports . . . that your excellence has positive orders to arrest all citizens inclining to our assistance." They also asked Shelby to distribute "some of these handbills"— probably Genet's printed address to the people of Louisiana—"to that noble society of democrats," presumably the Democratic-Republican Society of Lexington.[53]

Although the letter from Jefferson and Knox advocated "suppression by the militia" to stop Clark's expedition, the cabinet officers knew they were on shaky legal ground when they urged Shelby to employ "peaceable means of coercion" (indictments, bonds for good behavior, and "such other legal process as those learned in the laws of your state may advise"). President Washington had issued a proclamation of neutrality, but in point of law it was merely advisory and not enforceable. Similarly, General St. Clair's proclamation of December 7, 1793, exhorting "inhabitants of the territory of the United States North West of the Ohio . . . to observe a strict neutrality towards Spain [and] to abstain from every hostility against the subjects or settlements of that Crown," had no legal force in Kentucky.[54]

Jefferson and Knox wanted Shelby to act on his authority as governor of Kentucky. Beyond that all Jefferson could offer was his "hope that the citizens of Kentuckey will not be decoyed into any participation in these illegal enterprizes . . . by any effect they may expect from them on the navigation of the Mississippi." Whistling in the dark, Jefferson expressed his confidence that "their good sense will tell them . . . that their surest dependance is on those regular measures which are pursuing and will be pursued by the general government, and which flow from the United authority of all the states."

Time and again, Kentuckians had complained of "the feeble attempts which have been made by the executive under the present government, and the total silence of Congress on this important subject." Now, with Clark's sabers rattling in the background, Governor Isaac Shelby applied exquisite pressure on the Washington administration.

After conferring with his like-minded attorney general, James Brown, on January 13, 1794, Governor Shelby dispatched a forceful letter to the secretary of state. "I have great doubts," he wrote, "whether there is any legal authority to restrain or punish" Clark and his expedition,

> for if it is lawful for any one citizen of this State to leave it, it is equally lawful for any number of them to do it. It is also lawful for them to carry with them any quantity of provisions, arms and ammunition; and if the act is lawful in itself, there is nothing but the particular intention with which it is done that can possibly make it unlawful, but I know of no law which inflicts a punishment on intent only.

Shelby also felt "little inclination to take an active part in punishing or restraining any of my fellow citizens for a supposed intention, only to gratify or remove the fears of the ministers of a foreign prince who openly withholds from us an invaluable right." Nevertheless, "whatever may be my private opinion, as a man, as a friend to liberty, an American citizen, and an inhabitant of the Western Waters," he concluded, "I shall at all times hold it as my duty to perform whatever may be constitutionally required of me as Governor of Kentucky, by the President of the United States."

While Governor Shelby's ultimatum made its way east, Clark's call for volunteers appeared in the January 25 issue of Cincinnati's weekly *Centinel of the North-Western Territory* and the February 4 issue of John Bradford's *Kentucky Gazette* in Lexington:

> George R. Clark, Esq.
> Major General in the armies of France, and Commander in Chief of the French Revolutionary Legions on the Mississippi River.
>
> PROPOSALS
>
> For raising the volunteers for the reduction of the Spanish posts on the Mississippi, for opening the trade of the said river, and giving freedom to its inhabitants, etc. All persons serving the expedition to be entitled to one thousand acres of Land—those that engage for one year, will be entitled to two thousand acres—if they serve two years or during the present war with France, they will have three thousand acres of any unappropriated Land that may be conquered. . . . All lawful Plunder to be equally divided agreeable to the custom of War. . . . Those that serve the expedition will have their choice of receiving their land or one dollar a day.
>
> G. R. CLARK

In the east, the first published report of Clark's plans, a mid-November letter from Fort Washington, appeared in Philadelphia newspapers on January 4 and reached the *Connecticut Courant* by January 13. "A revolution is on foot in Louisiana," exclaimed another letter from Cincinnati that was published in the *Maryland Journal,* the *Virginia Centinel,* and the Haverhill, Massachusetts, *Guardian of Freedom:*

> The French inhabitants on the west side of the river Mississippi inspired by the glorious cause of their brethren in Europe, are determined to shake off the despotic yoke of Spain. . . . By the best accounts, the French and American settlements on the Mississippi, can bring into the field an army of 6,000 men, all excellent marksmen. . . . A contemplative mind will easily conceive the great advantages that would accrue to the world in general, and the United States in particular, should such an event actually take place—it would open the road for millions of the human race to emigrate to this favor'd

spot, on which nature has lavished its gifts. . . . The road once opened, would be the means of civilizing not only the natives of the soil, but . . . the Spaniards themselves over the Gulf of Mexico, whom priest-craft and ignorance has made useless to society. Such a revolution would produce more: it would put Americans in the full possession of the navigation of the most noble river within their territory, the right of which (contrary to nature's law) has been arbitrar[il]y withheld, and by them shamefully given up to a people whom we neither ought to love or fear.[55]

The tricolor of France was a flag of convenience for George Rogers Clark and his Kentucky neighbors. In his hands, Citizen Genet's grand expedition against Louisiana had always been an American enterprise— designed to put "Americans in the full possession of the navigation of the most noble river within their territory." Clark's moment for military glory may have escaped, but his demonstration of Louisiana's vulnerability forced Spain and America back to the bargaining table in earnest.

When Governor Shelby's ultimatum reached the secretary of state's office in Philadelphia, Edmund Randolph, former governor of Virginia and formerly Washington's attorney general, was behind the desk. Jefferson had retired to Monticello on December 31, but the impending change of personnel at the French embassy was more immediately important. On March 6, 1794, promptly upon his arrival in Philadelphia, Genet's replacement, Jean Antoine Joseph Fauchet, issued a proclamation canceling all French support for Clark's expedition. Two weeks later, President Washington issued his own proclamation against enlisting citizens of the United States "for the purpose of invading and plundering the territory of a nation at peace with the United States." For good measure the commander in chief also dispatched General Anthony Wayne to "establish a strong military post at Fort Massac on the Ohio, and prevent by force, if necessary, the descent of any hostile party down the river." George Rogers Clark's boats, guns, ammunition, provisions, and men never got farther than "a Small Camp" on the Mississippi four hundred miles south of Louisville "Fortifyd within fifty Miles of the Enemys lines."[56]

The ultimate failure of George Rogers Clark's expedition was not the work of his adversaries but of his patron. Citizen Genet's deteriorating relationship with Washington's administration, exacerbated by the months of dawdling for which Genet and Michaux were solely responsible, gave Spanish Louisiana the "accidents" and "measures" for which Carondelet and Gayoso had desperately hoped.[57] In the decade ahead, the fate of Louisiana would not be decided by George Rogers Clark and an army of Kentucky frontiersmen. After 1794 the destiny of the Mississippi River and its watershed would be determined by American statesmen, by European armies and diplomats, by rebellious Caribbean slaves, and by ordinary American farmers and merchants.

"Causes unforeseen had put a stop to the march of two thousand brave Kentuckians, who were about to go and put an end to the Spanish despotism on the Mississippi," the French agent August Lachaise lamented to the Democratic-Republican Society of Lexington in May 1794, "where Frenchmen and Kentuckians, united under the banners of France, might have made one nation, the happiest in the world—so perfect was their sympathy." Perhaps. But the perspective of Governor Isaac Shelby was closer to the mark: "My letter of the 13th January, 1794," Shelby recalled,

> was calculated rather to increase than to diminish the apprehensions of the General Government as to the Western country. This letter had the effect desired, it drew from the Secretary of State information in relation to the navigation of the Mississippi, and satisfied us that the General Government was, in good faith, pursuing the object of first importance to the people of Kentucky.[58]

Responding to the pressure created by George Rogers Clark's expedition and Governor Isaac Shelby's ultimatum, on November 24, 1794, the Senate of the United States confirmed Thomas Pinckney, of South Carolina, as President Washington's envoy to Madrid, where he was charged to negotiate a commercial treaty in which "our right to the free use of the Mississippi River shall be most unequivocally acknowledged and established, on principles never hereafter to be drawn into contestation."[59] Goethe's new era of world history was dawning over the American frontier.

## CHAPTER TEN

# Mr. Pinckney's Mission

*The success of Mr. Pinckney's Mission . . . you will see from my late letters is already insured.*

—William Short to the Secretary of State, January 16, 1795[1]

*The Southern boundary of the United States which divides their territory from the Spanish Colonies of East and West Florida, shall be designated by a line beginning on the River Mississippi at the Northernmost part of the thirty first degree of latitude North of the Equator, which from thence shall be drawn due East to the middle of the River Apalachicola or Catahouche, thence along the middle thereof to its junction with the Flint, thence straight to the head of St. Mary's River, and thence down the middle there of to the Atlantic Ocean.*

—Article II, Pinckney's Treaty, October 27, 1795

*It is likewise agreed that the Western boundary of the United States which separates them from the Spanish Colony of Louisiana, is in the middle of the channel or bed of the River Mississippi . . . and his Catholic Majesty has likewise agreed that the navigation of the said River in its whole breadth from its source to the Occean shall be free only to his Subjects, and the Citizens of the United States, unless he should extend this privilege to the Subjects of other Powers by special convention.*

—Article IV, Pinckney's Treaty, October 27, 1795

*His Catholic Majesty will permit the Citizens of the United States for the space of three years from this time to deposit their merchandize and effects in the Port of New Orleans and to export*

*them from thence without paying any other duty than a fair price
for the hire of the stores, and his Majesty promises either to continue this permission if he finds during that time that it is not
prejudicial to the interests of Spain, or if he should not agree to
continue it there, he will assign to them on another part of the
banks of the Mississippi an equivalent establishment.*

—Article XXII, Pinckney's Treaty, October 27, 1795

O N MONDAY, July 7, 1794, Carlos IV and his court were in Madrid,
moving from the spring gardens of Aranjuez to La Granja de San
Ildefonso, the summer palace in the mountains near Segovia, about forty
miles northwest of the capital. The king and his chief minister, Manuel
Godoy, now duke of Alcudia, had convened a meeting of their Council of
State for a sweeping reconsideration of Spain's diplomatic situation in
Europe and the Americas. The war against France was not going well. In
fact, at that moment a French army was advancing across the Pyrenees,
despite reports of turmoil in Paris where *sans culottes* were rioting in the
streets again over food shortages and the rising price of bread. In three
weeks, more drastic news would arrive from Paris when the sinister
Joseph Fouché, Napoleon's future head of secret police, and a coalition
of Maximilien Robespierre's political enemies brought the arch-Jacobin
and the radical party's leaders to the guillotine at the Place de la Révolu-
tion on the evening of July 28—the eleventh day of Thermidor by the
revolutionary calendar.

Across the Atlantic, the deposed French minister to the United
States, Edmond Charles Genet, having declined a return trip to Paris and
a probable date with the guillotine, was heading for the Arcadian bliss of
a three-hundred-twenty-five-acre farm near Jamaica, Long Island, and
the loving arms of the New York belle Cornelia Tappan Clinton, daughter
of the state's ardently republican governor. In the Mississippi Valley,
George Rogers Clark was establishing himself in St. Louis, on the Spanish side of the Mississippi, to escape creditors hounding him with bills for
provisions, boats, and arms assembled for the aborted expedition against
Louisiana.

In New Orleans, Governor François-Louis Hector, baron de Carondelet et Noyelles, was tallying up the cost of his defenses against Clark—
about $294,562, including $12,000 in bribes to General James Wilkinson
and $8,640 in reimbursements for Wilkinson's expenses "to retard, dis-
joint and defeat the mediated irruption of General Clark in L[ouisian]a."

The governor was also writing to Colonel John Graves Simcoe, the British lieutenant governor for Upper Canada, to suggest a joint campaign of Canadian troops and "warlike Indian tribes" against the American frontier settlements.

While Governor Carondelet dreamt of employing Spain's current alliance with Britain in the defense of Louisiana against the Americans, Godoy, however, was preparing to abandon that alliance in order to end Spain's disastrous war with France. With this impending turnabout in mind, Godoy was troubled by the news from London of the arrival on June 8, 1794, of United States chief justice John Jay, dispatched as a special envoy by President Washington to negotiate a treaty that maintained American neutrality and averted a war over British affronts on the high seas and in the vicinity of the Great Lakes. Caught once again in a monumental clash between Britain and France, both the Americans and the Spanish were negotiating from weakness.[2]

Godoy advised the Council of State that "if the United States should succeed in reaching a reconciliation with England," Spain's "situation in respect to the States [would become] even more critical." Great Britain, he feared, "was already acting as if she intended to declare war on [Spain] on some pretext or another . . . [and] establish her sovereignty over all the seas."

For the past five years, since Diego de Gardoqui's departure from New York in October 1789, Spain and the United States had made scant progress in the negotiations begun by John Jay and Gardoqui in 1785. As instructed, Gardoqui's successors in New York and Philadelphia, Josef Ignacio de Viar and Josef de Jaudenes, had done little—while their American counterparts in Spain, the ailing William Carmichael and Jefferson's trusted protégé William Short, had been shunted back and forth between Godoy and Gardoqui in a transparent game of deliberate procrastination.[3]

Part of the problem, Short explained, was the Americans' status as diplomats of the third rank—ordinary chargés d'affaires. By the diplomatic etiquette of the Spanish court, Carmichael and Short had "no opportunity of speaking with the Minister until [their foreign rivals] of the first and second order have finished their audience." By then, Short groaned, Godoy "has had his head already saturated with their communications and is on tip-toe generally with his watch in his hand to be precisely at the hour assigned with the King or elsewhere."[4]

As long as it had suited their purposes, Godoy and Gardoqui had impatiently glanced at their watches, hurried to other appointments, and generally put off the Americans with one excuse after another—but all that was about to change. Now it was time, Godoy told Gardoqui and the other members of his council of state, "to take the precautions which prudence and necessity" required. "One of these was to procure friends" among those nations "who could help us most and who as enemies could most harm us," Godoy announced, and "such precisely were the United States."[5]

"In addition to insuring our possessions on that continent," Godoy advocated friendship toward the United States as a means of "depriving the English of the great assistance which they got from those provinces in the war before the last"—the French and Indian War, or Seven Years' War. Carried away by his rhetoric, Godoy even voiced the unlikely thought that a friendly overture to the United States might "enable us to count them for our own defense, and for offense against the enemy." Then he promptly focused again on the real situation. "The time had come," Godoy believed, when negotiations with the United States

> could no longer be delayed as had been done up till now, because of not consenting to the principal point of the free navigation of the River Mississippi to the sea, which the United States pretend should be conceded to them.

At this point in this pivotal meeting, Godoy asked the council "to weigh and combine the different matters, points and circumstances." Then he sat down to hear their suggestions.

For Godoy, more than the fate of the Mississippi River was at stake. In a meeting of the council just three months earlier, with Carlos IV present, the veteran minister Pedro Pablo Abarca de Bolea, count of Aranda, had attacked not only Godoy's handling of the war with France but his capacity for high office as well. Godoy had responded tolerably well (depending on whose account of the incident one trusts), but it was Aranda who lost the encounter when the king took offense at a sarcastic zinger aimed at the royal favorite. "With my father you were stubborn and insolent," Carlos IV interrupted, "but you never went so far as to insult him in council." Within two hours the count of Aranda was locked in a carriage heading south to Granada, where he spent the next year in confinement at the palace of the Alhambra.

Manuel Godoy was twenty-seven years old, "conscious of the paucity of his years and experience," and acutely aware of the dangers he faced. The court was buzzing about the three-month-old Princess Francisco de Paula—born to Queen Maria Luisa in March—whose striking resemblance to Godoy, at least in the eyes of those who doubted the king's paternity, revived old gossip with a new Jacobin spin: "Godoy," taunted a verse circulated by a republican conspirator,

> . . . how can I admire him
> if the queen aroused him
> with her lustful desire—O rage!—
> and pulled him out of the barracks
> so as to have sex with
> Señor Duke of Alcudia.[6]

Aranda's criticisms also had the sting of truth. The year-old war with France was not going well. Royal troops who had advanced gloriously against the republican enemy last year were being pushed back across the Pyrenees. Their British ally had demonstrated more enthusiasm for destroying the French fleet than for helping Spain on the ground. Carondelet's and Gayoso's reports from Louisiana about Clark's impending attack were consistently bleak, and the separatist plots of Wilkinson and others had come to nothing. Spain faced serious choices.

As Godoy sat down, Diego de Gardoqui took the floor. "In corroboration of what the Duke of Alcudia explained," the crown's resident American expert began, "the greatest evil that could happen to Spain was that that new power [the United States] should succeed in uniting with England to work in common accord against this monarchy." Gardoqui then produced a three-year-old memorandum he had written to Floridablanca advocating a settlement of the question of Mississippi navigation. He went on to describe his negotiations with John Jay, their tentative agreement in 1786, and "the failure of Congress to accept the same." Brandishing a map of North America to illustrate his arguments, Gardoqui described a "strong pro-British party in America, particularly in the northern states," and warned that these commercial interests "might succeed in dominating the whole country if Spain did not take advantage of their irritation" over English "spoilations" against the rights of neutral shipping on the high seas.[7]

Gardoqui's views were seconded by the veteran councilor Pedro Rodríguez, count of Campomanes, who advocated securing the friendship of the United States by "grant[ing] them some extension of lands as they desired." If a generous settlement of the boundaries won American friendship, Campomanes argued, "the sacrifice of between thirty and fifty leagues . . . was not of so much importance" compared to the risk of "losing all." As for the Mississippi, Campomanes conceded that England had had no authority to grant the right of navigation to the United States in 1783. Nevertheless, when "he observed the ardor which those States had for it, and the efforts which they were making to get it," Campomanes reminded the council "that the free navigation of a river through the territories of different princes was no new thing." Godoy and Gardoqui had offered "powerful reasons . . . for gaining the friendship of the [United] States," Campomanes concluded, and "he was of the opinion that the free navigation of the Mississippi might be considered in terms . . . most useful to Spain."[8]

With the support of Spain's resident expert on American affairs and a veteran statesman whose experience reached back into the golden days of Carlos III's reign, Godoy stood on firm ground in recommending that Spain offer the United States "favors as to boundaries and the navigation of the Mississippi, as long as they would assure us . . . a good and sincere friendship." Without dissent, the council agreed that instructions be sent "straightway" to Viar and Jaudenes in Philadelphia, charging them to welcome a renewal of negotiations with the American government and the appointment by both sides of "commissioners plenipotentiary to meet on the spot to fix the boundary line by common agreement." For the moment, Great Britain was to be informed only that "an adjustment of outstanding issues was under way," while Spain cultivated the United States "carefully in order to fix them for our friendship and in time secure a real alliance." Godoy, Gardoqui, and Campomanes had made the case for a complete reversal of Spanish policy toward its boundaries with the United States and the navigation of the Mississippi River, and on July 7, 1794, "all of this the Council approved and His Majesty resolved that it should be done immediately."

Manuel Godoy's letter to Viar and Jaudenes in Philadelphia outlined the terms they were to propose to President Washington's administration. "Little will be risked," he wrote,

> in fixing the [boundary] according to the claims of the [United] States, as much as may be compatible with our treaties with the Indians, and in granting the [navigation of the Mississippi] with the restrictions which the interest of his [Majesty's] subjects requires; but the King desires . . . a solid alliance and reciprocal guarantee of our possessions and those of the States in America. To this end His Catholic Majesty desires that the President send a person with full power . . . for a treaty of alliance to be independent of the circumstances and relationships of the [current European] war.

Not surprisingly, in light of its importance, four drafts of this new state-ment of policy were prepared and discussed between the council meet-ing on July 7 and the departure on July 31 of a special courier who carried the final instructions to Philadelphia. On July 26, reviewing the penulti-mate draft, Godoy struck out all reference to Kentucky's disposition "to separate themselves from dependence on Congress and . . . place them-selves under His Majesty's protection." As far as the king and his minis-ters were concerned, the frontier intrigues with James Wilkinson and others were over, too. Ironically, however, Godoy's last-minute deletion of the reference to Kentucky separatism (coupled with the fact that he and Gardoqui kept Short and Carmichael entirely in the dark about Spain's new intentions) occasioned a full year of confusion between the two nations.[9]

When Godoy's instructions reached Josef de Jaudenes early in December 1794—his colleague Viar having turned his attention to com-mercial affairs as consul-general—Jaudenes promptly deciphered the new instructions and acknowledged their receipt in a letter to Godoy dated December 8. Then he did absolutely nothing about them for nearly four months.

In early spring, William Short informed Secretary of State Edmund Randolph, Jefferson's successor, that Godoy had sent an important new overture to the Spanish envoy in Philadelphia, but that its exact nature remained a mystery. When asked, Jaudenes evaded Randolph's queries about Godoy's intentions with a false assertion that he had been unable to decode the ciphered text with absolute certainty, and that he was there-fore waiting for clarification from Madrid. A few weeks later, in March 1794, Randolph learned from Short that Jaudenes had acknowledged his receipt of Godoy's new instructions back in December. Summoning Jau-denes to his office, Randolph demanded to know the substance of Godoy's message. Finally, on March 25, 1794—more than eight months after Carlos IV and his Council of State had decided upon their new pol-icy toward the United States—Jaudenes produced a document that pur-ported to represent his new instructions from Godoy.[10]

Why the long delay? And why was Jaudenes so reluctant to convey Godoy's friendly overture to the American secretary of state? Something more than procrastination was afoot.

As a senior aide in the Spanish embassy in the 1780s, Jaudenes had been party to Gardoqui's various conversations and confidential reports about separatist schemes in the American west. Now, during the summer of 1794, while the Washington administration was coping with local insurrections in western Pennsylvania against the excise tax on whiskey, someone from a "secret committee of correspondence of the West" and some unnamed "Kentucky Senators" approached Jaudenes about yet another attempt at separation. Eager to exploit the opportunity (about which Godoy's new instructions were conveniently silent owing to that last-minute deletion), Jaudenes had given encouragement and $100 to a Kentucky separatist who called himself Mitchell. Jaudenes had simply been stalling for time, deferring compliance with his instructions from Godoy in favor of his own maverick project.

Perhaps the real indication of Jaudenes's ineptitude, however, was the skimpy payment of $100, for the mysterious Mitchell never came back to Philadelphia. Instead, the western plotters took their plans to Governor Carondelet in New Orleans, where the royal purse was known to be deep and open. Months would pass before Manuel Godoy had all the pieces of this strange puzzle in view, but Jaudenes had been scammed. The whole episode—and all the delay and confusion it caused—was just one more scheme by General James Wilkinson, for which he would expect another reward in Spanish gold dollars.[11]

To save face about the pretended garbling of Godoy's instructions, when Jaudenes finally presented Godoy's overture to Secretary Randolph on March 25, 1795, the envoy hedged its language with so many conditional phrases that no one in the Washington administration could recognize the document for what Godoy intended: an invitation to negotiations based on the pivotal transformation in policy decided nine months earlier by the Spanish Council of State.[12]

Like most eighteenth-century bureaucratic prose, the reports and correspondence of Spanish colonial officials have a deferential tone that strikes the modern ear as verbose. The opening and closing sentences of Jaudenes's communication to Secretary Randolph are far worse—so much worse, in fact, that their subterfuge had to have been intentional. Rather than admit that Randolph had caught him in a lie about the garbling of Godoy's instructions, Jaudenes began his summary with this paragon of equivocation:

> The points on which I understand it to be the will of the King my master to adjust the pending negotiations with the United States, are, subject to the receipt of further explanatory declarations for which I am waiting, as follows.

And he closed the message with similar evasions:

The preceding is what I persuade myself I ought to deduce from the despatch in question and what I have received from my superior to the present time, to be the will of the King.

Sandwiched between this amazing mumbo jumbo, the rest of the document honestly summarizes the chief elements of Godoy's original proposal. All the main points are present: an offer to settle boundary questions "favorably" and another to "grant the navigation of the Mississippi with the restrictions demanded by the interests of his subjects," the hope for a treaty of alliance and commerce, and the request for an ambassador with "full powers." Delayed for months, however, and then bracketed by these remarkable equivocations, the profound significance of Godoy's overture was completely buried in Jaudenes's guilty rhetoric. As a result, Secretary Randolph and President Washington did not bother with a reply, for Jaudenes had left them nothing substantive to which they *could* reply—indeed nothing to suggest that anything might have changed.[13]

In a letter to William Short a week after Jaudenes delivered his version of Godoy's overtures, Secretary Randolph reflected the confusion caused by the envoy's obfuscation. Randolph wondered whether "the hints of propositions in Mr. Jaudenes's letter" indicated that Spain might be willing to negotiate the matters in question. On the other hand, the "evasions" and "depressions of their temper at one moment and exstacy at another, as events smile or frown," seemed to demonstrate that Spanish policy was "governed by a species of political cowardice . . . which deceives itself by merely postponing the evil day, and which will grant nothing upon principles of liberal policy."[14]

Luckily for both nations, the future of Spanish-American relations did not depend on the petty talents of Josef de Jaudenes and could no longer be interrupted by the intrigues of James Wilkinson. By the spring of 1795, when Jaudenes finally reported to Godoy about the delivery of his overture, entirely independent events in America enabled Jaudenes to "flatter [him]self" that his king's request for a new ambassador "is covered by the nomination recently made by the executive power of the United States." By another curious twist of fate (but *not* in response to Godoy's new proposals), President Washington had appointed Thomas Pinckney as "envoy extraordinary and sole commissioner plenipotentiary" to the court at Madrid. Pinckney's appointment was rather a direct consequence of George Rogers Clark's aborted expedition against Louisiana and of the pressures exerted on the American government by Governor Isaac Shelby and his constituents in Kentucky.[15]

. . .

In May 1794—two months prior to the pivotal July 7 meeting of Spain's Council of State and while he was still pursuing his policy of procrastination and delay, Manuel Godoy had instructed Spain's commissioners in Philadelphia to complain that their diplomatic counterparts in Madrid, William Carmichael and William Short, lacked the authority or personal stature necessary for successful negotiations. "Unless the ministers whom the United States should nominate were to be considered by His Majesty in every circumstance as possessing that character, splendor, and carriage which corresponds with residence near the royal person and with the gravity of the subjects to be treated," Godoy had declared, how could anyone expect His Most Catholic Majesty to pay the infant republic any heed? The objective sought by this former cadet of the palace guard was merely delay, but there was just enough truth in his brazen exaggeration to make the complaint plausible. Carmichael was near death's door, his health deteriorating so rapidly that he could no longer sign his own name, and despite real talent and ample experience, William Short was not an Adams, a Franklin, or a Jefferson.[16]

At home, as President Washington contemplated the choice of a suitably impressive ambassador to Spain, William Short's European experience was a domestic liability. He was virtually unknown to anyone on the western waters—where people cared about the Mississippi—because he had been living abroad since 1784, when he began his diplomatic apprenticeship as Jefferson's secretary in Paris. In addition, because Jaudenes's antics had entirely obscured Godoy's real intentions, the president's expectations for success were so low that William Short's qualifications seemed superfluous. "Peace and harmony with all nations being the supreme policy of the United States," Washington thought it "best to cast upon Spain the odium of the miscarriage of the negotiation, if at length it should miscarry." Nothing great was expected from a diplomatic assignment meant only to "yield to the subtleties of [Spain's] procrastination."[17]

Jefferson was President Washington's first choice for the job, but the master of Monticello was enjoying his retirement from political affairs. When Jefferson declined, the president turned his thoughts toward an old colleague and great admirer whose political reputation *was* familiar in Madrid and legendary among men of the west. From his modest law office at Red Hill overlooking the Staunton River Valley—a view that remains unspoiled to this day—Patrick Henry declined the honor as well.

Washington's third choice was both inspired and expedient. With Chief Justice John Jay embarking as Washington's special envoy to the

Court of St. James's, why not send America's resident ambassador from London to Madrid with the same special status? Thomas Pinckney was an urbane southerner, a political moderate, no less committed to the navigation of the Mississippi River than his cousin Charles Pinckney, who had vindicated America's claim to the river on the floor of Congress in August 1786—and, conveniently, he was at that very moment already on the correct side of the Atlantic Ocean.

Born in Charleston in 1750, Thomas Pinckney and his elder brother Charles Cotesworth Pinckney, like their cousin Charles, stood among the preeminent low-country aristocrats of South Carolina. Their father (also named Charles) had served as speaker of the colonial legislature and a member of the royal governor's council, and had taken the family to London during the 1750s, when he served as South Carolina's agent to the British Board of Trade and Plantations. From her horticultural experiments in the 1740s at Belmont plantation, on the Cooper River near Charleston, their remarkable mother, Eliza Lucas Pinckney, had single-handedly introduced silk and indigo production to the colony, where the valuable blue dye quickly joined rice as one of South Carolina's major commodities for export.

When the family had returned to South Carolina in 1758, Thomas and his brother Charles Cotesworth had stayed in England to study at the Westminster School, Christ Church, Oxford, and the Middle Temple—and had traveled extensively in Europe. Admitted to the bar in 1774, Thomas had promptly rejoined his elder brother in South Carolina and taken an active role, both political and military, in support of the American Revolution. The younger Pinckney served in 1777 as the American liaison to the comte d'Estaing, commander of the French fleet, had been wounded and captured at the Battle of Camden in 1780, and was exchanged in time to serve again with Washington in the Yorktown campaign that ended the war.

After the war, Thomas Pinckney served two terms as governor of South Carolina in 1787 and 1788 while his brother and cousin safeguarded their state's interests in the Philadelphia Convention of 1787, defending both slavery and the slave trade and insisting that treaties be ratified by a two-thirds majority of the Senate. Thomas Pinckney presided over the state convention that ratified the Constitution. In the politics of the new republic, the brothers offered firm but temperate support for Alexander Hamilton's economic and commercial policies (while their cousin Charles's suspicion of northern partisanship inclined him toward Jefferson and the Democratic-Republicans). Eventually the Federalist party advanced both brothers as candidates for vice president,

Thomas in 1796 and Charles Cotesworth in 1800, but in the meantime President Washington employed both men on diplomatic missions, Thomas as ambassador to Great Britain in 1791 (and from there to Madrid in 1795) and Charles Cotesworth as minister to France in 1796. If Spain demanded a man of "character, splendor, and carriage," America had few candidates more eligible than a wealthy Pinckney from Charleston, South Carolina.

President Washington's choice of Thomas Pinckney as the new minister to Madrid was a devastating disappointment to William Short. "I have been long enough in public service," he lamented in a private letter to friends, and "I have had all the thorns—others have gathered the roses." By 1795 the young man now recognized as America's first professional diplomat had "experienced this in two instances"—Gouverneur Morris's appointment as ambassador to France and Pinckney's appointment to Madrid. "It shall be my fault if I experience it in a third." In a gracious letter to the secretary of state, however, Short declared that his personal disappointment "will in no degree diminish my earnest wishes for the success of Mr. Pinckney's Mission (which you will see from my late letters is already insured) nor my best efforts to serve him."[18]

Despite Short's personal disappointment, he and Pinckney worked well together in Spain, in part because the gentleman from South Carolina was sensitive to the parallel between Short's feelings and his own reaction to Washington's decision to send John Jay to London. "If I were to say I had no unpleasant feelings" about Jay's appointment, Pinckney admitted to Secretary of State Edmund Randolph, "I should not be sincere; but the sincerity with which I make this declaration will, I trust, entitle me to credit, when I add, that I am convinced of the expediency of adopting any honorable measures which may tend to avert the calamities of war," and "that I consider Mr. Jay's . . . diplomatic experience and general talents, as the most probable method of effecting this purpose." "Under these circumstances," he assured Randolph, "I will cheerfully embrace every opportunity of promoting the objects of Mr. Jay's mission and of rendering his residence here [in London] agreeable."[19]

Had he known as much about Spain's situation as William Short did, Thomas Pinckney probably would have rushed to Madrid as soon as his credentials reached him in London on February 23, 1795—though in fairness to Pinckney and Jay in London, and to Randolph and Washington in Philadelphia, we must remember that Josef de Jaudenes's mishandling of Godoy's proposal had so completely obscured its important message that none of them recognized the urgency of the moment. True to his word, Pinckney lingered in London until Jay completed his negotiations (and even waited a few more weeks to see whether the Senate might ratify it quickly), then left for Madrid on May 15. Traveling by way of the Netherlands and France, Pinckney stopped briefly in Paris to confer with James Monroe, who had succeeded Gouverneur Morris as ambassador to France—a post "which the public good requires to be filled by a Republican"—before arriving in Madrid at what proved to be the absolutely perfect moment on June 28, 1795.[20]

Godoy was ready to negotiate. At first he assumed that Pinckney's appointment was a direct response to the offer of alliance, trade, western boundaries, and Mississippi navigation that he thought Jaudenes had communicated to Washington. More significantly, he knew that his representatives in Basle were secretly concluding a treaty with France that would not only break Spain's alliance with Great Britain but lead, he hoped, to a French alliance. Peace was essential, for French armies had moved south of the Pyrenees, but Godoy feared it would prompt a military retaliation from Britain. These fears were compounded by the possibility that Jay's Treaty (the terms of which remained unknown to Godoy)[21] would create an Anglo-American alliance to the detriment of Spanish interests in the Americas and on the seas.

Despite the worries that plagued Godoy, nothing in the wider world, not even a French invasion force, deterred the Spanish court from its seasonal migrations, which dated back to the reign of Philip II. Spring meant Aranjuez, that oasis of Baroque gardens and orchards in the dusty plains south of Madrid. Summer meant the slopes of the Guadarrama Mountains, the magnificent palace at La Granja de San Ildefonso, and the adjacent hunting park at Riofrío, where the smallest of Carlos IV's "cottages" was built in Italianate style with about two acres under its roof.

Pinckney saw all these royal residences. Arriving in Madrid on June 28 while the court was still at Aranjuez, he hastened south just in time to follow Their Catholic Majesties and the queen's paramour back to Madrid for ten days and then on July 10 to San Ildefonso. During the interval in Madrid, Pinckney was able to present himself and his credentials to Carlos IV, meet twice with Godoy, and spend days in consultation with William Short. Happily for both nations (and for the clarity of our story), Short had recently received from Randolph a verbatim copy of Jaudenes's garbled version of the proposal that the Spanish Council of State had outlined a full twelve months earlier. Godoy was astonished at all that had gone wrong, but in resolving their mutual confusion over this comedy of errors, Pinckney's negotiations were off to a good start.

As negotiations resumed at the summer palace of San Ildefonso, Godoy set aside his hope for a treaty of alliance and commerce (which was beyond Pinckney's authority) and focused on the boundary lines and the Mississippi navigation that Pinckney *was* authorized to negotiate. Progress came slowly until a courier arrived with the Treaty of Basle between France and Spain. Signed on July 22 and ratified in Paris on the 29th, it reached Carlos IV on August 3 and he signed it immediately. On August 7 the peace was joyously announced in Madrid, and the pace of Godoy's negotiations with Pinckney quickened. Worried about the prospect of British retaliation and the possibility of an alliance between the United States and Britain based on the still unknown terms of Jay's Treaty, the Spanish Council of State authorized the acceptance of a boundary with the United States at 31 degrees north latitude and the concession of American navigation on the Mississippi River, confident that Spain retained "in those and other parts of America . . . possessions, peoples and rights of great importance and sufficient for our commerce and navigation."[22]

Pinckney's negotiations with Godoy, who had been elevated to the title of Prince of the Peace in recognition of his success at Basle, now entered their final stage. As the two men exchanged drafts and counter-drafts for the final treaty, the last sticking point was American access to the port of New Orleans. Unless the treaty gave American traders a place to unload their flatboats and bateaux near the port of New Orleans so they could transfer their cargoes to oceangoing vessels, Pinckney asserted, the abstract right of Mississippi navigation was "illusory, without utility, and without effect." Securing this "right of deposit," Pinckney told Godoy, was "one of the principal objects of his mission." Godoy responded with a series of vague assurances about a place of deposit near the mouth of the river, but Pinckney stood firm. Their standoff persisted well into October, while the Spanish royal court moved from its summer palace at San Ildefonso to spend the autumn at San Lorenzo, where Carlos IV's imperial predecessors rested in the marble vault beneath El Escorial.

At this critical moment in the negotiation, the Americans discovered that their two heads—a resident minister long familiar with the ways of the Spanish court and the temporary "envoy extraordinary and sole commissioner plenipotentiary" assigned to close the deal—were better than Godoy's one. Pinckney and Short agreed that the Spanish "government will certainly give as little as they can" and that only a dramatic "ultimatum" would force Godoy to make good on his verbal "promise as to the depot at N[ew] Orleans."

The moment had arrived when someone had to blink. The Americans had everything going for them, including the all-important freedom to fail. They knew that President Washington and their colleagues at home had no real hope for the success for the mission beyond "cast[ing] upon Spain the odium of the miscarriage of the negotiation, if at length it should miscarry"—and they sensed that the terms under discussion were the best they could get and the most that Spain could expect. With the prospect of British retaliation looming in Godoy's mind and the possibility of an Anglo-American alliance haunting his dreams, the Americans sensed that Manuel Godoy, Prince of the Peace, and His Most Catholic Majesty Carlos IV needed (or thought they needed, which amounts to the same thing) a friendly treaty with the United States. Final success required only some kind of jolt to make the Spanish recognize that the terms under discussion were the best that they could ever expect.

When the Spanish had asked for a special ambassador of "character, splendor, and carriage," they had inadvertently dealt to the visiting Thomas Pinckney a powerful trump card that could not have been played by the resident William Short. President Washington and his cabinet expected little from his mission (which had actually made more progress than anyone else had in the past dozen years), and Short was on hand in case anything useful developed in the months ahead, so on Saturday, October 24, 1795, the aristocratic South Carolinian requested his passport and began packing for home.

Pinckney's intended departure was no ruse, no ploy, no stratagem—and for that very reason it was supremely effective. Threatening to quit never works unless one is actually ready to go, but Pinckney was dead serious about leaving, and Godoy knew it. Equally important, the royal Council of State knew it, too, which eliminated future grounds for carping about yielding to Pinckney everything the council had agreed to accept back in August.[23]

On Sunday, October 25, instead of his passport, Manuel Godoy offered Pinckney a right of deposit at New Orleans. That evening, Pinckney reported on the day's turn of events to William Short, who was then in Madrid. "You were right in your conjecture, my dear Sir," Pinckney wrote.

> The negotiation has been again brought forward and is newly determined—the two points on which we before divided were the facilities of navigation and the spoilations [claimed by neutral Americans for capture by Spanish warships]. On the first we have agreed upon N[ew] Orleans for 3 years paying only storage, but this permission to

be continued unless an equal establishment is assigned elsewhere on the Mississippi. The principle of [Jay's] British Treaty [which Pinckney had suggested to Godoy] . . . is agreed upon for the spoilations. We only wait for the wording of this article to be agreed on all points.[24]

On Tuesday, October 27, 1795, Thomas Pinckney and Manuel Godoy affixed their signatures to the final Treaty of San Lorenzo, as Pinckney's Treaty is also known.

A few days later, Pinckney and Short traveled together to Paris, leaving Pinckney's secretary, Charles Rutledge, son of South Carolina's chief justice, John Rutledge, as temporary deputy of the American legation in Madrid. Short retired to private life in Paris, where he resumed his earlier liaison with the now widowed duchesse de La Rochefoucauld before eventually returning to America at Jefferson's behest in 1802. Pinckney carried his treaty on to London and promptly home in triumph. The treaty that bears his name—"one of the greatest successes in American diplomacy," according to the great diplomatic historian Samuel Flagg Bemis, with "almost immeasurable consequences for the future territorial expansion of the United States"—was ratified by a unanimous vote of the Senate on March 7, 1796, and proclaimed in force on August 2.[25]

In addition to fixing the American boundary with Spanish Florida and Louisiana at the thirty-first parallel, the Mississippi River was at last open to American trade, with a permanent right of deposit either at New Orleans, for the first three years, or "an equivalent establishment." When news of Pinckney's Treaty reached Kentucky, the public reaction was nearly universal jubilation. "The general joy of all ranks and descriptions of citizens," proclaimed the Kentucky Gazette on March 26, 1796, "was never so conspicuous . . . of which, the firing of artillery, tolling of bells, bonfires etc. etc. were evident testimonies."[26]

## CHAPTER ELEVEN

# Affairs of Louisiana

*The science of the engineer and the artillerist can be learned from
books, almost like geometry, but the knowledge of the heroic facts
of war can only be acquired by study of the history of wars, the
battles of great captains, and by experience.*

—Napoleon Bonaparte at St. Helena, 1815–1821[1]

*The art of putting people in their places is foremost in the science
of government, but the art of finding a place for the malcontent is
certainly the most difficult. [Colonies in] far-off places with landscapes equal to their dreams and desires . . . [are] one good solution for this social difficulty.*

—Charles Maurice de Talleyrand-Périgord, December 26, 1797[2]

THOMAS JEFFERSON was not the only man contemplating the
future of the world from a book-strewn study in Paris in the 1780s.
In his room at the Ecole Militaire at the Champ de Mars (now overshadowed by the Eiffel Tower) on the Left Bank of the Seine, about a mile
distant as the *corneille* flies, a brilliant Corsican gentleman-cadet was also
contemplating the destinies of nations. Born into a struggling gentry family from Ajaccio, Corsica, on August 15, 1769, Nabolione was the second
child of Carlo Maria di Buonaparte, a lawyer and Corsican patriot, and
Letizia Ramolino Buonaparte. His father served as a prosecutor and
judge during the French occupation of Corsica, and was eventually
elevated to the lower aristocracy as a count. Through his influence,
Napoleon Bonaparte (as his name was translated into French) accepted
a scholarship from Louis XVI to study at the royal military college
at Brienne and then at the Ecole Militaire. He was graduated on September 28, 1785, at the age of sixteen, and joined the army as a second
lieutenant.[3]

Artillery was young Bonaparte's military specialty, but his genius was far-reaching. "Reserved and studious," his final examiners at the Ecole Militaire reported in August 1785, "he prefers study to any type of amusement, finding pleasure in the reading of good authors." Napoleon's instructors saw his aptitude for "abstract sciences" and his solid knowledge of geography and mathematics (including algebra, geometry, and trigonometry). "Quiet and solitary, capricious, haughty, and frightfully egotistical," according to his artillery instructor, Bonaparte spoke little in class but was "spirited in his answers." Outside of class he was "swift and sharp in his repartee" and imbued with "pride and boundless ambition." In his evenings of solitude Bonaparte indulged a passion for reading the lives of great men and the history of wars and empires, writing essays in the privacy of his room, and haunting the bookshops of Paris or Valence, where he was stationed after graduating from the Ecole Militaire.[4]

Both at Valence and on two lengthy sojourns home to Corsica, Bonaparte read voraciously, filling his notebooks (thirty-six of which survive) with reflections about military science, Corsican liberation, and ancient

*Sixteen-year-old Napoleon Bonaparte was graduated in September 1785 from the Ecole Militaire, the academy founded by Louis XV and designed by Jacques-Ange Gabriel. The adjacent Champ de Mars, originally a parade ground for the military academy, was the site of the Paris Exposition of 1889, for which the Eiffel Tower was constructed opposite the Ecole Militaire. A few blocks to the northwest, the tomb of Napoleon rests beneath the golden dome of the Hôtel des Invalides, where the emperor's body was reinterred in 1840.* (Collection of the author)

and modern history. He devoured French translations of Plutarch, Plato, Cicero, Livy, and Tacitus, as well as the great authors of the Renaissance and Enlightenment—Corneille, Machiavelli, Montaigne, Montesquieu, Rousseau, and Voltaire—and Buffon's *Histoire Naturelle, Générale et Particulière*. Bonaparte's obsession with the liberation of Corsica found a larger context in James Boswell's *Account of Corsica* (published in 1768 by Samuel Johnson's companion and biographer), in Rousseau's *Social Contract*, and in the radical works of Guillaume-Thomas, Abbé de Raynal.

Born in 1713 and trained by the Jesuits, the Abbé Raynal had left the church for a career as a writer and philosophe, winning fame less for his originality than his gift for popularizing the insights of other Enlightenment thinkers. Raynal's most successful and influential work was his six-volume *Philosophical and Political History of the Settlements and Trade of the Europeans in the East and West Indies*. Published in 1770 and proscribed by the Catholic Church's *Index Librorum Prohibitorum* four years later, the influential history sold out thirty editions by 1789. Owing in part to the editorial influence of Denis Diderot, who coordinated the Enlightenment's great cooperative project, the *Encyclopædia*, each edition of Raynal's grew more radical in its denunciations of slavery, royalty, and the Church—until French royal authorities ordered the book burned in 1781 and sent its author into exile.

The Abbé Raynal's *History of the Two Indies*, as it was widely known, inspired grand thoughts about liberation. The author's persecution by the ancien régime only accentuated the validity of his arguments for young men like Bonaparte, whose enthusiasm for Raynal went beyond the pages of his notebooks. After three years in exile, the abbé had been permitted to return to France in 1784 (although not to Paris until after the fall of the Bastille) and was living in Marseilles. On a trip home in 1786 Bonaparte sought out Raynal and showed him an early draft of his impassioned history of the "unjust French domination of Corsica."[5] The abbé encouraged him to finish and publish it.

"How is it possible," Bonaparte's essay demanded, "that an enlightened nation like France is not touched by our plight, a direct result of their actions? . . . Mankind! Mankind! How wretched you are in the state of bondage, but how great you are impassioned by the flame of liberty!" Drawing a lesson from the Abbé Raynal's *History*, Bonaparte believed that Corsica needed a liberating champion, a Spartacus, "a courageous chief." But when and where, he wondered, "shall a William Tell appear?"[6]

The twenty-year-old officer visited the aging Abbé Raynal at least twice on his travels between Corsica and France. Bolstered by his encouragement and advice, Bonaparte reworked his polemic into the epistolary form that Montesquieu had employed in his *Persian Letters*. Then he proudly sent a few chapters to his boyhood hero, the Corsican patriot General Pasquale Paoli, and dispatched the introduction to a former instructor at the military college at Brienne. Their verdicts were harsh but wise. General Paoli thought it "would have made a much greater impression if it had said less and if it had shown less partiality," while the Abbé Dupuy sent a flurry of criticisms and suggestions culminating in the prudent warning that "this language is too strong in a monarchy."[7]

Had Napoleon Bonaparte ignored Paoli and Dupuy and followed Raynal's counsel, his "Corsican Letters" surely would have brought a summary dismissal from the French army. As it happened, however, the daring words of the Abbé Raynal that directly influenced the course of history came not from his private advice to an aspiring author but from his *History of the Two Indies*. In retrospect, the keepers of the *Index* and protectors of the ancien régime had good reason to worry about the Abbé Raynal's ideas as they were disseminated throughout the world in thirty editions of his history. Bonaparte was not the only reader inspired to watch for the deliverance of a Spartacus or a William Tell.

While "interest alone can exert its influence over [the nations of Europe]," the Abbé Raynal had written in a stirring passage of his *History of the Two Indies*, slaves had no need of European generosity "to break the yoke of their oppression":

Nature speaks a more powerful language than philosophy or interest. Already have two colonies of fugitive negroes been established, to whom treaties and power give a perfect security. . . . These are so many indications of the impending storm, and the Negroes only want a chief, sufficiently courageous, to lead them on to vengeance and slaughter. Where is this great man, whom nature owes to her afflicted, oppressed, and tormented children? Where is he? He will undoubtedly appear, he will shew himself, he will lift up the sacred standard of liberty. This venerable signal will collect around him the companions of his misfortunes. . . . Spaniard, Portuguese, English, French, Dutch, all their tyrants will become the victims of fire and sword. The plains of America will suck up with transport the blood which they have so long expected. . . . The name of the hero, who shall have restored the rights of the human species will be blest, in all parts trophies will be erected to his glory. Then will the black code be no more, and the white code will be a dreadful one, if the conqueror only regards the right of reprisals.

At least one copy of Raynal's history found its way to a sugar plantation in the French colony of St. Domingue. Thousands of miles away from Valence and Marseilles, on the island of Hispaniola in the Caribbean, a slave named Toussaint L'Ouverture read the Abbé Raynal's words over and over again. "Where is he? He will undoubtedly appear." When the French Revolution came, Napoleon would fashion his own version of William Tell, and Haiti would embrace Toussaint L'Ouverture as "the black Spartacus who, as [the Abbé] Raynal predicted, has come to revenge all the evil done to his race."[8]

"Revolutions," Napoleon Bonaparte told a fellow artillerist in September 1789, "are ideal times for soldiers with a bit of wit and the courage to act." He had both, and they quickly overwhelmed his aspirations as a writer. After a stint in the Corsican national guard, Bonaparte returned to France in 1793 and was assigned to a revolutionary army laying siege to the port city and naval base of Toulon, where royalists assisted by the British fleet had revolted against the French republic. The city's defenses fell before his cannon, and the British fleet fled the harbor. On December 19, 1793, Major Bonaparte turned his guns on hundreds of royalist collaborators gathered in the town square for their slaughter, and then he leveled the public buildings of Toulon as a warning to royalists elsewhere. "I cannot find praiseworthy enough words to describe Bonaparte's full worth," the commanding officer reported to the war ministry in Paris. "He has a solid scientific knowledge of this profession and as much intelligence, if too much courage, *voilà*. . . . It now only remains for you, Minister, to consecrate his talents to the glory of the Republic!" Three days later the twenty-four-year-old military genius was promoted to the rank of brigadier general.[9]

General Bonaparte was among seventy-four officers detained as a precaution after the fall of Robespierre in July 1794 and then released and reinstated. Wary of Jacobinism and the excesses of the guillotine, the new and more conservative Directory recognized "the services his military talents can still provide . . . at a time when men of his high caliber are extraordinarily rare." Early in October, still uncertain about his future, Napoleon called upon Paul François Nicolas de Barras, one of the most influential members of the five-man Directory that now ruled France, at the seat of government in the Tuileries (a building destroyed in 1871 and now the site of I. M. Pei's pyramid at the Louvre). Much later in the day, about midnight, a crowd of several thousand working-class Parisians and royalists led by a self-proclaimed General Danican gathered ominously at the Tuileries. In the wee hours of the morning of 13 Vendémiaire (October 4) Barras summoned Bonaparte to defend the government.[10]

Soon after dawn General Bonaparte arrived with forty cannon, the largest of which he positioned at the Eglise St.-Roch, just north of the Tuileries and its gardens. Twice the rebellious crowd surged toward the building, peppering the defending regiments with small-arms fire. Twice the defenders held their ground, and the second time they pushed the armed rebels back toward the Eglise St.-Roch, where Bonaparte opened fire with his cannon. "The enemy attacked us at the Tuileries," he wrote that night to his brother Joseph.

> We killed a great many of them. They killed thirty of our men and wounded another sixty. . . . Now all is quiet. As usual I did not receive a scratch. I could not be happier.

Fourteen hundred rebellious citizens lay dead in the streets, and the government was safe. Two weeks later he was promoted to major general, and on October 25 he succeeded Barras as commander of the Army of the Interior. Bonaparte, having dropped the letter *u* from his last name, was the man of the hour. The next spring, on March 6, 1796, he married Barras's former mistress, Josephine de Beauharnais, who was adorned in republican simplicity with a white muslin dress, a tricolor sash, and his wedding gift of an enameled locket with the inscription "To Destiny." Two days after the wedding, Bonaparte headed for Nice and the headquarters of the Army of Italy, his new command.[11]

Thirty-two-year-old Josephine de Beauharnais had lost her husband to the guillotine during the Terror and taken up with Barras as his principal mistress—a fact that now spawned ugly scuttlebutt about Bonaparte's new assignment. The gossip, as the baron de Frénilly recorded it in his memoirs, was that Barras had "tired of her and got rid of her by giving the Army of Italy as a dowry," and that "the little General of 13 Vendémiaire took the dowry and the mistress, and made of her an Empress."[12]

Barras was, in fact, instrumental in making the appointment, but for all the members of the Directory, the choice was sweetened by Bonaparte's proven abilities and his previous obscurity. Better to entrust the Army of Italy to a talented but unknown general, the reasoning went, than to place it in the hands of others whose power and fame might threaten the government. Bonaparte, of course, confounded these calculations.[13]

In Italy he defeated four Austrian generals in succession, each with superior numbers, and forced Austria and its allies to sue for peace. In the north he founded the Cisalpine Republic, later known as the kingdom of Italy, and bolstered his influence at home by sending treasure worth millions of francs to the nearly bankrupt Directory. Plagued by financial problems, factional strife, corruption, and a series of attempted coups d'état, the Directory governed without distinction for four years, its income always dependent on the plunder sent home from Bonaparte's conquests. "The directors believe that they are using him," warned Bonaparte's former mathematics instructor, General Jean Charles Pichegru, "but one fine morning he is going to gobble them up, without their being able to do anything about it."[14]

That fine morning dawned in October 1799 after Bonaparte's conquest of Egypt. While in Italy Bonaparte had realized "for the first time" that he "no longer considered [him]self a mere general, but a man called upon to decide the fate of peoples." Sensing his resolve, aware of their own vulnerability, and relieved at the prospect of sending this dashing hero on a white horse to the far end of the Mediterranean, in February 1798 the members of the Directory had happily agreed to Bonaparte's expedition against Egypt. His aide Louis Antoine Fauvelet Bourrienne had asked how long they would be gone. "A few months, or six years," Bonaparte had replied, "it all depends on events"—events in Paris.[15]

By October 1799 Paris was a confusing snake pit of plots and intrigue. The panoply of conspirators—including royalists, British agents, former Jacobins, members of the Directory itself, and a group of self-styled communists for whom "the Revolution is not over" because "the rich still have all the money"[16]—agreed only that the Directory's days were numbered. For their part, on October 8 the five directors took what proved to be a final decisive and symbolic act when they ordered the ringing of church bells and firing of artillery salutes in celebration of a dispatch from Bonaparte announcing his final victory over the Turks at Abukir Bay near the mouth of the Nile.[17]

Five days later came daunting news that Napoleon Bonaparte himself had landed at the tiny harbor of Fréjus, on the Mediterranean coast midway between Toulon and Nice. He was rushing toward Paris, greeted by cheering crowds, "unanimous applause," and "general euphoria." The final morning of the Directory was in sight.[18]

The coup d'état that overthrew the Directory on November 9–10,

1799 (18–19 Brumaire, the month of fog), was the work of a wide coalition of politicians—including Charles Maurice de Talleyrand-Périgord, Joseph Fouché, Emmanuel-Joseph Sieyès, and many others—and it is generally regarded as the end of the revolution that began with the fall of the Bastille ten years earlier. The new Constitution of the Year VIII (1799) created offices for three consuls, sixty senators, one hundred tribunes, and three hundred legislative representatives, but in fact it soon made First Consul Napoleon Bonaparte a virtual dictator.

Of approximately five million votes cast in a national referendum, the new constitution was approved by a margin of 3,011,007 to 1,562—at least according to the official tabulation made by Lucien Bonaparte, Napoleon's brother, who conveniently ignored 3.5 million negative votes and double-counted 1.5 million favorable ballots. "Citizens," the first consul proclaimed after the coup d'état of 18–19 Brumaire, "the revolution remains faithful to the principles which gave it birth. It is finished." Two years later, with similar assistance at the polls, French voters approved a constitutional revision that made Bonaparte consul for life, and in 1804 they sanctioned yet another revision that created him Emperor Napoleon I.[19]

On the eve of a new century, the once reserved and studious youth of the Ecole Militaire had conquered Italy and Egypt and now ruled France. Much had changed, but that inquisitive young man who spent his evenings reading good authors had not disappeared. Napoleon enjoyed the company and conversation of learned and witty men—and in his heart he knew that the trophies and acclaim of a warrior were fleeting. "The people," he had commented while gazing from his carriage upon throngs of admirers who filled the streets of Paris, "would crowd as fast to see me if I were going to the scaffold." Of his many honors and triumphs, none pleased him more than his election to the prestigious National Institute of Science and Arts (now the Institut de France) in 1797.[20]

First proposed by the liberal statesman and bishop of Autun, Charles Maurice de Talleyrand-Périgord, in a report on public education delivered to the national legislature in May 1791, the National Institute was established in 1795 as the republican successor to the royal academies of the ancien régime, which had been abolished in 1792. With 144 full members and 144 associate members, the institute gathered the nation's preeminent intellectuals into three sections—physical sciences and mathematics, moral and political sciences, and literature and the fine arts—and charged them with "improving the arts and sciences" and pro-

*Forced into the priesthood by a childhood injury that gave him a perma-
nent limp, Charles Maurice de Talleyrand-Périgord had risen to bishop
of Autun when he embraced the French Revolution in 1789. He was
instrumental in drafting important provisions of the Declaration of
Rights of Man and Citizen, and he remained, through all the vagaries of
his remarkable career, a persistent advocate of its goals. One of history's
consummate survivors, Talleyrand escaped the Reign of Terror as an exile
in England and the United States. Although he disliked Philadelphia, Talleyrand admired American religious liberty and advocated toleration
and colonization in the public lectures that marked his return to France
and to power in 1797. He broke with Napoleon in August 1807 and subsequently helped engineer the reconstruction of Europe as Louis XVIII's
representative at the Congress of Vienna in 1814 and 1815. Talleyrand
died in Paris on May 17, 1838. This engraving, based on an oil portrait
by François Gérard, a student of Jacques-Louis David, depicts Talleyrand at the height of his powers.* (Collection of the author)

moting discovery and invention. "True conquests," Bonaparte proclaimed on the occasion of his induction into the National Institute of
Science and Arts on December 26, 1797, "are those made over ignorance. . . . The true power of the French Republic should consist henceforth in allowing no single new idea to escape its embrace."[21]

As if to demonstrate the validity of Bonaparte's sentiments, Paris was swiftly embracing two singular ideas advanced in lectures at the National Institute by another new member on April 4 and July 3, 1797. The lecturer was Charles Maurice de Talleyrand-Périgord, who had survived the Terror by exiling himself first to London and then to Philadelphia. His themes, derived in large measure from his observation in England and America, were the importance of religious toleration and the benefits of colonization.[22]

Unlike a palace coup, Citizen Talleyrand told the audience at the National Institute on April 4, 1797, a general revolution in which "everybody took part" arouses popular hatreds and "shakes up everything." In its wake comes "a general uneasiness in people's souls, a vague disposition toward risky enterprises, and a craving for incessant change and destruction." Since these feelings "cannot be muffled, they must be regulated"—controlled "not at the expense but for the benefit of public happiness."[23]

Freedom of religion, the former bishop of Autun had learned in America, promoted social and political harmony. "The freedom and especially the equality of religious beliefs is one of the strongest guarantees of social tranquillity, since where beliefs are respected, the other rights are necessarily respected as well." To enjoy the general blessings of liberty, Talleyrand declared, France must transcend its long history of violent religious wars, embrace freedom of religion, and "learn how to give up our hatreds if we do not want to forever give up our happiness."[24]

Returning to the podium of the National Institute on July 3, Citizen Talleyrand offered colonization as his second prescription for social and political order in the aftermath of the revolution. Once again his advice to France reflected his experience in America, where vast unexplored territories offered restless souls and malcontents—"*cette multitude de malades politiques*"—places to seek adventure and make a fresh start in life. "The art of putting people in their places is foremost in the science of government," Talleyrand believed, "but the art of finding a place for the malcontent is certainly the most difficult." Colonies in "far-off places with landscapes equal to their dreams and desires," Talleyrand suggested, were "one good solution for this social difficulty."[25]

Egypt and some "fertile but uninhabited" islands along the coast of Africa were the specific far-off places that Talleyrand had in mind as homesteads for French malcontents, but neither the rebellious island of St. Domingue nor the provinces of Canada and Louisiana had been forgotten by the influential crowd who attended his lectures at the National Institute. In this regard, Talleyrand knew his audience when he invoked the name of Etienne François duc de Choiseul as "one of the great men of our time, who had a keen sense of the future" while serving as chief minister during the Seven Years' War and the last dozen years of the reign of Louis XV. It suited the purpose of Talleyrand's lecture to remind his audience that, years before the events happened, Choiseul had predicted both American independence and the partitioning of Poland, and that he had also advocated French colonization in Egypt. Talleyrand did not need to remind his listeners that Choiseul had also been interested in regaining control of Louisiana.[26]

Talleyrand advocated colonization as a means of dispersing malcontents in order to achieve political and social stability in France. He invoked Choiseul's interest in Egypt as support for his vision, while Napoleon would also embrace Choiseul's interest in Louisiana and St. Domingue.

Since the loss of Canada and Louisiana at the end of the Seven Years' War, the idea of regaining possession of the former French colonies in North America was a recurrent dream that blossomed whenever war or diplomacy went well for France or poorly for Great Britain. Rumors of French designs on Louisiana began with the Franco-American alliance of 1778 and spread widely after the defeat of Great Britain—so much so that in 1786 Louis XVI's ministers directed the French envoy in New York to disavow them. "There has never been a question of an exchange of Louisiana for a French possession in the West Indies," Charles Gravier, comte de Vergennes, bluntly told Louis-Guillaume Otto, "and if it is again mentioned to you, you will formally deny it." Otto published Vergennes's denial in the *New York Packet* on January 19, 1787,[27] but vague rumors proved as persistent in America as the dream was in France.

That summer a French trader who lived in Kentucky, Barthélemi Tardiveau, revived the idea in a letter to the comte Eléonore François Elie Moustier, Otto's successor as chargé d'affaires to the United States. Moustier, in turn, incorporated Tardiveau's information in a lengthy report, forwarded to Paris in January 1789, in which he argued that returning Louisiana to France was in the best interests of both nations.

French control of the province, Moustier contended, offered Spanish Louisiana a more effective barrier against American aggression and France a profitable and self-sufficient empire in the Caribbean. From a diplomatic perspective, possession of the Mississippi Valley would enable France to counterbalance American and British territorial ambitions on the continent of North America. Commercially, the produce of Louisiana and the American settlements—food, timber, firewood, naval stores, and "the kinds of merchandise required by negroes"—would pass through the port of New Orleans to support the lucrative sugar, coffee, and cocoa industries of St. Domingue and the French West Indies.[28]

The idea of a Spanish retrocession of Louisiana alarmed Americans, but Moustier's stay in the United States was brief. His influence was limited. And his memorandum was fated to arrive in Paris weeks before the fall of the Bastille. For several years thereafter—during the bloody Reign of Terror, the war with Spain, and Citizen Genet's fiasco with George Rogers Clark—Moustier's memorandum advocating negotiations for a retrocession of Louisiana gathered dust in the files while a parade of ministers passed through the foreign office.[29]

Back in New York, Citizen Genet's successor, Jean Antoine Joseph Fauchet, dusted off a copy of Moustier's report early in 1795 as he formulated a similar dispatch in the anxious moments when France and Spain worried that Jay's Treaty would bring an alliance between the United States and Great Britain. Intercepted by the British and later presented to the American secretary of state, Fauchet's proposal maintained that unless Spanish policies changed or France stepped in, Louisiana was sure to end up in American hands.[30]

While Jean Fauchet's intercepted message was being read by British authorities, at the royal palace of Aranjuez (for it was spring) Carlos IV's minister Manuel Godoy was reaching similar conclusions about the future of Louisiana. As he monitored the French army's relentless advance toward Madrid in the spring of 1795 and the gloomy predictions and grandiose defensive schemes of Governor Carondelet in New Orleans, Godoy silently prepared to get the best deal he could for relinquishing Louisiana to France.[31]

In the secret negotiations at Basle that ended Spain's war with France and alliance with Great Britain in August 1795, Godoy had declined French overtures about a retrocession of Louisiana. At the time, France was preoccupied with its war with Austria and Godoy was reluctant to risk war with America—especially with John Jay busy at the negotiating table in London. By October, however, after he had failed to secure from Thomas Pinckney an American pledge for the territorial integrity of Louisiana and the Floridas, Godoy was ready to let France shoulder the burden of defending Spain's buffer zone along the Mississippi.[32]

As the American minister in Paris, James Monroe in 1796 once again found himself, as he had in Congress ten years earlier, monitoring secret machinations about the Mississippi River on which the happiness and peace of his country depended. Angry over the Jay Treaty—which it saw as a betrayal of the Franco-American alliance of 1778—the Directory threatened to begin apprehending American ships trading with Great Britain and, as Monroe recalled in his autobiography, to assume "a still more hostile attitude toward us." In the halls and salons of Paris, it was said

> that a treaty with Spain had been or would be soon concluded whereby Louisiana and the Floridas would be ceded to France, and that an attempt would be made to sever Canada from England, unite it with those provinces, and invite the western parts of our union to separate from [the United States] and join this new power which was thus to be reared in that quarter.

Privately, Monroe was able to get assurances from a member of the Directory that "their sole object in regard to Canada was to dismember it from England and weaken her." France, the unnamed director continued, would only take Louisiana "in the event of a war between Spain and England . . . to keep the British from . . . seiz[ing] the mouth of the Mississippi," and "with respect to our interior we had no cause for inquietude." Nevertheless, as President Washington attempted to steer his administration on a neutral course between the warring powers, America's relations with France continued to deteriorate. When Monroe left Paris a few months later—his recall engineered by the Federalist secretary of state Timothy Pickering during the bitter fight over Jay's Treaty—the Directory refused to recognize his successor, Charles Cotesworth Pinckney, and the two republics drifted toward armed conflict.[33]

The only surprising aspect of the American reaction to these events was the anger in the Federalist press over the possibility that Spain might cede Louisiana to the hated Republic of France. Northern politicians who had been willing to surrender the Mississippi River in 1786 (and who would oppose the Louisiana Purchase in 1803) suddenly found themselves embracing the views of the westerners they had been eager to push out of the union only a decade earlier.

If France took possession of Louisiana, warned the *New York Herald*, "the United States would be encircled by an artful, insinuating, active nation, and must forever renounce the hope of obtaining by purchase or amicable means, the territory west of the Mississippi, to the ocean." Interposed between the United States and the west, France was sure to threaten Mexico and the rest of the Spanish American empire as well.

"In the hands of the plodding Spaniards they do no harm and little good to the world at large," the Federalist writer continued, "but in the hands of an active nation, Mexico would be a dangerous engine of power." Self-interest demanded that America "prevent any powerful nation from making establishments in our neighborhood."[34]

It should not be surprising that America's reaction to developments in Europe was accurately reflected in letters from Secretary of State Timothy Pickering to his ambassador at the Court of St. James's. "We have often heard that the French government contemplated the repossession of Louisiana," Pickering wrote,

> and it has been conjectured that in their negotiations with Spain the cession of Louisiana and the Floridas may have been agreed upon. The Spaniards will certainly be more safe, quiet and useful neighbors. For her own sake Spain should absolutely refuse to make these cessions.

"France means to regain Louisiana," he added, "and to renew the ancient plan of her monarchs of *circumscribing* and encircling what now constitute the Atlantic states."[35]

At first glance, these sentiments seem an entirely predictable expression of American attitudes at the end of the eighteenth century. The aversion to having French troops on North American soil was commonplace, and the dread of being surrounded by hostile neighbors and cut off from westward expansion is older than the republic, for the restrictive provisions of the Quebec Act of 1774 were listed as evidence of tyranny in the Declaration of Independence.

The surprise in these letters is not in the sentiments expressed but in the identities of the author and recipient. The words were written by Timothy Pickering, one of the participants in the separatist movement of 1786, the chief engineer of Monroe's recall from France, and a future ringleader both of the 1803–1804 separatist reaction to the Louisiana Purchase and the separatist Hartford Convention of 1814. He wrote them to Rufus King, the congressional floor manager of the 1786 scheme to close the Mississippi, push the south and west out of the union, and establish a northern confederacy. What caused this drastic change in their attitude toward the west? Federalist antipathy toward Jacobin France, bitter partisan politics over the ratification of the Jay Treaty, and the rising specter of Napoleon's armies are only part of the answer.

·  ·  ·

In the major settlements of Kentucky and along the Cumberland and Tennessee Rivers, the frontier world of isolated log cabins and hunters who frightened Governor Carondelet by wandering for months with "a carbine and a little maize in a sack" was already history. By the mid-1790s, log stockades and "strong cabins" built by the likes of Daniel Boone were being supplanted by frame houses with glass windows and brick chimneys standing in tidy rows along rectilinear streets that anticipated the midwestern farming towns of Laura Ingalls Wilder.

Kentucky led the way, but within eight years of its founding in 1791 even Knoxville, Tennessee, had "about 100 houses all built of wood: the newest are mostly two-story frame structures." King and Crozier's mercantile store was offering, "in addition to their former assortment" of imported commodities,

> Irish Linens, Saddles and Bridles, Books and Stationary; Steel; Nails, Window Glass, Queen's Ware; Glass Ware; Pipes, Lead; Gun Powder; coffee; chocolate; Bohea, Green, Sequin, and Hyson Teas; Loaf and Brown Sugar; Pepper; All spice; Allum, Brimstone; Copperas, etc. etc. . . . All of which they will sell on reasonable terms, for Cash, Deer and Bear Skins, Furs, Hemp, Bees' Wax, Keg Butter, Tallow, Country linen, Flax, etc. etc.

Another Knoxville firm touted their new shipment of goods "from the Philadelphia market; all of which they will sell . . . on moderate terms for corn, rye, oats, bees wax, flax, old congress money, and Martin's certificates."[36]

By the mid-1790s, well-established trade routes linked eastern suppliers with the rapidly growing populations of Kentucky, Tennessee, and the Ohio Country. The consumer demands of frontier families bolstered ties of kinship, culture, or politics that stretched across the Appalachian Mountains. In any contest for the allegiance of western settlers—as Talleyrand recognized in his lecture about colonization and trade—American consumers "by far prefer English merchandise" over anything that Spain could provide. "Seven-tenths of the manufactured articles consumed in Kentucky," a French traveler calculated, "are imported from England."[37]

In the 1790s, the temptation to secede and join with Spanish Louisiana grew weaker with every Conestoga wagon that made the sixteen-day trip from Philadelphia to Pittsburgh, where consumer goods were shipped down the Ohio to merchants and their customers in Lexington and Louisville, Marietta and St. Louis, Natchez and Knoxville.

This movement of British and American manufactured goods across the mountains in the 1790s ended the threat of separatism in the Ohio River Valley just as surely as blue jeans and rock music helped bring down the Berlin Wall in the 1980s.[38]

The first retail store opened in Lexington, Kentucky, in 1783. Within a year the town boasted six stores, and by 1792 Lexington alone had twenty retail stores. The surviving invoices and shipping lists kept by merchant John Wesley Hunt provide a glimpse of the consumer goods sent "scrambling over the hills" in seven-ton wagonloads for shipment downriver. In October 1795, for example, Hunt sent five wagons full of merchandise from Philadelphia for delivery to his stores in Kentucky. On October 24, Mathias Vankirk's wagon left Pittsburgh loaded with two bales of muslin, two cases of dry goods, a chest of tea, and a hogshead of brandy. On the 26th, John Hack departed with four casks of wine, a bale of dry goods, a keg of shot, two crates of Queens ware china, two boxes of wool cards, a keg of alum, kegs of Morocco red and Turkey red dyestuff, and six trunks, two cases, a bale, and a tierce* of dry goods. William Graham left on the 28th carrying a hogshead of port wine, eight boxes of glass and china, and four trunks and a case of dry goods. That same day Elisha Phipps set out with two tierce of sugar and coffee, three boxes of linen, two barrels of snuff, two barrels of hats, a barrel of brushes, two boxes of wool cards, a keg each of ginger, indigo, brimstone, and shoe polish, and two tierce, four trunks, and a bale of dry goods. Finally, on October 29, Minshal Williams left Pittsburgh with four barrels of sugar, a case of looking glasses, a barrel of shoes, a tierce of dry goods, and three tierce of sugar and coffee.[39]

By the end of the decade, John Wesley Hunt's shipments of dry goods were even larger and his inventories more detailed (with notes indicating which commodities were especially fine or fashionable). The consumer preferences in Kentucky included imported men's cotton hose, plain or ribbed, in several colors, and silk hose in white, gray, or "fashionable" black. Men's gloves came in "fashionable silk," beaver, or white—women's in white, gray, "Black fashionable," and kid. Buttons arrived by the gross, plated or pearl, sized for coats or vests. For the gentlemen Hunt also stocked shaving boxes, razors, steel spurs and plated spurs, and the "best finished pen knives."

For Kentucky households Hunt had frying pans and copper tea kettles, sets of cups and saucers, dozens of teapots, sugar bowls and creamers, glass and common salts, pint and quart bowls, pint and half-pint

---

*Two hogsheads = 3 tierce = 6 barrels = 12 kegs = 24.5 cubic feet.

tumblers, wineglasses, and pepper mills. He stocked reams of "good quality" writing paper and letter paper, English and American playing cards, four dozen "Webster's Spelling Books," seven dozen Bibles, and half a dozen copies of the "late edition of [Jedidiah] Morse's Geography." His inventories included bolt after bolt of imported fabrics. "Fine flannel" in red, scarlet, white, or yellow. Fine dimity and common dimity with narrow or broad stripes. Cotton gingham in checks, stripes, and "apron check." Bed ticking and "fine diaper" fabric, two dozen assorted tablecloths, yards of Irish and German sheeting, "jaconet suitable for cravats," and "Black Sprig or Spotted gauze (for Vails)." Homespun fabric was for "none but the inferior inhabitants." The ladies of Louisville wove and exported 2,588 yards of country linen in 1801, but they used their income to buy stylish fabrics imported by merchants like John Wesley Hunt.[40]

An invoice from the Pittsburgh Glass Works described a consignment of six boxes of window glass, thirty-one dozen porter bottles, eight dozen half-gallon bottles, four dozen quart and pint bottles, and an assortment of jars "filling up the above boxes." Then there were the books. Invoice and shipping list "No. 19" from Philadelphia publisher and bookseller Mathew Carey to John Wesley Hunt began with two copies of Dr. Samuel Johnson's *Dictionary*. Eight large pages and two hundred forty titles later it ended with the Reverend Richard Baxter's *Saints Everlasting Rest* (probably the 1790 American abridgment edited by John Wesley). In between were novels and sermons, the Abbé Raynal's *Indies*, Buffon in an abridged quarto edition, John Locke's *Essays*, six copies each of Thomas Paine's *Age of Reason* and Thomas Jefferson's *Notes on the State of Virginia* and eighteen of Daniel Defoe's *Robinson Crusoe*. Hunt also had four copies of Richard Steele's prescriptive *Ladies' Library* and three of Susanna Rowson's sentimental *Fille de Chambre*, but six copies of Mary Wollstonecraft's *Vindication of the Rights of Woman*, with its dedication to "M. Talleyrand-Périgord, late bishop of Autun" (and author of the inclusive language of Article VI of the Declaration of the Rights of Man and Citizen). If the shelves of books that John Wesley Hunt offered his customers in Lexington, Kentucky, are any indication, the manly frontier days of a log cabin, a carbine, and a sack of maize were long past.[41]

The wealth amassed by John Wesley Hunt paid Benjamin Henry Latrobe to design Hopemont (now the Hunt-Morgan House on Gratz Park in Lexington) in the neoclassical style. It also supported his acquisition of the English thoroughbreds Baronet, Paymaster, and Royalist, which were standing stud on his Fayette County farm as early as 1803.

Perhaps the west's first millionaire ran a more successful commercial network than his rivals because his partners were family. Hunt's parents, Mary and Abraham, a miller in Trenton, New Jersey, who bred horses on the side, watched prosperity embrace their four older boys and tuberculosis claim their four younger children. John Wesley's elder brothers Pearson and Wilson worked the wholesale trade and shipping in Philadelphia, while his younger brother Theodore chose a career in the navy. As chronic illness claimed his other siblings, John Wesley Hunt did business with his cousins. Jesse Hunt traded out of Cincinnati, and Jeremiah Hunt was his uncle's agent in Detroit. Abijah started as John Wesley's partner in Lexington and in 1798 opened the partners' store in Natchez, a pivotal location for their export trade to New Orleans.[42]

Coin and currency always being in short supply, only 15 percent of John Wesley Hunt's customers paid for their purchases in cash. Seventeen out of twenty of his Lexington clients settled their accounts in "country produce," merchandise that Hunt exported by river to New Orleans, as did countless other western merchants. Flatboats carried their flour, tobacco, hemp, beef, pork, whiskey, butter, and other commodities to buyers downriver. The income generated by this Kentucky and Tennessee produce was then transferred on merchants' accounts with businessmen in Philadelphia, Baltimore, and other eastern cities. There, it bought American and British manufactured goods that men like John Wesley Hunt shipped over the mountains to Kentucky and Tennessee, where the cycle of commerce started anew. The shipments of flour alone exceeded eighty thousand barrels in 1801, a trade valued at $2.6 million. By the beginning of the new century, 70 percent of this export trade was transported in American ships: of 265 vessels that cleared the port of New Orleans in 1802, 158 were American, 104 were Spanish, and 3 were French.[43] Regardless of the Bay State's earlier disdain for the trans-Appalachian west, Timothy Pickering, Rufus King, and their maritime friends in New England had learned to care about Louisiana and the Mississippi River because what was good for Kentucky was good for the American merchant marine.

The publication in 1799 of Talleyrand's National Institute lecture, *Essai sur less Avantages à Tirer de Colonies Nouvelles dans Circonstances Présentes,* testified not only to its merits but to its author's return to the highest levels of French political life. On July 18, 1797, two weeks after his second lecture, the Directory had invited Talleyrand to become its foreign minister. In that capacity, Talleyrand quickly developed a working relationship with Napoleon rooted both in their shared interest in the conquest of Egypt and their mutual contempt for the Directory. Briefly forced from office by critics of his greed for bribes in what Americans called the XYZ Affair, Talleyrand was prominent among the conspirators who overthrew the Directory on November 9–10, 1799 (18–19 Brumaire) and established Bonaparte as first consul. Within days Talleyrand was reinstated as minister of foreign affairs. "He understands the world," Bonaparte said. "He knows thoroughly the courts of Europe; he has *finesse* to say the least of it; [and] he never shows what he is thinking."[44]

With slight differences in emphasis, Talleyrand's and Bonaparte's interests in colonies coincided. Both recognized their utility as pawns in the game of imperial warfare and diplomacy. The former bishop of Autun also valued colonies as a social safety valve, a place for malcontents to harmlessly exert and exhaust themselves. Napoleon was chiefly interested in their wealth and their produce—especially the sugar of St. Domingue.

Long a luxury enjoyed only by royalty, sugar by the end of the eighteenth century had become a staple in the European diet. Like flour, its scarcity had occasioned riots in Paris as early as January 1792 when its market price soared within weeks from 22 to 25 sous to 3 to 3½ livres per pound. Parisian crowds blamed both the shortage and the 280 percent spike in sugar prices on merchants and monopolists, whose shops and warehouses they raided. In fact, both were the direct result of the outbreak of civil war in St. Domingue, and more was at stake than sweets for angry housewives and their families.[45]

On the eve of the French and Haitian Revolutions, sugar processed in France and sold throughout Europe accounted for nearly 20 percent of the nation's exports. The slave plantations of Martinique and Guadeloupe, with some help from Saint Lucia, Tobago, and French Guiana, provided about 30 percent of the raw sugar for this massive French industry—but 70 percent came entirely from St. Domingue. When the Haitian Revolution and British warships cut off the supply of raw sugar coming into French ports, the industry utterly collapsed.[46]

When Bonaparte thought about colonies, he focused on the Caribbean, sugar, and St. Domingue. When he thought about Louisiana, his musings followed the arguments advanced by Eléonore Moustier's report in January 1789 and by French diplomats in their negotiations with Manuel Godoy's representatives at Basle in 1795, at San Ildefonso in 1796, and again at Madrid in 1798. The familiar argument had three main points: First, the produce of the Mississippi Valley could support French sugar, coffee, and cocoa plantations in the West Indies. Second,

French possession of Louisiana would realign the balance of power in North America to the detriment of Great Britain and as a brake on American ambitions. Third (and the incentive for Spain's agreement), France could do a better job of defending Louisiana from the United States or Great Britain than could Spain.[47]

By the end of the century, Spain and France were in basic agreement about the retrocession of Louisiana. For Carlos IV and Queen Maria Luisa (deprived for the moment of the advice of Manuel Godoy, who had been forced into a short retirement from politics),[48] the only remaining question was, What could France offer Spain in exchange for Louisiana?

"Frankly," Godoy's temporary replacement, Mariano Luis de Urquijo, remarked to the Spanish ambassador in Paris,

> [Louisiana] costs us more than it is worth. In giving it to the French we would incur the disadvantage of a contraband trade into Mexico, but . . . it would be very useful to maintain a barrier between the [Americans] and ourselves—a barrier against their plans of colonization—by means of a nation like France.

Under the Directory, France had offered the most attractive swap that Spain could imagine, a promise to restore Gibraltar to Spanish sovereignty. The only hitch was that France did not own the strategic 2.3-acre rock that controls the straits between the Atlantic and the Mediterranean. England had captured Gibraltar in 1704 and the United Kingdom has held it ever since. Godoy had always declined this and other mere promises from France.[49]

On July 22, 1800, Bonaparte and Talleyrand instructed their ambassador to Spain, Charles Jean Marie Alquier, to reopen negotiations for Louisiana, and in August Bonaparte dispatched his confidant General Louis Alexandre Berthier as minister plenipotentiary to augment the mission. Within a month Alquier and Berthier found the right price for the retrocession. In exchange for Louisiana and six Spanish warships, Bonaparte offered to create a kingdom in north-central Italy for Maria Luisa's brother, Ferdinand, duke of Parma. On October 1, 1800, Spain secretly agreed to the Second Treaty of San Ildefonso ceding Louisiana back to France. A few months later, by the Convention of Aranjuez, signed on March 21, 1801, France took title to Louisiana and the fateful island of Elba in return for placing Prince Louis of Parma (the duke's son and Queen Maria Luisa's nephew and son-in-law) on the newly created throne of the kingdom of Etruria, which included Tuscany, Parma, Florence, and the principality of Piombino.[50]

The deal assuaged Maria Luisa's family interests, delighted Carlos IV with the expectation of shifting to France the cost of maintaining his American frontier (a drain of about $337,000 a year on the Spanish treasury). The treaty pleased the French because it opened the way for the revival of the French sugar empire in the Caribbean. Both nations agreed to keep the retrocession secret for fear that either the British or the Americans would react by capturing Louisiana before Bonaparte could take possession.[51]

With arrangements in place for the recovery of Louisiana, Bonaparte threw his energies into two visionary schemes. One was his intended conquest of England. The other was the recovery of St. Domingue. Both would require large and expensive seaborne expeditionary forces. To buy himself an interval of "maritime peace" to prepare for these invasions, Bonaparte signed a truce with Great Britain on October 1, 1801—one year to the day after the secret retrocession of Louisiana—that was confirmed on March 25, 1802, as the Treaty of Amiens.[52]

For America, the important by-product of these developments was a linkage between the fate of Louisiana and the fortunes of the French expedition against Toussaint L'Ouverture. Bonaparte's intended invasion of England never materialized, and his vision for the Caribbean would collapse with the defeat of his expedition by the rebellious slaves of St. Domingue. "Louisiana had been destined to supply the other colony with provisions, cattle, and wood," the consulate's secretary of the treasury, François Barbé-Marbois, wrote years later, "and as St. Domingo was lost to France, the importance of Louisiana was also diminished."[53]

## CHAPTER TWELVE

# The Embryo of a Tornado

*One of the greatest follies I ever was guilty of was sending that army out to St. Domingo. . . . I committed a great oversight and fault in not having declared St. Domingo free, acknowledged the black government, and, before the peace of Amiens, sent some French officers to assist them. Had I done this, it would have been more consonant with the principles under which I was acting.*

—Napoleon Bonaparte at St. Helena, September 4, 1817[1]

*There is on the globe one single spot, the possessor of which is our natural and habitual enemy. It is New Orleans, through which the produce of three-eighths of our territory must pass to market.*

—Thomas Jefferson to Robert R. Livingston, April 18, 1802[2]

M Y DEAR SIR," American diplomat William Vans Murray informed John Quincy Adams from The Hague on March 30, 1801, "I fear that we have another iron in the fire—that France is to have the Floridas and Louisiana!!!" A moderate Federalist congressman from Maryland prior to his appointment by President John Adams as minister to the Netherlands, Murray wrote that he was "endeavoring to ascertain the truth, but think, now, that there is great reason to believe it."[3] After five years of false reports and speculation about French designs in the Caribbean, it was not surprising that early hints of the actual retrocession of Louisiana were somewhat exaggerated. Spain, of course, had refused to surrender Florida and was at that moment doing its best to delay the surrender of Louisiana, too. Bonaparte had the secret Treaty of San Ildefonso in hand, but all the Spanish ministers who had negotiated the deal were out of power. The royal favorite, Manuel Godoy, was once again in charge.

Officially the Prince of the Peace was the commanding general of the

Spanish armies, a post he accepted after declining Carlos IV's invitation to resume his former position as chief minister. When Godoy had offered a list of alternate candidates, one Pedro Cevallos had caught the king's eye. Asked for his opinion of the man, Godoy responded, "He's my cousin by marriage."

"So much the better," the king replied. "I can then count on him not to reject your advice." For the next seven years Godoy ruled Spain through the office of First Minister Pedro Cevallos, who carefully heeded his counsel and routinely forwarded state papers to the royal favorite, even during the Portuguese campaign. Godoy also maintained an intimate correspondence with Queen Maria Luisa. "Do not imperil yourself too much," she pleaded. "Do not tire yourself. . . . Ah, Manuel, what battles my imagination conjures up!"[4]

Impatient to take possession of Louisiana, Bonaparte vented his anger at Godoy in a letter to his Spanish ambassador. "Tell the Queen and the Prince of the Peace," he warned, "that if they continue this system [of procrastination], it will end with a thunderbolt." Godoy countered by pressing for clarification of one important detail about the retrocession of Louisiana that his predecessor had left too vague in the secret Treaty of San Ildefonso and its conventions. At Godoy's behest, Pedro Cevallos formally requested a "guarantee not to sell or alienate in any manner the property and use of this Province." In reply, on July 22, 1802, the French ambassador assured Carlos IV that

> the desire of France in this respect is perfectly in conformity with the intentions of the Spanish Government, and the sole motive for entering Louisiana was the restoration of a possession which had constituted a part of French territory. I am authorized to declare to you in the name of the First Consul that France will never alienate it.

With that final assurance in writing, on October 15, 1802, Carlos IV signed at Barcelona a royal order authorizing the delivery of Louisiana to France.[5]

Godoy had been out of office when Carlos IV had naively accepted Bonaparte and Talleyrand's verbal promise never to sell Louisiana. Oral contracts, the saying goes, are not worth the paper they are written on, but Bonaparte's written assurances were not much better. Although sincere enough at the time, his pledge never to alienate Louisiana lasted about ten months.

·   ·   ·

"Pauline was the prettiest and also the worst-behaved person imaginable," one of Bonaparte's officers said of the first consul's promiscuous younger sister. "I'm on good terms with my brother," she proclaimed shortly after the coup of 18–19 Brumaire. "He's slept with me twice already." True or not, Pauline's lust was notorious and many of her liaisons were with men Bonaparte despised. "Before she left for Santo Domingo," one of them wrote, "there were no fewer than five of us in the same house sharing Pauline's favors. She was the greatest tramp imaginable and the most desirable."[6]

One afternoon in May 1799 during a lull in the Italian campaign, Bonaparte was working in his study in the Baroque palace of Montebello outside Milan when he heard rustling noises behind a folding screen in the next room. Rising to investigate, Bonaparte discovered Pauline in the embrace of Colonel Charles Victor Emmanuel Leclerc, a staff officer who had served with him since the siege of Toulon. A month later, on June 17, 1799, the handsome and promising young officer was married to Pauline. Along with a substantial dowry from her brother came a promotion in rank.[7]

On October 24, 1801—three weeks after the preliminary signing of the Treaty of Amiens brought temporary peace to the high seas— General Leclerc took command of a French expedition to recover St. Domingue. Gathering in the wings at Dunkerque were ships and provisions intended for a second expedition of four thousand men to take possession of Louisiana under the command of General Claude Perrin Victor.[8]

Delayed by foul weather in November, Leclerc launched his expedition on December 14, 1801, from the natural harbor at Brest, near the entrance to the English Channel at the westernmost tip of Brittany. With decent winds and the preliminary truce of Amiens in force, the warships of Leclerc's squadron crossed the Atlantic and reached the coast of St. Domingue without incident, luffing their sails off Cap Français on Monday, February 1, 1802. Augmented by ships carrying troops from other ports in France and the Netherlands—three thousand each from Rochefort and Toulon, twelve hundred from Nantes, fifteen hundred each from Cádiz and Flushing, a thousand from Le Havre, and eight hundred from Guadeloupe—Leclerc's invasion force was huge. Tobias Lear, the American consul at Le Cap and President Washington's former personal secretary, reported that forty-six ships carrying forty thousand troops had arrived and twenty-five more ships and another twenty thousand soldiers were expected.[9]

Since 1796, when he was hailed as the black Spartacus foretold by the

*Born of slave parents in 1743, the self-educated tactician and statesman Toussaint L'Ouverture began his rise to prominence as a physician to the insurgent army during the 1791 slave uprising against the French colonial regime in St. Domingue (Haiti) and soon became a leader of the black troops. After the National Convention abolished slavery throughout the French empire in 1794, he supported the French against British invaders and was promoted to general in 1795. By 1801, still professing allegiance to revolutionary France and its ideals of liberty, equality, and fraternity, Toussaint L'Ouverture had consolidated his own authority on the liberated island. Although his troops repulsed the expedition sent by Napoleon to reinstate slavery on St. Domingue, Toussaint L'Ouverture was captured by treachery, sent to France, and imprisoned high in the Jura Mountains near the Swiss border. He died there of cold and starvation on April 7, 1803—five months after yellow fever claimed the life of Napoleon's brother-in-law, General Charles Victor Emmanuel Leclerc, commander of Napoleon's disastrous Haitian expedition.* (Courtesy Library of Virginia)

Abbé Raynal, Toussaint L'Ouverture had professed a consistent loyalty to republican France, which had abolished slavery throughout its territories two years earlier. Watching the arrival of Leclerc's flotilla from the hills above the capital, L'Ouverture's well-grounded suspicions of Napoleon's intentions grew stronger. Why send such a force if one's intentions were amicable? "Friends," muttered Toussaint L'Ouverture as he gazed at Leclerc's warships, "we are doomed. All of France has come. Let us at least show ourselves worthy of our freedom." In the city below, General Henri Christophe, the future president of Haiti, stood ready to torch the capital rather than surrender it to Leclerc.[10]

About noon on February 2 Leclerc sent a cutter into the harbor bearing copies of a proclamation from Napoleon. "Whatever may be your origin, and your colour," Leclerc proclaimed in the name of the first consul, "you are all Frenchmen, you are all free and equal before God and the Republic." Hoping to avert the loss of lives and property, including as many as seventy American merchant vessels in the harbor, Lear met with General Christophe the next evening. When Toussaint L'Ouverture had successfully turned back a British invasion, Lear reminded Christophe, he had frequently avowed that, so long as freedom was guaranteed to the blacks, "the Island belonged to France and they had a right to take it when they pleased." Christophe replied "in the most decided tone, that he could put no confidence in their declaration to confirm the freedom of the Blacks—that they meant to deceive him."[11]

For two days Leclerc's fleet hovered off Cap Français, "the wind so light that they did not attempt to come in," while oarsmen carried empty reassurances and stern warnings back and forth across the harbor and while citizens packed their treasures and fled to the country (or in the case of the Americans to the merchant ships anchored in the harbor). Christophe's orders from Toussaint L'Ouverture were no secret, and everyone knew that despite Leclerc's friendly rhetoric he had landed "a large body of troops" and taken Fort Dauphin, ten miles to the west. "Hostilities having commenced," Christophe advised Lear, his orders were to "oppose the entrance of the fleets—and that the first Gun fired should be a signal for setting fire to the town."[12]

Just before sunset on Thursday, February 4, two French warships moved toward Fort Picolett at the entrance to the harbor. "A shot was fired at her from the Fort, which was returned, and a short cannonading took place." Then came the sound of cannon fire from two small forts five or six miles away. "This firing was the signal for begining to set fire to the town and plantations in the plain and neighborhood," Lear wrote.

Our situation on board the Vessels gave us a full view of every thing which was done in every quarter. About seven o'clock the City began to blaze, and by ten it appeard to be inveloped in a general flame and exhibited an awful scene of conflagration.

"The destruction of the Town is far greater than in 1793," Lear wrote on Friday. "I judge there are not more than 70 houses . . . saved. The loss of property is total." Henri Christophe had set fire to Cap Français, but by carefully following Bonaparte's deceitful plans Charles Victor Emmanuel Leclerc ignited the war for Haitian independence and made it an especially vicious and dishonorable conflict—but one in which Toussaint L'Ouverture's countrymen did show themselves capable of freedom.[13]


The remarkably candid duplicity of the first consul's secret instructions to General Leclerc matched the fundamental lie upon which the entire expedition was based: in the name of the ideals of the French Revolution—liberty, equality, fraternity—forty thousand French troops were sent to reimpose the slave system of the ancien régime in St. Domingue. "In order to better understand the[se] instructions," Bonaparte wrote, "the time of the expedition should be divided into three periods." In the first two or three weeks, Leclerc was to land and organize his forces and acquaint "the mass of [his] army with the customs and the topography of the country." In the second phase, "the rebels are pursued to the death." In the final phase—to begin when generals Toussaint, Moïse, and Dessalines "no longer exist"—all scattered elements of their armies were to be "destroyed with time, perseverance, and a well contrived system of attack." Finally, "after the third period . . . the old pre-Revolutionary regulations [shall be] put into force." Plain and simple, Leclerc's overall objective was to turn back the clock and revive the slave-based sugar colony of the ancien régime.[14]

Deceit was a key element of the mission. "The conduct of the captain-general," Bonaparte wrote,

> will vary with the three periods above mentioned. In the first period, only the blacks who are rebels will be disarmed. In the third, all will be so treated. . . .
>
> All Toussaint's principal agents, white or colored, should, in the first period, be indiscriminately loaded with attentions and confirmed in their rank; in the last period, all sent to France. . . .

If Toussaint, Dessalines, and Moyse are taken in arms, they shall be passed before a court-martial within twenty-four hours and shot as rebels.

No matter what happens, during the third period all the Negroes, whatever their party, should be disarmed and set to work.[15]

Bonaparte never used the word *slavery* in his instructions to Leclerc—blacks were to be "set to work" and "the old pre-Revolutionary regulations put into force"—but this verbal deceit was in keeping with the entire racist tenor of the mission. "White women who have prostituted themselves to negroes, whatever their rank, shall be sent to Europe." And "any individual who should undertake to argue about the rights of blacks who have caused so much white blood to flow, shall under some pretext be sent to France, whatever his rank or services." In private, Bonaparte's attitudes were consistently racist. "The moment the blacks are disarmed and their principal generals deported to France," he wrote Leclerc in July, "you will have accomplished more for the commerce and civilization of Europe than has been done in the most brilliant campaigns." "I am for the whites," he told his Council of State, "because I am white. I have no other reason, and it is a good reason."[16]

Except for the burning of cities, plantations, and crops, at first Leclerc's invasion of St. Domingue went according to Bonaparte's plan. The French army moved inland from Le Cap on the north coast and Port Républicain (formerly Port-au-Prince) on the west, while Toussaint, Christophe, and the ruthless Jean-Jacques Dessalines waged a terrifying guerrilla war from the island's rugged hills. By the end of March, however, as Bonaparte's "first period" strayed into its eighth week, doubt began to blunt the revolutionary zeal of French troops dying in jungle ambushes at the hands of former slaves fighting for freedom and singing "La Marseillaise" and "Ça Ira." "Have our barbarous enemies justice on *their* side?" Leclerc's men wondered. "Are we no longer the soldiers of Republican France? And have we become the crude instruments of policy?"[17]

"I have tried several times to make Toussaint and all the generals surrender," Leclerc complained on April 21, but "I would not be able to adopt those rigorous measures which are needed to assure to France the undisputed possession of San Domingue until I have 25,000 Europeans present under arms." Five thousand of the seventeen thousand men he had brought ashore were dead, another five thousand were in hospital—and the rainy season was about to begin.[18]

At this critical moment, by lies and bribes and a clever ruse based on the fortuitous interception of rebel communications, Leclerc enticed Henri Christophe to change sides on April 26, with twelve hundred cavalry and a hundred cannon. His treachery changed everything for the moment. Early in May the Haitian Revolution paused. On the promise of freedom for all blacks and maintenance of rank for themselves and their officers, L'Ouverture and Dessalines made their peace with Leclerc.[19]

Despite these developments, the strength of Leclerc's army was waning fast as the rainy season brought yellow fever into play. "I have at this moment 3,600 men in hospital," Leclerc reported, "and no day passes without from 200 to 250 men entering the hospitals, while not more than 50 come out." Then, in compliance with Bonaparte's instructions, Leclerc arrested Toussaint L'Ouverture on June 7 and shipped him off to France. Imprisoned by Bonaparte in an unheated medieval dungeon at Fort de Joux, high in the Jura Mountains about fifty miles north of Geneva, the black Spartacus foretold by the Abbé Raynal succumbed to cold and starvation on April 7, 1803.[20]

Toussaint L'Ouverture's arrest and deportation began to peel away the deceitful veneer of Leclerc's expedition. "In overthrowing me, you have cut down in San Domingue only the trunk of the tree of liberty," the black general said as he was hustled aboard the frigate *Héros*. "It will spring up again by the roots for they are numerous and deep." Late in July, when the frigate *Cockarde* anchored in the harbor at Le Cap, any remaining doubt about Leclerc's secret intentions ended as news spread of Bonaparte's restoration of slavery in Guadeloupe.[21]

"I entreated you . . . to do nothing which might make [St. Domingue's blacks] anxious about their liberty until I was ready," Leclerc complained to Bonaparte early in August, but

> suddenly the law arrived here which authorizes the slave-trade in the colonies . . . [and] more than all that, General Richepanse has just taken a decision to re-establish slavery in Guadeloupe. In this state of affairs, Citizen Consul, the moral force I had obtained here is destroyed. I can do nothing by persuasion. I can depend only on force and I have no troops. . . . Your plans for the colonies are perfectly known. . . . This colony is lost, and once lost, you will never regain it. . . . My letter will surprise you, Citizen Consul . . . but what general could calculate on a mortality of four-fifths of his army? . . .
>
> The decrees of General Richepanse have repercussions here and are the source of great evil. The one which restored slavery, from hav-

ing been issued three months too early, will cost the army and the colony of San Domingue many men. . . . The rebels . . . die with an incredible fanaticism; they laugh at death; it is the same with the women.[22]

As yellow fever continued to ravage the French, who resorted to burying their dead after dark to conceal the extent of their losses, insurrection spread among the masses of St. Domingue. "Brigands," the French called them.

Christophe, Dessalines, and other Haitian generals stayed with Leclerc only because they distrusted one another, but his time was running out. An extensive plot discovered at the end of August, Leclerc reported, "was only partially executed for lack of a leader. It is not enough to have taken away Toussaint, there are 2,000 leaders to be taken away." The restoration of slavery in Guadeloupe revived the rebellion in St. Domingue. "One does not speak of rebellious blacks and peaceful blacks," a Spanish observer reported. "With the exception of the few who are in the domestic service of the whites . . . all the rest, including women and boys, are stubborn rebels."[23]

On October 11, Leclerc and his generals—French and Haitian, white, black, and mulatto—attended a reception held by his wife, Pauline, the first consul's sister. There at last the mulatto general Clairveaux broke the spell. "I have always been free," he said for all to hear, "but if I fancied that the restoration of slavery would ever be thought of, that instant I would become a brigand." Two days later he deserted Leclerc and rejoined the rebellion, as did Christophe and Dessalines. By mid-October the rebels controlled the countryside. The remnants of Leclerc's army—about two thousand men—held only the cities of Le Cap, Port-au-Prince, and Les Cayes. Of the thirty-four thousand troops Bonaparte had sent to St. Domingue, twenty-four thousand were dead and eight thousand were in hospital.[24]

Yellow fever finally claimed the life of Charles Victor Emmanuel Leclerc on November 2, 1802. That same day—at Archahaye, about fifteen miles north of Port-au-Prince on the western coast—Jean-Jacques Dessalines assumed overall command of Haiti's war for independence.[25]

Only the arrival of ten thousand reinforcements enabled Leclerc's successor, General Donatien Marie Joseph de Vimeur, vicomte de Rochambeau, to prolong the conflict for another year. Rochambeau's father had fought for liberty with Washington at the battle of Yorktown. The son was a vicious racist committed to a war of extermination against blacks and mulattoes. "To regain St. Domingue," he wrote, France must send hither 25,000 men in a body, declare the negroes slaves, and destroy at least 30,000 negroes and negresses—the latter being more cruel than the men. These measures are frightful, but necessary. We must take them or renounce the colony.[26]

Rochambeau combined techniques of mass murder from the Reign of Terror with the grotesque individual tortures of the island's slave regime. Sixteen of Toussaint L'Ouverture's former officers were chained to a rock at the harbor of Cap Français. Death claimed the last of them seventeen days later. General Maurepas, who had fought with Toussaint since the beginning, was tied to a mast and forced to watch the drowning of his wife and children while sailors nailed his epaulettes to his bare shoulders. Blacks were chained together and drowned by the boatload, torn to shreds by dogs, and hanged by the score. With greater dispatch and somewhat less depravity, Dessalines and his forces butchered French soldiers and white planters in similar numbers.[27]

Some three hundred fifty thousand Haitians of all colors died in the decade of carnage on Hispaniola along with as many as sixty thousand French soldiers. Napoleon's dream of a revived colonial empire in the Caribbean died with them. On November 28, 1803, Dessalines drove Rochambeau and the tattered remnants of the French expedition off the island and into the custody of a British fleet. A month later, on January 1, 1804, the Haitian republic established its independence.[28]

In March 1801 American diplomats began sending reports of the intended retrocession of Louisiana to Secretary of State James Madison. Since the fall of Robespierre and the collapse of Citizen Genet's western intrigues in 1793, rumors of a possible transfer of Louisiana from Spain to France had surfaced from time to time in the United States and in foreign capitals. As the new century opened, however, the military successes of Napoleon and his armies made the prospect of French intervention in North America more likely and more dangerous. The secrecy that cloaked Bonaparte's negotiations and preparations only increased American anxieties about the fate of New Orleans and the Mississippi.

The first hint of the intended retrocession came from Madrid, where the American minister David Humphreys reported a conversation with Lucien Bonaparte on the day after Napoleon's brother signed an agreement to create the kingdom of Etruria for Maria Luisa's nephew and son-in-law, Louis of Parma. *"To me,"* Humphreys correctly inferred, *"it affords an additional reason for believing the cession of Louisiana to*

*France."* A few days later Rufus King sent a similar message from the Court of St. James's, where he was monitoring developments on both sides of the Channel in the absence of a permanent American envoy in the French capital. "The opinion which at this time prevails both at Paris and London," King reported, was "that Spain has . . . actually ceded Louisiana and the Floridas to France." King also reported "that it is the opinion of certain influential Persons in France that nature has marked a line of Separation between the People of the United States living upon the two sides of the range of Mountains which divides their Territory"— an attitude that he and John Jay had expressed during the negotiations with Gardoqui in 1785 and 1786. Finally, taking note of a recently published French pamphlet advocating possession of Louisiana as a means to gain *"an influence over the United States,"* King worried "that this cession is intended to have, and may actually produce, Effects injurious to the Union and consequent happiness of the People of the United States." His sources indicated, in accord with Talleyrand's idea of using colonies as a safety valve for restless souls and malcontents, that Bonaparte was thinking of peopling Louisiana with veterans from his armies.[29]

By the end of May—as Robert Livingston arrived in Washington to confer with the president and secretary of state about his appointment as minister to France—Madison was describing "the Cession of Louisiana by Spain to the French Republic . . . as an event believed to have taken place." Owing to the secrecy that surrounded Napoleon's negotiations with Spain, however, no one could be certain about the retrocession or its terms. By November Rufus King had been able to obtain an unauthorized copy of the Convention of Aranjuez, which confirmed the cession of Louisiana. (He probably got it from the British, who were being asked by the French to acquiesce in the creation of the kingdom of Etruria.) Nevertheless, he was still trying to obtain a reliable copy of the secret Treaty of San Ildefonso, which "would enable us to determine whether [the cession] includes New Orleans and the Floridas."[30]

While Rufus King was carefully monitoring the French diplomacy from his station in London, his conversations with Robert Banks Jenkinson, Baron Hawkesbury, also eliminated any chance for conflict between the United States and Great Britain over Louisiana. On May 29, 1801, the foreign secretary invited King to visit him in Downing Street, where Hawkesbury "very unreservedly expressed" his nation's aversion to seeing Louisiana "pass under the dominion of France." Hawkesbury regarded the retrocession of Louisiana as nothing less than a reversal of the outcome of the Seven Years' War. "The acquisition might enable France to extend her influence and perhaps her Dominion up the Mississippi and through the [Great] Lakes even to Canada," while also threatening the security of British islands in the West Indies. Pleasantly surprised by Hawkesbury's candor, King responded by expressing his view of America's interests,

> taking for my text, the observation of Montesquieu "that it is happy for trading Powers, that God has permitted Turks and Spaniards to be in the world since of all nations they are the most proper to possess a great Empire with insignificance."

"The purport of what I said," King reported to Madison, "was, that we are content that the Floridas remain in the hands of Spain but should be unwilling to see them transferred except to ourselves." The result of this solid understanding between Rufus King and Baron Hawkesbury was Great Britain's quiet support for the American effort to acquire Louisiana.[31]

As they grew increasingly certain, despite French denials, that a retrocession of Louisiana *was* in the works, Americans quickly perceived the danger inherent in Bonaparte's preparations for the Leclerc expedition against St. Domingue. These American suspicions were more accurate than they knew. As soon as Leclerc could spare them, Bonaparte envisaged sending several thousand French troops ahead to Louisiana. That bright day never came, of course. The Haitian debacle swallowed up men and provisions originally intended for New Orleans. It also delayed, and ultimately aborted, a separate Louisiana expedition under the command of General Claude Perrin Victor.

Advance planning for the Louisiana expedition began in April 1801, and military and naval preparations commenced along the Dutch coast in the following spring. Bonaparte's instructions to his talented minister of marine, Denis Decrès, on June 4, 1802, outlined the essence of his plan. "My intention," the first consul wrote,

> is that we take possession of Louisiana with the shortest possible delay, that this expedition be organized in the greatest secrecy, and that it have the appearance of being directed on St. Domingue. The troops that I intend for it being on the Scheldt, I should like them to depart from Antwerp or Flushing. Finally, I should like you to let me know the number of men you think necessary to send . . . and that you present me with a [plan of] organization for this Colony.

More ominously, Bonaparte directed Decrès to plan "for the fortifications and batteries we should have to construct there in order to have a harbor and some men-of-war sheltered from superior forces." Equally revealing of the first consul's ambitions was his request that Decrès "have made for me a map of the coast from St. Augustine Florida to Mexico."[32]

By the end of summer, Bonaparte had chosen thirty-seven-year-old Lieutenant General Claude Perrin Victor, whose talents he had first noticed at the siege of Toulon in 1793, to command the expedition. Forty-five-year-old Pierre Clément Laussat, an attorney and minor bureaucrat who had avidly supported Napoleon's coup d'état of 18–19 Brumaire, was given the subordinate post of civilian governor, or colonial prefect, for Louisiana. In September the ships and material assembled at Dunkerque for the expedition were moved to Hellevoetsluis, near the mouth of the Rhine in the Batavian republic (the French puppet state imposed upon the Netherlands in 1795).[33]

On October 25 the long-awaited royal order signed by Carlos IV authorizing the transfer of Louisiana arrived in Paris. At the end of November, General Victor left Paris with all the necessary maps, cash in the amount of 881,631 francs, and secret instructions concerning the boundaries and defenses of the colony. "The French government wishes peace," Victor was told, "but . . . if war should come, Louisiana would certainly become the theater of hostilities." The first consul was counting on Victor and three thousand troops "to give Louisiana a degree of strength which will permit him to abandon it without fear in time of war, so that its enemies may be forced to the greatest sacrifices merely in attempting an attack on it."[34]

Now came the first of many delays. Vessels and men assigned to the Louisiana expedition had been redirected to St. Domingue. Victor's departure was postponed to December 22. When more problems arose, Decrès and Bonaparte rescheduled Victor's military expedition for February and decided to send Laussat ahead "to make all necessary preparations." From the port of La Rochelle on the Atlantic coast north of Bordeaux, Laussat and his family sailed for New Orleans aboard the thirty-two-gun brig-of-war *Surveillant* on January 10, 1803. The talented military engineer Joseph Antoine Vinache accompanied Laussat, but the rest of General Victor's expedition stayed behind as freezing weather closed the port of Hellevoetsluis through January and February. By mid-March, when the ice melted, a British fleet appeared along the Dutch coast, and April brought a storm that damaged several ships. These final delays proved fortuitous. Early in May, as the repairs to the fleet were nearly complete and the expedition once again made ready to sail, a courier riding hard from Paris brought a letter from Denis Decrès dated May 3, 1803, informing General Victor that his expedition had been canceled. Bonaparte had sold Louisiana, given up on St. Domingue, and was about to renew his war with Great Britain.[35]

From his post in London, Rufus King was the first American to alert the Jefferson administration to the preparations for the Leclerc and Victor expeditions. "It is confidently believed," he wrote on October 31, 1801, "that a considerable Expedition composed of land and Sea forces, is preparing in france, and will soon proceed to St. Domingo, and perhaps to the mississippi." This development, King thought, underscored the importance of reestablishing America's diplomatic presence in Paris.[36]

America had been without an ambassador in Paris since the departure of James Monroe in 1796. The French Directory had not only refused to receive Monroe's designated replacement, Charles Cotesworth Pinckney. It had expelled the South Carolinian while simultaneously unleashing French privateers against American commercial shipping in the naval Quasi-War that persisted from 1797 to 1800. In the last months of his presidency (and the first weeks of Bonaparte's consulship), John Adams had negotiated a peace settlement in a selfless act of statesmanship that split the Federalist party and doomed his own hopes for a second term. As a result of the Convention of 1800 between the United States and France, when Thomas Jefferson took the oath of office on March 4, 1801, he could pledge his country to "peace, commerce, and honest friendship with all nations, entangling alliances with none."[37]

Despite his early admiration for the French Revolution, his fondness for Paris, and his taste for French cuisine and culture, Jefferson knew that his "countrymen have divided themselves by such strong affections, to the French and the English, that nothing will secure us internally but a divorce from both nations; and this must be the object of every real American." Jefferson and his countrymen were comfortable with their Spanish neighbors. Regardless of French denials, evasions, and secrecy, the new administration and its diplomats continued the guessing game about the retrocession of Louisiana and the goals of the Leclerc and Victor expeditions while President Jefferson weighed his options in light of changing circumstances and reports from abroad.[38]

Throughout the first year of his presidency, Jefferson prepared himself for the worst. Conversations with his French friend Pierre Samuel Du Pont de Nemours, who had fled Paris under the Directory and helped establish the family's gunpowder factory in Wilmington, Dela-

ware, helped the president clarify his thoughts about the problem of
Louisiana. The occasion of Du Pont's return to France in the spring of
1802 gave Jefferson a back-channel opportunity to warn Bonaparte of his
new policies. "The inevitable consequences of their taking possession of
Louisiana," he advised Du Pont, "will cost France, and perhaps not very
long hence, a war which will annihilate her on the ocean." Europeans
were prone to think that they alone had "any right in the affairs of
nations," Jefferson cautioned.

> But this little event, of France's possessing herself of Louisiana . . .
> this speck which now appears as an almost invisible point in the hori-
> zon, is the embryo of a tornado which will burst on the countries on
> both sides of the Atlantic and involve in its effect their highest des-
> tinies. . . . Peace and abstinence from European interference are our
> objects, and so will continue while the present order of things in
> America remain uninterrupted.

"That [war] may yet be avoided is my sincere prayer," Jefferson declared
to Du Pont, "and if you can be the means of informing the wisdom of
Buonaparte of all its consequences, you will have deserved well of both
countries." Jefferson knew the ways of diplomacy, and he was counting
on Pierre Du Pont to convey a virtual ultimatum to Bonaparte—an ultimatum disguised as a private letter of advice to a friend. "You know too
how much I value peace," Jefferson reminded Du Pont, "and how unwillingly I should see any event take place which would render war a necessary resource." When things really mattered, Jefferson's words must
be read as carefully as they were written: he would go to war unwillingly
to keep France from taking Louisiana, but he was not unwilling to go
to war.[39]

Lest there be any doubt of the back-channel diplomatic character of
Jefferson's letter, it is important to recognize that Du Pont was in Washington at the time, and that the president entrusted his ultimatum
directly to Du Pont along with a letter he wanted him to deliver in person
to Chancellor Robert R. Livingston, the American ambassador in Paris.
Jefferson's instructions were explicit and detailed.

> You will perceive the unlimited confidence I repose in your good
> faith . . . when you observe that I leave the letter for Chancellor Liv-
> ingston open for your perusal. The first page respects a cypher, as do
> the loose sheets folded with the letter. They are interesting to him and
> myself only, and therefore are not for your perusal. It is the 2d 3d and

4th pages which I wish you to read . . . completely, and then seal the letter with wafers stuck under the flying seal that it may be seen by no body else if any accident should happen to you. I wish you to be possessed of the subject, because you may be able to impress on the government of France the inevitable consequences of their taking possession of Louisiana.

Jefferson closed his letter with "one more request, that you deliver the letter to Chancellor Livingston with your own hands, and moreover that you charge Mad[am]e Dupont, if any accident happens to you, that she deliver the letter with her own hands. If it passes thro' only hers and yours, I shall have perfect confidence in its safety." When Du Pont sailed for France aboard the *Virginia Packet,* he would be carrying a message of the utmost importance.[40]

"The cession of Louisiana," Jefferson advised Livingston, "completely reverses all the political relations of the United States, and will form a new epoch in our political course." Of the world's major nations, Jefferson had regarded France as the one that shared America's common interests, "our natural friend . . . with which we never could have an occasion of difference." That had utterly changed. "There is on the globe one single spot," he wrote,

the possessor of which is our natural and habitual enemy. It is New Orleans, through which the produce of three-eighths of our territory must pass to market, and from its fertility it will ere long yield more than half of our whole produce, and contain more than half of our inhabitants. France, placing herself in that door, assumes to us the attitude of defiance.

Spain could have retained Louisiana "quietly for years," Jefferson told Livingston. In Spain's "feeble state," he thought "her possession of the place would be hardly felt by us." In due time (as he had advised Archibald Stuart from Paris sixteen years earlier) events were certain to force the Spanish to trade Louisiana to the United States as "the price of something of more worth to her." But "not so . . . in the hands of France."[41]

In French hands, Louisiana would become "a point of eternal friction with us." The retrocession of Louisiana

render[ed] it impossible that France and the United States can continue long friends. . . . They, as well as we, must be blind if they do not see this; and we must be very improvident if we do not begin to make arrangements on that hypothesis.

The day that France takes possession of New Orleans, fixes the sentence which is to restrain her forever within her low-water mark. It seals the union of two nations, who, in conjunction, can maintain exclusive possession of the ocean. From that moment, we must marry ourselves to the British fleet and nation . . . and having formed and connected together a power which may render reinforcement of her settlements here impossible to France, make the first cannon which shall be fired in Europe the signal for the tearing up any settlement she may have made, and for holding the two continents of America in sequestration for the common purposes of the United British and American nations.

Jefferson reminded Livingston, as he reminded Du Pont, that he was not eager for war: "This is not a state of things we seek or desire," he wrote, but "it is one which this measure, if adopted by France, forces on us." Nor did he fear the might of Bonaparte's armies, "for however greater her force is than ours, compared in the abstract, it is nothing in comparison of ours, when to be exerted on our soil."[42]

No one expected the Treaty of Amiens to last forever. If Bonaparte took possession of Louisiana, Jefferson warned, the United States would "necessarily" ally itself with Great Britain "as a belligerent power in the first war of Europe. In that case, France will have held possession of New Orleans during the interval of a peace, long or short, at the end of which it will be wrested from her."[43]

Bonaparte, Jefferson suggested, should ponder the meager benefits that he could expect from a "few years' possession of New Orleans." In time of peace, France did not need Louisiana, for American merchants stood ready to supply her islands in the West Indies with all the provisions they required—and in time of war, French shipping "would be so easily intercepted." He encouraged Livingston to bring these considerations to the attention of the French government "in proper form," not as a threat but merely "as consequences not controllable by us, but inevitable from the course of things." France, he hoped, would "look forward and . . . prevent them for our common interest."[44]

There was only one compromise that Jefferson was willing to entertain. If France insisted on taking possession of the western watershed of the Mississippi, he ventured, "she might perhaps be willing to look about for arrangements which might reconcile it to our interests. If anything could do this, it would be the ceding to us the island of New Orleans and the Floridas." Only that could "relieve us from the necessity of taking immediate measures for countervailing such an operation by arrangements in another quarter"—a military alliance with Great Britain.[45]

From all reports, Jefferson knew "that the troops sent to St. Domingo, were to proceed to Louisiana after finishing their work in that island," and he knew, better than did Bonaparte, that "the conquest of St. Domingo will not be a short work. It will take considerable time, and wear down a great number of soldiers"—and this reality bought valuable time for negotiation. "Every eye in the United States is now fixed on the affairs of Louisiana. Perhaps nothing since the revolutionary war, has produced more uneasy sensations through the body of the nation." France has still enjoyed "a strong hold on the affections of our citizens generally," Jefferson admitted. If Bonaparte came to his senses, peace and friendship might continue. If not, then war was "inevitable from the course of things."[46]

Jefferson again took pains to emphasize, as he had done with Du Pont, that his warnings were more candid and personal than Livingston's official correspondence with Secretary of State Madison. "I have thought it not amiss, by way of supplement to the letters of the Secretary of State," he said, "to write you this private one, to impress you with the importance we affix to this transaction." In closing he asked Livingston "to cherish Dupont. He has the best disposition for the continuance of friendship between the two nations, and perhaps you may be able to make a good use of him."[47]

The wily president was making good use of both men, for without mentioning the idea anywhere in his letter to Livingston, Jefferson was entrusting Du Pont with a tentative idea that the president was not yet ready to commit to paper, even in a private letter to his ambassador: perhaps the United States could buy New Orleans. As Du Pont saw it, the only way Jefferson could persuade "France to a friendly surrendering of her property" was through a "payment of money." Calculate the cost of a war, Du Pont advised.

> Consider what the most fortunate war with France and Spain would cost you. And contract for a part—a half, let us say. The two countries will have made a good bargain. You will have Louisiana . . . for the least possible expense; and this conquest will be neither [animated] by hatred nor sullied by human blood.

"It is my earnest advice that you place a good estimate on [New Orleans]," Du Pont urged, "even a liberal and generous one . . . calculated to impress a court." Once a price had been settled, arranging "the manner of payment . . . is a minor matter which would straighten itself out."[48]

When Pierre Du Pont sailed for Paris in May 1802, he carried Jefferson's private letter to Chancellor Livingston about the strategic importance of New Orleans as well as the president's secret thoughts about *buying* New Orleans. "Agreement as to the price is the main thing," Du Pont had assured Jefferson, "the rest of your instructions are easy to follow and will be followed exactly." Through the summer of 1802 Livingston and Du Pont, respectively, worked the official diplomatic channels of diplomacy and the informal networks around Bonaparte. By October they had a price in view: $6 million for "New Orleans and the two Floridas," with France reserving "for herself absolutely all other territory . . . situated on the right bank of the Mississippi." The negotiations for the Louisiana Purchase at last were under way.[49]

— CHAPTER THIRTEEN —

# Selling a Ship

*The cession of Louisiana is an excellent thing for France. It is like
selling us a ship after she is surrounded by the British fleet. It
puts into safe keeping what [France] could not keep herself; for
England could take Louisiana in the first moment of war, without
the loss of a man. France could neither settle it nor protect it: she
is therefore rid of an incumbrance that wounded her pride,
[while France] receives money and regains the friendship of our
populace.*

—George Cabot to Rufus King, July 1, 1803[1]

*The century which has recently expired . . . began with war, and
it terminated with war. Hence arises a melancholy reflection, that
a practice which, it might be supposed, could only exist in the
absence of civilization, has been found to prevail in an age of
refinement.*

—"Thoughts on the Opening of the Nineteenth Century," 1804[2]

PERHAPS IT WAS the family's Scots heritage that made Robert an
especially popular first name among the wealthy Livingstons of colonial New York. The colony's first Robert Livingston, an immigrant from
the Scottish border county of Roxburgh, had established himself as a
frontier merchant at Albany in the 1670s and married into the patrician
Van Rensselaer family. By his death in 1728 this great-grandfather of Jefferson's envoy to Napoleon was lord of the quasi-feudal Manor of Livingston, with one hundred sixty thousand acres stretching from the banks
of the Hudson River east to Massachusetts. Landed wealth and tenants
gave the Livingstons and their peers—De Lanceys, Van Rensselaers, and
Schuylers—preeminence in the society and politics of colonial New
York.[3]

The ambassador's grandfather, also named Robert, built his estate on the Hudson at Clermont, in Dutchess County, where in 1718 he christened his son, the ambassador's father and namesake, Robert Robert Livingston. The repetition was intended to distinguish "The Judge," as the envoy's father came to be known, from several cousins and uncles. Born in New York City on November 27, 1746, the younger Robert Robert Livingston, Jefferson's ambassador, was named for his father and known as "The Chancellor." He grew up in the city but spent his holidays at Clermont, where he was "very fond of country life, of shooting, and taking solitary walks with his gun." At King's College, now Columbia University, the future diplomat developed a close friendship with John Jay, who was a year ahead of him. Graduating in a class of eight in May 1765, Livingston presented a commencement address titled "In Praise of Liberty" at Trinity Church that won accolades from the *New York Gazette* for its "sublimity" and "graceful propriety." John Jay contrasted his friend's vivacity, self-confidence, and natural intuition about men and women with his own bashfulness and pride. Livingston, Jay thought, was "formed for a citizen of the world . . . [with] talents and inclination for intrigue."[4]

Admitted to the bar in 1770, Livingston practiced law in partnership with Jay and represented New York in Congress from 1775 through 1785, where he served with Jefferson on the committee appointed to draft the Declaration of Independence. In 1781 Livingston was chosen as America's first secretary of foreign affairs, where he worked closely with his old friend during Jay's diplomatic mission to Spain. A staunch supporter of the Constitution during New York's ratification contest, Livingston had the honor of administering the oath of office to President George Washington in 1789 by virtue of his position as chancellor of New York. Passed over for appointment by the Washington administration, however, Livingston soon aligned himself and his family with the Jeffersonian Republicans. He opposed Alexander Hamilton's funding program, "openly declar[ing] against these measures of the federal government which tend to introduce a moneyed aristocracy and to annihilate the State governments." Political differences also ended his friendship with Jay. Writing as "Aristides" in response to a nasty newspaper attack mistakenly attributed to his boyhood friend, Livingston denounced Jay as a man whose "cold heart, gradated like a thermometer, finds the freezing point nearest the bulb." The Chancellor fought vigorously against the Jay Treaty of 1795, and he ran unsuccessfully against Jay for the governorship of New York that same year.[5]

Livingston's premature retirement from national politics ended abruptly with Jefferson's election as president in 1800. "It is essential," the Virginian wrote him in December, "to assemble at the outset persons

*In addition to his role in negotiating the Louisiana Purchase, Chancellor Robert R. Livingston of New York financed Robert Fulton's experiments with the steamboat. Named for Livingston's estate on the Hudson River, Fulton's* Clermont *led to a new age of navigation on the Mississippi River. After his return from France, Livingston devoted the last years of his life to scientific agriculture. The title page of his* Essay on Sheep, *published in 1809, proudly listed its author's laurels as president of the Society for the Promotion of Useful Arts, member of the American Philosophical Society, president of the American Society of the Fine Arts, and corresponding member of the Agricultural Society of the Seine. Livingston died at Clermont on February 25, 1813.* (Collection of the author)

to compose our administration, whose talents integrity and revolutionary name and principles may inspire the nation at once, with unbounded confidence." Although Livingston declined Jefferson's first proffered nomination as secretary of the navy, just seven days after the House of Representatives confirmed Jefferson as president on its thirty-sixth ballot, Livingston accepted the post of ambassador to France. "No one," wrote the French chargé d'affaires, Louis André Pichon, "could receive this mission with qualities more apt to maintain and increase the good understanding which has just been re-established so happily between the two nations."[6]

Delaying his departure in accord with the president's wish to secure formal ratifications of the Convention of 1800 that ended the naval Quasi-War with France, Chancellor Livingston had ample time to explore every conceivable option in detail with Jefferson and Madison. Livingston knew the president's goals as well as anyone could when he sailed for Paris in October aboard the frigate *Boston*. Traveling with him were his wife, Mary Stevens Livingston, "a polite, sensible, well-bred woman," and their daughters Elizabeth Stevens Livingston and Margaret Maria Livingston, twenty and eighteen. Accompanying his immediate family were the girls' husbands (both of whom were distant nephews of the Chancellor), the secretary of legation, Thomas Sumter, a full complement of household servants, a mountain of trunks and suitcases, and a gaggle of livestock. "Poultry, hogs, sheep, and a cow and a calf," a sailor was told, "and they say that's not half." Lashed to the quarterdeck was Chancellor Livingston's carriage, its passenger compartment designated as a makeshift parlor for the ladies. Tucked safely among his papers were the usual credentials, but his most important diplomatic instructions— the result of several months' consultation with Jefferson and Madison— were entrusted solely to Chancellor Livingston's memory.[7]

Chancellor Livingston and his entourage arrived in Paris early in December and were greeted by the marquis de Lafayette, a frequent visitor to Clermont during the Revolutionary War, and François Barbé-Marbois, former chargé d'affaires to the United States and now Bonaparte's minister of finance. Livingston met with Talleyrand on the 5th, and was formally presented to the first consul on the 6th. Bonaparte asked Livingston whether he had visited Europe before. Livingston answered that he had not. "You have come," replied the first consul, "to a very corrupt world."[8]

Against a backdrop of routine consular business, including American claims for ships and property seized during the Quasi-War, Livingston became a full player in the American guessing game about Bonaparte's plans. There were three questions: Whether France had accepted Louisiana from Spain (which Talleyrand resolutely denied). Whether the Floridas were included in the cession that Talleyrand denied. And whether Bonaparte was sending troops beyond St. Domingue to secure New Orleans. Gathering intelligence about these matters, however, was incidental to Livingston's basic objective. Depending on how far things had gone with Spain, Jefferson wanted Livingston to persuade France to forgo the retrocession. Or, if it was too late for that, he wanted Livingston to persuade France "to make over to the United States the Floridas . . . or at least West Florida." Or finally, if the retrocession had not included the Floridas, he wanted France to persuade Spain to cede them to the United States. In short, Livingston's chief task was to press the American case against Bonaparte's ambitions in the Caribbean and Louisiana.[9]

As events unfolded between December 1802 and the spring of 1803, Jefferson, Madison, Livingston, Du Pont, and Monroe all would contribute to the American acquisition of Louisiana, with important support from Rufus King in London. Throughout the long and complicated process of diplomacy, however, it was Livingston who did the heavy lifting. With so many uncertainties in play, his written instructions had been perfunctory from the beginning. Jefferson had explained his goals in broad terms. He and Madison kept Livingston abreast of their reactions to changing situations, but they counted on Livingston to size things up in Paris and exercise broad discretionary powers if necessary. Livingston, in turn, kept them candidly informed of both obstacles and opportunities—and his constant communication with Rufus King prevented either Britain or France from sowing confusion in the American camp.

Affable in temperament, Livingston was also hard of hearing—a potential disadvantage in his dealings with the witty and inscrutably subtle Talleyrand. But the French minister's legendary knack for discovering and exploiting an opponent's weaknesses was nearly worthless in the face of Livingston's unusual self-confidence. Despite his firm attachment to republican values that Bonaparte regarded as dangerously Jacobin, Livingston was a Hudson Valley squire to the manor born, unruffled by the hauteur of the former bishop of Autun.

Talleyrand tried to keep the American minister at arm's length with trifling ploys—pretending all the while that France had no claim to Louisiana. Soon after arriving in Paris, Livingston suggested that France offer Louisiana in settlement of the nation's debts to American merchants. "None but spendthrifts satisfy their debts by selling their lands," Talleyrand objected. Then he added, after a short pause, "but it is not ours to give." Livingston found ways to work around him.[10]

No Frenchman was willing to admit that Spain's retrocession was in the works, so Livingston prepared a forceful memorandum addressing the question, "Whether it will be advantageous to France to take possession of Louisiana?" He had twenty copies of his memorandum privately printed. He sent one to Madison, and he sent copies to Talleyrand and Bonaparte. The rest he carefully distributed to influential men around the first consul. The genius of Livingston's pamphlet lay not in its obvious conclusion but in its careful demolition of Bonaparte's mercantilist vision of Louisiana as a breadbasket for the sugar islands. France "is no longer a republic," he advised Madison, "it is the government of one man whose will is law." In one respect Bonaparte's secrecy about Louisiana made Livingston's diplomatic task easier: if the retrocession had not been concluded, then his question was safely hypothetical.[11]

Since France, "like every other country, possesses a limited capital" for investment, "the sole object of inquiry should be, where can this capital best be placed? At home? In the islands? At Cayenne? In the East Indies? Or in Louisiana?" The question was *not* whether France should have "any colonies" but whether she needed Louisiana.

> France possesses colonies . . . and she is bound in good faith to retain and protect them. But she is not bound to create new colonies, to multiply her points of defense, and to waste [investment] capital which she needs both at home and abroad.

In arguments that fill fourteen printed pages and that echo Jefferson's suggestions, Livingston demonstrated that France did not need Louisiana in order to reap the benefits of St. Domingue. In peacetime the sugar islands could readily buy food, manufactured goods, cloth, wood, and other commodities on the open market. In time of war, however, "the mouth of the Mississippi will be blocked up and the planters of the French Colony [will] be reduced to the utmost distress."[12]

Nor could France expect to benefit by exporting its manufactured goods up the Mississippi into the western states. "Nothing could give birth to this idea," Livingston wrote, "but the most perfect ignorance of the navigation of the river; and of the wants of the inhabitants." French wines found no favor with "the palates or purses of the inhabitants," who preferred "their own liquors, cider, beer, whisky, and peach brandy; the last of which, with age, is superior to the best brandy of France." Glass, tableware, hardware, and dry goods all reached the west through Baltimore or Philadelphia "on cheap and easy terms," never by "the slow and expensive passage up the river against the current."[13]

"In a commercial view, the settlement of Louisiana shall not be advantageous to France, but, on the contrary really injurious," Livingston concluded. "In a political one, it will be found still more inconsistent with her interests." Here, too, Livingston put forward arguments that he had discussed with President Jefferson, taking care neither to "leave unsaid what truth requires to be spoken" nor to "give umbrage by freedom which haughty spirits may construe into menace." The United States and France "are so happily placed with respect to each other, as to have no point of collision," Livingston wrote, in yet another echo of his conversations with Jefferson:

> How strong, how powerful, should the inducement be that compels
> France to lose these advantages, and convert a natural and warm ally
> into a jealous and suspicious neighbor, and perhaps, in the progress of
> events, into an open enemy!

"If there is a situation in the world," Livingston warned, again echoing Jefferson, "that would lead to these melancholy consequences, it would be that of France in possession of New Orleans."[14]

In his cover letter to Madison, Livingston explained the purpose of his memorandum. "I have had several conferences on the subject of Louisiana," he reported, "but can get nothing more from them than I have already communicated," so "I have thought it best by conversation and by writing to pave the way . . . till I know better to what object to point." Talleyrand promised to give his memorandum "an attentive perusal after which . . . I will come forward with some proposition." As Du Pont had recognized, setting the right price was tricky, and Livingston hoped Madison could offer "some directions on this head and not leave the responsibility of offering too much or too little entirely at my door." Weighed against the costs of "guards and garrisons, the risk of war, the value of duties and [the revenue that] may be raised by the sale of lands," he ventured that the Floridas and New Orleans might be "a cheap purchase at twenty millions of dollars."[15]

The summer passed with few developments, for as Livingston told Rufus King in August, "every body of fashion is now out of town." By October, however, Livingston had opened a new channel around Talleyrand when he gave a copy of his printed memorandum to Joseph Bonaparte, the first consul's elder brother. "My brother is his own counsellor," Joseph confided to Livingston, "but we are good brothers . . . and as I have access to him at all times, I have an opportunity of turning his attention to a particular subject that might otherwise be passed over." At their next encounter, Joseph Bonaparte told Livingston that both he and the first consul had read Livingston's memorandum "with attention," and that Napoleon had told him "that he had nothing more at heart than to be on the best terms with the United States."[16]

While waiting for guidance from Jefferson or Madison about how much he might offer for New Orleans or Florida, in December 1802 Livingston concocted a scheme that required no money at all. In a series of conversations with Napoleon's elder brother, Livingston suggested that although Louisiana would be a ruinous burden for the French nation, it offered a lucrative haven for the Bonaparte family in the event of Napoleon's death. Napoleon could transfer sovereignty over Louisiana to the United States and transfer the ownership of its lands to his own family. Then the United States could buy half the land from the Bonapartes for, say, $2 million.[17]

Livingston's scheme was useful, and it was actually less bizarre than it may seem. Family interests, after all, had prompted Carlos IV to exchange Louisiana for the throne of Etruria for his queen's nephew—a deal that had been brokered by Napoleon's brother Lucien. The Bonapartes were not yet an imperial family, but they were beginning to act like one. "There are duties which a man owes to himself and his family," Livingston advised, "which ought not to be overlooked when they can be performed without the smallest injury to the public." Why not barter Louisiana to the United States to underwrite "the present splendour of your family," he asked Joseph Bonaparte, and "secure to your posterity a property [in America] which nothing attainable in France would in any degree equal."[18]

Regardless of the merits of his scheme, Livingston used it to keep Napoleon thinking about the arguments advanced in his memorandum about Louisiana while he waited for guidance from Jefferson about how much to offer and for what. Livingston's December conversations with Joseph Bonaparte also forced Talleyrand back into play. Talleyrand did not want Napoleon's brother taking the lead in foreign affairs, and he was not about to watch from the sidelines while anyone else explored lucrative opportunities for graft. In this respect, Livingston knew he had scored a direct hit when Joseph Bonaparte informed him, early in January, that all future negotiations about Louisiana must go through Talleyrand, "who alone could inform you of the intention of the government."[19]

Livingston also used his December conversations with Joseph Bonaparte to reemphasize the British threat. If France persisted in its efforts to reclaim Louisiana and the Floridas, her actions were certain to force America into an alliance with Great Britain. Livingston's personal Anglophobia and his affection for France were well known, but through his intrigue with Joseph Bonaparte he reminded Talleyrand and the first consul that his own republican sympathies, and those of his countrymen, had limits.

Livingston's conversations with Joseph Bonaparte in December had attracted Talleyrand's attention. Early in January he reinforced this message by openly conversing with the British ambassador about Louisiana and the Floridas. If France persisted, Charles, Earl Whitworth, reported back to his superiors at Whitehall, Livingston "gave it as his decided opinion that . . . it would have the immediate effect of uniting every individual in America, of every party, and none more sincerely than himself, in the cause of Great Britain." In light of Livingston's "known political bias" toward France, Lord Whitworth concluded that Britain would have "few enemies" in America if France took possession of Louisiana. Whitworth also noted "that the little intercourse which has arisen between [Livingston] and myself gives a considerable degree of jealousy to Mr. Talleyrand."[20]

During the autumn of 1802, before and during his conversations with Joseph Bonaparte, Livingston also advanced America's negotiating position in one additional, crucial way. Ever since they got wind of the secret Treaty of San Ildefonso, American officials had been striving to discover whether its terms provided for the retrocession of East and West Florida from France to Spain. In August 1802, Livingston discovered that "all the old French maps mark the river Perdi[d]o as the boundary between Florida and Louisiana." Livingston knew, of course, that the Perdido River (now the westernmost boundary of the State of Florida) marked the border between the Spanish provinces of East and West Florida. He now realized that Talleyrand's and Bonaparte's evasions about the retrocession of the Floridas derived in part from their inadequate knowledge of the geography of the Gulf Coast.[21]

Livingston, Jefferson, and Madison generally distinguished between "Louisiana proper" (by which they meant the western watershed of the Mississippi), and the city or isle of New Orleans east of the river and West Florida along the Gulf Coast. Perhaps as a result of their reliance on outdated maps, the French seem never fully to have understood the importance that the Americans attached to West Florida—that "narrow slip of very barren lands" that controlled the Alabama, Chattahoochee, Mobile, and Tombigbee Rivers, which extended north into the American frontier settlements in Tennessee and the Mississippi Territory.[22]

The Americans' superior knowledge of their own geography gave them a greater advantage over the French than Livingston or anyone else realized. Time and again the Americans targeted New Orleans and West

Florida as their chief objectives, while shrugging with indifference about the "immense wilderness" of the western watershed. Jefferson's letter to Livingston on April 18, 1802, sought "the island of New Orleans and the Floridas." His cover letter to Du Pont demanded "the cession of New Orleans and the Floridas" as the price of peace. Similarly, the news of Spain's intended retrocession of Louisiana to France had prompted Secretary of State James Madison to "turn the present crisis to [our] advantage" by directing Charles Pinckney, the American minister to Spain, to seek "a cession . . . of the two Floridas or at least of West Florida, which is rendered of peculiar value by it containing the mouths of the Mobile and other rivers running from the United States." America had plenty of land between the Appalachians and the Mississippi, and the nation had no need to fight for more. Western farmers and planters did need, and were prepared to fight for, secure access to the world market via the Mississippi.[23]

Until Livingston began his conversations with Joseph Bonaparte, the American objective was always limited, as Madison wrote in January 1803, to "a cession of New Orleans and Florida to the United States and consequently the establishment of the Mississippi as the boundary between the United States and Louisiana." The idea of extending the American territory beyond the Mississippi arose during Livingston's unscripted conversations with Joseph Bonaparte. In October 1802, when Bonaparte asked him "whether we should prefer the Floridas or Louisiana," Livingston replied that America "had no wish to extend our boundary across the Mississippi." America sought only "security," he said, "and not an extension of territory." As Livingston pitched his scheme to enrich the Bonapartes by the sale of American lands, however, he concocted the idea of an American colony north of the Arkansas River and west of the Mississippi. It could be justified as a buffer to protect French Louisiana from attack by British Canada, but its real purpose was to attract American farmers as the most plausible way to assure the Bonaparte family that Louisiana lands would quickly appreciate in value. Livingston dropped his quirky scheme when it had served his purposes and brought Talleyrand back into the game. Nevertheless, the idea of transferring land west of the Mississippi to the United States was a lagniappe first voiced in Livingston's conversations with Joseph Bonaparte.[24]

By early January 1803 Robert Livingston had everything in place for the success of the diplomatic mission that Jefferson had entrusted to him two years earlier. Bonaparte and Talleyrand knew exactly what Jefferson wanted—New Orleans, West Florida, and control of the Mississippi— and exactly why. They knew that Jefferson welcomed friendship between France and the United States. They also knew that if they took possession of New Orleans, America would regard France as its "natural and habitual enemy." With persistence and imagination over the course of many months, Chancellor Livingston had set the stage for the Louisiana Purchase, effectively conveying to the first consul and his advisors every subtle nuance of the strategy Jefferson defined in his famous letter of April 18, 1802. "Every eye in the U. S.," Jefferson had written, "is now fixed on this affair of Louisiana."[25]

As the new year began, American eyes were watching closely to see how Bonaparte would react to Livingston's overtures. They were watching, as well, to see how Bonaparte *and* Jefferson reacted to a flurry of recent events that brought Spain, France, Great Britain, and the United States once again to the brink of war.

On Saturday, October 16, 1802, Juan Ventura Morales, a zealous and headstrong forty-six-year-old career bureaucrat, hurled a stone into the Mississippi. He closed the port of New Orleans to Americans—an action that started a wave of indignation that reached Natchez on Monday, and then spread to Kentucky, Washington, and the capitals of Europe. "From this date," Acting Intendant Morales proclaimed on October 16, "the privilege which the Americans had of importing and depositing their merchandise and effects in this capital, shall be interdicted."[26] Since the age of twelve, when Morales started working as a clerk in the customhouse of Málaga on the Mediterranean coast, he had built a reputation for meddlesome efficiency. As acting intendant at New Orleans since 1796, Morales had demonstrated a strong antagonism toward Americans and a predilection for controversy. Often working at cross purposes with the Spanish governors, Morales was an inflexible secular counterpart to the self-righteous Père Antoine. "The intendant places more obstacles in my way than the enemy," Louisiana governor Manuel Gayoso de Lemos had complained in 1799, for "his unmitigated ambition forces him to intervene in military and political matters . . . [against] the true interests of the king."[27]

By the terms of Pinckney's Treaty of 1795, the right of deposit had been established at New Orleans for a period of three years. After 1798 the treaty permitted Spain to designate "another part of the banks of the Mississippi [as] an equivalent establishment." Morales's proclamation—which Gayoso's successor, Manuel Juan de Salcedo, denounced as "a direct and open violation of the Treaty"—asserted that the period of "privilege" could be extended no longer "without an express order of the King."[28]

Within two days, the news of Morales's suspension of what Americans regarded as their *right* of deposit, not privilege, had reached Natchez. From there it spread rapidly upriver to Kentucky and Ohio. By October 26 the news of the closing of the port had reached Lexington, Kentucky, and the following Wednesday it was on the front page of Frankfort's weekly *Guardian of Freedom.* "Whether this order was given by the Spaniards, or by the French," the *Guardian* reported, "was [a] matter of uncertainty," but after months of speculation about Bonaparte's intentions, many westerners were ready to believe the worst. Early in November rumors flew through the bluegrass country, embellishing the story of the closing of the port with claims "that a French army had actually taken possession of Orleans." The next Wednesday's *Guardian* happily contradicted that rumor, "on the authority of a gentleman late from Natchez," who assured the editor "that no army has arrived . . . but that the French would take possession of the Colony shortly." Newspapers throughout the west also buzzed with information from another gentleman "just arrived from Bordeaux, who stated that arrangements were making by France to take possession of the colony, with 10,000 troops" commanded by General Victor.[29]

More immediately alarming were the reports of Spanish officials turning away flatboats laden with cotton, which gave all Kentucky farmers reason to fear that their autumn harvests "will be in the same predicament." A subsequent letter stating that some boats arriving at the closed port were being allowed "to land their cargoes, on paying a duty," offered *Guardian* readers a moment for optimism early in December, until they read in the next column that the situation at Natchez was one of "very great and general consternation," with Americans and Spanish alike "much agitated, fully expecting a war."[30]

As American citizens and public officials scrambled to discover who had closed the port, and why, speculation quickly focused on Morales's motives. "It is said by some," the *Guardian of Freedom* reported on December 1,

> that this behavior proceeds from a grudge the Intendant bears to our countrymen—Others suppose that as avarice has heretofore been his ruling passion, it still operates, and that nothing short of it could render him capable of such madness. Perhaps, say they, he has now received satisfactory information that the French will soon be possessors of this province, and he is determined to make the most of the little time that is left.

American traders in New Orleans doubted that any Spanish official would initiate so drastic a measure without explicit instructions. Morales was "too rich, too sensible and too cautious to take such responsibility on himself," the unofficial American consul in New Orleans believed, and had often expressed his indifference to "the consequences of measures which he undertook in compliance with orders."[31]

It took five weeks for news of the New Orleans crisis to reach Washington, but as soon as it arrived Jefferson and Madison adopted the position that Morales had acted on his own. Only a prompt reopening of the port could dissuade the western states from marching on New Orleans as they had been ready to do many times in the past. Since it is easier for a sovereign to disavow an overzealous subordinate than to be seen reversing his own policy, ascribing the closing of the port to a maverick Spanish bureaucrat gave the Jefferson administration room for diplomatic and political maneuvering toward a peaceful resolution of the crisis.

The closing of the port "is so direct and palpable a violation of the Treaty of 1795," Madison wrote, "that in candor it is to be imputed rather to the Intendant solely, than to instructions of his Government." Equally surprised by the proclamation, the Spanish ambassador in Washington had hastily assured Madison that Morales had overstepped his authority, while firsthand reports from New Orleans indicated "that the Governor did not concur with the Intendant" either. On the other hand, Kentucky's *Guardian of Freedom* regarded the text of Morales's proclamation itself as convincing "evidence that the shutting the port of New Orleans was not an act of the Intendant's, but of the Spanish government"—and the *Guardian's* editor called upon the president and Congress to do everything in their power to avenge the "insult" and "redress the grievance thus created."[32]

"From whatever source the measure may have proceeded," Madison advised Charles Pinckney, the American envoy to Spain, "the President expects that the Spanish Government will neither lose a moment in countermanding it, nor hesitate to repair every damage which may result from it." The wrath of America's western citizens, Madison believed,

> is justified by the interest they have at stake. The Mississippi is to them every thing. It is the Hudson, the Delaware, the Potomac, and all the navigable rivers of the atlantic states formed into one stream. The produce exported through that channel last year amounted to $1,622,672 from the Districts of Kentucky and Mississippi [alone], and will probably be fifty per cent more this year . . . a great part of

which is now or shortly will be afloat for New Orleans and consequently exposed to the effects of this extraordinary exercise of power.

After writing to Pinckney, Madison also met with the French chargé d'affaires, Louis André Pichon. It was anyone's guess, he warned Pichon,
what the five or six thousand Americans who were at that moment floating their harvest downriver might do when they reached New Orleans
and found the port closed to their exports. "We have rumours flying
through the woods from Pensacola to St. Louis," General James Wilkinson informed Kentucky senator John Brown, "that inflame our latent
combustibility." Unless the port is quickly reopened, "our citizens will
*kick up a dust,*" James Morrison wrote from Lexington to Virginia senator
Wilson Cary Nicholas. "They already *talk of war.*" Kentucky was "all in a
Hubbub," Robert Barr advised Kentucky senator John Breckinridge, "all
ready and waiting to step on board and sail down and take possession of
New Orleans."[33]

With French troops expected to arrive in New Orleans at any
moment, the timing of the Spanish intendant's action was especially
alarming. Many Americans jumped to the conclusion that Bonaparte had
pressured Spain to close the port. Northern Federalists began clamoring
for war—less because they cared about Louisiana than because their
enemy would be France. Congressman John Stratton, of Northampton
County on Virginia's Eastern Shore, reflected the exasperation of southern Federalists when he decried "the timidity of our executive in meeting
this flagrant violation of our Treaty with Spain." New Orleans could be
taken by "the Kentucky Militia alone," Stratton exclaimed. "No better
opportunity ever can occur for furnishing . . . a pretext for seizing the
East Bank of the Mississippi." Stratton and other southern Federalists
believed that "Securing perminantly the free Navigation of that River"
was "all important to America." Angry westerners were in full agreement.
They were ready to oust "the reptile Spaniards" from New Orleans before
Bonaparte took possession.[34]

With demands for war coming from either side, the Jefferson administration upheld the convenient fiction that Juan Ventura Morales's revocation of the American right of deposit and closing of the port of New
Orleans was simply a colossal blunder by one overzealous, avaricious,
bigoted, and probably stupid colonial official. A colossal but perhaps
reversible blunder.

Withdrawing the American right of deposit may have been short-
sighted, but it was not the work of a maverick local official. On July 14,
1802, the order to close the port had been issued by Carlos IV himself, as

Daniel Clark and other New Orleanians suspected that autumn. Earlier that spring Intendant Morales and other colonial officials had complained to the ministers of the Spanish treasury that Americans were abusing the right of deposit and heavily engaged in smuggling. Upon the advice of his chief minister, Pedro Cevallos (Manuel Godoy's successor and cousin by marriage), Carlos IV had secretly directed the intendant of Louisiana to prohibit the deposit of American goods in New Orleans—and Carlos had specifically instructed Morales not to justify his action as "the order of the king." Instead, he was to pretend that he had reviewed the terms of Pinckney's Treaty on his own initiative "and found that the limit of three years fixed by article XXII bound his hands so that he could not allow the introduction and deposit of American goods without the express permission of the king." By following his secret instructions to the letter, Juan Morales deflected responsibility from the king to himself so effectively that a full century passed before historian Edward Channing discovered and published the direct order from Carlos IV that precipitated the Mississippi crisis of 1802.[35]

Bonaparte was delighted when the news of Morales's proclamation arrived in a letter from his American envoy early in January 1803. By closing the port, Talleyrand wrote to his ambassador in Madrid, "Spain had taken a step equally in accordance with its rights and with the interests of France." The American right of deposit was incompatible with Bonaparte's plans to nurture trade between Louisiana and the French West Indies, "replace" the Americans, and "concentrate [Louisiana's] commerce into the national commerce." The first consul and his foreign minister welcomed Morales's proclamation as a measure that would curb American competitors and encourage French commerce. The closing of the port, however, was the only bit of good news from the New World that reached Bonaparte that winter.[36]

During the first week of January 1803, as troops assigned to reinforce General Charles Leclerc in St. Domingue waited in the cold at Hellevoetsluis, news of General Leclerc's death on November 2—and of the catastrophic losses and dismal failure of the Caribbean expedition—reached the first consul. Bonaparte's dream of reviving the French sugar empire in the West Indies died with his brother-in-law. His anger burst forth after a dinner party on Wednesday, January 12—just two days after Pierre Clément Laussat and the *Surveillant* cleared the harbor at La Rochelle for New Orleans. "Damn sugar, damn coffee, damn colonies!" Bonaparte exclaimed. (These were the "exact words of the First Consul,"

Pierre Louis Roederer, director general of public education, noted in his diary.)[37]

At the end of January the government newspaper in Paris, *Le Moniteur*, published a story hinting that the first consul was turning his attention to the east and thinking about reconquering Egypt. Great Britain reacted promptly to this threatened breach of the year-old Treaty of Amiens, by which Great Britain had promised to surrender the island of Malta to France and Bonaparte had agreed to return Egypt to the Ottoman Turks. On March 2, George III informed Parliament of Bonaparte's "very considerable military preparations . . . in the ports of France and Holland." The king advocated "additional measures of precaution" against the possibility, which Bonaparte was in fact entertaining, that the French troops and vessels assembled for Louisiana and St. Domingue might be redirected toward an invasion of England. As the ice melted in the harbor of Hellevoetsluis, British warships moved into the English Channel, trapping General Victor's forces in their harbors as they made ready for war.[38]

On Sunday afternoon, March 12, Chancellor Livingston and the foreign diplomatic corps attended a salon held by Josephine Bonaparte. "After going the usual round of Ladies in one room," her husband exchanged a few polite words with Livingston, a few more with the Danish ambassador, "and then went to the other end of the room . . . and went up to Lord Whitworth," the British ambassador. Bonaparte told Whitworth "that they would probably have a storm." Whitworth replied that he "hoped not."

"I find, my Lord, your nation wants war again," said Bonaparte.

"No, sir," Whitworth replied, "we are very desirous of peace."

"You have just finished a war of fifteen years," Bonaparte said.

"It is true, sir, and that was fifteen years too long," Whitworth replied.

"But you want another war of fifteen years," Bonaparte asserted.

"Pardon me, sir," Whitworth replied, "we are very desirous of peace."

Bonaparte then expressed "a few more very strong terms evoking the vengeance of heaven upon those who broke the treaty."

"I must either have Malta or war," he declared. Then, being told that "Madame B[onaparte] and the ladies in the next room expected him," Bonaparte departed.[39]


The United States had recoiled in republican indignation at Talleyrand's insistence upon substantial bribes in the XYZ Affair, so when Robert Livingston tempted the first consul's elder brother with the idea of giving the

*Napoleon Bonaparte, about 1803—a character study of genius and hubris. Jefferson regarded Bonaparte as "a great man" until the coup d'état of 18–19 Brumaire, and thereafter "set him down as a great scoundrel only." Talleyrand, who initially opposed the Louisiana Purchase in the hope of diverting him from another war in Europe, wrote that "I served Bonaparte while he was emperor as I had served him when he was Consul . . . so long as I could believe that he himself was devoted to the interests of France. But as soon as I saw him beginning to undertake those radical enterprises which were to lead him to his doom, I resigned my ministry. For this, he never forgave me." Exiled on the island of Elba, where he died on May 5, 1821, Napoleon described Talleyrand as "merde in a silk stocking."* (Courtesy Library of Virginia)

Bonaparte family land in Louisiana in exchange for American sovereignty, the scheme was as close to outright venality as any American official could come. Great Britain, on the other hand, had fewer qualms about bribery as an instrument of foreign policy.

Within days of the first consul's confrontation with Lord Whitworth at Josephine Bonaparte's salon, Joseph and Lucien Bonaparte sent an intermediary (a Swiss-born acquaintance named Bartholomew Huber who was familiar with officials in London and Paris) to suggest that in return for "a valuable consideration" the Bonapartes might be able to persuade their brother to relax his insistence on Malta or war. Whitworth immediately reported the proposal to the British foreign secretary, Robert Banks Jenkinson, Lord Hawkesbury. "I lose no time in informing you," Hawkesbury replied three days later, "that if an arrangement could be concluded which should be satisfactory to His Majesty, and by which His Majesty should retain the Island of Malta, the Sum of one Hundred thousand Pounds might be distributed as Secret Service."[40]

The sum of £100,000—worth about $16 million today—was indeed a valuable consideration, but with so many men around Bonaparte "partaking in the Pillage of this country," Whitworth determined that more money was required, especially if the British hoped to enlist Talleyrand's support. "I have no fixed Idea of what Sum may be necessary," Whitworth wrote on March 24, "but on calculating what we may expend in one month of War, the sacrifice of a Million, or even two Millions, would be economy." By the middle of April, the British were secretly negotiating with Joseph and Lucien Bonaparte, Talleyrand, and even Napoleon's fearsome chief of secret police, Joseph Fouché.[41]

In the end, the war was not averted and no money changed hands. Nevertheless, the British attempt to bribe Napoleon's brothers and ministers, which probably came to the first consul's attention through Fouché, underscored Talleyrand's and the Bonapartes' opposition to Napoleon's decision to sell Louisiana. Talleyrand, of course, had been advocating colonization since his lectures at the National Institute in 1797. He and Napoleon's brothers hoped that the first consul's projects in St. Domingue and Louisiana might divert his interest in Malta and Egypt. The attempted bribery also helps to explain both the famous bathroom encounter between Napoleon and his brothers as well as the first consul's eventual decision to negotiate with the Americans through his incorruptible finance minister, François Barbé-Marbois, rather than Foreign Minister Talleyrand.

The bathroom episode began one evening when Lucien Bonaparte came home to change clothes for the theater. Joseph was waiting for him. "Here you are at last," Joseph said, "I was afraid you might not come. This is no time for theater-going; I have news for you that will give you no fancy for amusement. The General wants to sell Louisiana."[42]

"Come now," Lucien replied, "if he were capable of wishing it, the Chambers would never consent."

"He means to do without their consent," Joseph answered. "What is more," he continued, "this sale would supply him the first funds for the war. Do you know that I am beginning to think he is much too fond of war?"—an opinion that Talleyrand shared. The brothers resolved to talk with Napoleon the next morning.

Lucien reached the Tuileries first, where he found the first consul soaking in a bath of rosewater. They exchanged pleasantries until Joseph arrived, whereupon Napoleon asked their opinion of his determination to sell Louisiana.

"I flatter myself," Lucien warned, "that the Chambers will not give their consent."

"You flatter yourself," Napoleon answered sarcastically. "That is precious, in truth!"

"And I flatter myself," Joseph interjected, "as I have already told the First Consul."

"And what did I answer?" Napoleon growled.

"That you would do without the Chambers," said Joseph.

"Precisely!" said Napoleon. "And now, gentlemen, think of it what you will; but both of you go into mourning about this affair—you, Lucien, for the sale itself; you, Joseph, because I shall do it without the consent of any one whatsoever. Do you understand?"

"You will do well," Joseph snarled as he stepped toward the tub, "not to expose your project to parliamentary discussion; for . . . I will put myself first at the head of the opposition."

Napoleon laughed scornfully. "You will have no need to lead the opposition, for I repeat that there will be no debate."

Months of relentless advocacy by Chancellor Livingston now paid off, as the first consul claimed the New Yorker's arguments as his own. "It is my idea," Napoleon declared as he rose from the tub. "I conceived it, and I shall go through with it, the negotiation, ratification, and execution, by myself. Do you understand? by me who scoffs at your opposition."

"Good!" Joseph shouted in a rage. "I tell you, General, that you, I, and all of us, if you do what you threaten, may prepare ourselves soon to go and join the poor innocent devils whom you . . . have transported to Sinnamary," site of the infamous prison colony near Cayenne in French Guiana.

"You are insolent!" Napoleon thundered as he fell back into the tub, dousing Joseph and Lucien with a torrent of rose-scented water.

Soaked to the skin, Lucien Bonaparte had the presence of mind to invoke the words of Neptune from Virgil's *Aeneid*,

I will show you . . . ! But no, first I had better set the waves at rest; after that you are going to pay dearly for your offence.

As Napoleon's valet fainted and fell to the floor, the three brothers regained their composure.[43]

After Joseph left to change his clothes, Lucien and Napoleon continued the argument. "Do you want me to tell you the truth?" Napoleon asked. "I am today more sorry than I like to confess for the expedition to St. Domingue." His decision to sell Louisiana stemmed from his realization that the dream of reviving the French empire in the Caribbean had indeed died with their brother-in-law General Leclerc. "Our national glory," Napoleon told Lucien, "will never come from our marine."[44]

The exact date of this conversation among the Bonaparte brothers is uncertain, and the incident itself may well be apocryphal. Nevertheless, by April 10, 1803, Napoleon had resolved to offer Louisiana to the Americans—and he would not be dissuaded. His timing was exquisite. Chancellor Livingston had put everything in order, and James Monroe had landed at Le Havre. He would arrive in Paris on April 12.

After mass on Easter Sunday, April 10, 1803, Bonaparte summoned Denis Decrès, minister of marine and colonies, and François Barbé-Marbois, minister of finance, to his palace at St. Cloud. A well-educated nobleman from the province of Champagne, Decrès had served with Admiral de Grasse in the West Indies and breached the British blockade at Malta during Bonaparte's Egyptian campaign. Gruff and authoritarian in his manner, hardworking and unswervingly loyal to the first consul, forty-two-year-old Rear Admiral Decrès was one of the few sailors to whom Bonaparte presented a sword of honor. For the previous two years he had been coordinating, with mixed success, preparations for the intended expeditions against St. Domingue, Louisiana, and now perhaps England.[45]

At fifty-eight, Barbé-Marbois was a career diplomat and administrator with a literary and scientific bent and proven affection for the United States. Serving in the 1780s as secretary to the French legation in Philadelphia and later as chargé d'affaires, he had worked with Livingston, Monroe, Jay, and many other American leaders. Barbé-Marbois

*During the final negotiations of the Louisiana Purchase in April 1803, Napoleon Bonaparte conferred with his principal negotiator, François Barbé-Marbois, on long walks in the gardens at St. Cloud, a few miles west of Paris. The palace was destroyed in 1870 during the Franco-Prussian War. Two miles northwest stands the seventeenth-century Château de Malmaison, Bonaparte's gift to Josephine in 1799.* (Collection of the author)

had compiled the twenty-two questions circulated to the thirteen American states that inspired Thomas Jefferson to compose his *Notes on the State of Virginia* in answer to his queries. In 1784 he had married Elizabeth Moore, daughter of the president of Pennsylvania's executive council. Although he had never seen Louisiana, Barbé-Marbois had traveled north to the Mohawk River in upstate New York. He had also served four years as Louis XVI's last intendant in St. Domingue, where "the ability and the virtue he practices in both public and private life" earned him "a host of enemies in the colony."[46]

A moderate in the French Revolution, Barbé-Marbois was exiled during the Terror and then imprisoned by the Directory for twenty-six months at Sinnamari and Cayenne, in French Guiana. Returning to France after the coup d'état of 18–19 Brumaire, Barbé-Marbois took charge of the public treasury in February 1801. Recognized as "a man of talents and integrity," Barbé-Marbois worked closely with Bonaparte for the next five years, amazed by the first consul's "capacity for comprehending everything, [and] the quickness and depth of his reflections."[47]

✓ "I know the full value of Louisiana," Bonaparte told Decrès and Barbé-Marbois, "and I have been desirous of repairing the fault of the French negotiator who abandoned it in 1763." Nevertheless, he continued, effective French control of Louisiana would be threatened by the British navy in the event of war, so "I must expect to lose it." The British had twenty ships in the Gulf of Mexico, Bonaparte said, "whilst our affairs in St. Domingue have been growing worse every day since the death of Leclerc." Rather than letting the British capture Louisiana, the first consul announced, "I think of ceding it to the United States."[48]

"They only ask of me one town in Louisiana," Bonaparte said, echoing the arguments that Jefferson had advanced through Livingston, "but I already consider the colony as entirely lost." Once again echoing the arguments he had read in Livingston's printed memorandum, Bonaparte concluded "that in the hands of this growing power, [Louisiana] will be more useful to the policy and even to the commerce of France, than if it should attempt to keep it."[49]

"We should not hesitate to make a sacrifice of that which is . . . slipping from us," Barbé-Marbois replied.

> War with England is inevitable; shall we be able with very inferior naval forces to defend Louisiana against that power? . . . Can we restore fortifications that are in ruins, and construct a long chain of forts upon a frontier of four hundred leagues?

The expense would drain French resources, Barbé-Marbois continued, again echoing Livingston's arguments, giving Britain "a secret joy in seeing you exhaust yourself in efforts of which she alone will derive the profit." Louisiana has been settled for one hundred years, the finance minister observed, borrowing yet another argument from Livingston, "and in spite of efforts and sacrifices of every kind the last accounts of its population attest its weakness."[50]

Admiral Decrès disagreed. "We are still at peace with England," he said, and "the colony has just been ceded to us." If peace continued, the sale of Louisiana would be seen as a "premature act of ill-founded apprehension," contrary to the honor of France. "There does not exist on the globe," the minister of marine and colonies asserted, "a single city susceptible of becoming as important as New Orleans." Its proximity to the American west already made it one of the most commercial ports in the world, Decrès asserted. "The Mississippi does not reach there till it has received twenty other rivers, most of which surpass in size the finest rivers of Europe." Gazing a century into the future, Admiral Decrès imagined the construction "at the isthmus of Panama [of] a simple canal . . . to connect one ocean with the other." Louisiana, he said, "will be on this new route, and it will then be . . . of inestimable value." If France were forced to abandon St. Domingue, he concluded, "Louisiana will take its place."[51]

Having heard the candid advice of his ministers, Bonaparte ended the conversation and the three men retired to their rooms.

Early Monday morning, April 11, Bonaparte sent for Barbé-Marbois. "Irresolution and deliberation are no longer in season," he declared.

I renounce Louisiana. It is not only New Orleans that I will cede, it is the whole colony without any reservation. I know the price of what I abandon, and I have sufficiently proved the importance that I attach to this province. . . . I renounce it with the greatest regret. To attempt obstinately to retain it would be folly.

"I direct you to negotiate this affair with the envoys of the United States," the first consul said. "Do not even await the arrival of Mr. Monroe: have an interview this very day with Mr. Livingston." The conflict with Great Britain was about to resume. "I want fifty millions" for Louisiana, Bonaparte said, "and for less than that sum I will not treat. . . . I require money to make war on the richest nation of the world."[52]

Now it was the first consul's turn to gaze far into the future. "In two or three centuries," he observed, "the Americans may be found too powerful for Europe . . . but my foresight does not embrace such remote fears. . . . It is to prevent the danger, to which the colossal power of England exposes use, that I would provide a remedy."[53]

Barbé-Marbois listened carefully as Bonaparte outlined his strategy for the negotiation. "Mr. Monroe is on the point of arriving," and was surely carrying secret instructions from President Jefferson about how much money to offer for New Orleans. The first consul anticipated that neither Livingston nor Monroe was "prepared for a decision which goes infinitely beyond any thing that they are about to ask of us." Therefore, he instructed Barbé-Marbois:

Begin by making them the overture, without any subterfuge. You will acquaint me, day by day, hour by hour, of your progress. . . . Observe the greatest secrecy, and recommend it to the American ministers.

The treaty talks that culminated in the Louisiana Purchase commenced that evening, while James Monroe's carriage was still rolling toward Paris.[54]

## CHAPTER FOURTEEN

# Midnight in the
# Garden of Rue Trudon

*The purchase [was] a pretty expensive one ... but we have*
*removed by it a dangerous rival (whether this government or that*
*of Britain possessed the country) for ever from our shores. We*
*have enabled our government to live in perpetual peace,*
*and ... acquired the means of living at no very distant period,*
*absolutely independent of Europe or the east indies, since the pro-*
*duce of every soil and of every climate may now be found or*
*placed within our own country. Whatever the opinion of the pres-*
*ent day may be I am content to stake my political character with*
*posterity upon this treaty.*

—Robert R. Livingston to Rufus King, May 11, 1803[1]

THE FIRST NEWS of Juan Ventura Morales's proclamation closing
the Mississippi to American trade reached President Jefferson on
Thursday, November 25, 1802, two weeks before he was slated to present
his State of the Union address. Despite the angry reactions of the press
and public, Jefferson sidestepped the news from New Orleans in what
Alexander Hamilton called his *"lullaby* message" to Congress on December 8. Retired from public office but not from politics, the great New
York Federalist was not shy about offering martial advice in the newspapers over pen names like Titus Manlius and Pericles.[2]

The crisis in Louisiana threatened "the early dismemberment of a
large portion of the country," Hamilton warned his countrymen, using
the pen name Pericles, and "more immediately the safety of all the
Southern States." In the long run it threatened "the independence of the
whole union." Of America's two options, the choice was clear to a statesman who regarded Julius Caesar as the greatest man who ever lived.
Hamilton sneered at the first option: "to negociate and endeavour to pur-

chase, and if this fails to go to war." He favored the second: "to seize at once on the Floridas and New-Orleans, and then negociate."[3]

If President Jefferson called ten thousand men to arms and embraced these "decisive measures," Hamilton wrote,

> he might yet retrieve his character; induce the best part of the com-munity [that is, Hamilton's Federalist friends] to look favorably upon his political career, exalt himself in the eyes of Europe, save the coun-try, and secure a permanent fame.

"But for this, alas!" the American Caesar frowned, "Jefferson is not destined!"[4]

Firmly and quietly, the president had already initiated negotiations through Pierre Du Pont and Robert Livingston for possession of New Orleans and the Floridas. Now, facing "the agitation of the public mind on occasion of the late suspension of our right of deposit at N[ew] Orleans," something more dramatic was needed. "The measures we have been pursuing being invisible," Jefferson admitted, "do not satisfy."[5]

Among those invisible measures was Jefferson's plan for a scientific expedition up the Missouri River and across the Rocky Mountains to the Pacific. Soon after taking office, Jefferson had invited Lieutenant Meri-wether Lewis to serve as his private secretary—citing his "knolege of the Western country" as a valuable attribute for the position. With Lewis close at hand, planning for the mission began in earnest, building upon the instructions he had drawn up for André Michaux in 1793. The project was cloaked in secrecy, but *not* for diplomatic reasons—indeed Jefferson consulted secretly the Spanish, French, and British representatives about his plans for "a small caravan" to explore the Missouri River, and he secured foreign passports for its commanders.[6]

The secrecy answered domestic political considerations: Jefferson did not believe that the Constitution authorized the outfitting of a scientific and "literary" expedition at public expense. Nevertheless, "the President has been all his life a man of letters, very speculative, and a lover of glory," the Spanish envoy reported to his superiors, and he was eager

> to perpetuate the fame of his administration not only by measures of frugality and economy which characterize him, but also by discover-ing . . . the way by which the Americans may some day extend their population and their influence up to the coasts of the South Sea [i.e., the Pacific Ocean].

To indulge his scientific curiosity and advance the good of the country, Jefferson emphasized the commercial significance of the expedition in his secret message to Congress on January 18, 1803. "While other civilized nations have encountered great expense to enlarge the boundaries of knowledge by undertaking voyages of discovery," Jefferson asked for only $2,500 and only for a constitutional purpose. "The interests of commerce place the principal object within the constitutional powers and care of Congress," he wrote. "That it should incidentally advance the geographical knowledge of our own continent," the president cagily admitted, "can not but be an additional gratification." Congress approved the money, and planning was well under way before Robert Livingston and James Monroe bought Louisiana. Their diplomatic coup transformed the expedition led by Meriwether Lewis and William Clark into a great national adventure—and both opportunities forced the apostle of strict construction to stretch the Constitution beyond what he regarded as the limits of its expressly delegated powers.[7]

Federalist critics condemned Jefferson's response to the Mississippi crisis as "in every respect the weakest measure that ever disgraced the administration of any country." The French chargé d'affaires saw things differently. "However timid Mr. Jefferson may be," Louis André Pichon advised Talleyrand, in words that would bolster the American bargaining position in Paris, "I cannot help seeing that there is a tendency toward adopting an irrevocably hostile system [toward France]. This circumstance will be decisive for Mr. Jefferson. If he acts feebly, he is lost."[8]

On Monday, January 10, President Jefferson dispatched an urgent note to James Monroe, who had completed his second term as governor of Virginia at noon on Christmas Eve. "I have but a moment to inform you," the president wrote, "that the fever into which the western mind is thrown by the affair at N[ew] Orleans . . . threatens to overbear our peace." The note arrived in Richmond as Monroe and his family were packing for New York. Elizabeth Kortright Monroe and the girls planned to visit her parents while her husband joined Kentucky senator John Breckinridge on a jaunt to inspect his landholdings in the west. After twenty years in public office, Monroe was looking forward to opening a law practice in Richmond, settling his debts, and making some money.[9]

Instead, Jefferson's letter presented him with a fait accompli, the "temporary sacrifice" of a new public assignment. "I shall tomorrow nominate you to the Senate for an extraordinary mission to France," the president wrote, "and the circumstances are such as to render it impossible to decline."

The whole public hope will be rested on you. I wish you to [stay] either in Richmond or Albemarle till you receive another letter from me, which will be written two days hence if the Senate decide immediately. . . . In the meantime pray work night and day to arrange your affairs for a temporary absence; perhaps for a long time.[10]

The capital was busy on Tuesday, January 11. While the Senate considered Monroe's appointment as special envoy to France and Spain to secure "our rights and interests in the river Mississippi and in the territories eastward thereof," the House gathered in secret session to appropriate $2 million for "any expenses which may be incurred in relation to the intercourse between the United States and foreign nations." This bland legislative language veiled the intended object of purchasing New Orleans and the Floridas.[11]

By a strict party-line vote, the Senate confirmed Monroe's appointment on Tuesday afternoon. Congress authorized the money on Wednesday, and Jefferson's allies quickly sent word to their constituents. On January 12, for example, Republican congressman David Holmes, of Harrisonburg, Virginia, put the administration's spin on recent events in a letter to his neighbor James Allen (the early national politician's equivalent to a sound bite for the evening news). Holmes knew he could count on Allen, a state senator who was then in Richmond for the legislative session, to spread the administration's perspective among his colleagues, who in turn would inform wider circles of friends and constituents.

"The proceedings of congress have been uninteresting except upon one Subject," Holmes wrote, summarizing the talking points about Jefferson's public policy toward Louisiana.

The conduct of the Spanish officer at Orleans in refusing to permit our Western Citizens from landing their produce at that place as usual and refusing to assign any other on the Banks of the River . . . has exerted much Sensibility. The intimate connection between the free Navigation of the Mississippi, and the existence of a Union with the Western country is felt by the administration. . . . It is Not only the intention of the Executive to Secure Permanently that object but to enlarge our Privileges. Mr. Monroe whos Nomination has been confirmed by the Senate (15 to 12) Will join Messrs. Livingston and Pinckney to negociate upon this Subject. It is generally believed that the conduct of the Spanish Officers at Orleans, has not received the Sanction of their Government but [is] a Swindling act of their own. If this Should not be the case and negociation fails . . . War or what is more to be deprecated a dismemberment of the Union Must take place.

Holmes, who was later elected the first governor of Mississippi, hoped that "the impatience of the Western People will not drive them to any improper acts, before Peacefull measures Can be Tried."[12]

As promised, on Thursday, January 13, Jefferson informed Monroe of his confirmation by the Senate. Regardless of whether his talents were actually necessary in Europe, where Chancellor Livingston and Charles Cotesworth Pinckney were ably representing American interests in Paris and Madrid, Monroe's political appeal at home was irresistible. In private friendship and in politics, no man except James Madison was more closely identified with the president. Monroe's reputation as a stalwart defender of western interests in the Mississippi Valley dated to the Jay-Gardoqui negotiations of 1785–1786 and the debates over the ratification of the Constitution. He owned land in the west and had many friends there. He also knew the salons and officials of Paris from his days as President Washington's minister, and he had friends among the French republicans, although fewer among the members of Bonaparte's court.

The two minor liabilities that Monroe brought to the assignment stemmed from his tenure as minister to France in the 1790s. First, many of his French political friends were out of favor with Bonaparte. Second, Monroe was a proud man—a "man of the sword" ready to defend his reputation on the field of honor. His sensitivity to French public opinion had been heightened by the embarrassment of being recalled by President Washington in 1796. The inconvenient friends were easily managed. Monroe gave his Parisian butler a list of names "with instruction [that] should any of them call, not to admit them, always giving some excuse which should not be offensive." Although his vanity never interfered with the work at hand, Monroe's interest in gauging the warmth of his welcome was almost obsessive, and it did incline him to undervalue Livingston's accomplishments in the months prior to his arrival.[13]

The announcement of Monroe's appointment was a master stroke in domestic politics. "The measure has already silenced the Federalists here," President Jefferson wrote, "and the country will become calm as fast as the information extends over it." For the moment, all Monroe needed to do was show up. In the longer view, however, both men knew they were gambling Monroe's (and the administration's) political reputation and future. "All eyes, all hopes, are now fixed on you," Jefferson advised his friend.

*James Monroe, in an engraving from the 1816 portrait by John Vander-lyn. When Monroe abandoned his new law office in Richmond and accepted the appointment as special minister to France in 1803, his decision proved a turning point both for his political career and his personal finances. After returning from Europe, Monroe served in James Madison's cabinet and then as the last president of the Virginia dynasty. With each year of public service after 1803, Monroe slid further into debt until his death in New York City on July 4, 1831. The Barings Bank of London had made millions financing the Louisiana Purchase. Only the bank's forbearance on a substantial personal loan and a last-minute congressional appropriation of $30,000 saved the remnants of Monroe's estate from his creditors.* (Collection of the author)

Were you to decline, the chagrin would be universal . . . for on the event of this mission depends the future destinies of this republic. If we cannot by a purchase of the country insure to ourselves a course of perpetual peace and friendship with all nations . . . war cannot be distant.

.  .  .

The domestic implications of the Mississippi crisis were paramount in Jefferson's decision to send a second and highly visible emissary to France. The president also had other compelling arguments for sending someone, and for choosing Monroe.

Based on his own diplomatic experience, Jefferson knew that written instructions, no matter how carefully composed, were cumbersome and chronically out of date by the time they crossed the Atlantic. Much had happened in the fifteen months since Chancellor Livingston had sailed for Europe. In 1802 the president's eloquence had been equal to the task of revising American policy toward France after the discovery of the retrocession of Louisiana: "The day that France takes possession of New Orleans . . . we must marry ourselves to the British fleet and nation." Now, however, because he *was* a skillful writer and because so many things had changed, Jefferson knew that the complexities of diplomacy involving Great Britain, France, Spain, and the United States—with two of the four on the verge of sweeping them all into war—required something more supple than ink on paper. (As writers, perhaps Abraham Lincoln, Woodrow Wilson, and Teddy Roosevelt were in Jefferson's league, but in time of crisis they also had the telegraph.)[14]

Jefferson's goal had not changed. He wanted possession of New Orleans and the Floridas so that America controlled the rivers into the Gulf of Mexico. Neither had his diplomatic methods. Come what may, the president had to have reliable spokesmen in Paris who knew what he wanted and who possessed authority sufficient to attain it. As Jefferson had recently advised an ally in Congress, the crux of effective statesmanship was "doing what good we can; when we cannot do all we would wish."[15]

As he had with Chancellor Livingston (and informally with Pierre Du Pont), Jefferson offered Monroe "full and frequent oral communications" in preparation for the French mission. The negotiations toward "our object of purchasing N[ew] Orleans and the Floridas," Jefferson recognized, are "liable to assume so many shapes, that no [written] instructions could be squared to fit them." The president wanted his new emissary to be "well impressed with all our views and therefore qualified to meet and modify . . . every form of proposition which could come from the other party." Monroe was a perfect choice because he "possess[ed] the unlimited confidence of the administration and of the western people; and generally of the republicans everywhere."

"Were you to refuse to go," Jefferson cautioned, "no other man can be found who does this." Not surprisingly, when Jefferson's letters of January 10 and 13 reached him in Richmond, the former governor canceled his trip to New York and the west, put the new law office on hold, and began packing his bags for Paris.


By Sunday, March 6, 1803, Jefferson's minister extraordinary and plenipotentiary and his family had their baggage aboard the *Richmond,* a vessel of about four hundred tons, as they wrapped up their visit with Elizabeth Kortright Monroe's family. Clearing the port of New York in a snowstorm on Tuesday, the *Richmond* made an uneventful crossing in thirty-one days. At Le Havre a salute from the battery protecting the mouth of the Seine welcomed the ship into the harbor on Friday, April 8, 1803. Stepping onto French soil at about two o'clock in the afternoon, the returning minister and his family were escorted to their hotel by an honor guard of fifty French soldiers.[16]

Conveniently, one of the other passengers from the *Richmond* was heading immediately for Paris. Monroe entrusted him with a note informing Livingston of his safe arrival and his intention to rest for a day and then travel to the capital. Soon thereafter, however, municipal officials told Monroe that news of his arrival had already reached Bonaparte—a hundred miles away in Paris—by semaphore telegraph. Devised by engineer Claude Chappe and adopted by the French legislative assembly in 1792, this "optical telegraph" was based on a semaphore with three arms that could be placed in a combination of ninety-two discrete positions. Chappe's system made it possible—using a coded vocabulary of ninety-two words on each of ninety-two pages for a total of nearly eighty-five hundred words—to relay messages by semaphore from one signal tower to the next. For the first time in history, information moved faster than a horse could carry a dispatch rider. News of Monroe's arrival reached Paris in hours rather than days.[17]

On Sunday, Monroe's note reached Robert Livingston, confirming the nearly instantaneous news via Chappe's semaphore telegraph. At that moment, only five other people in the world—Talleyrand, Barbé-Marbois, Decrès, and possibly Joseph and Lucien Bonaparte—were aware of the drastic shift in Napoleon's attitude toward Louisiana. Chancellor Livingston was not yet among them. Nor could he know that within days the first consul would be echoing his own arguments as justification for selling the province.

Excited perhaps as much by the telegraph as by his curiosity about events in America, Livingston dashed off a quick, genial, and fateful note of self-deprecating welcome to his old friend and new colleague. "Dear Sir," Livingston wrote,

I congratulate you on your safe arrival, and have long and anxiously wished for you. God grant that your mission may answer yours and the public expectations. War may do something for us—nothing else would. I have paved the way for you, and if . . . we are now in possession of New Orleans, we should do well. . . . I have apprized the Minister of your arrival; and told him you would be here on Tuesday or Wednesday.[18]

Forever after, ignoring Livingston's phrase about paving his way, Monroe regarded this polite and hastily written note as proof, as the Virginian wrote in his autobiography, that "Mr. Livingston gave a very discouraging prospect of the success of his mission." Surely the surprising turn of events that awaited them in Paris owed principally to the triumphant return of James Monroe, minister extraordinary and plenipotentiary.[19]

The arrival of Jefferson's new emissary, regardless of his identity, signaled that the Americans meant business. But so did the arrival in Paris on April 8 of copies of the *New York Chronicle* bearing the entire text of Pennsylvania senator James Ross's militant resolutions asserting America's "indisputable right to the free navigation of the river Mississippi." As a resident of the west, former college Latin teacher, and unsuccessful candidate for governor of Pennsylvania, Ross, a forty-one-year-old Pittsburgh lawyer, was the Federalists' point man in the Mississippi crisis. He introduced the heart of their war plan on February 16, 1803. Ross proposed an appropriation of $5 million and authorization to call up as many as fifty thousand militia—from South Carolina, Georgia, Tennessee, Kentucky, Ohio, and the Mississippi Territory, "together with the naval and military force of the union." With these resources, the president was "to take immediate possession of . . . a convenient deposit for [American] produce and merchandize in the island of New Orleans . . . or the adjacent territories."[20]

The Republican alternative came in the form of substitute resolutions introduced by Kentucky senator John Breckinridge, Monroe's personal friend and Jefferson's political ally. Breckinridge's resolutions authorized the president to direct the state governors "to organize, arm and equip" as many as eighty thousand militia and "hold [them] in readiness to march at a moment's warning." This Republican alternative gave the president more room for diplomacy and was more respectful of state prerogatives. Either way, however, the senators' message to France and Spain—and to the American westerners—was firm and clear.[21]

"Upon what then do we really differ?" Senator Ross asked his colleagues. "Upon nothing but the time of acting—Whether we shall take measures for immediate restoration and security," as Alexander Hamilton's Pericles essays advocated, "or whether we shall abstain from all military preparation, and wait the [result] of negociation," as Jefferson was doing. "There is no disagreement but on this point," Ross accurately concluded, "for if negociation fails, every man who has spoken has pledged himself to declare war."[22]

On February 25 the United States Senate had substituted Breckinridge's resolutions for Ross's by a strict party-line vote of fifteen to eleven—and then promptly passed the measure by a unanimous vote of all the senators present. Bonaparte was a strategic genius, but when Robert Livingston sent Talleyrand a copy of the *New York Chronicle* on April 8, 1803, it did not require genius to read the implications of James Ross's resolutions. Had the wording of Breckinridge's substitutes been known, the French reaction would have been the same. Both sets of resolutions sent the same message to foreign powers, as Senator Ross himself admitted, "except that one set of resolutions puts greater power into the hands of the President than the other."[23]

One more bit of news that reached Talleyrand and Bonaparte in the first week of April—completely unknown to Monroe or Livingston—was pivotal to the success of the American negotiations in Paris. Congress had authorized Monroe as a minister to France and, if necessary, Spain. President Jefferson and Secretary of State Madison, however, had intimated to the French chargé d'affaires, Louis André Pichon, that if Monroe were disappointed in France he would seek an alliance with Great Britain. "According to all I can gather," Pichon warned Talleyrand, "I see that Mr. Monroe has *carte blanche* and that he will go to London if he is badly received at Paris."[24]

War with Great Britain was imminent. Leclerc was dead, his Haitian expedition was a disaster, and the reinforcements for St. Domingue and Louisiana were trapped at Hellevoetsluis. New Orleans was vulnerable, and the westerners were armed and angry. On April 8, 1803—while James Monroe and his family were coming ashore at La Havre in the pilot boat of the *Richmond*—Talleyrand and Bonaparte took Ross's resolutions and Pichon's warning to heart. Talleyrand, who had strongly opposed the idea of selling Louisiana, was now ready to see it as "an advantageous arrangement" to compensate for "the inevitable loss of a country that war was going to place at the mercy of another nation."[25] Two days later, on Easter Sunday, the first consul summoned François

Barbé-Marbois and Denis Decrès to the garden of his palace at St. Cloud and announced his intention to sell Louisiana to the United States.[26]

Early Monday morning, April 11, Napoleon Bonaparte renounced Louisiana to Barbé-Marbois and directed him to sell it to the United States. "Do not even wait for the arrival of Mr. Monroe," the first consul said, "have an interview this very day with Mr. Livingston." That afternoon, however, it was Foreign Minister Talleyrand, not the treasury minister, who invited Chancellor Livingston to his office on rue du Bac, on the Left Bank in St.-Germain-des-Prés.[27]

Livingston opened the conversation by reiterating his conviction that in reaction to Spain's revocation of the right of deposit the United States was certain to seize New Orleans and the Floridas either now or at the first outbreak of the next European war. Talleyrand listened patiently. Then he wondered aloud "whether we wished to have the whole of Louisiana."[28]

"No," Livingston replied (accurately reflecting Jefferson's objectives), "our wishes extended only to New Orleans and the Floridas." However, as he had suggested on earlier occasions, it would be wise policy on the part of France "to give us the Country above the River Arkansas in order to place a barrier between [French Louisiana] and Canada."

If France sold New Orleans to the United States, Talleyrand responded, the rest of Louisiana had little value. "What," he asked Livingston, would you "give for the whole"?

Livingston doubted the sincerity of Talleyrand's question. His skepticism, Barbé-Marbois wrote long after the event, was "justified by the many deceptions that had been previously practiced upon him." Dickering over land prices was nothing new, however, so the Chancellor started low. He "supposed we should not object to twenty Millions provided our Citizens were paid." (Twenty million francs was about $3.75 million, and Livingston wanted to keep Talleyrand and Bonaparte from evading their promise to settle American claims from the Quasi-War of 1797–1800.)[29]

"This was too low an offer," Talleyrand replied, inviting Livingston to "reflect upon it and tell him tomorrow."

"As Mr. Monroe would be in Town in two days," Livingston suggested that he "would delay my further offer until I had the pleasure of introducing him."

After fifteen months in Paris, Livingston knew the former bishop of Autun well enough to see an immediate connection between Talleyrand's next remark and the recent news of the saber rattling by the United States Senate. With the shrug of indifference by which he habitually veiled matters of utmost importance, Talleyrand ventured "that he did not speak from authority, but that the idea had struck him."[30]

That evening the Chancellor wrote a letter to Madison, with key passages in code, explaining the full significance of his conversation with Talleyrand. "I have reason . . . to think," he surmised, "that this resolution [to sell Louisiana] was taken in council [with Bonaparte] on Saturday, for on Friday I received Mr. Ross's motion [and] I immediately sent it to Mr. Talleyrand with an informal note expressive of my fears that it would be carried into effect." Livingston had also sent a French translation of Ross's motion to General Jean-Baptiste Bernadotte, who had immediately taken it to Joseph Bonaparte. The Ross resolutions, Livingston believed, were the "exciting causes" of Napoleon's change of heart about Louisiana, "which . . . we shall be able on the arrival of Mr. Monroe to pursue to effect."[31]

The next day—Tuesday, April 12—Livingston met again with Talleyrand, and then added a postscript at the bottom of his letter to Madison before sealing it and entrusting it to the secretary of the French legation for delivery to America:

> Orders are gone this day to stop the sailing of vessels from the French ports. War [with Great Britain] is inevitable. My conjecture as to their determination to sell [Louisiana] is well founded. Mr. Monroe is just arrived here.[32]

Tuesday evening Monroe called upon Livingston at his house on the Right Bank at rue Trudon (a street that disappeared in the nineteenth century with the opening of rue Auber and the opera at the Palais Garnier, home of the Phantom). They agreed to spend the next day reviewing their joint instructions from Jefferson and their files of official correspondence.

It is not easy to sort out exactly who said what to whom and when during the second week of April. Events were moving quickly. Monroe had just arrived and his credentials had not yet been formally presented to, or accepted by, the first consul. This fact troubled Monroe and Livingston. If their negotiations failed, they did not want to be criticized for any lapse in diplomatic protocol. Bonaparte, who could be a stickler for protocol when it suited his purposes, knew that these negotiations were not likely to fail and was less concerned with procedural formalities.

Although eager to reach an agreement, Bonaparte added another layer of complexity to the discussions by working through at least two independent intermediaries, Talleyrand and Barbé-Marbois, who spoke sometimes to one American and not the other. And if this were not confusing enough, Monroe injured his back in the middle of April—the pain was "very excruciating" and he was bedridden for several days.[33] Not surprisingly, then, these complex negotiations left some ambiguities in the documentary record.

Livingston's and Monroe's contemporary notes and correspondence about the Louisiana Purchase are replete with vague or inaccurate dates, loose ends, dead ends, and occasional misinformation. No one observer witnessed everything at the time, and documents could be misdated in haste or fatigue. Monroe and Livingston wrote several joint reports to Madison, but each man also wrote private letters to Madison or Rufus King, the American minister in London, that reflected his individual perception of his personal role in the negotiations. Retrospective accounts such as Monroe's *Autobiography* and Barbé-Marbois's *History of Louisiana* were susceptible to the usual frailties of human memory— further compounded by differences between the Julian and the French revolutionary calendars. April 12 on the Julian calendar, for example, was 22 Germinal an XI on French correspondence and documents.

All this said, however, the final unpleasant truth is that after the success of the Louisiana Purchase, Livingston and Monroe each tried to play up his claim to glory for an achievement that ultimately belonged, more than to any others, to Jefferson and Bonaparte. Goaded by admirers or detractors, nudged by ambition and pride, both American ministers tampered with their files (Livingston to a much greater extent than Monroe) and adjusted their memories of the negotiations.[34]

Chancellor Livingston's terse postscript of April 12 confirming to Madison that his conjecture about the French intention to sell Louisiana was "well founded" was based on his second meeting with Talleyrand, hours before Monroe's arrival in Paris. "On the 12th," Livingston explained in his next letter—written after midnight on April 14—"I called upon [Talleyrand] to press this matter further."[35]

The foreign minister was evasive. He again thought it proper "to declare that his proposition was only personal," Livingston reported, "but still requested me to make an offer" for Louisiana. When the Chancellor declined because Monroe was soon to arrive with fresh instructions from the American government, Talleyrand "shrugged up his shoulders" and tried to change the subject. Livingston, however, had prepared himself for Talleyrand's ploys. Stating that he "wished merely to have the negotiation opened by any proposition," the Chancellor presented Talleyrand with "a note which contained that request."

Talleyrand responded that "he would answer my note, but that he must do it evasively because Louisiana was not theirs." Livingston "smiled at this assertion and told him that I had seen the Treaty . . . [and] knew the Consul had appointed officers to govern the country, and that [Bonaparte] had himself told me that Gen[era]l Victor was to take possession."

When Talleyrand "still persisted that they had it in contemplation but had it not," Livingston responded firmly. "If so," he said, "we should negotiate no further on the subject but advise our Government to take possession."

Talleyrand "seemed alarmed . . . and told me he would answer my note but that it would be evasively."

"We were not disposed to triffle," the Chancellor warned. "The times were critical and though I did not know what instructions Mr. Munroe might bring, I was perfectly satisfied that they would require a precise and prompt notice." Livingston then joked that he was "fearful from the little progress I had made that my Government would consider me a very indolent negociator." Talleyrand "laughed and told me that he would give me a certificate that I was the most importunate he had yet met with."

As Livingston ended his conversation with Talleyrand on January 12, he sensed that something bigger was going on, but he could not yet put his finger on it. "There was," he wrote Madison a day and a half later, "something so extraordinary in all this that I did not detail it to you till I found some clue to the labyrinth."[36] The clue surfaced Wednesday evening after he and Monroe had dinner at Livingston's house.

Livingston and Monroe spent Wednesday, April 13, reviewing their papers and then shared dinner with their assistants. From the table that evening the Chancellor "observed the Minister of the Treasury walking in my garden." Livingston sent his son-in-law to greet François Barbé-Marbois, who "told him he would return when we had dined." An hour later, while the group was "taking coffee," Barbé-Marbois "came in, and after being some time in the room," he and Livingston "strolled into the next room" where they could speak privately.[37]

Barbé-Marbois said that upon returning to Paris from St. Cloud (where Bonaparte had dramatically renounced his interest in Louisiana), "he heard that [Livingston] had been at his house two days before"—on the 11th—"when he was at St. Cloud." Thinking that the Chancellor "might have something particular to say to him," Barbé-Marbois "had taken the first opportunity to call." Chancellor Livingston "saw that this was meant as an opening to one of those free conversations which [he] frequently had with him," so he mentioned that he had twice spoken with Talleyrand. He also mentioned "the extraordinary conduct of the Minister" at their second meeting.[38]

Despite their mutual affection, Livingston noticed that Barbé-Marbois was choosing his words very carefully—waiting, it seemed, to hear more about Livingston's conversations with the former bishop of Autun before saying more about his own reasons for meandering into the ambassador's garden at rue Trudon. There were two reasons for Barbé-Marbois's caution. One was that although Bonaparte had directed Barbé-Marbois to open negotiations immediately, men who worked closely with the first consul knew that he sometimes acted impulsively. Perhaps he had had second thoughts about supplanting Talleyrand entirely from the negotiations—we can be certain that Talleyrand had such thoughts.

The other reason for caution was more obvious at the time, but easily forgotten two centuries later. All the participants in these negotiations had firsthand experience with the tumults of revolution. How many regimes had risen and fallen since the storming of the Bastille? How many people had been exiled? How many heads had rolled? By April 1803 Bonaparte and the consulate government had survived for three years, but who could be certain of its future? The Bourbon monarchy had lasted for decades, and the Directory had lasted for five years—and in both cases, at critical moments, the former bishop of Autun had helped bring them down. Talleyrand's conversion to the idea of selling Louisiana was only a few days old, but his political cunning, his *prescience barométrique,* was legendary—as was his capacity for betrayal. Barbé-Marbois had every reason for caution until Livingston's account of his odd conversation with Talleyrand signaled that it really was safe to be involved in the sale of Louisiana.

Further conversation, Barbé-Marbois whispered, would "lead to something important that had been cursorily mentioned to him at St. Cloud." But since the "house was full of Company," the treasury minister invited Livingston to come to his office "any time before Eleven that night." After Barbé-Marbois left, Monroe recalled five months later, Livingston rejoined his colleagues "appearing much agitated." Barbé-Marbois, as Monroe remembered it, had confirmed their suspicions that

Bonaparte had in fact informed him "at St. Cloud on Sunday . . . of his decision to cede [Louisiana] to the U[nited] States."[39]

Monroe and Livingston then conferred about the wisdom of further conversation with Barbé-Marbois that evening. "I hesitated on the idea of his going alone," Monroe confided to Madison, "before I was presented" and they had "adopted any plan." Monroe also worried that "too much zeal might do harm, that a little reserve might have a better effect." Livingston, however, "could not see the weight of these objections." He urged the "necessity of dispatch" and the impossibility of bringing Monroe with him before he had been formally presented to the foreign minister and first consul. Monroe reluctantly agreed ("ceased to oppose his going," is how he described it to Madison), but advised Livingston to be "reserved in the conference . . . in short to hear and not to speak."[40]

After Monroe and the others went home, Livingston "followed" Barbé-Marbois to his office. Once there, the treasury minister "wished me to repeat what I had said relative to Mr. Talleyrand requesting a proposition from me as to the purchase of Louisiana," Livingston reported. "I did so and concluded with the extreme absurdity of [Talleyrand's] evasions." Livingston then reminded Barbé-Marbois that "delay . . . would enable Britain to take possession" of Louisiana.[41]

Barbé-Marbois challenged Livingston's assumption that Britain would be "so successful [in] a war as to be enabled to retain her conquests." But the Chancellor responded that the Americans might well determine that it was in "their interest to render [Britain] successful." Was it prudent, Livingston asked, for France to "throw us into her scale"?

After a long digression about possible outcomes in the event of war—"discussions" that Livingston dismissed to Madison in the wee hours of the next morning as "of no moment to repeat"—"we returned to the point." Livingston's account of his conversations with Talleyrand, Barbé-Marbois said, "led him to think that what the Consul had said to him on Sunday at St Cloud . . . had more of earnest than he thought at the time."

Now it was Barbé-Marbois's turn to recount *his* Easter Sunday conversation about Louisiana. "The Consul had asked him what news from England?" Barbé-Marbois began. He had replied "that he had seen in the London papers the proposition for raising 50,000 men to take New-Orleans"—Ross's resolutions. "The Consul said he had seen it too," Barbé-Marbois said, "and he had also seen that something was said about 2,000,000 of D[ollar]s being disposed among the people about him to bribe them."

A little later, Barbé-Marbois continued, while he was "walking in the Garden, the Consul came again to him, and spoke to him about the troubles that were excited in America." Barbé-Marbois said that he was sorry "that any cause of difference should exist between our countries."

"Well you have the charge of the treasury," Barbé-Marbois said that Bonaparte replied. "Let them give you one hundred millions and pay their own claims, and take the whole country." (At St. Cloud, Bonaparte had actually told Barbé-Marbois that he wanted fifty million francs—in the end the treasury minister's exaggeration to Livingston got them an extra ten.)[42]

Although not quite on this scale, Chancellor Livingston was no novice at haggling for a good price. "Seeing by my looks that I was surprised at so extravagant a demand," Livingston assured Madison, Barbé-Marbois quickly added that he, too, "considered the demand as exorbitant, and had told the First Consul that [the United States] had not the means of raising it." Bonaparte's response was that they "might borrow it."

At last, Livingston told Madison, the cryptic hints of the past few days added up. "I now plainly saw the whole business."

> First the Consul was disposed to Sell. [But] he distrusted Talleyrand on account of the business of the supposed intention to bribe and [therefore] meant to put the negotiation into the hands of Marbois whose character for integrity is established.

In light of Barbé-Marbois's revelations, Livingston pled poverty and found fault with the merchandise. Because the United States "would be perfectly satisfied with New Orleans and the Floridas and had no disposition to extend across the River," he told the treasury minister, "of course we would not give any great sum for the purchase." Certainly not 100 million francs. Barbé-Marbois "was right in his Idea of the extreme exorbitancy of the demand," the Chancellor said, "however we would be ready to purchase [Louisiana] provided the sum was reduced to a reasonable limit."

At this point in the evening, near midnight, both men knew their conversation had turned a significant corner. They were no longer discussing *whether* France might sell Louisiana or *whether* the United States might buy it. Livingston and Barbé-Marbois had begun to negotiate a price.

Barbé-Marbois "then pressed me to name the sum," Livingston told Madison. "This was not worth while," he had replied, for "any declaration of mine would have no effect." If, on the other hand, "a negotiation was to be opened," the Chancellor had said, "we should, Mr. Munro and myself, make the offer after mature reflection." This response "compelled" Barbé-Marbois to admit "that tho' he was not authorized expressly to make the inquiry . . . yet if I could mention any sum that came near the mark that could be accepted he would communicate it to the First Consul."

Regardless of his assurances to Monroe after dinner, the opportunity was too good to pass up. "I told him that we had no sort of authority to go to a sum that bore any proportion to what he mentionned," Livingston reassured Madison, "but that as he considered [Bonaparte's] demand as too high he would oblige me by telling me what he thought to be reasonable." Barbé-Marbois had "replied that if we should name sixty million and take upon us the American claims to the amount of twenty more he would try how far it would be accepted." Two weeks later, Livingston and Monroe would sign a treaty for this exact price—but for the moment the Chancellor maintained that it was too much, invoking once again "the ardour of the Americans to take [Louisiana] by force."

Barbé-Marbois was now ready to clinch the deal, in words that Livingston quoted directly in his report to Madison:

> Says he, you know the temper of a youthful conqueror—every thing he does is rapid as lightening[.] We have only to speak to him as an opportunity presents itself, perhaps in a crowd when he bears no contradiction. When I am alone with him I can speak more freely and he attends but this opportunity seldom happens and is always accidental.

"Try then if you can not come up to my mark," Barbé-Marbois had urged. "Consider the extent of the country, the exclusive navigation of the River, and the importance of having no neighbour to dispute with you, no war to dread."

The hour was late, but the two men had made remarkable progress. They had reached a preliminary understanding about the sale of Louisiana and the approximate price, so the Chancellor pushed on to the next issue. "I asked him," Livingston reported to Madison, "in case of a purchase whether they could stipulate that France would never possess the Floridas . . . and relinquish all right that she might have to them. He told me that she would go thus far!"

Now it was Livingston's turn to consolidate the evening's progress by opening formal negotiations in which everything they had discussed could be made official. "I could now say nothing more on the subject," Livingston told Barbé-Marbois, "but that I would converse with Mr. Munroe, and that I was sure I would find him disposed to do every thing that was reasonable."

And now it was Livingston's turn to be wary of Talleyrand by making an observation intended, as the Chancellor explained to Madison, "to see whether my conjectures relative to [Talleyrand] were well founded." If formal negotiations were to begin, Livingston suggested to Barbé-Marbois, "I could wish that the First Consul would depute some body to treat with us who had more leisure than the Minister for foreign affairs." Barbé-Marbois replied "that as the First Consul knew our personal friendship . . . there would be no difficulty when the negotiation was somewhat advanced to have the management of it put into his hands."

"Thus, Sir," Livingston informed Madison, "you see a negotiation is fairly opened."

> The field opened to us is infinitely larger than our instructions contemplated. . . . I speak now without reflection and without having seen Mr. Munroe, as it was midnight when I left the treasury office [and] it is now three O'clock. . . . We shall do all we can to cheapen the purchase but my present sentiment is that we shall buy. . . .
>
> Mr. Munroe will be presented to the Minister to morrow when we shall press for as early an audience as possible from the First Consul.

Wednesday, April 13, 1803, had been a long and productive day, ending in the office of the treasury minister about midnight, when François Barbé-Marbois and Robert Livingston had defined the basic outline of the Louisiana Purchase.

On Thursday, April 14, Livingston and Monroe attended the office of the foreign minister, where Talleyrand accepted the Virginian's credentials "in a Manner which was perfectly satisfactory." Talleyrand, Monroe reported to Madison, assured them that the first consul welcomed "the disposition which our Government has shewn" and "also expressed himself in Terms very favorable to my Colleague and myself."[43]

Nevertheless, the matter of diplomatic protocol—and the potential for delay—loomed in the Americans' minds. Talleyrand promised them that he would confer with Bonaparte that evening about Monroe's formal presentation to the first consul. Their obstacle was precedent: "No minister," Monroe wrote, "has yet been presented except at public audiences, which are monthly. If I am held to that Rule it will not take place 'till the 5th of next month." Talleyrand, nevertheless, was confident that "a person would be designated to treat with us, with whom we might communicate before [Monroe] was presented." And in the end, as Talleyrand indicated, Bonaparte was more than willing to bend the rules of protocol. The fact that Monroe could not be formally presented to the first consul until the monthly reception at the Louvre on Sunday, May 1, 1803, had no adverse effect upon the American ministers' negotiations with Barbé-Marbois.[44]

Recalling his service in the United States during and after the American Revolution, Barbé-Marbois noted in his *History of Louisiana* that

> the three negotiators had seen the origin of the American republic, and for a long time back their respective duties had established between them an intercourse on public affairs, and an intimacy, which does not always exist between foreign envoys.

"Deliberation succeeded to astonishment," the French minister recalled. The Americans, "without asking an opportunity for concerting measures out of the presence of the French negotiator," accomplished their purpose in a matter of days—"the conferences rapidly succeed[ing] one another."[45]

"The negotiations had three objects," wrote Barbé-Marbois, which corresponded precisely with the three issues that he and Livingston had explored at midnight in his office on April 13.

> First, the cession, then the price, and, finally, the indemnity due [to American merchants] for the prizes and their cargoes [captured during the Quasi-War].

Each was discussed separately, and in time each became the focus of a separate document.[46]

After Livingston had introduced Monroe to Talleyrand on Thursday, the Americans conferred about their strategy for negotiating the price in the formal negotiations that commenced the next day. Neither American was aware that Bonaparte had named 50 million francs as his price when he had "renounced" his interest in Louisiana to Barbé-Marbois. Based on Livingston's midnight conversation with the treasury minister, however, the Americans set their upper limit at 50 million, "including our debts," but decided "only to mention forty in the first instance." Livingston communicated this opening bid to Barbé-Marbois on Friday, April 15. For the next week the treasury minister shuttled back and forth between Paris and St. Cloud, taking full advantage of his role as intermediary between the Americans and Bonaparte to squeeze as much as he could out of the deal.[47]

The first round of the formal negotiations was typical of what followed. Barbé-Marbois expressed great sympathy for the Americans and their "situation," but worried aloud that 40 million was such a low offer "that perhaps the whole business would be defeated." Nevertheless, he volunteered to carry the offer "that very day to St Cloud, and let [them] know the result." On Saturday, after hearing Barbé-Marbois's story that Bonaparte had received the American offer "very coldly," Livingston and Monroe offered 50 million and then resolved "to rest for a few days upon our oars."[48]

By April 27, after two weeks of intermittent formal negotiations, Livingston, Monroe, and Barbé-Marbois settled upon the basic terms that Livingston had discussed at the treasury minister's office on the evening of the 13th: 60 million francs for Louisiana and 20 million to settle the American claims.

Despite the back injury that confined him to his apartments for a week or so, Monroe worked in close partnership with Livingston even on the days that the Chancellor had to meet alone with Barbé-Marbois. After formally covering the same ground that Livingston and Barbé-Marbois had explored in their midnight meeting (a circumstance that bolstered Monroe's impression that his colleague had made little progress prior to his arrival in France), at last the moment arrived to get the deal onto paper.

On Wednesday afternoon, April 27, at two o'clock, Barbé-Marbois and Livingston met at Monroe's apartment, where the Virginian, still "indisposed" by his back injury, "might repose as it suited [him]" on a sofa. Barbé-Marbois arrived with two draft treaties, or "projects" (from *projet de loi,* the French term for draft legislation), as Monroe described them in his journal. The first project, which set the price at 100 million francs plus 20 million for the American claims, was "a treaty given him by the gov[ernmen]t to be presented to us." Immediately Barbé-Marbois dismissed his government's demands as "hard and unreasonable," and asked the Americans to consider instead

> another project which he called his own, and which had not been seen by the gov[ernmen]t, but to which he presumed the first-consul would assent.

Barbé-Marbois's draft "reduced that demand to 80, including the debt." The rest of the afternoon was spent discussing the American claims, which had almost become an obsession to Livingston during his months in Paris.[49]

By Thursday morning, April 28, Livingston had prepared, and he and Monroe had discussed, a revised draft based on Barbé-Marbois's second project. "We called on Mr. Marbois the 29th and gave him our project," Monroe wrote in his journal, "which proposed to offer 50 millions to France and 20 on acc[oun]t of her debts to the citizens of the United States." Barbé-Marbois responded that "it would be useless" for him to accept a treaty offering less than a total of 80 million francs, "as the consul had been sufficiently explicit on that point."[50]

"After explaining to him the motives which led us to open that sum," Monroe wrote, "we agreed to accede to his idea and give 80 millions." When Barbé-Marbois "asked us if we would not advance something immediately," the Americans outlined a plan to finance the Louisiana Purchase through European bankers, sweetening their offer with a twelve-year preferential trading privilege for French merchants at the port of New Orleans.[51]

Trading privileges did not interest Barbé-Marbois or his government, but they were concerned for the citizens of Louisiana. "He seemed desirous," Monroe wrote in his journal, "to secure by some strong provisions the incorporation of the inhabitants of the entire country with our union." To this the Americans voiced no objection. "We told him that we would try to modify the article to meet his ideas as fully as we could."[52]

In the final treaty, perhaps it is fitting that the forthright promises of Article III, the most controversial and democratic element in the entire document—

> The inhabitants of the ceded territory shall be incorporated in the Union of the United States and admitted as soon as possible according to the principles of the federal Constitution to the enjoyment of all these rights, advantages and immunities of citizens of the United States, and in the mean time they shall be maintained and protected in the free enjoyment of their liberty, property and the Religion which they profess.[53]

—were instigated by a moderate but incorruptible republican serving as treasury minister to the virtual dictator of France.

In three days, the treaty negotiations were effectively complete. As the Americans left Barbé-Marbois's office on the 29th, he kept a copy of the American draft, "as he said he would see the consul the next morning on the subject." Barbé-Marbois then said that Talleyrand had inquired about Monroe's health, asking specifically whether he "was in health to be presented to the first consul." The next morning, Saturday, April 30, Livingston called on Talleyrand to assure him that Monroe "had recovered." Then he stopped at Monroe's apartment and "informed me," as the Virginian wrote in his journal, "that it was arranged that I should be presented next day, that is on the first of May."[54]

"May 1st Sunday," Monroe noted in his journal. "I accompanied my colleague to the Palace of the Louvre where I was presented by him to the Consul." Bonaparte greeted the Americans warmly.

"I am glad to see you," he said to Monroe. "You have been here 19 days?" Monroe told him he had.

"You speak French."

Monroe replied, "A little."

"You had a good voyage?"

"Yes."

"You came in a frigate?"

"No, in a merchant vessel chartered for the purpose."

Addressing Livingston, the first consul inquired about his family's health. Then, Monroe wrote, Bonaparte "turned to Mr. Livingston and myself and observed that our aff[ai]rs stood as settled." Bonaparte was quietly focusing his attention on the resumption of his war against Great Britain. "This accession of territory," he told Barbé-Marbois, "strengthens for ever the power of the United States; and I have just given to England a maritime rival that will sooner or later humble her pride."[55]

The Louisiana Purchase treaty and its two conventions were dated April 30, 1803, but it took as long to prepare the official documents in French and English as it had taken Barbé-Marbois, Livingston, and Monroe to agree on their provisions. Monroe and Livingston signed the original treaty and first convention on Monday, May 2. Recognizing "that it was impossible to have two original texts in two languages," the negotiators adopted the Franco-American Treaty of 1778 as their precedent and determined "that the original had been agreed on and written in the French language." As the three negotiators shook hands, Livingston voiced the sentiment they all shared. "We have lived long," he said,

> but this is the noblest work of our whole lives. The treaty which we have just signed has not been obtained by art or dictated by force. . . .
> It will change vast solitudes into flourishing districts. From this day the United States take their place among the powers of the first rank.

Three days later, on Thursday, May 5, the negotiators signed the English translation of the treaty, and finally they signed the remaining conventions "about May 8 or 9th."[56] Precisely a month had passed since the convergence of Louis André Pichon's warning, James Ross's resolutions, and James Monroe's arrival at Le Havre had finally convinced Bonaparte and Talleyrand that they had no real choice but to adopt Robert Livingston's arguments as their own and sell Louisiana to the United States.

While Robert Livingston and James Monroe were waiting to sign the English language copies of the conventions that accompanied the Louisiana Purchase treaty, news of their success began its eight-week-long transit across the Atlantic. In Washington, however, the impending outbreak of war had already prompted President Thomas Jefferson to summon his cabinet to the new White House at midday on Saturday afternoon, May 7, 1803. (They generally met at noon so Jefferson had time to exercise his horse with a ride before dinner.) On this important occasion—meeting "on the supposition that war between England and France is commenced"—Attorney General Levi Lincoln and all four department secretaries were present to consider several questions of Louisiana policy: James Madison from State, Albert Gallatin from the Treasury, General Henry Dearborn from the War Department, and Robert Smith from the Navy. The postmaster general, Gideon Granger, was absent, for he did not participate in these policymaking sessions.[57]

The first decision was on the question of whether to issue a proclamation of neutrality, as Presidents Washington and Adams had done in the 1790s. Jefferson and his cabinet unanimously agreed that proclaiming American neutrality was unwise and unnecessary because it would reassure "foreign nations . . . of our neutrality without price, whereas France may be willing to give N[ew] Orleans for it, and England to engage a just and respectful conduct."[58]

The second item for discussion was New Orleans. Thinking it "premature till we hear from our ministers," and until he could gauge the "probable course and duration of the war," Jefferson did not press the cabinet for a "specific opinion." He noted that their general sentiment was "that we must avail ourselves of this war to get it." If Monroe's mission failed, Jefferson concluded, "we shall take it directly, or encourage a declaration of independence and then enter into alliance." Under no circumstances would the United States permit "Gr[eat] Br[itain]'s taking possession of it."

Everyone agreed that the United States needed more than the restoration of "merely our right of deposit." By closing the river, Carlos IV and Juan Ventura Morales had upped the stakes for everyone. Jefferson and his cabinet were determined to accept nothing "short of the sovereignty of the island of N[ew] Orleans, or a [site] sufficient for a town to be located by ourselves." For the moment, however, they could await the result of Monroe's and Livingston's diplomacy. "We have," Treasury Secretary Albert Gallatin reminded the president, "time enough to consider."[59]

## CHAPTER FIFTEEN

# An Immense Wilderness

*I am astonished when I see so great a business finished which but
a few months since we whispered to one another about; it has the
air of enchantment. . . . It must strike . . . every true friend to freedom in these United States as the greatest and most beneficial
event that has taken place since the Declaration of Independence.*

—General Horatio Gates to Thomas Jefferson, July 7, 1803[1]

*Will republicans, who glory in their sacred regard to the rights of
human nature, purchase an immense wilderness for the purpose
of cultivating it with the labor of slaves?*

—The Balance and Columbian Repository, September 20, 1803[2]

Boston's *Independent Chronicle* and the *New-York Evening Post*
broke the news of the Louisiana Purchase on Thursday, June 30,
1803. "The wise, seasonable and politic negociation," crowed the Boston
editor, a friend of the administration,

> has gloriously terminated to the immortal honor of the friends of
> peace and good government and to the utter disappointment of the
> factious and turbulent throughout the nation.

That same day Rufus King landed in New York City, back from his post as
minister to Great Britain, carrying notes to the president from Monroe
and Livingston confirming their success.[3]

During the last weeks of their negotiations, as France and Great
Britain slid toward war, Livingston and Monroe had kept King apprised
of their progress. "In case of war," King had warned them on Saturday,
May 7,

it is the purpose of this Government to send [a British] expedition to occupy New Orleans. If it be ceded to us, would it not be expedient openly or confidentially to communicate the fact here? I have reason to be satisfied that it would prevent the projected expedition.

That same day, by coincidence, Monroe and Livingston dispatched a short note to King confirming that the treaty had been signed. Both messages went by courier, but in effect they crossed in the mail. As a result, before heading home to America, King was able to inform Lord Hawkesbury, the British foreign minister,

that a treaty was signed at Paris on the 30th of April . . . by which the complete sovereignty of the town and territory of New Orleans, as well as of all Louisiana, as the same was heretofore possessed by Spain, has been acquired by the United States.

Sailing on April 21 aboard the *John Morgan,* King stepped ashore ten weeks later to bring Americans the first official news that the Louisiana Purchase Treaty had been signed. King also brought assurances of "harmony and good understanding between Britain and the United States" from George III and Lord Hawkesbury—although British military planners at the Admiralty and the War Department just bundled up their papers for the invasion of New Orleans and filed them away in case they might be useful—perhaps a dozen years hence.[4]

America's twenty-seventh celebration of the Fourth of July was an especially festive Monday for the author of the Declaration of Independence. Everything that Rufus King knew about the Louisiana Purchase—but no details about price or boundaries[5]—had reached President Jefferson and Secretary of State Madison in Washington on the evening of July 3.

"We received a letter from Mr. King arrived in N[ew] York," Jefferson announced to his son-in-law on July 5,

covering one from Livingston and Monroe to him in which they informed him that on the 30 of April they signed a treaty with France, ceding to us the island of N[ew] Orleans and all Louisiana as it had been held by Spain. The price is not mentioned, we are in hourly expectation of the treaty by a special messenger.

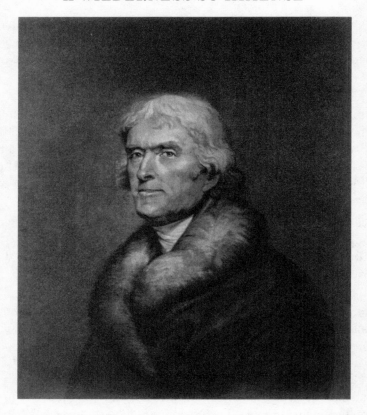

*President Thomas Jefferson in January 1805 from the portrait by Rembrandt Peale. As the debate over the extension of slavery into the territory of the Louisiana Purchase grew strident, the implications of the Missouri Compromise alarmed Jefferson. To maintain a balance of power in the Senate, Maine joined the union as a free state in March 1820, Missouri joined as a slave state in August 1821, and slavery was henceforth prohibited north of 36° 30' north latitude. "A geographical line, coinciding with a marked principle, moral and political," Jefferson wrote in April 1820, "once conceived and held up to the angry passions of men, will never be obliterated, and every new irritation will mark it deeper and deeper."* (Courtesy Library of Virginia)

"It is something larger than the whole U.S.," Jefferson continued, "probably containing 500 millions of acres, the U.S. containing 434 millions." "By the acquisition of Louisiana," London's *European Magazine* reported, "the whole extent of the United States will then be 1,680,000 square miles . . . or about sixteen times and a half larger than Great Britain and Ireland!!!" Louisiana's boundaries were vague, even in the treaty, but Jefferson's guess was close. Sixteen years later, when the lines were finally drawn, the Louisiana Purchase territory comprised 529,402,880 acres. Jefferson was right on the mark, however, about the first and paramount consequence of his Louisiana Purchase: "This removes from us the greatest source of danger to our peace."[6]

As the astonishing news spread, letters of congratulations poured into the White House. "It has the air of enchantment," seventy-five-year-old General Horatio Gates wrote from his home at Rose Hill, New York, "as the greatest and most beneficial event that has taken place since the Declaration of Independence." An admirer from Tennessee, David Campbell, wrote that "in its magnitude it approaches to a second Declaration of Independence." So common was the analogy between the Louisiana Purchase and independence that even the French chargé d'affaires, Louis André Pichon, described the transaction as "the greatest achievement in the history of the United States since their independence."[7]

Ohio senator John Smith voiced the other common comparison. The "permanent and exclusive" control of the Mississippi was the greatest contribution toward "peace and harmony among ourselves," Smith wrote, "since the establishment of the federal constitution." For the moment at least, as Pichon reported to Talleyrand, "the enemies of the President seem to be truly stupefied."[8]

Jefferson's "hourly expectation of the treaty by a special messenger" was too optimistic by more than a week. Livingston and Monroe had sent copies by three different messengers. The fastest courier delivered the Louisiana Purchase Treaty, the two conventions, and their cover letter to the president on Thursday evening, July 14—Bastille Day.[9]

Despite their achievement, Livingston and Monroe adopted an almost apologetic tone in their letter transmitting the text of the Louisiana Purchase Treaty to Jefferson and Madison. "An acquisition of so great an extent was, we well Know, not contemplated by our appointment," they wrote,

> but we are persuaded that the Circumstances and Considerations which induced us to make it, will justify us, in the measure, to our Government and Country.

"Before the negotiation commenced," they wrote, "the first Consul had decided to offer to the U[nited] States by sale the whole of Louisiana, and not a part of it." As their discussions continued they had discovered "that Mr. Marbois was absolutely restricted to the disposition of the whole" as well, and "that he would treat for no less portion, and . . . that it was useless to urge it."[10]

Had Bonaparte been willing to sell only New Orleans, they admitted, acquiring possession of the east bank of the Mississippi River would have fulfilled their instructions. But in time "a divided Jurisdiction over the River" was certain to "beget jealousies, discontents and dissentions which the wisest policy on our part could not prevent." By acquiring both banks of "this great River and all the streams that empty into it . . . the apprehension of these disasters is banished for ages."[11]

They saw many advantages in the acquisition of the entire Louisiana territory. The purchase bolstered American neutrality. "We separate ourselves in great measure from the European World and its concerns, especially its wars and intrigues." It was a step toward economic self-sufficiency—"a great stride to real and substantial independence . . . in all our foreign and domestic Relations." They hoped that it might cement "the Bond of our Union . . . by the encreased parity of interest" between west and east, south and north. And finally, on the world stage, "without exciting the apprehensions of any Power," it gave the young American republic "a more imposing attitude, with respect to all."[12]

With the text of the treaty at last in hand, Jefferson summoned his cabinet to meet on Saturday, July 16, to plan their next steps. At Bonaparte's insistence, the Louisiana Purchase Treaty set an October 30 deadline for ratification. Jefferson's first question to the cabinet was, "Shall Congress be called, or only Senate and when?" Their unanimous recommendation was to convene both houses of Congress on October 17. In preparation, Secretary of State Madison would send copies of the treaty to the senators and congressmen with a letter explaining "that the call 3 weeks earlier than they had fixed was rend[ere]d necessary by the treaty, and urging a punctual attendance on the 1st day."[13]

Jefferson and his cabinet also decided that "the substance of the treaty [should] be made public, but not the treaty itself." They wanted Daniel Clark, the American consul at New Orleans, to turn "his attention to the public property [to be] transferred to us" including "archives, papers and documents." In case the Spanish reacted angrily, Jefferson and his cabinet resolved to send William C. C. Claiborne, governor of the Mississippi Territory, to take possession of New Orleans "and act as Governor and Intendant under the Spanish laws, leaving every thing to go on as heretofore [and] making no innovation, nor doing a single act which will bear postponing." Two companies of troops would be put on alert at Fort Adams, which commanded the Mississippi River at the American boundary, midway between Natchez and Baton Rouge. Jefferson wanted to "get the Spanish troops off as soon as possible."[14]

After considering the domestic implications of the treaty, the cabinet turned its attention to Livingston and Monroe, voicing unanimous approval for "their having treated for Louisiana and the price given." Jefferson, Madison, Dearborn, and Smith agreed to inform their diplomats that they saw "no reason to doubt ratification of the whole." Mr. Gallatin, the president noted, had scruples about the separation of powers and "disapprove[d] of this last as committing members of the Congress. All the other points unanimous."[15]

As the meeting drew to a close, Jefferson and his cabinet addressed one last concern. Ever since Juan Ventura Morales had precipitated the Mississippi crisis on October 16, 1802, Jefferson and his friends had been proclaiming the critical importance both of New Orleans *and the Floridas*. His ministers had accomplished vastly more than anyone expected. Still, if measured against the letter of their instructions, they had sent home only half a loaf. How important were the Floridas?

In light of the Louisiana Purchase Treaty, the cabinet's answer was a frugal and resounding shrug. "We are more indifferent about the purchase of the Floridas," Jefferson noted, "because of the money we have to provide for Louisiana." Their indifference was also rooted in a typically Jeffersonian anticipation of the future—"because we think they cannot fail to fall in our hands." Westerners immediately agreed. "As to the Floridas," Senator John Breckinridge wrote from Lexington, Kentucky, "I really consider their acquisition as of no consequence for the present. We can obtain them long before we shall want them, and upon our own terms."[16]

Although the success of Jefferson's emissaries astonished the entire nation, the president's political adversaries did not remain "stupefied" for very long. Indeed, the first Federalist criticisms of the Louisiana Purchase came ashore with Rufus King. Ten weeks at sea gave King ample time for reflection upon the implications of the Louisiana Purchase. As to the western territory, King's opinions dated back to his flirtation with New England separatism during the Jay-Gardoqui negotiations of 1785–1786. Once again, as King was preparing for his departure from London in May 1803, Americans there heard him complain that the Louisiana territory "will be too extensive" and "impossible to govern."[17]

James Monroe and his friend Fulwar Skipwith warned the administration of King's hostile opinions (and of the political ambitions that led to his candidacy for the vice presidency in 1804), but George William Erving was more blunt about his colleague the ambassador. Educated in England but a staunch republican from King's adopted New York, Erving had been sharply attacked by the Federalist press when his appointment as the American consul in London displaced Timothy Pickering's nephew, Samuel Williams, "a favorite child of the Essex tribe." Erving was "an offensive aristocrat in manners and habits," the *New-England Palladium* sneered from Boston, "but a jacobin in principle."[18]

Ambassador King, Erving warned Secretary of State Madison, was "a very artificial and dangerous character—a man with two faces." He was "a sort of Janus in his common intercourse with the world," Erving contended, "and he would be a *Sejanus* in certain political circumstances"— an allusion to the ambitious praetorian guard Lucius Aelius Sejanus, who had poisoned the son of the Roman emperor Tiberius while plotting to place himself on the imperial throne.[19] Madison and Monroe had their own misgivings about the returning ambassador, for each had witnessed Rufus King's duplicity firsthand during the congressional intrigues over the Mississippi River in the 1780s.

While nay-saying New England Federalists fumed about the Louisiana Purchase, Alexander Hamilton's immediate reaction—an intricate blend of realism, partisanship, and regional pride—influenced his compatriots in the middle states, the south, and the west. The Louisiana Purchase was beneficial, Hamilton announced in an unsigned *New-York Evening Post* editorial published on July 5, just days after the news reached America, not because it expanded American territory but because it "was essential to the peace and prosperity of our Western country," and because it opened "a free and valuable market to our commercial states." So long as the price was not "too dear," Hamilton condoned the "exultation which the friends of the administration display, and which all Americans may be allowed to feel."[20]

"This purchase has been made during the period of Mr. Jefferson's presidency," Hamilton had to admit,

> and will, doubtless, give éclat to his administration. Every man, however, possessed of the least candour and reflection will readily acknowledge that the acquisition has been solely owing to a fortuitous concurrence of unforeseen and unexpected circumstances, and not to any wise or vigorous measures on the part of the American government.

"The real truth is," Hamilton continued after several paragraphs about Spain and France and St. Domingue, "Bonaparte found himself absolutely compelled . . . to relinquish his darling plan of colonizing the banks of the Mississippi." This alone enabled Jefferson's administration to achieve "what the feebleness and pusillanimity of its miserable system of measures could never have acquired." Moreover, "after making due allowance for great events," if Hamilton were to assign credit for the Louisiana Purchase to anyone, "the merit of it . . . [was] due to our ambassador Chancellor Livingston [of New York], and not to the Envoy Extraordinary" from Virginia, James Monroe.[21]

Louisiana's immense acreage was "extremely problematical" for Hamilton. New Orleans would have been "perfectly adequate to every purpose," he thought, "for whoever is in possession of that, has the uncontrouled command of the river." Perhaps in time the United States might barter the Louisiana territory "for the Floridas," which Hamilton regarded as "obviously of far greater value to us than all the immense, undefined region west of the river." Calculating that only one sixteenth of American territory east of the Mississippi was "yet under occupation," Hamilton regarded expansion west of the river as "too distant and remote to strike the mind of a sober politician with much force."[22]

Hamilton saw the dangers of the Louisiana Purchase as readily apparent. America was sure to suffer "all the injuries of a too widely dispersed population"—and worse. "By adding to the great weight of the western part of our territory," Hamilton predicted, the Louisiana Purchase "must hasten the dismemberment of a large portion of our country, or a dissolution of the Government." And finally there was the existing population. "How they are to be governed is another question," Hamilton wrote. "Whether as a colony"—with the risk of transforming the American republic into an empire—"or . . . an integral part of the United States"— despite differences of language, culture, religion, and ethnicity. "The probable consequences" of the Louisiana Purchase, Alexander Hamilton concluded,

> and the ultimate effect it is likely to produce on the political state of our country, will furnish abundant matter of speculation to the American statesman.

In a parting shot at the president, Hamilton attributed all credit for the treaty to his fellow New Yorker, Chancellor Livingston. "The cession was voted in [Bonaparte's] Council of State on the 8th of April," Hamilton wrote (adopting a chronology that must have been supplied by Rufus King), "and Mr. Munro did not even arrive till the 12th."[23]

A week after Hamilton's unsigned editorial appeared in New York, more strident opinions began to fill New England's Federalist newspapers. On Thursday, July 13, a letter in Boston's *Columbian Centinel* opened the litany of complaint. The author, who identified himself as Fabricius, was none other than the High Federalist of Dedham, Massachusetts, Fisher Ames. Forced into retirement in 1797 by the lung disease that would claim his life at the age of fifty on the Fourth of July 1808, Ames had led the Federalist party in the House of Representatives during the Washington administration. Through his brilliant newspaper essays and an extensive private correspondence, this self-described leader of the Essex Junto retained an influence among New England Federalists rivaled in 1803 only by Hamilton's.[24]

Louisiana, Ames declared, was "a great waste, a wilderness unpeopled with any beings except wolves and wandering Indians." Although the exact figure had not yet been announced, Fabricius reckoned that the price was too high: "We are to give money of which we have too little for land of which we already have too much." Fresh land in the west was sure to "drain our people away from the pursuit of . . . manufactures and commerce." Worst of all, the watershed of the Mississippi "may be cut up into States without number, but each with *two votes in the Senate*." Supported by their vassals in the west, the slaveholders of the Old Dominion would dominate the enlarged nation—"imperial Virginia, arbitress of the whole."[25]

Fisher Ames and his Federalist friends regarded Virginia's lust for possession of the Mississippi watershed—dating back to the congressional dispute over the Jay-Gardoqui negotiations of 1785–1786—as proof of the Old Dominion's malevolent passion for preeminence in national politics. "The *great* state," Ames wrote Timothy Dwight, editor of the *Hartford Courant* and the *Connecticut Mirror,* "has the ambition to be the *great nation*." While New Englanders "make turnpikes and busy ourselves with local objects," Ames complained to Rufus King, "Virginia rides the great horse." The Old Dominion, Ames fretted in an essay published after his death, was large enough to subvert the American republic into an imperial monarchy. By expanding the nation into the "unmeasured world beyond that river," he lamented to Boston Federalist Christopher Gore, the republic was rushing

like a comet into infinite space. In our wild career, we may jostle some
other world out of its orbit, but we shall, in every event, quench the
light of our own.

"Is Virginia to be our Rome?" Ames asked, as he projected Jefferson into
the role of Caesar or the Emperor Bonaparte. "Why should it be supposed," he wondered,

> that the Northern States, who possess so prodigious a preponderance
> of *white* population, of industry, commerce, and civilization over the
> Southern, will remain subject to Virginia?[26]

Race and ethnicity—as well as calculations of regional self-interest—
figured prominently in Federalist attitudes. "Virginia holds her preponderance, as mistress of the Union," Ames complained in an essay for the
*Repertory* that was reprinted in the *Boston Gazette,* because the three-
fifths clause of the Constitution gave the south an advantage in congressional representation and the Electoral College. "Without the black
votes, Mr. Jefferson would not have been president," Ames wrote, refer-
ring not to black *voters* but to the extra weight that the three-fifths compromise of the Constitution added to the votes of their masters. In order
to terminate an "inequality [that] will be still more extended by the
acquisition of Louisiana," Timothy Pickering introduced a constitutional
amendment to compute state representation solely on the basis of free
population—but it died on the table in the United States Senate. Decisions about America's future, Fisher Ames wrote in the *New-England
Palladium,* were being decided by "*three fifths* of the ancient dominion,
and the offscourings of Europe."[27]

Federalists regarded the residents of Louisiana with similar disdain
and Article III of the treaty with disgust. "Having bought an empire,"
Ames asked, "who is to be emperor? The sovereign people? and what
people? all, or only the people of the dominant states?" Otters, he fumed,
were more capable of self-government than Louisiana's

> *Gallo-Hispano-Indian omnium gatherum* of savages and adventurers,
> whose pure morals are expected to sustain and glorify our republic.
> Never before was it attempted to play the fool on so great a scale.

"New Orleans," a meandering Federalist reported to Alexander Hamilton from the relative safety of Natchez, is

a place inhabited by a Mixture of Americans, English, Spanish, and French and crouded every year . . . with two or three thousand boatmen from the back country, remark[able] for their dissipated habits, unruly tempers, and lawless conduct . . . and where the white population bears so small a proportion to the black . . . [that] the Blacks have already been guilty of two or three insurrections within a few years back.

"Should this precious treaty go into operation," warned Josiah Quincy, a future president of Harvard College, "I doubt not [that] thick skinned beasts will crowd Congress Hall, Buffaloes from the head of the Missouri and Alligators from the Red River." The size of Louisiana and the diversity of its population were threats to the republic. "In a territory so extensive as the United States, comprising within its limits . . . peoples whose sentiments, habits, manners, and prejudices, are very different, and whose local interests and attachments are various," a Fourth of July orator reminded the citizens of tiny Conway, Massachusetts, in 1804, "it is not strange that the seed of division should exist."[28]

When the Louisiana Purchase sent the big red playground ball of separatism bouncing once again through the adolescent republic, Fisher Ames, Alexander Hamilton, and Rufus King held fast to the nationalist vision of High Federalism, never wavering in their commitment to the union. Many of their friends in Massachusetts and Connecticut, however, were ready (as King had been in 1786) to grab the ball and go home. "The Virginia faction have certainly formed a deliberate plan to govern and depress New England," Salem-born Timothy Higginson, a founding director of the Bank of Massachusetts and member of the Essex Junto, told Pickering, "and this eagerness to extend our territory and create new States is an essential part of it."[29]

The separatist reaction to the Louisiana Purchase was missing three veterans from 1786. Nathaniel Gorham had died in 1796, bankrupt after financing 2.6 million acres of New York land with depreciated state currency that Hamilton's funding plan restored to its original value. Essex attorney Nathan Dane was on the sidelines, too deaf for politics and hard at work on a nine-volume *General Abridgment and Digest of American Laws,* which would establish his reputation in the field of American jurisprudence. Dane would attribute his subsequent participation in the separatist Hartford Convention of 1814 to the conviction that "somebody must go to prevent mischief." Theodore Sedgwick had recently become an associate justice of the Supreme Judicial Court of Massachusetts and was opposed to any "abandonment of the union." Sedgwick

agreed with his good friend Alexander Hamilton that the "Dismembre-
ment of our Empire" offered "no relief to our real Disease; which is
DEMOCRACY, the poison of which by a subdivision will only be . . . the
more virulent."[30]

At the head of the separatist reaction to the Louisiana Purchase
was Massachusetts senator Timothy Pickering, of Essex County. Self-
righteous, suspicious, and conspiratorial by nature, Pickering was one of
the most disagreeable personalities in all of American political history. A
man who entertained himself by compiling dossiers on his political enemies.[31] A man whose fervent prayer at the age of eighty-two was:

> I pray God to spare my life and preserve my faculties, until I can, by a
> correct history of Jefferson's public life . . . exhibit his character with
> those dark shades which belong to it—in order to enlighten the public
> mind, and hold him up [as] a warning beacon, for the benefit of the
> present and future generations.

"The Great Land-Jobber" was one of the milder epithets that Pickering
coined after the Louisiana Purchase to describe "the Moonshine philoso-
pher of Monticello," whom he regarded as "one of the worst men who
ever directed the affairs of a free country."[32]

On Christmas Eve 1803, Coyle's boardinghouse on Capitol Hill in
Washington—home away from home for New England congressmen—
became the headquarters of the separatist reaction to the Louisiana
Purchase.[33] "Although the end of all our Revolutionary labors and expec-
tations is disappointment," Pickering wrote to his old friend Judge
Richard Peters,

> I will not yet despair: I will rather anticipate a new confederacy,
> exempt from the corrupt and corrupting influence and oppression of
> the aristocratic Democrats of the South. There will be—and our chil-
> dren at farthest will see it—a separation. The white and black popula-
> tion will mark the boundary. The British Provinces . . . will become
> members of the Northern confederacy.

A month later Pickering outlined the separatist plan in greater detail to
Salem-born George Cabot, a former senator and future president of the
separatist Hartford Convention of 1814. "Shall we sit still," Pickering
asked,

until even in the Eastern States the principles of genuine Federalism shall be overwhelmed? . . . The principles of our Revolution point to the remedy,—a separation. That this can be accomplished, and without spilling one drop of blood, I have little doubt. . . . I do not believe in the practicability of a long-continued union. A Northern confederacy would unite congenial characters, and present a fair prospect of public happiness; while the Southern States, having a similarity of habits, might be left "to manage their own affairs in their own way."

"*When* and *how* is a separation to be effected?" Pickering asked rhetorically.

It must begin in Massachusetts. The proposition would be welcomed in Connecticut; and could we doubt of New Hampshire? But New York must be associated . . . [and] made the centre of the confederacy. Vermont and New Jersey would follow of course, and Rhode Island of necessity.

From Coyle's boardinghouse, Pickering and his lieutenants, including Uriah Tracy and Roger Griswold, of Connecticut, were discreetly rallying their forces. "The Connecticut gentlemen have seriously meditated upon it," Pickering reported, and "we suppose the British Provinces in Canada and Nova Scotia . . . may become members of the Northern league. A liberal treaty of amity and commerce will form a bond of union between Great Britain and the Northern confederacy highly useful to both." Griswold, who became the separatist leader in the House, calculated that the states "to be embraced by the Northern confederacy" could readily pay off their share of the national debt, "leaving out the millions given for Louisiana."[34]

New Hampshire congressman Samuel Hunt recruited his Senate colleague William Plumer into the separatist movement with the assurance that Hunt's uncle, Massachusetts governor Caleb Strong, was already on board. "The ratification of this treaty and the possession of that immense territory will hasten the dissolution of our present government," Plumer had told his colleagues in October 1803.

We must form different empires. . . . Admit this western world into the union, and you destroy with a single operation the whole weight and importance of the eastern states . . . [and] precipitate them to erect a separate and independent Empire.

By the end of January, Senator Plumer had written some four hundred letters rallying his friends to the separatist banner, and he was working closely with Pickering as well as Connecticut senators Uriah Tracy and James Hillhouse and congressmen Roger Griswold and Calvin Goddard. "My hopes," Plumer told his friends, "rest on the union of New England."[35]

Another key participant in the separatist reaction to the Louisiana Purchase was the distinguished jurist Tapping Reeve, who had tutored Aaron Burr after his graduation at Princeton and married Burr's sister after leaving the Princeton faculty to practice law. Now settled in Fairfield, Connecticut, where he had established the first law school in the United States, the sixty-year-old Reeve perhaps made the disgruntled Federalists' first informal approach to the mercurial Democratic-Republican vice president, Burr.[36]

The New Englanders agonized over their doubts about Burr's character—"his spirit of ambition and revenge"—but an effective northern confederacy needed the commercial State of New York, where the vice president was contemplating a run for the governorship. Although the party of the rich and the wise and the good had no hope of electing a Federalist governor, factional rivalries among New York Republicans gave them leverage at the polls "if Colonel Burr is elevated in New York to the office of Governor by the votes of Federalism." Congressman Roger Griswold outlined the pros and cons of this tactic in a long letter to Connecticut congressman Oliver Wolcott. He admitted that

> objections of a very serious nature oppose the election of Colonel Burr, whether that election is viewed in relation to a general union of the Northern States, or in relation to the power which the office will give a man of Colonel Burr's talents. . . . But, my dear sir, what else can we do? If we remain inactive, our ruin is certain.

"As unpleasant as the thing may be," Griswold concluded, supporting "the election of Colonel Burr [w]as the only hope . . . of rallying in defence of New England."[37]

Griswold had met Burr in December at the private dinner at which Senators Pickering, Hillhouse, Plumer, and Tracy broached their northern confederacy plan to the vice president. "Mr. Hillhouse unequivocally declared that it was his opinion that the United States would soon form two distinct and separate governments," Plumer recorded in his diary. "On this subject Mr. Burr conversed very freely," creating the impression "that he not only thought *such an event would take place—but that it was necessary it should."* Later that evening, as he analyzed Burr's "every sentiment and even expression," Senator Plumer had doubts about the vice president's candor. Burr "possessed the talent of making an impression of an opinion . . . without explicitly stating or necessarily giving his sentiments," Plumer realized. "In every thing he said or did, he had a design— and perhaps no man's language was ever so apparently explicit, and at the same time so covert and indefinite." Since Congress was about to adjourn, Griswold and Burr agreed to meet in New York on Wednesday, April 4— about three weeks prior to the gubernatorial election.[38]

Although Griswold and Pickering's group promoted Burr's candidacy in New York, they were opposed by the formidable voice of Alexander Hamilton. Early in February, when the state's Federalist leaders met in Albany for a strategy session, Hamilton denounced Burr as "a man of irregular and insatiable ambition" whose "elevation by the aid of foederalists" would only "give him fair play to disorganize New England" by joining forces with the separatists to become "chief of the Northern portion" of the nation. And again in April, at a private Federalist meeting in New York City, Hamilton warned his compatriots that the New Englanders supporting Burr contended "that a dismemberment of the Union is expedient."[39]

As the election drew near, Burr was optimistic and the New England Federalists began planning for an autumn meeting—a November convention in Boston. But the New York election was becoming unusually mean-spirited. With ten days to go the *New York City Commercial Advertiser* quoted Burr's opponent, New York's chief justice, Morgan Lewis, to the effect that "had he known how the election would have been conducted" he would have let the government go to hell rather than be a candidate. As yet unnoticed in the metropolis, however, were two angry letters printed in the pages of the *Albany Evening Post* and the *Albany Register* describing Hamilton's warnings about the dangers of Aaron Burr.[40]

The balloting, expected to be close, was spread over five days. Aaron Burr carried Manhattan by a margin of one hundred votes, but by Monday, April 30—the first anniversary of the Louisiana Purchase Treaty— upstate election returns buried Burr's political career in a landslide. In the previous gubernatorial election, "Governor [George] Clinton, the most popular man in the state," one editor crowed, "had a majority of 3,945 only." By Saturday, May 5, everyone knew that Morgan Lewis had crushed Aaron Burr by 30,829 votes to 22,139—a margin of almost nine thousand. "So much for Burrism and Federalism in 1804!"[41]

Burr was humiliated. And then someone sent Burr a couple of week-old newspaper clippings. The first—published in the *Albany Evening Post*—was the complete text of a private letter written by Dr. Charles Cooper about Hamilton's comments at a private dinner after the Federalist meeting in Albany back in February. Hamilton "has come out decidedly against Burr," Cooper had written, "indeed when he was here he spoke of him as a dangerous man [who] ought not to be trusted." The second clipping was worse. Angered that Burr supporters had published his letter, and outraged when they accused him of exaggerating Hamilton's comments, Cooper had fired off a letter in defense of his veracity that found its way into the *Albany Register* on April 24. The good doctor protested that he had exercised restraint in his description of Hamilton's comments, "for really sir, I could detail to you a still more despicable opinion which Gen. Hamilton has expressed of Mr. Burr." The second clipping—with its reference to Hamilton's despicable opinion—was the one that Burr enclosed with a note demanding from Hamilton "a prompt and unqualified acknowledgment or denial" of his reported remarks. The note was the first step toward a duel.[42]

Burr regarded Hamilton's response—"that I could not, without manifest impropriety, make the avowal or disavowal which you seem to think necessary"—as a further insult. Although Hamilton claimed that nothing he had said "exceed[ed] the limits justifiable among political opponents," Burr disagreed. More angry notes were exchanged until the date of their fateful "interview" was set for Wednesday, July 11, 1804. Citing religious and moral principles—as well as the possibility that his remarks may, in fact, "have injured Col. Burr"—Hamilton confided to a piece of paper his resolve

> to *reserve* and *throw away* my first fire, and *I have thoughts* even of *reserving* my second fire—and thus give a double opportunity to Col. Burr to pause and reflect.

Many duels ended without bloodshed when both adversaries shot wide of the mark—vindicating their reputations on the field of honor by risking mortal combat without actually taking a life. Had Burr known of Hamilton's decision to throw away his first shot, both men might well have survived their interview at Weehawken.[43]

Hidden by foliage below and virtually inaccessible from above, there was a small ledge in the rock palisades below Weehawken, New Jersey, a five-minute boat ride across the Hudson River from Greenwich Village. There, at about seven o'clock on Wednesday morning, July 11, the heavy

.544 caliber ball from Hamilton's gun snapped off a tree limb twelve feet above the ground. Had Hamilton thrown away his first shot? Or did his pistol discharge as he fell mortally wounded by Burr's shot, which struck above his right hip, tore through his liver, and lodged in his spine? Only Burr and two men attending as seconds knew, and the two witnesses disagreed about who shot first. At two o'clock the next afternoon, Alexander Hamilton died.[44]

After putting his personal affairs in order the night before the fatal "interview," Hamilton had written two final letters. The second was to his wife. The first had gone to his Federalist friend Theodore Sedgwick, stating that "Dismemberment of our Empire" offered "no relief to our real Disease; which is DEMOCRACY."[45]

Burr's defeat in the gubernatorial election and Hamilton's death on the field of honor at Weehawken disrupted the movement for a northern confederacy in reaction to the Louisiana Purchase. The Boston separatist meeting planned for November 1804 was put off for years—but the impulse toward separation only lay dormant. New England separatism surfaced again in 1808–1809 in response to Jefferson's embargo, and it culminated during the War of 1812 in the Hartford Convention of 1814. John Quincy Adams regarded the separatist reaction to the Louisiana Purchase as "the key to all the great movements of . . . the Federal party in New England, from that time forward, till its final catastrophe in the Hartford Convention."[46]

As late as the third week of January 1815, the inveterate separatist Timothy Pickering was still eager with anticipation. "With regard to the admission of new States into the Union," Pickering wrote on January 23,

> events with which the present moment is teeming may take away the subject itself. If the British succeed in their expedition against New Orleans—and . . . I see no reason to doubt of their success—I shall consider the Union as severed.

"By taking and holding New Orleans," and by gaining command of "the whole Western country," Senator Pickering wrote the next day, Great Britain

> will break the Union, essentially diminish the power of the United States, and thus remove from us . . . the whole Western world . . . and leave the Atlantic States free from their mischievous control—a control every day becoming more powerful and dangerous.[47]

The New England separatist reaction to the Louisiana Purchase had been mortally wounded on the palisades overlooking the Hudson River at Weehawken in 1804. It was ultimately destroyed—a thousand miles away from Senator Pickering's desk in Washington—by Andrew Jackson's cannon on January 8, 1815, at Chalmette, on the east bank of the Mississippi River below New Orleans.

The Federalists were not alone in their contention that the Louisiana Purchase went against the Constitution. President Thomas Jefferson, champion of limited government and a strict construction of the Constitution, had his own doubts about its constitutionality—doubts that he discussed openly with New Hampshire senator William Plumer, a subsequent participant in the separatist reaction, and many others. "The general government has no powers but such as the constitution has given it," Jefferson explained in letters to Pennsylvania statesman John Dickinson, Kentucky senator John Breckenridge, and others, "and it has not given it a power of holding foreign territory, and still less of incorporating it into the Union." The Louisiana Purchase Treaty was an act "beyond the Constitution," Jefferson believed. He saw the adoption of a suitable amendment as the way for "the nation to sanction an act done for its great good, without its previous authority."[48]

For seven weeks, from June 30 when the news had reached him in Washington through August 17, Jefferson tinkered with an amendment to set things right. The language to authorize the purchase itself came easily. The difficulty for Jefferson and his New England critics lay in the implications of Article III of the treaty, which provided "that the inhabitants of the ceded territory shall be incorporated in the Union of the United States and admitted . . . to the enjoyment of all these rights, advantages and immunities of citizens of the United States."[49] Civilized New Englanders wanted no truck with "the half savage *omnium gatherum* of Louisiana," with its "Frenchmen, Spaniards and Indians," with the prospective immigration of "United Irish and rogues," or with any "red, yellow or black brethren beyond the Mississippi." The *Columbian Centinel and Massachusetts Federalist* complained that "the treaty changes the identity of our nation—the United States are no longer the same."[50] President Jefferson was more concerned about the Indians.[51]

Jefferson's admiration for American Indians was rooted in his boyhood encounters with the Cherokee at Shadwell, his father's home in Albemarle County, near Monticello, and in the eloquence of Chief

Outacity, which he witnessed as a student at the College of William and Mary. Admiration and optimism permeated his comments about Indians in his *Notes on Virginia,* and for years Jefferson had advocated Indian relations based on both justice and fear. "Fear to keep them from attacking us," he wrote from Paris in 1786, for

> after the injuries we have done them, they cannot love us. . . . But justice is what we should never lose sight of, and in time it may recover their esteem.

Seventeen years later, the view from the White House was different. While Livingston and Monroe were negotiating the Louisiana Purchase in Paris, President Jefferson was advising William C. C. Claiborne, governor of the Mississippi Territory, that it was "all important to press on the Indians, as steadily and strenuously as they can bear." American settlements, the president informed General William Henry Harrison, governor of the Indiana Territory,

> will gradually circumscribe and approach the Indians, and they will in time either incorporate with us as citizens of the United States, or remove beyond the Mississippi. . . . As to their fear, we presume our strength and their weakness is now so visible that they must see we have only to shut our hand to crush them, and that all our liberalities to them proceed from motives of pure humanity only.

"The preceding views," Jefferson cautioned Claiborne, "are such as should not be formally declared."[52]

The Louisiana Purchase accelerated the shift in Jefferson's policy. His draft amendment to the Constitution would have given Congress authority to take possession of Indian lands east of the Mississippi and exchange them "for those of white inhabitants on the West side thereof and above the latitude of 31 degrees." If Congress acted "with the wisdom we have a right to expect," the president wrote to Horatio Gates in his July 11 acknowledgment of the general's praise for America's diplomatic triumph, "they may make [Louisiana] the means of tempting all our Indians on the East side of the Mississippi to remove to the West," thereby "condensing instead of scattering our population." The sale of vacated Indian lands in the east, he suggested in a similar letter to his old revolutionary colleague John Dickinson, of Pennsylvania, might "pay the whole debt contracted before it comes due."[53] The Louisiana Purchase prompted an ominous transition in the government's policies toward American Indians. "Should any tribe be foolhardy enough to take up the hatchet," Jefferson wrote with chilling prescience, "seizing the whole country of the tribe, and driving them across the Mississippi . . . would be an example to others, and a furtherance of our final consolidation."[54]

Years later, when President Andrew Jackson offered the Choctaw Indians "a country beyond the Mississippi," he described it as one of the "valuable objects which Mr. Jefferson promised you."[55] America's barely visible first steps along the Trail of Tears were taken in the White House as Thomas Jefferson pondered the implications of the Louisiana Purchase.

Already reluctant to acknowledge openly his changing Indian policy,

*This late-nineteenth-century lithograph, titled* Traité avec les Etats Unis, *presents a romanticized depiction of Bonaparte signing the Louisiana Purchase on May 22, 1803. In fact, when he ratified the treaty that Monroe, Livingston, and Barbé-Marbois had signed earlier in May, Bonaparte was preoccupied with the resumption of war against Great Britain and more interested in getting his money for Louisiana than in staging an elaborate ceremony—while the American commissioners were impatient to get the treaty on its way to the United States for prompt ratification in advance of the six month deadline.* (Courtesy Louisiana State Museum and Dr. and Mrs. E. Ralph Lupin)

Jefferson was suddenly forced to evade all the troubling constitutional implications of the Louisiana Purchase as well. On August 18 the president and his secretary of state opened urgent messages from Livingston and Monroe. Bonaparte was having second thoughts. The entire transaction might be in jeopardy. If Jefferson wanted Louisiana, "it is highly important that the Congress be immediately called and the treaty and conventions . . . be carried into immediate effect," Monroe wrote.

> No delay should occur in performing what we are to perform, since a failure in any one point in the time specified may defeat and I think will defeat the whole.

After the treaty was ratified, Livingston wrote, Bonaparte began raising "a great deal of trouble with . . . an opinion prevailing that we have made too favorable a bargain." Public opinion as we know it today was a minor problem. Weeks after signing the treaty, Bonaparte's Senate on May 18 had agreed to create him Emperor Napoleon I, so his concern for appearances may have been heightened by the national plebiscite to confirm the title scheduled for November 6—but the real issue was money.[56]

The first consul was looking for "the slightest pretence . . . to undo the work," Livingston warned the president, unless he got ready cash for his war with Great Britain. "I hope the President will convene the Congress to create the funds," Monroe reiterated, "since I repeat again a failure to comply strictly within the terms limited" could give Napoleon reason to break the treaty as Americans had seen him do with other nations. "I hope [to] God that nothing will prevent your immediate ratification and without altering a syllable of the terms," Livingston wrote again on the 25th.

> If you wish anything changed, ratify unconditionally and set on foot a new negotiation. Be persuaded that France is sick of the bargain and that Spain is much dissatisfied and the slightest pretence will lose you the treaty.[57]

At this crucial moment in France, James Monroe saved the Louisiana Purchase—for he had two advantages over Livingston. Monroe knew the president's intentions better than anyone in Paris (having conferred with Jefferson more recently than Livingston), and he could be uniquely confident that his closest personal and political friends (who just happened to be the president and secretary of state) would back him in a crisis. Napoleon wanted money, and Monroe had come to Europe with a $2 million appropriation from Congress for the purchase of New Orleans and

West Florida. He and Livingston had even mentioned these funds during early negotiations with Barbé-Marbois and Talleyrand—a detail that surely had not slipped Napoleon's mind. In the absence of clear instructions from home, however, Livingston raised a reasonable objection. Did they have the authority (and was it prudent) to pay Napoleon a huge sum of money when he was threatening to back away from the whole deal?

The answer was not without risk, but in the circumstances, an ocean away from the president, James Monroe and only James Monroe could say yes. Through the offices of Barings and of Hope & Co. in London, where he had succeeded Rufus King at the Court of St. James's, Monroe arranged an advance payment of $2 million "as a guaranty of the stipulations of the treaty." Livingston co-signed the order, and that was that.[58]

Which American minister deserves greater credit for the Louisiana Purchase? President Jefferson anticipated that question in his letter to Horatio Gates. "I find our opposition is very willing to pluck feathers from Monroe," he observed,

> although not fond of sticking them into Livingston's coat. The truth is both have a just portion of merit and were it necessary or proper it could be shewn that each has rendered peculiar service, and of important value.[59]

In short, Robert Livingston made the deal and James Monroe saved it.

After Monroe defused the crisis with Napoleon, however, Jefferson still faced the challenge of accommodating both his own constitutional scruples and the urgency of a prompt and unconditional ratification of the Louisiana Purchase Treaty. Livingston's and Monroe's warnings had reached him on Wednesday, August 17. On Thursday Jefferson abandoned his draft amendment and dispatched a series of letters that announced his strategy in clear and nearly identical terms. "I wrote you on the 12th instant on the subject of Louisiana" he advised Kentucky senator John Breckinridge, "and the constitutional provision which might be necessary for it," but

> a letter received yesterday shews that nothing must be said on that subject which may give a pretext for retracting; but that we should do sub-silentio what shall be found necessary.

"The less we say about the constitutional difficulties respecting Louisiana the better," he told Madison that same day. "What is necessary for surmounting them must be done sub-silentio." Responding to Attorney

General Levi Lincoln's suggestions for his draft amendment two weeks later, Jefferson observed "that the less that is said about any constitutional difficulty, the better. . . . It will be desirable for Congress to do what is necessary, *in silence.*"[60]

Early in September, in anticipation of the upcoming meeting of Congress, Jefferson outlined his thinking in somewhat greater detail to Virginia senator Wilson Cary Nicholas. The advice is vintage Jefferson, decisive and elusive. "Whatever Congress shall think it necessary to do," Jefferson wrote,

> should be done with as little debate as possible, and particularly so far as respects the constitutional difficulty. . . . I had rather ask an enlargement of power from the nation, where it is found necessary, than to assume it by a construction which would make our powers boundless. Our peculiar security is in possession of a written Constitution. Let us not make it a blank paper by construction. . . . I think it important, in the present case, to set an example against broad construction . . . confid[ent] that the good sense of our country will correct the evil of construction when it shall produce ill effects.[61]

The Constitution required a two-thirds vote for the ratification of a treaty (a provision inspired by the impasse over the Jay-Gardoqui negotiations of 1785–1786) and Jefferson had the votes in the Senate. There was nothing to be gained, and much to be lost, by spinning dangerous webs of constitutional theory. Federalist congressman John Rutledge, Jr., of South Carolina complained "that the measure cannot yet be even brought to the bar of argument."[62]

The Eighth Congress met on Monday, October 17, 1803—and Jefferson's Third Annual Message contained nothing about the constitutionality of the Louisiana Purchase. Two days later—time enough for the required three readings on three separate days—the Senate ratified the Louisiana Purchase Treaty by a vote of twenty-four to seven. (New Jersey senator Jonathan Dayton, who had visited New Orleans in June and objected to the French presence in North America, was the only Federalist who crossed the aisle.) "The Senate have taken less time to deliberate on this important treaty," New Hampshire separatist William Plumer grumbled, "than they allowed themselves on the most trivial Indian contract."[63]

Once the treaty had been pushed through the Senate, the necessary provisions for its implementation required action by both houses of Congress. And it was here, despite Federalist complaints to the contrary, that the constitutional implications of the Louisiana Purchase *were* "brought to the bar of argument."[64] Party discipline enabled Jefferson to enforce a virtually silent vote in the Senate, but the members of the House of Representatives were more unruly and rambunctious. His floor managers enjoyed a three-to-one majority in the House, but on October 24, 1803, they carried their first procedural showdown by a margin of only two votes—fifty-nine to fifty-seven. Only five years earlier, Jefferson's party had championed states' rights and strict construction in the Virginia and Kentucky Resolutions of 1798. Now their words could have been scripted by the Hamiltonian Federalists. They invoked the inherent powers of a sovereign nation, granted by the once hated "necessary and proper" and "general welfare" clauses of the Constitution.[65]

"I cannot perceive," said Caesar Augustus Rodney, "why within the fair meaning of this general provision is not included the power of increasing our territory, if necessary for the general welfare or common defence"—all too conveniently ignoring that just a few years earlier he and the Democratic-Republicans had readily perceived the dangers of such a broad construction. "Have we not vested in us," the Republican leader from Delaware asked,

> every power necessary for carrying [the Louisiana] treaty into effect, in the words of the Constitution which give Congress the authority to "make all laws which shall be necessary and proper for carrying into execution the foregoing powers, and all other powers vested by the Constitution in the government of the United States" . . . ?

Such were the constitutional rationalizations, voiced by his own party, that Jefferson wanted to keep off the record, sub-silentio. The bulwark of American liberty, our written Constitution, was threatened by "those who consider the grant of the treaty making power as boundless," Jefferson had warned. "If it is, then we have no Constitution." When the good of the republic required action "beyond the Constitution," perhaps Jefferson was right that in the long run it was better to act silently than to render the Constitution "a blank paper by construction."[66]

Entwined with the debate about the constitutionality of the Louisiana Purchase was another vexing matter. Article III of the Louisiana Purchase Treaty promised that "the ceded territory shall be incorporated in the Union of the United States" and its inhabitants granted all the "rights, advantages and immunities of citizens of the United States." Once the nation had taken possession of "this new, immense, unbounded world," what would be its relationship to the existing union? How would it be governed?[67]

Here, too, the question had both theoretical and practical dimensions. Anxious to keep the Atlantic states from being outnumbered, several Federalists suggested that Louisiana must remain a colony, its alien population unrepresented in Congress, its affairs administered from Washington. "We can obtain territory either by conquest or compact . . . without violating the Constitution," Connecticut senator Uriah Tracy stated. "We can hold territory," he said, "but to admit the inhabitants into the Union, to make citizens of them, and States, by treaty, we cannot constitutionally do." Rather than see themselves outnumbered in an expanded *republic,* the Federalists were prepared, at least for the sake of argument, to hint at the creation of an *empire*—governing the west by force rather than consent, treating its inhabitants as subjects rather than citizens. "I have often thought," wrote Gouverneur Morris, "that when we . . . acquire Canada and Louisiana it would be proper to govern them as provinces, and allow them no voice in our councils."[68]

Beneath these hints about imperial rule lay the ethnic and racial prejudice that permeated Federalist newspaper commentary about the Louisiana Purchase. "Can it be conceived . . . that these people, bred up in the arms of despotism, will suddenly be fitted for self-government and republicanism?" jeered the *Gazette of the United States.*

> Are they with their ignorance of our constitution, language, manners and habits, qualified . . . ? Are two Spaniards from New-Orleans to have the same influence in the Senate with two Senators from Virginia, Pennsylvania or Massachusetts?

Similar words echoed through the next century. "Kings can have subjects," but "it is a question whether a republic can," statesman and diplomat George Kennan remarked about the xenophobic impulse in American westward expansion.

> If it is true that our society is really capable of knowing only the quantity which we call "citizens," . . . then the potential scope of our system is limited . . . to people of our own kind—people who have grown up in the same peculiar spirit of independence and self-reliance, people who can accept, and enjoy, and content themselves with our institutions.[69]

Jefferson had similar doubts about Louisiana's foreign population and about the Indians on either side of the Mississippi. In both instances he

expected them to be supplanted or assimilated by sturdy American yeoman farmers.

As governor of Virginia in the last year of the Revolutionary War, Jefferson had coined the phrase "empire of liberty" in a letter directing
George Rogers Clark to secure the American west by capturing Detroit.
"Our confederacy," he had written from Paris on that chilly January afternoon in 1786, "must be viewed as the nest from which all America, North
and South is to be peopled."[70] Now, two decades later, as he prepared to
ensure the expansion of his empire of liberty into the Louisiana territory,
Jefferson's embrace of imperial authority gave many congressmen pause.

## CHAPTER SIXTEEN

# Fluctuations of the
# Political Thermometer

*I see too many proofs of the imperfection of human reason to entertain wonder or intolerance at any difference of opinion on any subject . . . experience having taught me the reasonableness of mutual sacrifices of opinion [and] . . . the expediency of doing what good we can; when we cannot do all we would wish.*

—Thomas Jefferson to John Randolph of Roanoke, December 1, 1803[1]

*Rumours of the cession to the United States were gaining ground. The fluctuations of the political thermometer in this respect were indicated by the greater or lesser eagerness with which people sought me—and that eagerness was on the decline.*

—Pierre Clément Laussat, *Memoirs of My Life*[2]

T HE UNRULY debate in the House of Representatives over granting him the authority he wanted for the administration of Louisiana—and especially the reservations expressed by congressmen from his own party—startled Jefferson. "More difference of opinion seems to exist as to the manner of disposing of Louisiana, than I had imagined possible!" he exclaimed to New York senator De Witt Clinton. "Our leading friends are not yet sufficiently aware of the necessity of accommodation and mutual sacrifice of opinion," he lamented, while "the opposition is drilled to act in phalanx on every question."[3] Jefferson felt that the inhabitants of Louisiana were "as yet as incapable of self-government as children"—the same characterization he later applied to slaves[4]—"yet some [congressmen] cannot bring themselves to suspend [their democratic] principles for a single moment." Even his floor leader in the House, Virginia's quick-tempered Republican John Randolph of Roanoke, got a presidential lecture on Aristotelian politics and "the reasonableness of mutual sacrifices of opinion [and] . . . the expediency of doing what good we can; when we cannot do all we would wish."[5]

According to accepted international law, Louisiana's existing laws remained in force until the United States altered them. Jefferson intended to "introduce the trial by jury in *criminal* cases, first," followed by "habeas corpus, the freedom of the press, freedom of religion etc. as soon as can be." Thereafter, as each passing year drew "their laws and organization to the mould of ours by degrees," Jefferson expected the inhabitants of Louisiana to "ripen for receiving these first principles of freedom" so that "Congress may from session to session confirm their enjoiment of them."[6]

On the premise that the inhabitants of Louisiana stood "in nearly the same relation to us as if they were a conquered country," as Republican William Eustis put it, the administration proposed an interim government with all powers vested in a governor and legislative council appointed by the president. "The government laid down in this bill is certainly a new thing in the United States," he admitted, "but the people of this country differ materially from the citizens of the United States." Because they were accustomed to Spain's authoritarian rule and unfamiliar with self-government, "the approach of such a people to liberty must be gradual." Although many in Jefferson's own party expressed serious misgivings, the administration was prepared to "countenance the principle of governing by despotic systems" until the inhabitants of Louisiana were ready, "in due time, [to] receive all the benefits of citizens." Senator William Plumer, the separatist from New Hampshire, was appalled. Jefferson's plan for the administration of Louisiana was "an act of practical tyranny," he wrote. "It is a Colonial system of government— It is the first the United States have established—It is a bad precedent— The U. S. in time will have many colonies—precedents are therefore important."[7]

Jefferson's first choice as paternal despot for the children of Louisiana was South Carolina senator Thomas Sumter, a staunch Virginia-born Jeffersonian who had earned his reputation and the rank of general in the bitter guerrilla warfare in the Carolinas during the Revolution. Youthful at seventy—Sumter died a full twenty-eight years later just shy of his ninety-eighth birthday—the Palmetto State's legendary Game-Cock was

*William Charles Cole Claiborne by E. B. Savary. Born in Sussex County, in the heart of Southside Virginia, in 1775 and schooled at Richmond Academy and briefly at the College of William and Mary, W. C. C. Claiborne began his political apprenticeship at fifteen as a clerk in the office of John Beckley, clerk of the House of Representatives and Jeffersonian political organizer. As a congressman from Tennessee, Claiborne held the state's vote for Jefferson in the contested presidential election of 1800 and was rewarded with the appointment as territorial governor of Mississippi in May 1801 and governor of the Orleans Territory after the Louisiana Purchase. Initially, Claiborne's ignorance of French and conviction "that the people of Louisiana are not prepared for Representative Government" won him few friends. In time, however, his marriage to a Louisianian, his compassionate response to the Cuban refugees from St. Domingue in 1809–1810, and his prompt suppression of the Pointe Coupée slave revolt of 1811 won him a decisive victory over the native Jacques Villeré in the 1812 election for the first governor of the State of Louisiana. Ineligible for reelection, Governor Claiborne was named to the United States Senate in January 1817 but died on November 23 before taking his seat.* (Courtesy Louisiana State Museum)

"as perfect in all points as we can expect," Jefferson confided to Madison. "Sound judgment, standing in society, knolege of the world, wealth, liberality, familiarity with the French language and having a French wife."[8]

When General Sumter decided to remain in the Senate, Jefferson's thoughts turned to his old friend the marquis de Lafayette and then to James Monroe—neither of whom could be enticed to take up residence in the isle of Orleans.

In time, however, the president lowered his sights and found two men whose combined talents—and immediate availability—sufficed. For the civil administration of Louisiana, Jefferson turned to another scion of an old Virginia family, twenty-nine-year-old Tennessee-born William Charles Cole Claiborne. Born in Tennessee and trained by the Republican organizer and clerk of the House of Representatives John Beckley, young Claiborne's political loyalty was equal to Sumter's. As a congressman during the Burr-Jefferson presidential deadlock of 1801, Claiborne had held the Tennessee vote for Jefferson, and as the current governor of the Mississippi Territory he was close at hand and familiar with the situation in Louisiana. Only his youth, limited experience, and complete ignorance of French and Spanish were drawbacks. In case a show of force proved necessary, Jefferson backed Claiborne with forty-seven-year-old General James Wilkinson, who commanded American troops in the southwest and whose talents for intrigue were multilingual. Wilkinson's assignment was temporary, and Claiborne's post remained an interim appointment until January 17, 1806. Nevertheless, subject only to instructions from Jefferson and Congress, Claiborne held nearly dictatorial powers over the Louisiana territory and its populace, whose language he did not speak, and whose society he did not comprehend.[9]

"Two trees that the Mississippi River carried along with it down to the Gulf of Mexico brushed the sides of our ship this morning," Pierre Clément Laussat noted in his journal on Wednesday, March 9, 1803, as the thirty-two-gun *Surveillant* crossed the Tropic of Cancer and carried him toward New Orleans—the sole remnant of Napoleon's intended expedition for the subjugation of Louisiana. After weathering a fierce storm that drove them back out to sea for ten days, the brig finally crossed the bar of the Mississippi on Sunday, March 20. As the *Surveillant* made its way upriver, its frequent stops for meals or the occasional night spent ashore gave Laussat opportunities to talk with French residents. "I am patiently awaited in New Orleans," Laussat wrote.

> The agents of the Spanish government are behaving like a moribund people. The Anglo-Americans in general are furious; [while] those in the West shall be ours.

"We must," he added ominously, "foster this diversity of feelings and interests."

At three o'clock on Saturday afternoon, March 26, Laussat and his family landed a few miles below New Orleans, and within an hour they were "greeted with salvos by the artillery from the forts" as their carriage approached the governor's gate. That evening Laussat met the aging Spanish governor, Manuel Juan de Salcedo, and they attended mass together the next morning. At Salcedo's dinner Sunday afternoon, "toasts were raised to the respective governments" and "the rounds of drinks were endless." Laussat was exuberant as he jotted down his thoughts at the close of his first full day in New Orleans. "Here we are in our new country, our new home, in the midst of new duties," he beamed. "All Louisianans are Frenchmen at heart!"[10]

Endless rounds of drinks may have contributed a little, but Laussat's good spirits on that Sunday evening late in March were possible only because he had been out of touch since December, when he had left General Claude Perrin Victor's troops and ships behind at Hellevoetsluis. During his long carriage ride to the port of La Rochelle, his long wait for a break in the weather, and his long voyage across the Atlantic, Laussat "dreamed constantly of reform, improvement, and new establishment." As Napoleon's colonial prefect for Louisiana he

> hoped to spend six or eight years in an administration that . . . at least doubled the population and agriculture of the country and tripled or quadrupled its trade, thus leaving behind a lasting and honorable memorial.

"Every day I congratulated myself," Laussat wrote, "for having so well estimated the resources of the colony." He was utterly enchanted by the city of New Orleans, its inhabitants, its air.[11]

Laussat enjoyed the luxury of wearing "merchandise of a superior quality . . . imported from India, England, and France." He found society and culture "as developed here" as in Paris. The people were

> far more frank, docile, and sincere than in Europe. They are pleasant and very polite, and they give a general impression that delights. . . . There is a great deal of social life; elegance and good breeding prevail throughout. . . . There are numerous hairdressers and all sorts of masters—dancing, music, art, fencing, etc. All the people in New Orleans love to read. There are no book shops or libraries, but books are ordered from France.[12]

Above all, "Louisianans are Frenchmen at heart!" Except that the first consul of France was experiencing a change of heart about Louisiana.

Throughout the spring and early summer of 1803, grumblings about Spain's closing of the Mississippi receded as rumors of an American takeover gained currency. "The fluctuations of the political thermometer in this respect," Laussat wrote in his memoirs, "were indicated by the greater or lesser eagerness with which people sought me—and that eagerness was on the decline." Laussat kept up a brave front, however, assuring French inhabitants that the rumors were fabrications somehow linked to the end of Jefferson's first term as president—all the while complaining in letters to French officials (as late as August 17) that he had heard nothing from France since March. Be careful what you wish for— the next day's mail brought from Louis André Pichon in Washington official news of the sale of Louisiana, followed immediately by the letters from François Barbé-Marbois and Denis Decrès, minister of the marine and colonies. It was all true, Laussat finally admitted, "leaving me only the regret of a year of idleness, of a useless migration by my family to the New World, and of many expenses, troubles, and fruitless inconveniences."[13]

In the face of Spain's protests against Napoleon's sale of Louisiana, neither French nor American officials could be sure that the Spanish officials in New Orleans would transfer the territory peacefully. Uncertainty heightened tensions in the city, which often flared into violent confrontations at social events, especially at dances, even after the transfer of Louisiana to the United States. To keep the peace, municipal officials enforced a strict sequence at public balls: "two rounds of French quadrilles, one round of English quadrilles . . . and one round of waltzes." In his memoirs Laussat recounted an evening of threats and fisticuffs that might have been filmed at Rick's in Casablanca. This particular fracas began when some Americans wanted to dance another English quadrille, and it ended with

> General Wilkinson inton[ing] the "Hail Columbia," accompanied by the music of his staff, then "God Save the King," then huzzas. The French, on their side, sang "Enfants de la Patrie, Peuple français, peuple de frères," and shouted "Vive la République!" It was an infernal brawl. After this cabaret scene, Claiborne and Wilkinson, escorted by Americans and the band, returned to their homes.

Eventually the Americans arranged a "reconciliation banquet" to assuage hard feelings aroused by this skirmish in what Laussat called a "war of esteem"—but not before the American consul, Daniel Clark, "let it be rumored around that 'until two or three Frenchmen have been hanged, we will not rule over this country.' "[14]

At 11:45 on Wednesday morning, November 30, 1803, Pierre Clément Laussat set out from his house in the faubourg Marigny, just outside the downriver wall of the city, accompanied on foot by a party of sixty Frenchmen. From the river, the brig *Argo* fired a salute as the procession moved toward the large crowd gathered at the Place d'Armes and the Cabildo. Spanish troops stood at attention on one side of the square, the colonial militia on the other, and "the drums rolled in front of the guardroom when [he] passed."[15]

*Pierre Clément Laussat governed Louisiana for three weeks before he signed the documents transferring the province to the United States on December 20, 1803. His departure from New Orleans was complicated by the resumption of warfare between France and Great Britain. Selling his library and its incriminating bookplates and inscriptions, Laussat slipped out of New Orleans in April 1804 using an American passport with the fictitious name Peter Lanthois. Laussat went on to serve as prefect of Martinique from 1804 to 1809 and prefect of Guiana from 1819 to 1823, when he retired to his native Pau, published his memoirs, and died in 1831.* (Courtesy Library of Virginia)

*The Sala Capitular of the Cabildo, now part of the Louisiana State Museum in New Orleans, was the site of the major transfer ceremonies of the Louisiana Purchase from Spain to France on November 30 and from France to the United States on December 20, 1803.* (Courtesy Louisiana State Museum)

As Laussat entered the meeting room on the second floor known as the Sala Capitular, "the commissioners of His Catholic Majesty came midway across the room to meet me." Governor Salcedo, "an impotent old man in his dotage," took his seat in an armchair with Laussat to his right and the marqués de Casa Calvo, "a violent man who hated the French," to his left. Laussat presented his credentials and the order from Carlos IV authorizing the transfer of Louisiana to Napoleon's representative. After Casa Calvo formally announced that any Spanish subjects who chose to stay in Louisiana were, "from that moment on, rightfully released from their oath of allegiance," Governor Salcedo presented Laussat with a silver tray bearing the keys to Fort St. Charles and Fort St. Louis.[16]

Struggling to his feet, the aging governor then yielded the middle chair to Laussat. The documents of cession were read aloud in Spanish and French. "We signed and affixed the seals," Laussat recalled,

> then we rose and went out on the side of the balconies of the city hall. Upon our appearance, the Spanish flag, which had been flying atop the flagstaff, was lowered, and the French flag raised. The company of grenadiers of the Spanish Regiment of Louisiana went forward to take the Spanish flag, and the Spanish troops filed off after it in double time.

After escorting Salcedo and Casa Calvo to the head of the stairs—with "poor old Salcedo collapsing from decrepitude" and Casa Calvo sustaining "that calm and serene appearance which even the most second-rate politicians of his nation never lose"—Laussat descended to the Place d'Armes and addressed the militia. "In the name of the French Republic," he intoned over the thunder of cannon salutes from the forts and the *Argo,*

> I entrust these flags to you. . . . They are raised in your midst for the good of your country; they are here as they are in their native land. French blood is in the veins of most of you.

"The remainder of the day was one continuous holiday," Laussat recalled, with a succession of dinners and parties, toasts and champagne, dancing and card playing that lasted through the night until seven o'clock the next morning.[17]

Laussat's three weeks as prefect of Louisiana were filled with activity. His reenactment of the French Code Noir began a movement (which accelerated in the American period) toward stricter regulation of slaves and free blacks. Laussat also abolished the Spanish Cabildo, or governing council, and replaced it with a mayor and council system of municipal government—a step less significant for its impact on the machinery of municipal government than for changes in personnel, as Laussat replaced the entrenched Spanish officeholders with many Frenchmen and "some merchants, some Americans, and some experienced businessmen." The abolition of the Cabildo delighted incoming interim governor Claiborne. The old "body was created on principles altogether incongruous with those of our Government," Claiborne wrote, but "in their place I found a Municipality established . . . of approved characters, and well disposed toward the expected change of Government, and I therefore did not long hesitate to sanction the new arrangement."[18]

The organization of the militia presented Laussat (as it would Claiborne) with "the thorniest article" of his short administration. Laussat supplanted the Spanish Regiment of Louisiana with independent companies of Frenchmen and Americans.[19] He also provided for the preservation of public records and established a new volunteer fire company. Americans were quick to realize that Laussat's most significant contributions to the Louisiana Purchase were his role in the peaceful transfer of the province from Spain to France and his assurance of a prompt transfer of authority to the president's commissioners. Together these two achievements meant, as William C. C. Claiborne informed President Jefferson before leaving Fort Adams for New Orleans on December 8, "that no serious resistance would be made to the surrender of Louisiana to the U.S."[20]

Back in July, Jefferson and his cabinet had decided to "get the Spanish troops off as soon as possible," and had put William C. C. Claiborne and two companies of troops at Fort Adams on alert. Meeting again on October 4, the cabinet had unanimously determined that "forcible poss[essio]n of N[ew] Orleans [would] be taken" if the Spanish refused to surrender the territory peacefully. On Sunday, December 4, Claiborne and Wilkinson rendezvoused at Fort Adams—on the Mississippi River thirty-eight miles south of Natchez—for their descent to New Orleans. Marching with them were two hundred militia volunteers from the Mississippi Territory and the fort's garrison of regular troops, a total "force of between 450 and 500 Men." Claiborne was confident that a "speedy consummation of the Negociation for Louisiana [was] likely to be accomplished without the effusion of Blood, or the further expenditure of public Treasure."[21]

As Claiborne and Wilkinson approached the city, Daniel Clark, the American consul, reported that everything was quiet in New Orleans. With Britain and France at war again, however, he passed along worries about a possible disruption from another quarter. On Monday, December 12, a British officer from Kingston, Jamaica, informed Clark that twelve hundred French troops fleeing St. Domingue—remnants of Leclerc's ill-starred expedition—had been captured by the British and taken to Jamaica. Eager "to get rid of the Expence and trouble of Keeping them," the governor of Jamaica was taking advantage of the fact that New Orleans was now a French port and had loaded the troops in three Danish vessels that "were to sail in a very few days . . . for the Mississippi." Clark was happy to report that when he informed Laussat of this development, the prefect "immediately gave orders that they should not be admitted" and began gathering provisions so that if they did arrive they could be sent somewhere else—anywhere but New Orleans. Half of Spain's Louisiana garrison had already sailed, Clark reported, and the rest had already boarded "a sloop of War which sails to morrow." The delicate political situation in New Orleans was thus compounded by temporary military vulnerability. "Every delay is a day of fear and suspense for the whole Country," Clark wrote, "and you Cannot possibly make use of too much expedition to arrive and put an end to it."[22]

As Brigadier General Wilkinson and his five hundred troops made camp outside New Orleans on Friday, December 16, Laussat was scurrying to publish "yet one more decree relative to the regulation of the Negroes," his declaration that the Code Noir of 1724 was once again in effect except for any provisions that contradicted the Constitution of the United States. Claiborne arrived the next day, delayed by an accident on the river when his sloop ran aground at Pointe Coupée, midway between Fort Adams and Baton Rouge. "Everything is quiet," he assured Secretary of State James Madison, "and I persuade myself that in three Days the American Flag will be raised, amidst the shouts of a grateful People."[23]

December 20, 1803, "was to be the first of a truly new era for the Mississippi shores," Laussat wrote.

> The day was beautiful and the temperature as balmy as a day in May. Lovely ladies and city dandies graced all the balconies on the Place d'Armes. The Spanish officers could be distinguished in the crowd by their plumage . . . [and] the eleven rooms of the city hall were filled with all the beautiful women of the city.

Claiborne, Wilkinson, and the American troops entered at the city's Tchoupitoulas Gate and marched along the riverfront to the Place d'Armes. Laussat's chief engineer, Major Joseph Antoine Vinache, and other dignitaries greeted the American commissioners at the foot of the stairs and accompanied them to the Sala Capitular above.

As Salcedo had done just three weeks earlier, Laussat now greeted Jefferson's emissaries "halfway across the room," offered Claiborne an armchair on his right and Wilkinson another on his left, and announced the purpose of the ceremony. A secretary read aloud the Americans' commissions, the treaty of transfer, Laussat's authorization from the first consul, and the certificates of ratification. Proclaiming that he was "transferring the country to the United States," Laussat then presented General Wilkinson with "the keys to the city, tied together with tricolor

Hoisting the American Colors, *by Thure de Thulstrup, was painted about 1903 to celebrate the centennial of the Louisiana Purchase. It hangs in the Sala Capitular of the Cabildo in New Orleans, where Claiborne, Wilkinson, and Laussat signed the formal transfer of sovereignty from France to the United States on December 20, 1803. Early in 1804, Americans re-created the symbolism of this dramatic event at three other locations. Captain Amos Stoddard represented both France and the United States at St. Louis, the administrative center for Upper Louisiana. Acting for Laussat, Stoddard accepted Upper Louisiana from the Spanish lieutenant governor, Carlos Dehault Delassus, on March 9, 1804. The next day Stoddard lowered the French tricolor and raised the Stars and Stripes as he took formal possession of St. Louis and Upper Louisiana for the United States. A week later, on March 18, Captain Daniel Bissell raised the American flag in a similar ceremony at New Madrid. And, finally, in April 1804 Captain Edward Demaresque Turner raised the American flag over Natchitoches, the oldest European settlement in the Louisiana territory. "I took possession of this post on the 26th," Turner reported to Claiborne. "The French Flag superseded the Spanish at eleven, and the American the French at 12 o'clock—to the seeming satisfaction of everyone."* (Courtesy Louisiana State Museum)

ribbons."[24] As Casa Calvo had done in November for the Spanish, Laussat "absolved from their oath of allegiance to France [any] inhabitants who chose to remain under the dominion of the United States."[25] Laussat, Wilkinson, and Claiborne then affixed their signatures to the formal documents transferring possession of the city of New Orleans and the entire western watershed of the Mississippi to the American republic, doubling its size with the strokes of three quills.

As the representatives of the two republics stepped onto the main balcony of the Cabildo,

> the French colors were lowered and the American flag was raised. When they reached the same level, both banners paused for a moment. A cannon shot was the signal for salvos from the forts and the batteries.

By day's end Wilkinson met privately with Casa Calvo and the visiting governor of West Florida, Don Vizente Folch, to protest that his secret Spanish pension had fallen $20,000 in arrears. From the Cabildo that evening, where he anticipated his own night "without repose" while Claiborne attended a series of lavish balls that once again lasted far into the morning, Wilkinson dashed off a "hasty Scral" to Secretary of State Madison. Rumors "of an intention to fire the Town" had Wilkinson and one hundred seventy American troops patrolling the city on foot and on horseback. "I apprehend no Danger," the general wrote, "but the horrors of a sinister attempt, makes it my duty to prevent one."[26]

At about one o'clock in the morning, Wilkinson added a postscript to his note. "Every thing in the City is still tranquil," he wrote, but to ensure "the continuation of this tranquility" he asked Madison to send "a Garrison of 500 Regulars . . . as soon as possible." As they had stood on the balcony of the Cabildo that afternoon, Wilkinson and Claiborne had been shocked by the sight of free colored militiamen helping to raise the Stars and Stripes over New Orleans. Of all the potential threats to the new regime in Louisiana, "the formidable aspect of the[se] armed Blacks and Malattoes, officered and organized," was the one that Wilkinson found most "painful and perplexing." Although a few weeks later the general could report that the colored militiamen no longer sported the tricolor cockade of the French Revolution and had "universally mounted the Eagle in their Hats and avow[ed] their attachment to the United States," this patriotic gesture could not diminish the new American administration's dilemma. Claiborne and Wilkinson knew that their actions were being watched closely in Louisiana and throughout the country. (As interim governor, Claiborne may also have been aware of Wilkinson's self-serving opinion that Louisiana needed "a Military executive Magistrate.")[27]

"My principal difficulty," Claiborne wrote, "arises from two large Companies of people of color, who are attached to the Service, and were esteemed a very Serviceable Corps under the Spanish Government." As in other Spanish Caribbean provinces, Louisiana's colored militia embodied the political and social elite of the free nonwhite population. The right to bear arms and to wear uniforms distanced them from the slave population, while participation in the militia afforded men of color the opportunity to associate with whites as near equals—a situation virtually unknown elsewhere in the United States.[28]

Of the many differences between the rest of America and its new polyglot territory, the contrast between the Caribbean three-caste society and the American black-white, slave-free dichotomy was perhaps the most striking. There were, of course, free blacks living in the Atlantic states (especially in antebellum Maryland) but their presence in American society was anomalous compared to the free people of color in Louisiana and the Caribbean. Genteel toleration of cultural and ethnic difference was one thing—New Orleans cuisine was delicious, its music agreeable, its people handsome—but *armed* free people of color were dangerously reminiscent of St. Domingue. Militia companies of free men of color represented a frightening assertion of political demands and social aspirations.

Claiborne described his options in a letter to the secretary of state. If he granted new commissions for the colored militia companies it "might be considered as an outrage on the feelings of a part of the Nation"— slaveholders worried about upholding "principles of Policy which the Safety of the Southern States has necessarily established" (his wordy euphemism for slavery). "On the other hand," Claiborne lamented, "not to be re-commissioned, would disgust them" and create "an armed enemy in the very heart of the Country."[29]

Claiborne accurately characterized his confrontation with diversity as the "principal difficulty" he faced as governor of the new territory. And once again, the events of the Louisiana Purchase were shaped by events and attitudes from the world at large. "The People of Colour are all armed," Wilkinson wrote, "and it is my Opinion a single envious artful bold incendiary"—a man like Toussaint L'Ouverture—"might produce those Horrible Scenes of Bloodshed and rapine, which have been so frequently noticed in St. Domingo."[30]

While Americans and French-speaking whites demanded the suppression and even banishment of the colored militia officers, fifty-five leading free people of color offered themselves to Claiborne as a corps of volunteers. Proud of their military service under the Spanish and French regimes, they voiced "the fullest confidence in the Justice and Liberality of the [American] Government towards every Class of Citizens." Hoping that their confidence was warranted, they also petitioned Claiborne for assurances of their own "personal and political freedom" according to Article III of the Louisiana Purchase Treaty, which promised inhabitants of the territory "all rights, advantages and immunities of citizens of the United States."[31]

Notable among the fifty-five proud men who signed this petition were Pierre Bailly and his son. A decade earlier Governor Carondelet had deported the elder Bailly—then known as Pedro—to Cuba for his "diabolical ideas of freedom and equality" and for "having made remarks against the Spanish government . . . showing himself to be inclined to the principles of the French rebels." The Spanish governor of Louisiana had found Bailly guilty of advocating social equality between whites and free men of color. Now Pierre Bailly, his namesake son, and fifty-three other proud free men of color were only asking the new American governor to live up to his nation's ideals of "Justice and Liberality . . . toward every Class of Citizens."[32]

"Our population consists of people of allmost all nations," the American-born New Orleans merchant Benjamin Morgan had written after news of the Louisiana Purchase reached the city, but the most vexing question was

> upon what footing will the free quadroon mulatto and black people stand; will they be entitled to the rights of citizens or not. They are a numerous class in this city—say ½ or ¾ of the population—many very respectable and under [the Spanish] government enjoy their rights in common with other subjects.

On January 16, 1804, when the leaders of Louisiana's free colored militia petitioned William C. C. Claiborne for justice, the United States formally confronted the profound human consequences of the Louisiana Purchase for the first time. "On this particular Corps," Claiborne admitted as he asked the administration for guidance, "I have reflected with much anxiety."[33]

President Jefferson's response was telling. At a cabinet meeting on February 18 attended by all four secretaries and his attorney general, Jefferson resolved (mixing precision and cunning in a way that drove his enemies crazy) "that the militia of Colour shall be confirmed in their posts, and treated favorably, till a better settled state of things shall permit us to let them neglect themselves." Claiborne was instructed to confirm the colored militiamen in their ranks, provide them with a regimental banner, and buy time. White Louisiana planters, however, were too impatient to wait until Jefferson's better settled state of things allowed the free blacks and mulattoes time merely to neglect themselves. Having successfully pressured Laussat to reinstitute the restrictive provisions of the Code Noir, they pressed Claiborne in the same direction.[34]

In June, under the pretense of reorganizing the entire territorial militia, Claiborne put white officers in command of the free men of color— all the while dreading that in time "this quarter of the Union must, I fear, experience in some degree, the Misfortunes of St. Domingo." The compromise satisfied no one. Within weeks a free black named Stephen betrayed a plot among the city's slaves and free people of color (a substantial majority of the population). Their plan involved a revolt to free the slaves and overthrow American rule, it was said, and a Spanish invasion force from Florida led by former governor Casa Calvo—the same Casa Calvo who was managing Wilkinson's secret pension.[35]

Federalist critics of the Louisiana Purchase called the place "a howling wilderness" and "an immense wilderness." They damned it as "an untrodden waste for owls to hoot and wolves to howl in," "the realm of alligators and catamounts," and "an empire that is boundless, or whose bounds are as yet unexplored." They scorned the "unmeasured world beyond that river" as a "vast region [of] still wild land." What frightened Americans most, however, was not the familiar wilderness west of the Mississippi but the alien urban population at its mouth—that *"Gallo-Hispano-Indian omnium gatherum* of savages and adventurers."[36]

On any given day in 1803, New Orleans played host (as well as bartender, croupier, and madam) to a few hundred transient mercantile agents, riverboat men, barge hands, sailors, and naval officers whose antics helped earn the city its notoriety in the American imagination—for there *was* a place in New Orleans called the Rising Sun.[37] Of the city's 8,050 permanent residents in about 1803, however, 92 percent comprised the elements of the three-caste societies of the Caribbean and Latin America: 3,300 French-speaking Creoles, 2,800 slaves, and 1,300 free people of color. The remainder were Spanish officials and troops, enterprising Anglo-Americans, and refugees from St. Domingue (whose numbers would swell to ten thousand by the end of the decade).[38]

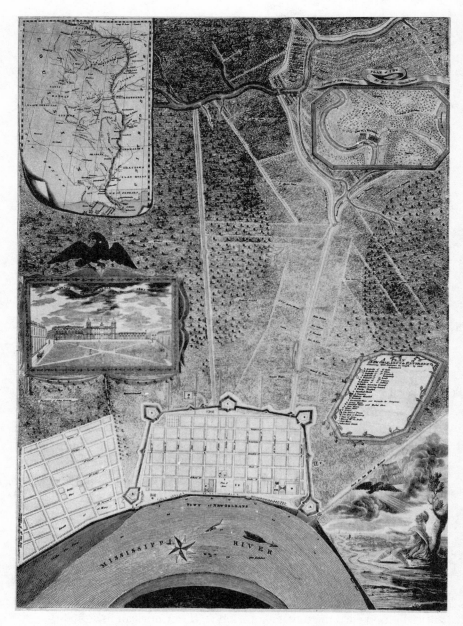

*John L. Bóqueta de Woiseri's 1803* Plan of New Orleans *depicts the walled city of New Orleans on the Mississippi River with fauburg St. Mary upriver (left). Bayou St. John, which flows to Lake Pontchartrain, is at the top of de Woiseri's map—connected to the city by the straight line of the Carondelet Canal and the winding roadway along a natural ridge to the right. Inset images show (top left) the Mississippi River; (top right) the environs of New Orleans; and (bottom left) the Cabildo, St. Louis Cathedral, and Presbytere on the Place d'Armes (now Jackson Square).* (Courtesy Louisiana State Museum)

Two centuries ago, amid a "gabble of tongues" and an array of ivory, café au lait, copper, and ebony complexions in the streets and markets of New Orleans, a nation that habitually and legally regarded people either as black or white began an encounter with ethnic and cultural diversity that has been sustained by subsequent expansion and immigration.[39]

American fascination with the "unmeasured world" beyond the Mississippi River had long preceded the fortuitous acquisition of the Louisiana territory. Had André Michaux and Citizen Genet been more effective in the 1790s, Jefferson and the American Philosophical Society would have sent explorers up the Missouri River ten years before the Corps of Discovery headed west from St. Charles, Missouri, under the command of Meriwether Lewis and William Clark on May 21, 1804.[40]

When they disparaged Louisiana as "an empire . . . whose bounds are as yet unexplored," the administration's Federalist critics were right. "The farther we go northward, the more undecided is the boundary," the French minister of marine and colonies, Denis Decrès, had written in 1802, for

> this part of America contains little more than uninhabited forests or Indian tribes, and the necessity of fixing a boundary never yet has been felt there. There also exists none between Louisiana and Canada.

The Louisiana Purchase Treaty merely repeated the language of earlier treaties—and the Americans got no help from Talleyrand.[41]

In a conversation a few weeks after signing the treaty, Robert Livingston had asked the sly diplomat if he could clarify the boundaries that France had ceded to the United States. "I can give you no direction," Talleyrand replied. "You have made a noble bargain for yourselves and I suppose you will make the most of it."[42] Between 1803 and 1819, as world events pressed the necessity of fixing the boundaries of Louisiana upon them, Americans did make the most of their noble bargain.

Spain had responded to the Louisiana Purchase with angry protests to the United States. The first ground of complaint was that Bonaparte had agreed not to sell the province. The second argument was that the secret Treaty of San Ildefonso of 1800, which had transferred Louisiana to France, was void because Bonaparte had failed to combine Tuscany, Parma, Florence, and the principality of Piombino into the kingdom of Etruria for Prince Louis of Parma, Queen Maria Luisa's nephew and son-in-law.[43] Secretary of State Madison's official correspondence is full of carefully reasoned rebuttals of both Spanish complaints, but political realities rather than legal niceties decided the issue. It was obvious, Madison had Charles Pinckney explain to Spanish authorities in Madrid, on the one hand that Spain was too weak to challenge Bonaparte's actions, and on the other that if Spain were somehow able to enlist French help in retaining Louisiana, Great Britain would step in and capture the province. "What is it that Spain dreads?" Madison asked.

> She dreads, it is presumed, the growing power of this country, and the direction of it against her possessions within its reach. Can she annihilate this power? No. Can she sensibly retard its growth? No.

"Does not common prudence then advise her," Madison wrote, "to conciliate . . . the good will of a nation whose power is formidable to her," rather than "adopting obnoxious precautions, which can have no other effect than to bring on the Calamity which she fears"? Spain's final answer, Madison was confident, could only be yes—and he was right.[44]

Caught between Great Britain and France, Spain itself was rapidly falling into disarray at home and abroad. On October 21, 1803, off Cape Trafalgar on the southern coast of Spain, a British fleet of twenty-seven ships commanded by Admiral Horatio Nelson utterly defeated a somewhat larger fleet of Spanish and French vessels commanded by Napoleon's Vice Admiral Pierre Charles de Villeneuve. Britain sustained about fifteen hundred casualties, their great admiral among them—but Villeneuve and thousands of his sailors were captured and twenty French and Spanish ships were destroyed or captured, while not a single British vessel had been lost. The defeat ended Napoleon's plan to invade England, gave Britain supremacy on the high seas for the rest of the century, and stripped Spain of its last vestige of military power in the Napoleonic Wars.

Checked at sea, Napoleon nevertheless ruled the Continent. He had crowned his brother Joseph Bonaparte king of Naples in 1806 and his brother Louis Bonaparte king of Holland. His Confederation of the Rhine gave him control of the German states except Austria, Prussia, Brunswick, and Hessen. By 1806 Britain and France were locked in the economic warfare defined by Napoleon's Continental System, forbidding British trade with all European nations, and Britain's Orders in Council, which prohibited neutral nations from trading in ports that complied with Napoleon's decrees. When President Jefferson responded in 1806 with his disastrous embargo, his attempt to avoid war and maintain neutrality by prohibiting American trade with European belligerents, the United States took its first steps toward the War of 1812.

America's situation as a neutral power was difficult enough, but Spain's position on the Continent was worse. Once again openly employed by Carlos IV and Maria Luisa as Spain's admiral-general and "Alteza Serenisima," or Most Serene Highness, Manuel Godoy had been secretly courting Napoleon's favor in the hope of obtaining a small kingdom when the emperor got around to carving up Portugal. Godoy's admiration turned to alarm, however, when Napoleon defeated the Prussians at Jena and captured Berlin in October 1806. "If Czar Alexander does not succeed in bringing down this colossus," Godoy whispered to the Russian ambassador, "our turn will come and we shall be the last victims."[45]

Napoleon promptly crushed the Russian army at Friedland in June 1807 and forced Alexander to sue for peace. Then he turned his attention south. "The Spanish Royal House are my personal enemies," Napoleon confided to the Austrian diplomat Prince Klemens von Metternich, the man who arranged Napoleon's marriage to the archduchess Marie Louise after his divorce from Josephine and who in 1814–1815 rearranged the face of Europe in the Congress of Vienna. "They and I," Napoleon said, "cannot be on thrones at the same time."[46]

Spain would be messier. Cultivating the hatred between Prince Ferdinand, Carlos IV and Maria Luisa's son, and Godoy, their favorite, Napoleon had planted seeds of destruction in very fertile soil. He toppled the Bourbon monarchy on May 6, 1808, sending the trinity of Carlos, Maria Luisa, and Godoy into permanent exile in Italy. When Napoleon put his brother on the throne vacated by His Most Catholic Majesty, however, the Spanish people rose in revolt and drove Joseph Bonaparte out of Madrid. "We cannot recognize as our king," one Spanish churchman said to another, "someone who is a freemason, a heretic, and a Lutheran, as are all the Bonapartes and indeed all the French people." The ensuing struggle for Spain, depicted on Goya's patriotic canvases and known as the Peninsular War, pitted a large French army against British forces led by Arthur Wellesley, future duke of Wellington. The war also inspired the term *guerrilla,* or "little war," to describe the Spanish irregulars and civilians who continued to fight despite the defeat of Spain's royal army.[47]

Napoleon's war on the Iberian Peninsula started ominously when Talleyrand resigned in protest (a departure that had become a reliable omen of any regime's impending doom). The Spanish Ulcer, as the French called the war, dragged on until 1813—a year before Napoleon's first abdication and two years before his final defeat at the Battle of Waterloo on June 18, 1815.[48] For six years the Peninsular War tied down an entire army that Napoleon might have used elsewhere to decisive advantage (or merely squandered in his disastrous campaign against Russia). And for six years Napoleon's Spanish Ulcer precluded any progress in America's negotiations about the boundaries of the Louisiana Purchase.

By the end of the first year of the Peninsular War, many of Spain's more talented and experienced career officials had allied themselves with the Junta Central, which aimed to put Prince Ferdinand on the throne. It was their foresight that sent forty-seven-year-old Luis de Onís y González to the United States as the representative of the patriotic provisional government based in Aranjuez. Born in Salamanca, Onís had studied Greek and Latin at eight, taken legal training at the University of Salamanca, and devoted thirty years to the Spanish diplomatic service. Onís spoke fluent French, German, and Italian, and passable English, and he was a protégé of Carlos III's great minister, the count of Floridablanca, president of the Junta Central until his death on November 20, 1808.[49]

Onís's credentials made little impression on President James Madison's administration when he landed in New York on Wednesday, October 4, 1809. Reluctant to offend Napoleon and his brother, the United States declined to recognize Onís as a representative of Spain, citing "the contending claims of Charles and Ferdinand" to the throne—despite former President Jefferson's private admission that by American principles "the right of the Junta to send a Minister could not be denied."[50]

By the time Secretary of State James Monroe did accept Onís's diplomatic credentials—on December 19, 1815—the Spanish Ulcer had been lanced. Bourbons were back on their thrones in Spain and France. Talleyrand was helping the Congress of Vienna restore a balance of power among the monarchies of Europe. And the French colossus, Napoleon, stood master of the forty-seven-square-mile island of St. Helena, twelve hundred miles off the African coast in the South Atlantic. In the Americas, Mexico and other Spanish colonies were striving for independence, Louisiana had been admitted to the union in 1812, and the United States had ended the unhappy War of 1812 with a flourish—Andrew Jackson's magnificent defeat of Wellington's veterans at the Battle of New Orleans on January 8.

Four more years of negotiation stood ahead. Years of "tiresome reiteration" and the "higgling and splitting of hairs," according to one chronicler, as Onís and John Quincy Adams, President James Monroe's secretary of state, nailed down the final boundaries of that vast unmeasured world beyond the river. They chose February 22, 1819—Washington's birthday (which happened to be a Monday)—to sign the Adams-Onís Treaty, "designed to end all the differences between the two governments which have been pending for eighteen years." A jubilant Senate unanimously ratified the treaty two days later, while the disgruntled Spanish ratified it two years later.[51]

The Adams-Onís Treaty secured Texas for Spain and surrendered the Floridas to the United States (provisions that were later controversial but readily accepted by Americans at the time). Together with the Convention of October 20, 1818, between the United States and Great Britain, the treaty set the northern boundary of the Louisiana Purchase at the forty-ninth parallel from the Lake of the Woods, in Minnesota, to the Rocky Mountains. It drew a boundary between Oregon and California at the forty-second parallel but left the northern boundary between the Rockies and Pacific undefined.[52]

As defined by the Adams-Onís Treaty, the western boundary of the Louisiana Purchase started at the mouth of the Sabine River on the Gulf of Mexico and ran northerly along the west bank of that river to the thirty-second parallel (near Logansport, Louisiana). From there the line ran due north to the Red River (near Ogden, Arkansas), followed the river west to the hundredth meridian (southwest of Hollis, Oklahoma), and then ran due north to the Arkansas River (at Dodge City, Kansas) and west along the river. At this point in the negotiation (and in the final treaty) geographic ignorance intruded upon legal precision. Based upon the John Melish map of 1818, Adams and Onís thought the Arkansas River began at the forty-second parallel. In fact it rises just above the thirty-ninth parallel west of Leadville, Colorado (two hundred forty miles due south of the forty-second parallel at Seminoe Reservoir, near Hanna, Wyoming). On the Melish map the Arkansas River intersected the forty-second parallel near the southwest corner of Idaho, whence Adams and Onís ran the boundary due west to the Pacific Ocean (now the northern boundary of California, Nevada, and Utah).*

"For the first time our government begins to see its way to the Northern Pacific Ocean with any thing like a clear and definite view of sovereignty," Joel K. Mead's *National Register* crowed from the capital in response to the Adams-Onís Treaty.

---

*The thirteen states carved from the Louisiana Purchase are Arkansas, Colorado east of the Rocky Mountains, Iowa, Kansas, Louisiana, Minnesota west of the Mississippi River, Missouri, Montana, Nebraska, North Dakota, Oklahoma, South Dakota, and Wyoming. Portions of New Mexico, Texas, Alberta, Saskatchewan, and Manitoba within the watershed of the Mississippi River were excluded by the Convention of 1818 and the Adams-Onís Treaty of 1819.

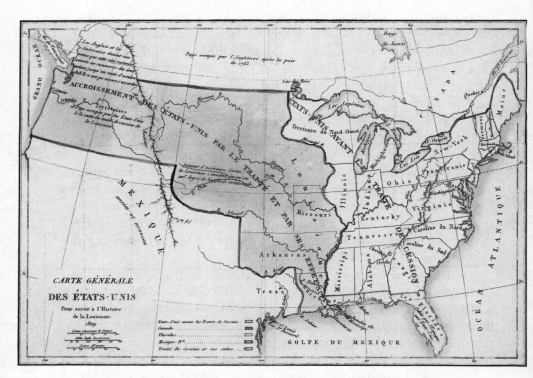

*This map of the Louisiana Purchase was published in the first edition of François Barbé-Marbois's* Histoire de la Louisiane et de la Cession de Cette Colonie par la France aux Etats-Unis de l'Amérique Septentrionale *(Paris, 1829). The boundaries shown were drawn in the Adams-Onís Treaty of 1819. An American edition of Barbé-Marbois's* History, *translated under the supervision of Jared Sparks, was published in 1830. Barbé-Marbois died in Paris in 1835.* (Collection of the author)

It is thus we stride, from object to object; and shall eventually light upon the banks of the river Columbia and the shores of the Pacific! What magnificent prospects open upon us!

But the Louisiana Purchase had other implications that were less magnificent. Within a year, in 1820, the American debate over slavery focused on the admission of Missouri as a slave state—as the immediate aftermath of the Louisiana Purchase led the nation inexorably toward the Civil War.[53]

# A Various Gabble of Tongues

*A thick fog enveloped every thing . . . and at sunrise we were in
front of [New Orleans] without being able to see it. We therefore
cast anchor . . . on the West or South bank, but so thick a fog
enveloped the city that the ear alone could ascertain its existence.
London is heard indeed at 7 or 8 miles distance, in the incessant
low rumbling of coaches and other carriages. On the arrival of a
stranger in [Philadelphia] an incessant crash of drays meets his
ear. But on arrival in New Orleans in the morning, a sound more
strange than any that is heard anywhere else in the world aston-
ishes him. It is a more incessant, loud, rapid, and various gabble
of tongues of all tones than was ever heard at Babel. . . .*

*The strange and loud noise heard through the fog . . . from the
voices of the market people and their customers was not more
extraordinary than the appearance of these noisy folks when the
fog cleared away, and we landed. Everything had an* odd
*look . . . and I confess that I felt myself in some degree, again a
Cockney, for it was impossible not to stare at a sight wholly new
even to one who has traveled much in Europe and America.*

Benjamin Henry B. Latrobe, January 12, 1819[1]

AT DAWN on Saturday, May 11, 1804, cannon sounded a "Grand
National Salute" from the Battery at the tip of Manhattan and the
fort on nearby Governors Island as New York City launched a grand celebration of the first anniversary of the Louisiana Purchase Treaty. The
event was orchestrated by the city's new mayor, and former United States
senator, De Witt Clinton. American flags were visible everywhere, flying
over the principal buildings of the city and from the masts of all the ships
in the harbor. As church bells pealed in triumph, Mayor Clinton, the
sheriff, and scores of municipal officials gathered in City Hall Park for a

gigantic parade. Rank upon rank of militiamen—cavalry, infantry, and artillery—marched through the streets of Manhattan behind their commander, who rode a profusely decorated white stallion as he held up the front end of a very long white silk banner inscribed with the words: "Extension of the Empire of Freedom in the Peaceful, Honorable, and Glorious Acquisition of the Immense and Fertile Region of Louisiana, December 20th, 1803, 28th Year of American Independence, and in the Presidency of Thomas Jefferson."[2]

Behind the soldiers and politicians came the members of New York's Tammany Society, carrying a fifteen-foot-long white muslin map of the Mississippi River and the territory of Louisiana. As the procession marched through lower Manhattan, cannons roared salutes to the three nations, and bands played rousing music, including "Hail, Columbia," an unnamed "Spanish piece," and "Bonaparte's March." At last the parade turned back up Broadway and arrived again at City Hall Park, where the soldiers fired crisp salutes and the assembled populace gave three resounding cheers for Thomas Jefferson and the Louisiana Purchase.[3]

Seven hundred miles to the south on the next day, May 12, the southern Federalist Dr. David Ramsay, the most able historian of the nation's founding generation, was mounting the pulpit of St. Michael's Church in Charleston, South Carolina, to deliver his *Oration on the Cession of Louisiana to the United States*. Ramsay was one of dozens of orators in cities and towns up and down the Eastern Seaboard raising their voices in a jubilee of oratory in the spring of 1804 to celebrate the one-year anniversary of the Louisiana Purchase.[4]

"Louisiana is Ours!" David Ramsay proclaimed. As to the significance of America's acquisition of that vast territory, Ramsay acknowledged "the establishment of independence, and of our present constitution" as "prior, both in time and importance; but with these two exceptions," Ramsay believed, "the acquisition of Louisiana, is the greatest political blessing ever conferred on these states."[5]

Historical perspective had not changed much one hundred forty-nine years later when the Pulitzer Prize–winning historian and "Easy Chair" columnist for *Harper's* magazine, Bernard DeVoto, wrote an essay commissioned by *Collier's* magazine about the Louisiana Purchase upon the occasion of its sesquicentennial in 1953. Because he lived after the shots at Fort Sumter and surrender at Appomattox, DeVoto added one event to the comparative list, but otherwise his opinion about the Louisiana Purchase echoed Ramsay's:

No event in all American history—not the Civil War, nor the Declaration of Independence nor even the signing of the Constitution—was more important.

DeVoto wrote about westward expansion, exploration, and commerce, and he wrote about constitutional change and the Civil War, and he came close to proving his point. But Bernard DeVoto knew that something was missing. "However it may be put," he lamented, the peaceful transfer of sovereignty from Spain, to France, to the United States for nine hundred thousand square miles of territory was a story "still too momentous to be understood."[6]

Despite some misgivings about the constitutional issues, most Americans agreed that the Louisiana Purchase was, in Talleyrand's words, "a noble bargain"—*la bonne affaire!* The Mississippi and its western tributaries alone drain a million square miles. The price of securing the Ohio-Mississippi waterway and doubling the size of the United States was 80 million francs ($15 million) financed for twenty years by the Barings Bank of London and Hope & Co. of Amsterdam. International negotiations, completed in 1819, refined the boundaries between American and Spanish territories and also transferred Florida to the United States.

Still, $15 million was a lot of money at the beginning of the nineteenth century, especially to strict-constructionist Jeffersonians paying off the national debt that Alexander Hamilton had created to strengthen the central government. "Some people have expressed fears lest our government may have given too much for Louisiana," a New Jersey wit advised the editors of the Trenton *True American:*

> I would wish you to inform your readers that a company of monied men in this and the neighboring states is forming, for the purpose of purchasing Louisiana [from] our government . . . for the purchase money and the expence of the negotiation.[7]

They would have made a killing. When the 6 percent loans were repaid, the total cost of Mississippi navigation and the whole Louisiana Territory was $23,527,872.57—about 4 cents an acre.[8]

Millions of acres of cheap fresh lands drained by the Mississippi and its tributaries were ideal for cotton—a commodity with a lucrative new market in the steam-driven mills of Manchester, a fiber readily processed by Eli Whitney's cotton gin, and a crop well suited to plantation agriculture and slave labor. Along the Lower Mississippi, enterprising planters switched their cash crop from indigo to cotton with amazing speed. In 1798 Julien Poydras was sending a barge back and forth from Pointe Coupée to New Orleans carrying thirty barrels of indigo on each trip and exporting thirty-nine thousand pounds of indigo to London at 10 bits per pound. That November, however, he sent one boat to New Orleans "loaded with cotton for an American." By the following October, Poydras was "applying myself entirely to cotton." "The price of indigo does not interest me this year," he told one merchant, "I hardly made any and will get little from others"—"we are all over head and ears in cotton." By December 1799 Poydras was bragging about his "superb double mill to gin the cotton" and his brisk business buying up cotton at 24 piastres a hundredweight and shipping and selling it quickly "to profit by the present high prices." The price of indigo, meantime, had fallen to 6 bits "but there is hardly any."

Within two years Poydras had a cotton press and a bevy of gins and was sending his boat to New Orleans filled with cotton every fifteen days. By August 1800 he had a contract with James Freret to export 100,000 250-pound bales of cotton and another for 22,000 bales through Lisle Sarpy—and he could assure both merchants that "should I not have enough of *my* cotton to fill your order, I have on hand a supply of other cotton to do so." In two short years, Julien Poydras had gone from exporting twenty tons of indigo to an annual wholesale trade of fifteen thousand tons of cotton.[9] Poydras may have been unusually quick to plant cotton, but American planters and other crops were not far behind.

When William C. C. Claiborne's ancestors had landed at Jamestown in 1616, English colonists regarded the lands they took in North America (as earlier in Ulster) as a wilderness peopled only with savages, the remnants of Native American tribes decimated by European disease. Thomas Jefferson lived in a plantation community of two hundred people on his mountaintop at Monticello. He walked daily among faces that exhibited a whole range of tones, even within his own family, but Jefferson saw only white and black, free and slave. The "amalgamation" of black Americans "with the other color," he wrote in 1814, "produces a degradation to which no lover of his country, no lover of excellence in the human character can innocently consent."[10] His representatives and his countrymen brought similar attitudes to their 1803 encounter with the racial diversity of Louisiana.

Claiborne and the twelve thousand Americans who flooded into Louisiana in the decade after 1803 almost overwhelmed New Orleans's baffling patterns of race, language, law, and culture. Jefferson and his countrymen had always assumed that the Creoles would be displaced, assimilated, or marginalized by English-speaking settlers—and they might have been, except for the aftermath of the Haitian and French Revolutions. Between May 1809 and January 1810, New Orleans welcomed ten thousand French-speaking refugees from St. Domingue by way of Cuba—equal numbers of whites, slaves, and free people of color whose arrival made the city even more Caribbean, reinforcing everything that Claiborne and his countrymen found exotic and dangerous about New Orleans for decades to come.[11]

Controversies over race, religion, law, language, and culture not only delayed Louisiana's statehood until 1812, they worked like the rumblings of an earthquake along the vulnerable fault lines of nineteenth-century American society and government. By 1818–1819, when treaties among the United States, Spain, and Great Britain gave America the rest of Florida and drew the final boundaries of the Louisiana Purchase, the second half of our national history was well under way. The land north of the thirty-third parallel was now called the Missouri Territory, to avoid confusion with the State of Louisiana south of it.

As Americans brought their internal improvements and their slaves to New Orleans and the new territory, the nation's long-deferred debate over slavery grew increasingly angry. The consequences of the Louisiana Purchase scoured at the mortar of the Constitution, as the New Englanders' arguments for state rights and secession—arguments that surfaced during the Jay-Gardoqui negotiations of 1786, after the Louisiana Purchase in 1803–1804, and again during the War of 1812—went south.

In 1820, when the Missouri crisis erupted over the creation of another slave state from the territory of the Louisiana Purchase, a grand compromise was necessary to preserve the union: henceforth the new states were admitted in pairs, one slave and one free, to keep a balance of power in the Senate. This Missouri Compromise worked until the 1850s, but the Missouri Question (as the "Louisiana Question" had come to be known, to avoid confusion) haunted the conscience of America until the cannon roared at Fort Sumter—and long beyond.

Americans today live their lives in the wake of the Louisiana Purchase. It reshaped our hemisphere so completely that we cannot easily imagine anything different. It spurred exploration and expansion. It lured the republic toward the temptations of empire. Lewis and Clark tracked the northern reaches of the vast territory in 1804–1806 and staked a claim to the Pacific Northwest. Zebulon Pike and others headed south and west. The landscape inspired artists from George Caleb Bingham and George Catlin to Thomas Hart Benton, Ansel Adams, and Georgia O'Keeffe. A nation that once may have been resigned to sharing the Mississippi with a foreign neighbor now embraced the Pacific Coast as its "Manifest Destiny." But DeVoto knew all this in 1953 when he said the event was "still too momentous to be understood." He knew the Louisiana Purchase brought geographic expansion, discovery and exploration, and sectional and constitutional conflicts that led to the Civil War. And he sensed that something was missing.

As we mark the two hundredth anniversary of the Louisiana Purchase, our vantage point suggests that David Ramsay and Bernard DeVoto were too close to their subject—too close in time—to comprehend its momentous implications. Even as recently as 1953, one hundred fifty years after the event, some of the long-term consequences of the Louisiana Purchase were not yet apparent. Today, as its two hundredth anniversary converges upon the four hundredth anniversaries of Jamestown Island and Plymouth Rock, our perspective may be clearer simply because we and our children have lived longer with the results of the Louisiana Purchase.

How different the United States was for our parents and grandparents in 1953: Eight of ten Americans then lived on a farm or in a small town; today eight of ten live in urban areas. The Korean War was ending. French soldiers were losing a war in Vietnam. Joseph Stalin was in the final year of his life, and Joseph McCarthy in the final year of his credibility. Fidel Castro was an obscure prisoner in a Cuban jail. Neither the Berlin Wall nor the Watergate Hotel had been built. Color television was experimental, and only 29 percent of American women worked outside the home, compared with 57 percent today. Spanish was a foreign language. Segregation was the law in the American south and widely practiced throughout the country. *Brown v. Topeka* was in the lower courts. The Salk vaccine was in field tests, and the Pill was just a dream. Today, in short, we have a vantage point denied to David Ramsay in 1804 and Bernard DeVoto in 1953.

In the two centuries of Anglo-American colonial history from Jamestown to the Louisiana Purchase, American public life had become the domain of Protestant, agrarian, English-speaking men. Whites were free, blacks were slaves, and Native Americans did not count. Starting at

New Orleans in 1803, five million Americans along the Atlantic Seaboard accelerated an encounter with diversity that has been sustained by geographic expansion and immigration in the nineteenth and twentieth centuries. Ramsay and DeVoto could not yet see it, but the Louisiana Purchase was a turning point at America's halfway mark toward an inclusive national history. Looking back from the year 2003, Americans should marvel at who we have become—the very antithesis of John Winthrop's Boston, Timothy Pickering's Salem, James Monroe's Virginia, or Thomas Jefferson's yeoman republic. We may wonder what the next two centuries have in store.

Travelers who actually visited New Orleans two centuries ago probably came closest to seeing the human significance of the Louisiana Purchase that eluded David Ramsay and Bernard DeVoto. The Jeffersonian polymath Benjamin Henry Latrobe, for example, arriving in 1819 to complete the construction of waterworks for the city of New Orleans, encountered "a more incessant, loud, rapid, and various gabble of tongues . . . than was ever heard at Babel." He found the three-caste society of New Orleans "wholly new even to one who has traveled much in Europe and America"[12]—a bustling urban place filled with Catholics, Creoles, French, Spanish, Africans, Native Americans, West Indians, and Anglo-Americans. With Irish, Germans, and countless others soon to arrive. At the Cabildo in New Orleans on December 20, 1803, the United States began a long encounter with diversity that has forced us, and that should inspire us, to think and to live far differently than the Founders expected.

Although Ramsay and DeVoto did not have the imagination to envisage it, we live at a moment when census officials report that Spanish-speaking Americans have become the nation's largest minority group. Is it not time for Americans to look beyond the colonial East Coast dichotomy of black and white? Without forgetting that the Louisiana territory witnessed ugly and vicious moments of racial discord and bloodshed, we want to hope that perhaps—standing at the beginning of a millennium and on the eve of a bicentennial—perhaps we can learn a lesson from the good people of that *"Gallo-Hispano-Indian omnium gatherum* of savages and adventurers" who lived in the "unmeasured world beyond that river" and scared the dickens out of Fisher Ames.

If a candid reconsideration of the Louisiana Purchase helps us see diversity rather than dichotomy in the history we share with one another and with the world, perhaps we Americans can begin to look back at the Louisiana Purchase as a tributary in a long and slow and often tragic story of eventual inclusion. And perhaps the most fascinating part of the story of the Louisiana Purchase—the destiny of America—remains farther downstream.

# Treaty of 1795 Between the United States and Spain

His Catholic Majesty and the United States of America desiring to consolidate on a permanent basis the Friendship and good correspondence which happily prevails between the two Parties, have determined to establish by a convention several points, the settlement whereof will be productive of general advantage and reciprocal utility to both Nations.

With this intention His Catholic Majesty has appointed the most excellent Lord Don Manuel de Godoy and Alvarez de Faria, Rios, Sanchez Zarzosa, Prince de la Paz Duke de la Alcudia Lord of the Soto de Roma and of the State of Albalá: Grandee of Spain of the first class: perpetual Regidor of the Citty of Santiago: Knight of the illustrious Order of the Golden Fleece, and Great Cross of the Royal and distinguished Spanish order of Charles the III. Commander of Valencia del Ventoso, Rivera, and Aceuchal in that of Santiago: Knight and Great Cross of the religious order of St. John: Counsellor of State: First Secretary of State and Despacho: Secretary to the Queen: Superintendant General of the Posts and High Ways: Protector of the Royal Academy of the Noble Arts, and of the Royal Societies of natural history, Botany, Chemistry, and Astronomy: Gentleman of the King's Chamber in employment: Captain General of his Armies: Inspector and Major of the Royal Corps of Body Guards etc. etc. etc. and the President of the United States with the advice and consent of their Senate, has appointed Thomas Pinckney a Citizen of the United States, and their Envoy Extraordinary to his Catholic Majesty. And the said Plenipotentiaries have agreed upon and concluded the following Articles.

## ARTICLE I

There shall be a firm and inviolable Peace and sincere Friendship between His Catholic Majesty his successors and subjects, and the United States and their Citizens without exception of persons or places.

## ARTICLE II

To prevent all disputes on the subject of the boundaries which separate the territories of the two High contracting Parties, it is hereby declared and agreed as follows: to wit: The Southern boundary of the United States which divides their territory from the Spanish Colonies of East and West Florida, shall be designated by a line beginning on the River Mississippi at the Northernmost part of the thirty first degree of latitude North of the Equator, which from thence shall be drawn due East to the middle of the River Apalachicola or Catahouche, thence along the middle thereof to its junction with the Flint, thence straight to the head of St. Mary's River, and thence down the middle there of to the Atlantic Occean. And it is agreed that if there should be any troops, Garrisons or settlements of either Party in the territory of the other according to the above mentioned boundaries, they shall be withdrawn from the said territory within the term of six months after the ratification of this treaty or sooner if it be possible and that they shall be permitted to take with them all the goods and effects which they possess.

## ARTICLE III

In order to carry the preceding Article into effect one Commissioner and one Surveyor shall be appointed by each of the contracting Parties who shall meet at the Natchez on the left side of the River Mississippi before the expiration of six months from the ratification of this convention, and they shall proceed to run and mark this boundary according to the stipulations of the said Article.[1] They shall make Plats and keep journals of their proceedings which shall be considered as part of this convention, and shall have the same force as if they were inserted therein. And if on any account it should be found necessary that the said Commissioners and Surveyors should be accompanied by Guards, they shall be furnished in equal proportions by the Commanding Officer of his Majesty's troops in the two Floridas, and the Commanding Officer of the troops of the United States in their Southwestern territory, who shall act by common consent and amicably, as well with respect to this point as to the furnishing of provisions and instruments and making every other arrangement which may be necessary or useful for the execution of this article.

## ARTICLE IV

It is likewise agreed that the Western boundary of the United States which separates them from the Spanish Colony of Louisiana, is in the middle of the channel or bed of the River Mississippi from the Northern boundary of the said States to the completion of the thirty first degree of latitude North of the Equator; and his Catholic Majesty has likewise agreed that the navigation of the said River in its whole breadth from its source to the Occean shall be free only to his Subjects, and the Citizens of the United States, unless he should extend this privilege to the Subjects of other Powers by special convention.

## ARTICLE V

The two High contracting Parties shall by all the means in their power maintain peace and harmony among the several Indian Nations who inhabit the country adjacent to the lines and Rivers which by the preceding Articles form the boundaries of the two Floridas; and the beter to obtain this effect both Parties oblige themselves expressly to restrain by force all hostilities on the part of the Indian Nations living within their boundaries: so that Spain will not suffer her Indians to attack the Citizens of the United States, nor the Indians inhabiting their territory; nor will the United States permit these last mentioned Indians to commence hostilities against the Subjects of his Catholic Majesty, or his Indians in any manner whatever.

And whereas several treaties of Friendship exist between the two contracting Parties and the said Nations of Indians, it is hereby agreed that in future no treaty of alliance or other whatever (except treaties of Peace) shall be made by either Party with the Indians living within the boundary of the other; but both Parties will endeavour to make the advantages of the Indian trade common and mutualy beneficial to their respective Subjects and Citizens observing in all things the most complete reciprocity: so that both Parties may obtain the advantages arising from a good understanding with the said Nations, without being subject to the expence which they have hitherto occasioned.

## ARTICLE VI

Each Party shall endeavour by all means in their power to protect and defend all Vessels and other effects belonging to the Citizens or Subjects of the other, which shall be within the extent of their jurisdiction by sea or by land, and shall use all their efforts to recover and cause to be restored to the right owners their Vessels and effects which may have been taken from them within the extent of their said jurisdiction whether they are at war or not with the Power whose Subjects have taken possession of the said effects.

## ARTICLE VII

And it is agreed that the Subjects or Citizens of each of the contracting Parties, their Vessels, or effects shall not be liable to any embargo or detention on the part of the other for any military expedition or other public or private purpose whatever; and in all cases of seizure, detention, or arrest for debts contracted or offences committed by any Citizen or Subject of the one Party within the jurisdiction of the other, the same shall be made and prosecuted by order and authority of law only, and according to the regular course of proceedings usual in such cases. The Citizens and Subjects of both Parties shall be allowed to employ such Advocates, Sollicitors, Notaries, Agents, and Factors, as they may judje proper in all their affairs and in all their trials at law in which they may be concerned before the tribunals of the other Party, and such Agents shall have free access to be present at the proceedings in such causes, and at the taking of all examinations and evidence which may be exhibited in the said trials.

## ARTICLE VIII

In case the Subjects and inhabitants of either Party with their shipping whether public and of war or private and of merchants be forced through stress of weather, pursuit of Pirates, or Enemis, or any other urgent necessity for seeking of shelter and harbor to retreat and enter into any of the Rivers, Bays, Roads, or Ports belonging to the other Party, they shall be received and treated with all humanity, and enjoy all favor, protection and help, and they shall be permitted to refresh and provide themselves at reasonable rates with victuals and all things needful for the sustenance of their persons or reparation of their Ships, and prosecution of their voyage; and they shall no ways be hindered from returning out of the said Ports, or Roads, but may remove and depart when and whither they please without any let or hindrance.

## ARTICLE IX

All Ships and merchandize of what nature soever which shall be rescued out of the hands of any Pirates or Robbers on the high seas shall be brought into some Port of either State and shall be delivered to the custody of the Officers of that Port in order to be taken care of and restored entire to the true proprietor as soon as due and sufficient proof shall be made concerning the property there of.

## ARTICLE X

When any Vessel of either Party shall be wrecked, foundered, or otherwise damaged on the coasts or within the dominion of the other, their respective Subjects or Citizens shall receive as well for themselves as for their Vessels and effects the same assistence which would be due to the inhabitants of the Country where the damage happens, and shall pay the same charges and dues only as the said inhabitants would be subject to pay in a like case: and if the operations of repair should require that the whole or any part of the cargo be unladen they shall pay no duties, charges, or fees on the part which they shall relade and carry away.

## ARTICLE XI

The Citizens and Subjects of each Party shall have power to dispose of their personal goods within the jurisdiction of the other by testament, donation, or otherwise; and their representatives being Subjects or Citizens of the other Party shall succeed to their said personal goods, whether by testament or ab intestato and they may take possession thereof either by themselves or others acting for them, and dispose of the same at their will paying such dues only as the inhabitants of the Country wherein the said goods are shall be subject to pay in like cases, and in case of the absence of the representatives, such care shall be taken of the said goods as would be taken of the goods of a native in like case, until the lawful owner may take measures for receiving them. And if question shall arise among several claimants to which of them the said goods belong the same shall be decided finally by the laws and Judges of the Land wherein said goods are.

And where on the death of any person holding real estate within the territories of the one Party, such real estate would by the laws of the Land descend on a Citizen or Subject of the other were he not disqualified by being an alien, such subject shall be allowed a reasonable time to sell the same and to withdraw the proceeds without molestation, and exempt from all rights of detraction on the part of the Government of the respective states.

## ARTICLE XII

The merchant Ships of either of the Parties which shall be making into a Port belonging to the enemy of the other Party and concerning whose voyage and the species of goods on board her there shall be just grounds of suspicion shall be obliged to exhibit as well upon the high seas as in the Ports and havens not only her passports but likewise certificates expressly shewing that her goods are not of the number of those which have been prohibited as contraband.

## ARTICLE XIII

For the beter promoting of commerce on both sides, it is agreed that if a war shall break out between the said two Nations one year after the proclamation of war shall be allowed to the merchants in the Cities and Towns where they shall live for collecting and transporting their goods and merchandizes, and if any thing be taken from them, or any injury be done them within that term by either Party, or the People or Subjects of either, full satisfaction shall be made for the same by the Government.

## ARTICLE XIV

No subject of his Catholic Majesty shall apply for or take any commission or letters of marque for arming any Ship or Ships to act as Privateers against the said United States or against the Citizens, People, or inhabitants of the said United States, or against the property of any of the inhabitants of any of them, from any Prince or State with which the said United States shall be at war.

Nor shall any Citizen, Subject, or inhabitant of the said United States apply for or take any commission or letters of marque for arming any Ship or Ships to act as Privateers against the subjects of His Catholic Majesty or the property of any of them from any Prince or State with which the said King shall be at war. And if any person of either Nation shall take such commissions or letters of marque he shall be punished as a Pirate.

## ARTICLE XV

It shall be lawful for all and singular the Subjects of his Catholic Majesty, and the Citizens People, and inhabitants of the said United States to sail with their Ships with all manner of liberty and security, no distinction being made who are the proprietors of the merchandizes laden thereon from any Port to the Places of those who now are or hereafter shall be at enmity with his Catholic Majesty or the United States. It shall be likewise lawful for the Subjects and inhabitants aforesaid to sail with the Ships and merchandizes aforementioned, and to trade with the same liberty and security from the Places, Ports, and Havens of those who are Enemies of both or either Party without any opposition or disturbance whatsoever, not only directly from the Places of the Enemy aforementioned to neutral Places but also from one Place belonging to an enemy to another Place belonging to an Enemy, whether they be under the jurisdiction of the same Prince or under several, and it is hereby stipulated that Free Ships shall also give freedom to goods, and that everything shall be deemed free and exempt which shall be found on board the Ships belonging to the Subjects of either of the contracting Parties although the whole lading or any part thereof should appartain to the Enemies of either; contraband goods being always excepted. It is also agreed that the same liberty be extended to persons who are on board a free Ship, so that, although they be Enemies to either Party they shall not be made Prisoners or taken out of that free Ship unless they are Soldiers and in actual service of the Enemies.

## ARTICLE XVI

This liberty of navigation and commerce shall extend to all kinds of merchandizes excepting those only which are distinguished by the name of contraband; and under this name of contraband or prohibited goods shall be comprehended arms, great guns, bombs, with the fusees, and other things belonging to them, cannon ball, gun powder, match, pikes, swords, lances, speards, halberds, mortars, petards, granades, salpetre, muskets, musket ball bucklers, helmets, breast plates, coats of mail, and the like kind of arms proper for arming soldiers, musket rests, belts, horses with their furniture and all other warlike instruments whatever. These merchandizes which follows shall not be reckoned among contraband or prohibited goods; that is to say, all sorts of cloths and all other manufactures woven of any wool, flax, silk, cotton, or any other materials whatever, all kinds of wearing aparel together with all species whereof they are used to be made, gold and silver as well coined as uncoined, tin, iron, latton, copper, brass, coals, as also wheat, barley, oats and any other kind of corn and pulse: tobacco and likewise all manner of spices, salted and smoked flesh, salted fish, cheese and butter, beer, oils, wines, sugars, and all sorts of salts, and in general all provisions which serve for the sustenance of life. Furthermore all kinds of cotton, hemp, flax, tar, pitch, ropes, cables, sails, sail cloths, anchors, and any parts of anchors, also ships masts, planks, wood of all kind, and all other things proper either for building or repairing ships, and all other goods whatever which have not been worked into the form of any instrument prepared for war by land or by sea, shall not be reputed contraband, much less such as have been already wrought and made up for any other use: all which shall be wholy reckoned among free goods, as likewise all other merchandizes and things which are not comprehended and particularly mentioned in the foregoing enumeration of contraband goods: so that they may be transported and carried in the freest manner by the subjects of both parties, even to Places belonging to an Enemy, such towns or Places being only excepted as are at that time besieged, blocked up, or invested. And except the cases in which any Ship of war or Squadron shall in consequence of storms or other accidents at sea be under the necessity of taking the cargo of any trading Vessel or Vessels, in which case they may stop the said Vessel or Vessels and furnish themselves with necessaries, giving a receipt in order that the Power to whom the said ship of war belongs may pay for the articles so taken according to the price thereof at the Port to which they may appear to have been destined by the Ship's papers: and the two contracting Parties engage that the Vessels shall not be detained longer than may be absolutely necessary for their said Ships to supply themselves with necessaries: that they will immediately pay the value of the receipts: and indemnify the proprietor for all losses which he may have sustained in consequence of such transaction.

### ARTICLE XVII

To the end that all manner of dissentions and quarels may be avoided and prevented on one side and the other, it is agreed that in case either of the Parties hereto should be engaged in a war, the ships and Vessels belonging to the Subjects or People of the other Party must be furnished with sea letters or passports expressing the name, property, and bulk of the Ship, as also the name and place of habitation of the master or commander of the said Ship, that it may appear thereby that the Ship really and truly belongs to the Subjects of one of the Parties; which passport shall be made out and granted according to the form annexed to this Treaty. They shall likewise be recalled every year, that is, if the ship happens to return home within the space of a year. It is likewise agreed that such ships being laden, are to be provided not only with passports as above mentioned, but also with certificates containing the several particulars of the cargo, the place whence the ship sailed, that so it may be known whether any forbidden or contraband goods be on board the same; which certificates shall be made out by the Officers of the place whence the ship sailed in the accustomed form; and if any one shall think it fit or adviseable to express in the said certificates the person to whom the goods on board belong he may freely do so: without which requisites they may be sent to one of the Ports of the other contracting Party and adjudged by the competent tribunal according to what is above set forth, that all the circumstances of this omission having been well examined, they shall be adjudged to be legal prizes, unless they shall give legal satisfaction of their property by testimony entirely equivalent.

### ARTICLE XVIII

If the Ships of the said subjects, People or inhabitants of either of the Parties shall be met with either sailing along the Coasts on the high Seas by any Ship of war of the other or by any Privateer, the said Ship of war or Privateer for the avoiding of any disorder shall remain out of cannon shot, and may send their boats aboard the merchant Ship which they shall so meet with, and may enter her to number of two or three men only to whom the master or Commander of such ship or vessel shall exhibit his passports concerning the property of the ship made out according to the form inserted in this present Treaty: and the ship when she shall have shewed such passport shall be free and at liberty to pursue her voyage, so as it shall not be lawful to molest or give her chace in any manner or force her to quit her intended course.

## ARTICLE XIX

Consuls shall be reciprocally established with the privileges and powers which those of the most favoured Nations enjoy in the Ports where their consuls reside, or are permitted to be.

## ARTICLE XX

It is also agreed that the inhabitants of the territories of each Party shall respectively have free access to the Courts of Justice of the other, and they shall be permitted to prosecute suits for the recovery of their properties, the payment of their debts, and for obtaining satisfaction for the damages which they may have sustained, whether the persons whom they may sue be subjects or Citizens of the Country in which they may be found, or any other persons whatsoever who may have taken refuge therein; and the proceedings and sentences of the said Court shall be the same as if the contending parties had been subjects or Citizens of the said Country.

## ARTICLE XXI

In order to terminate all differences on account of the losses sustained by the Citizens of the United States in consequence of their vessels and cargoes having been taken by the Subjects of his Catholic Majesty during the late war between Spain and France, it is agreed that all such cases shall be referred to the final decision of Commissioners to be appointed in the following manner. His Catholic Majesty shall name one Commissioner, and the President of the United States by and with the advice and consent of their Senate shall appoint another, and the said two Commissioners shall agree on the choice of a third, or if they cannot agree so they shall each propose one person, and of the two names so proposed one shall be drawn by lot in the presence of the two original Commissioners, and the person whose name shall be so drawn shall be the third Commissioner, and the three Commissioners so appointed shall be sworn impartially to examine and decide the claims in question according to the merits of the several cases, and to justice, equity, and the laws of Nations. The said Commissioners shall meet and sit at Philadelphia and in the case of the death, sickness, or necessary absence of any such commissioner his place shall be supplied in the same manner as he was first appointed, and the new Commissioner shall take the same oaths, and do the same duties. They shall receive all complaints and applications, authorized by this article during eighteen months from the day on which they shall assemble. They shall have power to examine all such persons as come before them on oath or affirmation touching the complaints in question, and also to receive in evidence all written testimony authenticated in such manner as they shall think proper to require or admit. The award of the said Commissioners or any two of them shall be final and conclusive both as to the justice of the claim and the amount of the sum to be paid to the claimants; and his Catholic Majesty undertakes to cause the same to be paid in specie without deduction, at such times and Places and under such conditions as shall be awarded by the said Commissioners.

## ARTICLE XXII

The two high contracting Parties hopping that the good correspondence and friendship which happily reigns between them will be further increased by this Treaty, and that it will contribute to augment their prosperity and opulence, will in future give to their mutual commerce all the extension and favor which the advantage of both Countries may require; and in consequence of the stipulations contained in the IV. article his Catholic Majesty will permit the Citizens of the United States for the space of three years from this time to deposit their merchandize and effects in the Port of New Orleans, and to export them from thence without paying any other duty than a fair price for the hire of the stores, and his Majesty promises either to continue this permission if he finds during that time that it is not prejudicial to the interests of Spain, or if he should not agree to continue it there, he will assign to them on another part of the banks of the Mississippi an equivalent establishment.

## ARTICLE XXIII

The present Treaty shall not be in force untill ratified by the Contracting Parties, and the ratifications shall be exchanged in six months from this time, or sooner if possible.

In Witness whereof We the underwritten Plenipotentiaries of His Catholic Majesty and of the United States of America have signed this present Treaty of Friendship, Limits and Navigation and have thereunto affixed our seals respectively.

Done at San Lorenzo el Real this seven and twenty day of October one thousand seven hundred and ninety five.

Thomas Pinckney [Seal]
El Principe De La Paz [Seal]

# Louisiana Purchase Treaty

## Treaty Between the United States of America and the French Republic, April 30, 1803

The President of the United States of America and the First Consul of the French Republic in the name of the French People desiring to remove all Source of misunderstanding relative to objects of discussion mentioned in the Second and fifth articles of the Convention of the 8th Vendémiaire an 9/30 September 1800 relative to the rights claimed by the United States in virtue of the Treaty concluded at Madrid the 27 of October 1795, between His Catholic Majesty and the Said United States, and willing to Strengthen the union and friendship which at the time of the Said Convention was happily reestablished between the two nations have respectively named their Plenipotentiaries to wit The President of the United States, by and with the advice and consent of the Senate of the Said States; Robert R. Livingston Minister Plenipotentiary of the United States and James Monroe Minister Plenipotentiary and Envoy extraordinary of the Said States near the Government of the French Republic; And the First Consul in the name of the French people, Citizen Francis Barbé Marbois Minister of the public treasury who after having respectively exchanged their full powers have agreed to the following Articles.

### ARTICLE I

Whereas by the Article the third of the Treaty concluded at St Ildefonso the 9th Vendémiaire an 9/1st October 1800 between the First Consul of the French Republic and his Catholic Majesty it was agreed as follows.

"His Catholic Majesty promises and engages on his part to cede to the French Republic six months after the full and entire execution of the conditions and Stipulations herein relative to his Royal Highness the Duke of Parma, the Colony or Province of Louisiana with the Same extent that it now has in the hand of Spain, and that it had when France possessed it; and Such as it Should be after the Treaties subsequently entered into between Spain and other States."

And whereas in pursuance of the Treaty and particularly of the third article the French Republic has an incontestable title to the domain and to the possession of the said Territory—The First Consul of the French Republic desiring to give to the United States a strong proof of his friendship doth hereby cede to the United States in the name of the French Republic for ever and in full Sovereignty the said territory with all its rights and appurtenances as fully and in the Same manner as they have been acquired by the French Republic in virtue of the above mentioned Treaty concluded with his Catholic Majesty.

## ARTICLE II

In the cession made by the preceding article are included the adjacent Islands belonging to Louisiana all public lots and Squares, vacant lands and all public buildings, fortifications, barracks and other edifices which are not private property.—The Archives, papers and documents relative to the domain and Sovereignty of Louisiana and its dependences will be left in the possession of the Commissaries of the United States, and copies will be afterwards given in due form to the Magistrates and Municipal officers of Such of the said papers and documents as may be necessary to them.

## ARTICLE III

The inhabitants of the ceded territory shall be incorporated in the Union of the United States and admitted as soon as possible according to the principles of the federal Constitution to the enjoyment of all the rights, advantages and immunities of citizens of the United States, and in the mean time they shall be maintained and protected in the free enjoyment of their liberty, property and the Religion which they profess.

## ARTICLE IV

There Shall be Sent by the Government of France a Commissary to Louisiana to the end that he do every act necessary as well to receive from the Officers of his Catholic Majesty the Said country and its dependences in the name of the French Republic if it has not been already done as to transmit it in the name of the French Republic to the Commissary or agent of the United States.

## ARTICLE V

Immediately after the ratification of the present Treaty by the President of the United States and in case that of the first Consul's shall have been previously obtained, the Commissary of the French Republic shall remit all military posts of New Orleans and other parts of the ceded territory to the Commissary or Commissaries named by the President to take possession—the troops whether of France or Spain who may be there shall cease to occupy any military post from the time of taking possession and shall be embarked as soon as possible in the course of three months after the ratification of this treaty.

## ARTICLE VI

The United States promise to execute Such treaties and articles as may have been agreed between Spain and the tribes and nations of Indians until by mutual consent of the United States and the said tribes or nations other Suitable articles Shall have been agreed upon.

## ARTICLE VII

As it is reciprocally advantageous to the commerce of France and the United States to encourage the communication of both nations for a limited time in the country ceded by the present treaty until general arrangements relative to the commerce of both nations may be agreed on; it has been agreed between the contracting parties that the French Ships coming directly from France or any of her colonies loaded only with the produce and manufactures of France or her Said Colonies; and the Ships of Spain coming directly from Spain or any of her colonies loaded only with the produce or manufactures of Spain or her Colonies shall be admitted during the Space of twelve years in in [*sic*] the Port of New-Orleans and in all other legal ports-of-entry within the ceded territory in the Same manner as the Ships of the United States coming directly from France or Spain or any of their Colonies without being Subject to any other or greater duty on merchandize or other or greater tonnage than that paid by the citizens of the United States.

During the Space of time above mentioned no other nation Shall have a right to the Same privileges in the Ports of the ceded territory—the twelve years Shall commence three months after the exchange of ratifications if it Shall take place in France or three months after it Shall have been notified at Paris to the French Government if it Shall take place in the United States; It is however well understood that the object of the above article is to favour the manufactures, Commerce, freight and navigation of France and of Spain So far as relates to the importations that the French and Spanish Shall make into the Said Ports of the United States without in any Sort affecting the regulations that the United States may make concerning the exportation of the produce and merchandize of the United States, or any right they may have to make Such regulations.

## ARTICLE VIII

In future and for ever after the expiration of the twelve years, the Ships of France shall be treated upon the footing of the most favoured nations in the ports above mentioned.

## ARTICLE IX

The particular Convention Signed this day by the respective Ministers having for its object to provide for the payment of debts due to the Citizens of the United States by the French Republic prior to the 30th September 1800 (8th Vendémiaire an 9) is approved and to have its execution in the Same manner as if it had been inserted in this present treaty, and it Shall be ratified in the same form and in the Same time So that the one Shall not be ratified distinct from the other.

Another particular Convention Signed at the Same date as the present treaty relative to a definitive rule between the contracting parties is in the like manner approved and will be ratified in the Same form, and in the Same time and jointly.

## ARTICLE X

The present treaty Shall be ratified in good and due form and the ratifications Shall be exchanged in the Space of Six months after the date of the Signature by the Ministers Plenipotentiary or Sooner if possible.

In faith whereof the respective Plenipotentiaries have Signed these articles in the French and English languages; declaring nevertheless that the present Treaty was originally agreed to in the French language; and have thereunto affixed their Seals.

Done at Paris the tenth day of Floreal in the eleventh year of the French Republic; and the 30th of April 1803.

Robt R Livingston [seal]
Jas Monroe [seal]
Barbé Marbois [seal]

# Louisiana Purchase Conventions

## A Convention Between the United States of America and the French Republic

The President of the United States of America and the First Consul of the French Republic in the name of the French people, in consequence of the treaty of cession of Louisiana which has been Signed this day; wishing to regulate definitively every thing which has relation to the Said cession have authorized to this effect the Plenipotentiaries that is to say: the President of the United States has, by and with the advice and consent of the Senate of the Said States nominated for their Plenipotentiaries, Robert R. Livingston, Minister Plenipotentiary of the United States and James Monroe Minister Plenipotentiary and Envoy-Extraordinary of the Said United States near the Government of the French Republic; and the First Consul of the French Republic, in the name of the French People has named as Plenipotentiary of the Said Republic the citizen Francis Barbé-Marbois: who in virtue of their full powers, which have been exchanged this day have agreed to the followings articles:

## ARTICLE 1

The Government of the United States engages to pay to the French Government in the manner Specified in the following article the Sum of Sixty millions of francs independent of the Sum which Shall be fixed by another Convention for the payment of the debts due by France to citizens of the United States.

## ARTICLE 2

For the payment of the Sum of Sixty millions of francs mentioned in the preceding article the United States shall create a Stock of eleven millions, two hundred and fifty thousand Dollars bearing an interest of Six per cent per annum payable half yearly in London Amsterdam or Paris amounting by the half year to three hundred and thirty Seven thousand five hundred Dollars according to the proportions which Shall be determined by the french Government to be paid at either place: The principal of the Said Stock to be reimbursed at the treasury of the United States in annual payments of not less than three millions of Dollars each; of which the first payment Shall commence fifteen years after the date of the exchange of ratifications—this Stock Shall be transferred to the Government of France or to Such person or persons as Shall be authorized to receive it in three months at most after the exchange of ratifications of this treaty and after Louisiana Shall be taken possession of in the name of the Government of the United States.

It is further agreed that if the french Government Should be desirous of disposing of the Said Stock to receive the capital in Europe at Shorter terms that its measures for that purpose Shall be taken So as to favour in the greatest degree possible the credit of the United States and to raise to the highest price the Said Stock.

## ARTICLE 3

It is agreed that the Dollar of the United States Specified in the present Convention Shall be fixed at five francs 3333/100000 or five livres eight Sous tournois.

The present Convention Shall be ratified in good and due form, and the ratifications Shall be exchanged in the Space of Six months to date from this day or Sooner if possible.

In faith of which the respective Plenipotentiaries have Signed the above articles both in the french and english languages, declaring nevertheless that the present treaty has been originally agreed on and written in the french language; to which they have hereunto affixed their Seals.

Done at Paris the tenth of Floreal eleventh year of the French Republic. (30th April 1803.)

Robt R Livingston [seal]
Jas Monroe [seal]
Barbé Marbois [seal]

# A Convention Between the United States of America and the French Republic

The President of the United States of America and the First Consul of the French Republic in the name of the French People having by a Treaty of this date terminated all difficulties relative to Louisiana, and established on a Solid foundation the friendship which unites the two nations and being desirous in complyance with the Second and fifth Articles of the Convention of the 8th Vendémiaire ninth year of the French Republic (30th September 1800) to Secure the payment of the Sums due by France to the citizens of the United

States have respectively nominated as Plenipotentiaries that is to Say The President of the United States of America by and with the advise and consent of their Senate Robert R. Livingston Minister Plenipotentiary and James Monroe Minister Plenipotentiary and Envoy Extraordinary of the Said States near the Government of the French Republic: and the First Consul in the name of the French People the Citizen Francis Barbé Marbois Minister of the public treasury; who after having exchanged their full powers have agreed to the following articles.

## ARTICLE 1

The debts due by France to citizens of the United States contracted before the 8th of Vendémiaire ninth year of the French Republic (30th September 1800) Shall be paid according to the following regulations with interest at Six per Cent; to commence from the period when the accounts and vouchers were presented to the French Government.

## ARTICLE 2

The debts provided for by the preceding Article are those whose result is comprised in the conjectural note annexed to the present Convention and which with the interest cannot exceed the Sum of twenty millions of Francs. The claims comprised in the Said note which fall within the exceptions of the following articles Shall not be admitted to the benefit of this provision.

## ARTICLE 3

The principal and interests of the Said debts Shall be discharged by the United States, by orders drawn by their Minister Plenipotentiary on their treasury, these orders Shall be payable Sixty days after the exchange of ratifications of the Treaty and the Conventions Signed this day, and after possession Shall be given of Louisiana by the Commissaries of France to those of the United States.

## ARTICLE 4

It is expressly agreed that the preceding articles Shall comprehend no debts but Such as are due to citizens of the United States who have been and are yet creditors of France for Supplies for embargoes and prizes made at Sea in which the appeal has been properly lodged within the time mentioned in the Said Convention 8th Vendémiaire ninth year (30th September 1800).

## ARTICLE 5

The preceding Articles Shall apply only, First: to captures of which the council of prizes Shall have ordered restitution it being well understood that the claimant cannot have recourse to the United States otherwise than he might have had to the Government of the French republic, and only in case of insufficiency of the captors—2d the debts mentioned in the Said fifth Article of the

Convention contracted before the 8th Vendémiaire an 9/30th September 1800 the payment of which has been heretofore claimed of the actual Government of France and for which the creditors have a right to the protection of the United States—the Said 5th Article does not comprehend prizes whose condemnation has been or Shall be confirmed: it is the express intention of the contracting parties not to extend the benefit of the present Convention to reclamations of American citizens who Shall have established houses of Commerce in France, England or other countries than the United States in partnership with foreigners, and who by that reason and the nature of their commerce ought to be regarded as domiciliated in the places where Such house exist.—All agrements and bargains concerning merchandize which Shall not be the property of American citizens are equally excepted from the benefit of the Said Convention Saving however to Such persons their claims in like manner as if this Treaty had not been made.

## ARTICLE 6

And that the different questions which may arise under the preceding article may be fairly investigated the Ministers Plenipotentiary of the United States Shall name three persons who Shall act from the present and provisionally and who shall have full power to examine without removing the documents, all the accounts of the different claims already liquidated by the Bureaus established for this purpose by the French Republic and to ascertain whether they belong to the classes designated by the present Convention and the principles established in it or if they are not in one of its exceptions and on their Certificate declaring that the debt is due to an American Citizen or his representative and that it existed before the 8th Vendémiaire 9th year/30 September 1800 the debtor shall be entitled to an order on the Treasury of the United States in the manner prescribed by the 3d Article.

## ARTICLE 7

The Same agents Shall likewise have power without removing the documents to examine the claims which are prepared for verification, and to certify those which ought to be admitted by uniting the necessary qualifications, and not being comprised in the exceptions contained in the present Convention.

## ARTICLE 8

The Same agents Shall likewise examine the claims which are not prepared for liquidation and certify in writing those which in their Judgment ought to be admitted to liquidation.

## ARTICLE 9

In proportion as the debts mentioned in these articles Shall be admitted they Shall be discharged with interest at Six per Cent by the Treasury of the United States.

## ARTICLE 10

And that no debt shall not have the qualifications above mentioned and that no unjust or exorbitant demand may be admitted, the Commercial agent of the United-States at Paris or Such other agent as the Minister Plenipotentiary of the United States Shall think proper to nominate shall assist at the operations of the Bureaus and cooperate in the examinations of the claims; and if this agent Shall be of the opinion that any debt is not completely proved or if he shall judge that it is not comprised in the principles of the fifth article above mentioned, and if notwithstanding his opinion the Bureaus established by the french Government should think that it ought to be liquidated he shall transmit his observations to the board established by the United States who without removing documents shall make a complete examination of the debt and vouchers which Support it, and report the result to the Minister of the United States.—The Minister of the United States Shall transmit his observations in all Such cases to the Minister of the treasury of the French Republic on whose report the French Government Shall decide definitively in every case.

The rejection of any claim Shall have no other effect than to exempt the United States from the payment of it the French Government reserving to itself, the right to decide definitively on Such claim So far as it concerns itself.

## ARTICLE 11

Every necessary decision Shall be made in the course of a year to commence from the exchange of ratifications and no reclamation Shall be admitted afterwards.

## ARTICLE 12

In case of claims for debts contracted by the Government of France with citizens of the United States Since the 8th Vendémiaire 9th year/30 September 1800 not being comprised in this Convention may be pursued and the payment demanded in the Same manner as if it had not been made.

## ARTICLE 13

The present convention Shall be ratified in good and due form and the ratifications Shall be exchanged in Six months from the date of the Signature of the Ministers Plenipotentiary or Sooner if possible.

In faith of which, the respective Ministers Plenipotentiary have Signed the above Articles both in the french and english languages declaring nevertheless that the present treaty has been originally agreed on and written in the french language, to which they have hereunto affixed their Seals.

Done at Paris the tenth of Floreal eleventh year of the French Republic. 30th April 1803.

Robt R Livingston [seal]
Jas Monroe [seal]
Barbé Marbois [seal]

# Draft Amendments to the Constitution, July–August 1803

In the summer of 1803, President Jefferson and his cabinet discussed the necessity of amending the Constitution for the acquisition of Louisiana. The following draft amendments were written during the course of their deliberations. None was formally proposed.

1. Between June 30 and July 9, 1803, President Jefferson prepared a lengthy draft of an amendment to Article 4, Section 3 of the United States Constitution.[1]

> The Province of Louisiana is incorporated with the U.S. and made part thereof. The rights of occupancy in the soil, and of self government, are confirmed to the Indian inhabitants, as they now exist. Pre-emption only of the portions rightfully occupied by them, and a succession to the occupancy of such as they may abandon, with the full rights of possession as well as of property and sovereignty in whatever is not or shall cease to be so rightfully occupied by them shall belong to the U.S.
>
> The legislature of the Union shall have authority to exchange the right of occupancy in portions where the U.S. have full right for lands possessed by Indians within the U.S. on the East side of the Mississippi: to exchange lands on the East side of the river for those of the white inhabitants on the West side thereof and above the latitude of 31 degrees: to maintain in any part of the province such military posts as may be requisite for peace or safety: to exercise police over all persons therein, not being Indian inhabitants: to work salt springs, or mines of coal, metals and other minerals within the possession of the U.S. or in any others with the consent of the possessors; to regulate trade and intercourse between the Indian inhabitants and other persons; to explore and ascertain the geography of the province, its productions and other interesting circumstances; to open roads and navigation therein where necessary for beneficial communication; and to establish agencies and factories [i.e., frontier

trading posts] therein for the cultivation of commerce, peace and good understanding with the Indians residing there.

The legislature shall have no authority to dispose of the lands of the province otherwise than as hereinbefore permitted, until a new Amendment of the constitution shall give that authority. Except as to that portion thereof which lies South of the latitude of 31 degrees; which whenever they deem expedient, they may erect into a territorial Government, either separate or making part with one on the eastern side of the river, vesting the inhabitants thereof with all the rights possessed by other territorial citizens of the U.S.

2. About July 9, 1803, after reviewing Jefferson's draft, James Madison offered him this alternative amendment.[2]

Louisiana as ceded by France is made part of the U. States. Congress may make part of the U.S. other adjacent territories which shall be justly acquired.

Congress may sever from the U.S. territory not heretofore within the U. States, with consent of a majority of the free males above 21 years, inhabiting such territory.

3. On July 9, 1803, after reviewing Jefferson's draft, Navy Secretary Robert Smith offered Jefferson the following draft:[3]

Louisiana being in virtue of the Treaty etc incorporated with the United States and being thereby a part of the Territory thereof Congress shall have power to dispose of and make all needful rules and regulations respecting the same as fully and effectually as if the same had been at the time of the establishment of the Constitution a part of the Territory of the U. States: provided nevertheless that Congress shall not have power to erect or establish in that portion of Louisiana which is situated North of the Latitude of /32/ degrees any new State or territorial government nor to grant to any citizen or citizens or other individual or individuals excepting Indians any right or title whatever to any part of the said portion of Louisiana until a new Amendment to the Constitution shall give that authority.

4. After July 9, 1803, Jefferson prepared this second draft amendment.[4]

Louisiana, as ceded by France to the U.S. is made part of the U.S. Its white inhabitants shall be citizens, and stand, as to their rights and obligations, on the same footing with other citizens of the U.S. in analogous situations. Save only that as to the portion thereof lying North of an East and West line drawn through the mouth of Arkansa river, no new State shall be established, nor any grants of land made, other than to Indians in exchange for equivalent portions of land occupied by them, until authorized by further subsequent amendment to the Constitution [which] shall be made for these purposes.

Florida also, whenever it may be rightfully obtained, shall become a part of the U.S. Its white inhabitants shall thereupon be Citizens and shall stand, as to their rights and obligations, on the same footing with other citizens of the U.S. in analogous situations.

5. On August 24, Jefferson enclosed his last draft in a letter to James Madison stating that upon "further reflection on the amendment to the constitution necessary in the case of Louisiana," he had decided that "it will be better to give general powers, with specified exceptions, somewhat in the way stated below."[5]

Louisiana, as ceded by France to the U.S., is made part of the U.S. Its white inhabitants shall be citizens, and stand, as to their rights and obligations on the same footing with other citizens of the U.S. in analogous situations.

Save only that as to the portion thereof lying North of the latitude of the mouth of Arcansa river, no new state shall be established, nor any grants of land made therein, other than to Indians in exchange for equivalent portions of land occupied by them, until an amendment to the Constitution shall be made for these purposes.

Florida also, whensoever it may be rightfully obtained, shall become a part of the U.S. Its white inhabitants shall thereupon be citizens, and shall stand as to their rights and obligations on the same footing with other citizens of the U.S. in analogous circumstances.

# A Note on Texts and Translations

This book relies heavily on documentary sources, both from manuscripts and from the variety of comprehensive editions that have become hallmarks of modern American scholarship. Based on the canons of modern documentary scholarship, so-called accidentals are handled consistently in quotations from all documentary sources. Terminal periods in abbreviations are omitted unless retained in modern usage, thus, James Monroe's *wold.* is presented as *wo[u]ld* but *Mr.* remains *Mr.* Superior letters are brought to the line of the text. Ampersands and *&c* are generally spelled out, and Jefferson's frequent use of *it's* for *its* is silently corrected. Jefferson and his contemporaries invented many ways to spell *Mississippi;* I employ the single modern spelling. When quoting from a modern documentary edition, I generally suppress the editorial apparatus used to identify interlineations, passages written in code or cipher, or readings supplied by a reliable editor. When it is important for the reader to be aware of the original orthography, I comment upon it in the text or notes. Underscored words from manuscript sources are set in italics, and italics are retained when they were used for emphasis rather than typographical decoration in printed sources. The notes identify those few instances in which I employ italics to convey my own emphasis within a quotation (e.g., when Rufus King wrote of his "*particular* country" in 1786), and the notes also indicate those few occasions when an author underscored the entire quoted passage for emphasis. When quoting from older translations of primary sources (principally the WPA-era Spanish Despatches), I have corrected obvious typographical errors and rendered a few awkwardly translated phrases into idiomatic English. For liturgical texts familiar in Latin to eighteenth-century men and women, I have used translations that echo the sturdy language of American hymns and liturgy.

All my interpolations in quoted passages are presented within brackets, including the occasional substitution of a noun for a pronoun (e.g., *Madison's* for *his*) or a third-person for a first-person pronoun (e.g., *her* for *my*). The notes direct anyone to my original sources. With few exceptions, the notes refrain from comment about historiographical debates, nor are they intended as a complete bibliography of works consulted. Information from the *Dictionary of American Biography, American National Biography, Biographical Directory of the American Congress, Hornbook of Virginia History,* and other standard reference works is used without citation.

## SHORT TITLES

| | |
|---|---|
| *AHR* | *American Historical Review* |
| Dangerfield, *Livingston* | George Dangerfield, *Chancellor Robert R. Livingston of New York, 1746–1813* (New York, 1960) |
| *HAHR* | *Hispanic American Historical Review* |
| *JAH* | *Journal of American History* |
| *Jefferson Papers* | Julian P. Boyd, Charles Cullen, John Catanzariti, Barbara Oberg et al., eds., *Papers of Thomas Jefferson* (Princeton, 1950– ) |
| *Letters of Delegates* | Paul H. Smith, Ronald M. Gephart et al., eds., *Letters of the Delegates to Congress, 1774–1789* (Washington, D.C., 1976–2000) |
| *LH* | *Louisiana History* |
| *LHQ* | *Louisiana Historical Quarterly* |
| *Madison Papers* | William T. Hutchinson, William M. E. Rachal, Robert A. Rutland et al., eds., *Papers of James Madison* (Chicago and Charlottesville, 1962– ) |
| *Madison Papers: State* | Robert J. Brugger, Mary A. Hackett, David B. Mattern et al., eds., *Papers of James Madison: Secretary of State Series* (Charlottesville, 1986– ) |
| *MVHR* | *Mississippi Valley Historical Review* |
| Robertson, *Louisiana* | James Alexander Robertson, *Louisiana Under the Rule of Spain, France, and the United States, 1785–1807* (New York, 1910–1911) |
| Schama, *Citizens* | Simon Schama, *Citizens: A Chronicle of the French Revolution* (New York, 1989) |
| Spanish Despatches | Despatches of the Spanish Governors (Works Progress Administration typescripts, 1937–1938), Special Collections, Howard-Tilton Library, Tulane University |
| *State Papers and Correspondence* | *State Papers and Correspondence Bearing upon the Purchase of the Territory of Louisiana* (Washington, D.C., 1903) |

| | |
|---|---|
| *Territorial Papers* | Clarence Edwin Carter, ed., *Territorial Papers of the United States,* vol. 9, *Territory of Orleans, 1803–1812* (Washington, D.C., 1940) |
| *VMHB* | *Virginia Magazine of History and Biography* |
| *Washington Papers* | W. W. Abbot and Dorothy Twohig, eds., *Papers of George Washington: Confederation Series* (Charlottesville, 1992–1997) |

# *Notes*

## TRIBUTARIES

1. Thomas Jefferson, *Notes on the State of Virginia,* ed. William Peden (Chapel Hill, 1954), 7–10.

2. Led to the headwaters of the Mississippi River by an Anishinabe guide named Ozawindib, the pioneering ethnologist Henry Rowe Schoolcraft gave Lake Itasca its name in 1832, a coinage from portions of the Latin words for *truth* and *head:* verITAS CAput. Statements of the length of the Mississippi River vary from 2,340 to 2,552 miles, in part because the river is constantly extending its delta into the Gulf and altering its course with bends and cutoffs. I have my parents' photographs of my sister Connie and me playing at the headwaters of the Mississippi on a 1953 excursion from Verndale, Minnesota, about seventy miles south of the little lake. The river left no lasting impression in my memory, but the steam locomotives and their coaling towers in Wadena did, as did the huge statues of Paul Bunyan and Babe, his blue ox, at a park in Bemidji, a few miles north of Lake Itasca.

## CHAPTER ONE: PIECE BY PIECE

1. Jefferson to Archibald Stuart, January 25, 1786, *Jefferson Papers,* 9: 217–19.

2. Thomas Jefferson to William Buchanan and James Hay, January 25, 1786, *Jefferson Papers,* 9: 219–22.

3. Jefferson to Thomas Mann Randolph, April 18, 1790, quoted in James A. Bear, Jr., and Lucia C. Stanton, eds., *Jefferson's Memorandum Books: Accounts, with Legal Records and Miscellany, 1767–1826.* Papers of Thomas Jefferson, 2d ser. (Princeton, 1997), 771.

4. *Jefferson's Memorandum Books,* 432–33, 713–14; Susan R. Stein, *The Worlds of Thomas Jefferson at Monticello* (New York, 1993), 18–28, 103, 350–63, 370, 428–33; Edward T. Martin, *Thomas Jefferson: Scientist* (New York, 1952), 131–91.

5. Howard C. Rice, *L'Hôtel de Langeac: Jefferson's Paris Residence, 1785–1789* (Paris and Monticello, 1947); Stein, *Worlds of Thomas Jefferson,* 18–28; interview with Susan R. Stein, December 1, 1999.

6. Interview with Lucia C. Stanton, December 6, 1999; Abigail Adams to Mary Smith Cranch, October 1, 1785, in Richard Alan Ryerson et al., eds., *Adams Family Correspondence:* vols. 5 and 6, *October 1782–December 1785* (Cambridge, Mass., 1993), 6: 396, cf. 391.

7. Stanton interview; Abigail Adams to Elizabeth Cranch, September 5, 1784, *Adams Family Correspondence,* 5: 433; *Jefferson's Memorandum Books,* 567.

8. George Green Schackelford, *Jefferson's Adoptive Son: The Life of William Short, 1759–1848* (Lexington, Ky., 1993), 13–132; Jon Kukla, "Flirtation and Feux d'Artifices: Mr. Jefferson, Mrs. Cosway, and Fireworks," *Virginia Cavalcade* 26 (Autumn 1976): 52–63.

9. Family details are from Dumas Malone, *Thomas Jefferson and His Time* (6 vols., Boston and New York, 1948–1981); Annette Gordon-Reed, *Thomas Jefferson and Sally Hemings: An American Controversy* (Charlottesville, 1997); Jan Ellen Lewis and Peter S. Onuf, eds., *Sally Hemings and Thomas Jefferson: History, Memory, and Civic Culture* (Charlottesville, 1999); and my conversations with Lucia C. Stanton and Diane Swann-Wright, November–December 1999. Genealogical charts are found in Malone, *Jefferson,* 1: 426–34, and Lewis and Onuf, *Hemings and Jefferson,* xii. The articles in the *National Genealogical Society Quarterly* 89, no. 3 (September 2001): 165–237, provide a reliable summary of the evidence about Jefferson and Hemings.

10. Malone, *Jefferson,* 1: 366.

11. Jefferson to Adams, September 25, 1785, *Adams Family Correspondence,* 6: 391; Jefferson to Monroe, May 20, 1782, *Jefferson Papers,* 6: 185.

12. Martha Jefferson's recollections, *Jefferson Papers,* 6: 199–200.

13. Ibid.

14. Ibid.

15. Ibid.

16. Ibid.

17. Jefferson to Chastellux, November 26, 1782, *Jefferson Papers,* 6: 203.

18. The correspondence about Polly Jefferson and Sally Hemings's voyage is collected in Lester J. Cappon, ed., *The Adams-Jefferson Letters: The Complete Correspondence Between Thomas Jefferson and Abigail and John Adams* (Chapel Hill, 1959), 178–86.

19. Ibid.

20. Ibid.

21. Ibid.

22. "Not until the summer of 1787 was the circle of his little family completed," Dumas Malone wrote in his monumental biography of Jefferson, "and not until then did the American Minister become fully reconciled to life in France" (Malone, *Jefferson,* 2: 12). Ironically, exactly fifty years after the publication of this statement, DNA evidence regarding Jefferson's paternity of Sally

Hemings's children amplified Malone's statement in ways that the admiring biographer never intended ("Jefferson Fathered Slave's Last Child," *Nature* 396 [Nov. 5, 1998]: 27–8; Eric S. Lander and Joseph J. Ellis, "Founding Father," ibid., 13–14).

23. Jefferson's correspondence of January 25–26, 1786, is published in *Jefferson Papers,* 9: 215–22.

24. Randolph C. Downes, "Trade in Frontier Ohio," *MVHR* 16 (1930): 469–71.

25. Stuart to Jefferson, October 25, 1785, *Jefferson Papers,* 8: 644–47.

26. B. L. Rayner, *Sketches of the Life, Writings, and Opinions of Thomas Jefferson, with Selections of the Most Valuable Portions of His Voluminous and Unrivaled Private Correspondence* (New York, 1832), 524; Fiske Kimball, *The Capitol of Virginia: A Landmark of American Architecture,* ed. Jon Kukla (Richmond, 1989), 12–13.

27. Kimball, *Capitol of Virginia,* 12–13, 22.

28. Ibid., 18, 58–59.

29. Ibid., 22–23.

30. Ibid., 25, 59, 60.

## CHAPTER TWO: CARLOS III AND SPANISH LOUISIANA

1. The earl of Bristol to William Pitt, August 31, 1761, quoted in Sir Charles Petrie, *King Charles III of Spain: An Enlightened Despot* (London and New York, 1971), 96–97.

2. Petrie, *Charles III of Spain,* 164–65.

3. Ibid., 165.

4. The original 1786–1788 portrait is owned by the duquessa de Fernán de Núñez in Madrid; four replicas hang in the Prado and other collections; Pierre Gassier and Juliet Wilson, *The Life and Complete Works of Francisco Goya* (Paris, 1970; New York, 1971), 31, 78, 95; *OED,* s.v. cordon.

5. Petrie, *Charles III of Spain;* John D. Bergamini, *The Spanish Bourbons: The History of a Tenacious Dynasty* (New York, 1974), 83–101; Marcel Brion, *Pompeii and Herculaneum: The Glory and the Grief* (New York, 1960), 38–59; Joseph Jay Davis, *The Town of Hercules: A Buried Treasure Trove* (rev. ed., Malibu, Calif., 1995), 37–49.

6. A. P. Whitaker, "James Wilkinson's First Descent to New Orleans in 1787," *HAHR* 8 (1928): 82–97; Leslie Bethell, ed., *Cambridge History of Latin America,* vol. 2 (1984), 34.

7. Anthony H. Hull, *Charles III and the Revival of Spain* (Lanham, Md., 1981), 403.

8. Bergamini, *Spanish Bourbons,* 86.

9. Hull, *Charles III,* 304.

10. Eleta's first name is mentioned in W. N. Hargreaves-Mawdsley, *Eighteenth-Century Spain, 1700–1788: A Political, Diplomatic and Institutional History* (Totowa, N.J., 1979), 115; Petrie, *Charles III of Spain,* 229.

11. Bergamini, *Spanish Bourbons*, 101.

12. Records and Deliberations of the Cabildo, Book no. 3, from January 1, 1788, to May 18, 1792; City Archives, New Orleans Public Library, 55–57.

13. Jacques Marquette, "The Mississippi Voyage of Jolliet and Marquette, 1673," in Louise Phelps Kellogg, ed., *Early Narratives of the Northwest, 1634–1699* (New York, 1917), 256.

14. Henri de Tonty, "Memoir on La Salle's Discoveries, by Tonty, 1678–1690," in Kellogg, *Early Narratives of the Northwest*, 302; Francis Parkman, *La Salle and the Discovery of the Great West* (Boston, 1903), 308.

15. D. A. Brading, "Mexican Silver-Mining in the Eighteenth Century: The Revival of Zacatecas," *HAHR* 50 (1970): 665–81; D. A. Brading and Harry E. Cross, "Colonial Silver Mining: Mexico and Peru," *HAHR* 52 (1972): 545–79; Herbert S. Klein, *The American Finances of the Spanish Empire: Royal Income and Expenditures in Colonial Mexico, Peru, and Bolivia, 1680–1809* (Albuquerque, 1998), 15–29.

16. Several eyewitness accounts of this fire are extant. One unofficial account dated March 26 was printed in *The London Chronicle* on August 19, 1788. Another composed ca. April 1 was published in the *Gaceta de Mexico* on May 6, 1788. Both are reprinted in Lauro A. de Rojas and Walter Pritchard, eds., "The Great Fire of 1788 in New Orleans," *LHQ* 20 (1937): 578–89, along with secondary accounts by Charles Gayarré, Alcée Fortier, and others. At its meeting on November 18, 1896, "President Fortier entertained the [Louisiana Historical] society by translating a valuable French document, published at Cap Français, and giving an account of the great fire of 1788 in New Orleans"; *Publications of the Louisiana Historical Society* 1, no. 4 (1896): 10–11. The official report dated April 1, 1788, exists in at least two versions. The Works Projects Administration (WPA) translation from Legajo 1394 is preserved in the Spanish Despatches. A shorter version, dated April 1, 1788, was published with Gilbert Pemberton's quirky " 'Noblesse Oblige': Why New Orleans Can Always Come Back," *Publications of the Louisiana Historical Society* 8 (1914–1915): 56–63. The subject warrants an authoritative documentary edition, for substantial differences between the WPA transcription and Pemberton's text suggest the existence of multiple versions of the report. The WPA translation is a long report signed by Miró that mentions the death of the "sick negress." Pemberton's translation is half as long, lacks many details including any mention of deaths, and is presented as a report from Miró *and* Navarro.

17. Robertson, *Louisiana*, 1: 177–78; Martín Navarro to Fernando José Mangino, superintendent of the royal mint, February 28, 1788, Kuntz Collection, Tulane University; Jack D. L. Holmes, "Some Economic Problems of the Spanish Governors of Louisiana," *HAHR* 42 (1962): 523.

18. Brian E. Coutts, "Martín Navarro: Treasurer, Contador, Intendant, 1766–1788: Politics and Trade in Spanish Louisiana" (Ph.D. diss., Louisiana State University, 1981), 514n.

19. James Alexander Robertson published the report and dated it "ca. 1785" (Robertson, *Louisiana*, 1: 235–61), but the manuscript was dated August 29 and

sent to imperial authorities on September 24, 1780 (Coutts, "Martín Navarro," 306n). In quoting Navarro's treatise, I use Robertson's edition as "copy text" unless Brian E. Coutts's chapter, "Trade and Commerce, 1780–1788" (Coutts, "Martín Navarro," 306–447) provides a superior translation.

20. Adam Smith, *An Inquiry into the Nature and Causes of the Wealth of Nations,* ed. R. H. Campbell, A. S. Skinner, and W. B. Todd (Oxford, 1976), 592–94.

21. Caroline Maude Burson, *The Stewardship of Don Esteban Miró, 1782–1792: A Study of Louisiana Based Largely on the Documents in New Orleans* (New Orleans, 1940), 86–87.

22. Coutts, "Martín Navarro," 505–8; *Dictionary of Louisiana Biography,* s.v. "Navarro, Adélaïde de Blanco," "Demarest, Louis George."

23. Coutts, "Martín Navarro," 505–8, 550–53; Robertson, *Louisiana,* 1: 247.

24. Robertson, *Louisiana,* 1: 247, 249–50.

## CHAPTER THREE: POOR COLONEL MONROE!

1. Sarah Vaughan to Catherine Wilhelmina Livingston, October 10, 1784, Massachusetts Historical Society, quoted in Harry Ammon, *James Monroe: The Quest for National Identity* (New York, 1971), 46.

2. Sarah P. Stetson, "The Philadelphia Sojourn of Samuel Vaughan," *Pennsylvania Magazine of History and Biography* 73 (1949): 459–74.

3. George Washington to Archibald Cary, May 30, 1779; Alexander Hamilton to John Laurens, May 22, 1779, Ammon, *James Monroe,* 27–28.

4. John Adams to Abigail Adams, September 18, 1774; Titus Hosmer to Jeremiah Wadsworth, July 19, 1778, *Letters of Delegates,* 1: 79; 25: 644.

5. Count Gijsbert Karel van Hogendorp's account of a spring 1784 conversation with Thomas Jefferson, ibid., 21: 494n.

6. Abiel Foster to Jonathan Blanchard, March 30, 1785, ibid., 22: 296–97.

7. Monroe to Jefferson, June 16, 1785, ibid., 22: 462.

8. Rufus King to Timothy Pickering, April 15, 1785; Richard Henry Lee to George Washington, May 7, 1785; Rufus King to Timothy Pickering, May 30, 1785; and William Grayson to James Madison, May 28, 1785, ibid., 22: 341–42, 383–84, 406, 416; Peter S. Onuf, *The Origins of the Federal Republic: Jurisdictional Controversies in the United States, 1775–1787* (Philadelphia, 1983), 149–72.

9. Richard Henry Lee to George Washington, February 14, 1785, *Letters of Delegates,* 22: 199. The American agent in Madrid, William Carmichael, notified Congress of Gardoqui's appointment in a letter dated October 12, 1784, that was read in Congress on February 10, 1785; ibid., 22: 197.

10. Journals of the Confederation Congress, February 15, 1785, quoted in *Letters of Delegates,* 22: 197.

11. Michael A. Otero, "The American Mission of Diego de Gardoqui, 1785–1789" (Ph.D. diss., University of California, Los Angeles, 1949), 25–48;

Light Townsend Cummins, *Spanish Observers and the American Revolution, 1775–1783* (Baton Rouge, 1991), 193–94.

12. Samuel Flagg Bemis, "John Jay," in Bemis, ed., *The American Secretaries of State and Their Diplomacy,* vol. 1 (New York, 1927), 240–41.

13. John Jay to Edward Rutledge, February 25, 1787, *Letters of Delegates,* 23: 172n2; Richard Henry Lee to Thomas Lee Shippen, June 4, 1785, ibid., 22: 432; Thomas Rodney's Diary, May 4, 1786, ibid., 23: 267. During his six years as a member of Congress, Rodney attended an average of two weeks per year.

14. Otero, "The American Mission of Diego de Gardoqui"; *Relaciones diplomáticas entre España y los Estados Unidos según los documentos del Archivo Histórico Nacional* (2 vols., Madrid, 1944–1945).

15. *Letters of Delegates,* 22: 200, 323, 355.

16. Ibid., 22: 355, 401, 405, 406, 418.

17. Ibid., 22: 431, 476.

18. Ibid., 22: 481, 499, 504.

19. Ibid., 22: 511.

20. Ibid., 22: 512.

21. Charles Thomson to John Jay, July 22, 1785; Monroe to Jefferson, August 15, 1785, ibid., 22: 526, 563. John P. Kaminski provides valuable insights into Secretary Jay's activities in "Shall We Have a King? John Jay and the Politics of Union," *New York History* 81 (2000): 31–58, and "Honor and Interest: John Jay's Diplomacy During the Confederation," ibid., forthcoming.

22. *Boston Independent Chronicle,* April 22, 1799, and Elbridge Gerry to Francis Dana, June 13, 1782, quoted in William C. Stinchcombe, *The American Revolution and the French Alliance* (Syracuse, 1969), 68, 190–91.

23. Nathan Dane to Edward Pulling, January 9, 1786, *Letters of Delegates,* 23: 85.

24. Rufus King to Caleb Davis, October 17 and November 3, 1785, *Letters of Delegates,* 22: 691n, 718–20.

25. Rufus King to Caleb Davis, November 3, 1785, ibid., 22: 718–20.

26. Ibid.

27. Ibid. Compare Article 6, section 2 of the Articles of Confederation—"No two or more states shall enter into any treaty, confederation, or alliance, whatever, between them, without the consent of the United States, in Congress assembled, specifying accurately the purposes for which the same is to be entered into, and how long it shall continue"—with the outright prohibition in Article I, section 10 of the Constitution: "No State shall enter into any Treaty, Alliance, or Confederation."

28. Rufus King to Caleb Davis, November 3, 1785, *Letters of Delegates,* 22: 718–20.

29. Nathaniel Gorham to Caleb Davis, February 23, 1786, ibid., 23: 161.

30. Five states were present at the Annapolis Convention: Delaware, New Jersey, New York, Pennsylvania, and Virginia; Mervin B. Whealy, " 'The Revolution Is Not Over': The Annapolis Convention of 1786," *Maryland Historical Magazine* 81 (Fall 1986): 230–35. Massachusetts elected delegates who

declined to attend, for reasons made clear in Rufus King to Jonathan Jackson, June 11, 1786; Rufus King to James Bowdoin, September 17, 1786; Rufus King's Address, October 11, 1786; and Nathan Dane's Address, November 9, 1786, *Letters of Delegates*, 23: 352, 561, 587–90; 24: 16–21.

31. For this rapid deterioration of Congress in relation to the history of the Constitution, see Forrest McDonald, *E Pluribus Unum: The Formation of the American Republic, 1776–1790* (Boston, 1965), Chapter 5.

32. James Monroe to Patrick Henry, August 12, 1786, *Letters of Delegates*, 23: 466.

33. Nathan Dane to Rufus King, August 11, 1786; Rufus King to Nathan Dane, August 17, 1786, *Letters of Delegates*, 23: 488–89.

34. Theodore Sedgwick to Caleb Strong, August 6, 1786, *Letters of Delegates*, 23: 436; Stephen E. Patterson, "The Roots of Massachusetts Federalism: Conservative Politics and Political Culture before 1787," in Ronald Hoffman and Peter J. Albert, *Sovereign States in an Age of Uncertainty* (Charlottesville, 1981), 38–39.

35. Louis-Guillaume Otto to the comte de Vergennes, September 10, 1786, Archives du Ministère des affaires étrangères: Correspondence politique, Etats-Unis, 32: 65–71; translated in George Bancroft, *History of the Formation of the Constitution of the United States* (New York, 1882), 2: 389–93.

36. Charles de Secondat, baron de Montesquieu, *The Spirit of the Laws* (Geneva, 1748), trans. Thomas Nugent; ed., Franz Neumann (New York, 1949): Book 8, section 16.

37. James Monroe to James Madison, May 31, 1786, *Letters of Delegates*, 23: 324–26.

38. Ibid.

39. Ibid.

## Chapter Four: A Long Train of Intrigue

1. *Letters of Delegates*, 23: 85.

2. Ibid., 23: 462–66.

3. Bettina Manzo, ed., "A Virginian in New York: The Diary of St. George Tucker, July–August, 1786," *New York History* 67 (1986): 197.

4. Ibid.; Russell Kirk, *John Randolph of Roanoke: A Study in American Politics* (4th ed., Indianapolis, 1997), 37; Robert Dawidoff, *The Education of John Randolph* (New York, 1979); Jonathan Daniels, *The Randolphs of Virginia: America's Foremost Family* (Garden City, N.Y., 1972), 97–98.

5. James Duane's Notes of Debates, September 6, 1774; John Jay to John Vardill, September 24, 1774, in *Letters of Delegates*, 1: 31, 95. References to secrecy or secrets occur 1,305 times in Smith's twenty-five volumes of congressional correspondence.

6. Manzo, ed., "Diary of St. George Tucker," 181–82.

7. Ibid., 186–91.

8. Ibid., 188–96.

9. The maps on pages 57–58 showing the series of concessions made in instructions to Gardoqui between 1784 and 1787 are based on Samuel Flagg Bemis, *Pinckney's Treaty: America's Advantage from Europe's Distress, 1783–1800* (Baltimore, 1926; rev. ed., New Haven, 1960), 33, 67–70.

10. Michael A. Otero, "The American Mission of Diego de Gardoqui, 1785–1789" (Ph.D. diss., University of California, Los Angeles, 1949), 74.

11. John J. Meng, ed., *Despatches and Instructions of Conrad Alexandre Gérard, 1778–1780: Correspondence of the First French Minister to the United States with the Comte de Vergennes* (Baltimore, 1939), 433–34, 494, 531; Edmund S. Morgan, "The Puritan Ethic and the American Revolution," *WMQ*, 3d ser., 24 (1967): 21; Jay to Jefferson, December 14, 1786, *Jefferson Papers*, 10: 599.

12. Diego de Gardoqui to the comte de Floridablanca, August 6, 1786, Legajo 3.893, Ap. 6 s.n., Archivo Históric Nacional, Madrid.

13. James Monroe to James Madison, May 31, 1786, *Letters of Delegates*, 23: 325n2; King to Monroe, July 30, 1786, ibid., 23: 423; Worthington C. Ford et al., eds., *Journals of the Continental Congress, 1774–1789* (Washington, D.C., 1904–1937), 31: 457, 467–84.

14. James Monroe to Thomas Jefferson, June 16, 1786, *Letters of Delegates*, 23: 360.

15. James Monroe to James Madison, May 31, 1786, ibid., 23: 325n2; King to Monroe, July 30, 1786, ibid., 23: 423; *Journals of the Continental Congress*, 31: 457, 467–84.

16. Theodore Sedgwick to Caleb Strong, August 6, 1786, *Letters of Congress*, 23: 436; Stephen E. Patterson, "The Roots of Massachusetts Federalism: Conservative Politics and Political Culture Before 1787," in Ronald Hoffman and Peter J. Albert, eds., *Sovereign States in an Age of Uncertainty* (Charlottesville, 1981), 38–39.

17. *American Quarterly Review* 1 (March 1827): 30–31; *Letters of Delegates*, 1: 12.

18. Charles Thomson to John Jay, August 1, 1786, *Letters of Delegates*, 23: 424–25.

19. Louis-Guillaume Otto to the comte de Vergennes, September 10, 1786; Archives du Ministère des affaires étrangères: Correspondence politique, Etats-Unis, 32: 65–71, translated in George Bancroft, *History of the Formation of the Constitution of the United States* (New York: Appleton, 1882), 2: 389–93; *Letters of Delegates*, 23: 546–48.

20. George C. Rogers, Jr., *Charleston in the Age of the Pinckneys* (2d ed., Columbia, S.C., 1984), 126–40.

21. Clarence S. Brigham, *History and Bibliography of American Newspapers, 1690–1820* (Worcester, Mass., 1947), 1: 610, 620, 680, 925, 1391; Jacob Axelrad, *Philip Freneau: Champion of Democracy* (Austin, 1967), 207–8. When the new federal government moved to Philadelphia, Childs followed and published the *National Gazette*, edited by Philip Freneau, from 1791 to 1793.

22. Pinckney to Washington, December 14, 1789, *Letters of Delegates*, 23:

458. "To refresh Your Memory on the subject of the agency [i.e., role] I had on the former Mississippi Question I send you the inclosed," Pinckney wrote to Madison on July 9, 1801, "being some of the copies I had left as it was printed for the Use of the then Southern Members"; *Madison Papers: State,* 1: 388. Madison had forwarded a copy of Pinckney's "printed sheet containing his ideas on a very delicate subject" to George Washington on October 14, 1787, *Letters of Delegates,* 24: 479–80n. The confusion occasioned by Francis Childs's substitution of "16th" for "10th" bedevils all published versions of Pinckney's speech except *Letters of Delegates,* 23: 446–58. Madison's copy is available on Evans microcards in many major libraries; the copy in the Continental Congress Broadside Collection, Library of Congress, no. 201, has annotations not found on the Evans microcard; and the "TR[anscript]" in the Thomson Papers (published in *Letters of Delegates,* 23: 446–58) may be a scribal copy given to the secretary by Pinckney, who presumably gave his speaking text to printer Francis Childs.

23. Fifteen congressmen took organized notes of debates between 1774 and 1789—a third of them in the month of August 1786; *Letters of Delegates,* 22 vols., passim.

24. Diego de Gardoqui to the comte de Floridablanca, August 20, 1786, Legajo 3.893, Ap. 6 s.n., Archivo Histórico Nacional, Madrid.

25. Worthington C. Ford et al., eds., *Journals of the Continental Congress, 1774–1789* (Washington, D.C., 1904–1937), 31: 509.

26. Quotations from Pinckney's speech are from the text published in *Letters of Delegates,* 23: 446–58.

27. *Journals of the Continental Congress,* 31: 510.

28. Stephen Mix Mitchell to William Samuel Johnson, February 15, 1786, *Letters of Delegates,* 23: 158.

29. William Grayson to Richard Henry Lee, March 22, 1786, ibid., 23: 201 and editorial notes, ibid., 54, 147, 152; James E. Wootton, *Elizabeth Kortright Monroe* (Charlottesville, 1987), 3–4; Harry Ammon, *James Monroe: The Quest for National Identity* (New York, 1971), 49; George Athan Billias, *Elbridge Gerry: Founding Father and Republican Statesman* (New York, 1976), 147.

30. Grayson to Lee, March 22, 1786, *Letters of Delegates,* 23: 201; Jay to John Adams, May 4, 1786, Henry P. Johnston, ed., *Correspondence and Public Papers of John Jay* (New York, 1881), 3: 193–94; Monroe to James Madison, February 11, 1786, and Rufus King to Benjamin Lincoln, Jr., April 16, 1786, *Letters of Delegates,* 23: 147, 240; Gerry to Monroe, May 28, 1786, quoted in Ammon, *James Monroe,* 61.

31. King to Lincoln, April 16, 1786, *Letters of Delegates,* 23: 240 (emphasis added).

32. All quotations from James Monroe to Patrick Henry, August 12, 1786, are from the text printed in ibid., 23: 462–66.

33. Diego de Gardoqui to the comte de Floridablanca, August 20, 1786, Legajo 3.893, Ap. 6 s.n., Archivo Histórico Nacional, Madrid.

34. Ibid.

35. Ibid. "No single issue during the entire Confederation era produced such a rigid and pervasive cleavage in Congress. . . . Clearly the Jay-Gardoqui question had some transcendent quality which polarized party politics." H. James Henderson, *Party Politics in the Continental Congress* (New York, 1974), 389. The thirteenth state, Rhode Island, was chronically absent from Congress.

## CHAPTER FIVE: THE TOUCH OF A FEATHER

1. George Washington to Governor Benjamin Harrison, October 10, 1784, *Washington Papers*, 2: 92–93.

2. Rufus King to Jonathan Jackson, September 3, 1786, *Letters of Delegates*, 23: 541.

3. *Journals of the Continental Congress*, 34: 534–35.

4. Jon Kukla, "Mr. Henry's Rat: The Jay-Gardoqui Negotiations and the Union of the States, 1785–1788," forthcoming.

5. Herbert S. Klein, *The American Finances of the Spanish Empire: Royal Income and Expenditures in Colonial Mexico, Peru, and Bolivia, 1680–1809* (Albuquerque, 1998), 15–29.

6. Arthur Preston Whitaker, *The Spanish-American Frontier, 1783–1795: The Westward Movement and the Spanish Retreat in the Mississippi Valley* (Lincoln, Neb., 1927), 68, 102; James Madison's Notes of Debates, March 13, 1787, *Letters of Delegates*, 24: 145.

7. James Madison's Notes of Debates, April 23, 1787; Rufus King to Jonathan Jackson, September 3, 1786, *Letters of Delegates*, 24: 248; 23: 541; Diego de Gardoqui to the comte de Floridablanca, February 1, 1786, Legajo 3.893, Ap. 3, no. 7., Archivo Histórico Nacional, Madrid, quoted in Michael A. Otero, "The American Mission of Diego de Gardoqui, 1785–1789" (Ph.D. diss., University of California, Los Angeles, 1949), 199. Otero's literal translation is "Would that there were no such Mississippi in the world!"

8. Jay to Jefferson, December 14, 1786, *Jefferson Papers*, 10: 599.

9. Jay to William Bingham, May 31, 1785, *Correspondence and Public Papers of John Jay*, 3: 154; Jay to Jefferson, April 24, 1787, ibid., 245.

10. John Dawson, Speech to the Virginia Convention, June 24, 1788, in John P. Kaminski et al., eds., *Documentary History of the Ratification of the Constitution, Ratification of the Constitution by the States: Virginia* 10 (Madison, Wis., 1993), 1491, 1493; James Winthrop, "Agrippa IV," December 4, 1787, ibid., *Massachusetts* 4 (Madison, Wis., 1997), 303, 383. Winthrop exaggerated: the nonslave population of the United States according to the census of 1790 was 3,231,647.

11. Theodore Sedgwick to Caleb Strong, August 6, 1786 (emphasis added), Ephraim Paine to Robert R. Livingston, May 24, 1784, *Letters of Delegates*, 21: 640, 23: 436; Stephen E. Patterson, "The Roots of Massachusetts Federalism: Conservative Politics and Political Culture Before 1787," in Ronald Hoffman and Peter J. Albert, *Sovereign States in an Age of Uncertainty* (Charlottesville, 1981), 38–39.

12. Robert A. Gross, ed., *In Debt to Shays: The Bicentennial of an Agrarian Revolution* (Charlottesville, 1993), 1–3, 101–18, 121–22, 129–30; Joseph Parker Warren, ed., "Documents Relating to the Shays Rebellion," *AHR* 2 (1896–1897): 694–95; Kaminski et al., eds., *Documentary History of the Ratification of the Constitution,* 4: xxxviii–xl.

13. Theodore Sedgwick to Caleb Strong, August 6, 1786, Rufus King to Jonathan Jackson, June 11, 1786, *Letters of Delegates,* 23: 436–37, 353.

14. Massachusetts Delegates to Governor James Bowdoin, September 3 and November 2, 1785, ibid., 22: 612, 716.

15. Grayson to Madison and to Monroe, November 22, 1786, ibid., 24: 31, 32.

16. Gouverneur Morris reflecting upon the framing of the Constitution in a letter to Henry W. Livingston, November 25, 1803; Max Farrand, ed., *Records of the Federal Convention of 1787* (rev. ed., New Haven, 1937), 3: 401. Robert William Fogel asserted the greater value of waterways in *Railroads and American Economic Growth: Essays in Economic History* (Baltimore, 1964).

17. Diary entry, October 4, 1784, Donald Jackson and Dorothy Twohig, eds., *The Diaries of George Washington* (Charlottesville, 1976–1979), 3: 67 (emphasis added).

18. Michael B. Chesson, *Richmond After the War, 1865–1890* (Richmond, 1981), 5.

19. *Virginia: A Guide to the Old Dominion* (New York, 1940; Richmond, 1992), 525.

20. For the *Daily Advertiser,* September 17, 1789, Kenneth R. Bowling and Helen E. Veit, eds., *The Diary of William Maclay and Other Notes on Senate Debates* (Baltimore, 1988), 406–10.

21. Donald Creighton, *The Commercial Empire of the St. Lawrence* (New York and Toronto, 1937 and 1956), 206–7. Creighton stated that his study "of the St. Lawrence as the inspiration and basis of a transcontinental, east-west system, both commercial and political in character" was "not meant to provide a final and self-sufficient interpretation of Canadian history" (ibid., iii, v), but it has much to offer Americans curious about our good neighbors to the north.

22. Steven E. Siry, *De Witt Clinton and the American Political Economy: Sectionalism, Politics, and Republican Ideology, 1787–1828* (New York, 1990).

23. W. W. Abbot, "George Washington, the West, and the Union," in Don Higginbotham, ed., *George Washington Reconsidered* (Charlottesville, 2001), 199–202.

24. George Washington to Jacob Reade, November 3, 1784, and to Henry Knox, December 5, 1784, ibid., 206–7.

25. George Washington to George Plater, October 25, 1784, ibid., 207.

26. Washington to Governor Benjamin Harrison, October 10, 1784, *Washington Papers,* 2: 92–93.

27. James Monroe to James Madison, September 29, 1786, *Letters of Delegates,* 23: 576. Monroe's letter to Mason is not extant, and Mason's actual sentiments are not directly known. Mason had long upheld Virginia's claim to

the Mississippi, and in 1786 Washington believed he "will advocate the navigation of that river," as Mason did in the Virginia ratification debates of 1788; Robert A. Rutland, ed., *Papers of George Mason, 1725–1792* (Chapel Hill, 1970), 852n and passim.

28. James Monroe to James Madison, September 29, 1786, *Letters of Delegates,* 23: 576.

29. Richard Henry Lee to George Washington, July 16, 1787, ibid., 24: 357. Richard Henry Lee described himself as "much interested in the establishment of a wise and free republic in Republic Massachusetts Bay, where yet I hope to finish the remainder of my days. The hasty, unpersevering, aristocratic genius of the south suits not my disposition"; quoted in Burton J. Hendrick, *The Lees of Virginia* (New York, 1935), 352.

30. Henry Lee to Washington, April 21, July 3, August 7, August 12, September 8, and October 11, 1786, *Letters of Delegates,* 23: 247, 382, 437–38, 440n, 554, 590–92. The evidence for Lee's complicity is in Gardoqui's confidential dispatches 14, 16, 17, 18, of November 29, 1786, May 12, July 6, and December 5, 1787, and his expense account for 1786–1787 (Archivo Central de Alcalá, Legajo 3895), cited in Samuel Flagg Bemis, *Pinckney's Treaty: America's Advantage from Europe's Distress, 1783–1800* (Baltimore, 1926; rev. ed., New Haven, 1960), 94–95.

31. James Madison to George Washington, November 8, Washington to Madison, November 18, Madison to Henry Lee, November 23, Madison to Thomas Jefferson, December 4, Edward Carrington to James Madison, December 18, and Henry Lee to Madison, December 20, 1786, *Madison Papers,* 9: 166–68, 170–71, 175–76, 189–92, 218–20; Thomas Boyd, *Light-Horse Harry Lee* (New York, 1931), 152–63; Bemis, *Pinckney's Treaty,* 96.

32. Thomas Jefferson to George Washington, March 15, 1784, *Jefferson Papers,* 7: 25–27.

33. For the *Daily Advertiser,* September 17, 1789, *Diary of William Maclay,* 410 (emphasis added).

34. Ibid.

## CHAPTER SIX: BOURBONS ON THE ROCKS

1. Edmund B. D'Auvergne, *Godoy: The Queen's Favorite* (Boston, 1913), 26–27; Douglas Hilt, *The Troubled Trinity: Godoy and the Spanish Monarchs* (Tuscaloosa, 1987), 17.

2. Quoted in Sir Charles Petrie, *King Charles III of Spain: An Enlightened Despot* (New York and London, 1971), 218.

3. Records and Deliberations of the Cabildo, Book no. 3, from January 1, 1788, to May 18, 1792; City Archives, New Orleans Public Library, 60–61.

4. Ibid.

5. Ibid. The founding of this hospital by Andrés Almonester is ably treated in Christina Vella, *Intimate Enemies: The Two Worlds of the Baroness de Pontalba* (Baton Rouge, 1997), 46–49.

6. Records and Deliberations of the Cabildo, Book no. 3, 60–61.

7. Robertson, *Louisiana,* 1: 247, 249–50.

8. John D. Bergamini, *The Spanish Bourbons: The History of a Tenacious Dynasty* (New York, 1974), 103; D'Auvergne, *Godoy,* 24; Douglas Hilt, *Troubled Trinity,* 17; Ramón Colón de Carvajal, "Clocks and Clock Workers for the King," in Jana Martin, ed., *The Majesty of Spain: Royal Collections from the Museo del Prado and the Patrimonio Nacional* (Jackson, Miss., 2001), 196; Petrie, *King Charles III of Spain,* 223–27.

9. Petrie, *King Charles III of Spain,* 224.

10. Hilt, *Troubled Trinity,* 15–16. Maria Luisa's given names were Luisa Maria Teresa and she signed her personal letters Luisa; Gabriel H. Lovett, *Napoleon and the Birth of Modern Spain* (New York, 1965), 5n.

11. D'Auvergne, *Godoy,* 26–29; Hilt, *Troubled Trinity,* 17.

12. Bergamini, *The Spanish Bourbons,* 104; Jana Martin, ed., *The Majesty of Spain,* 44, 70, 85; Petrie, *King Charles III of Spain,* 225.

13. D'Auvergne, *Godoy,* 26–35.

14. Hilt, *Troubled Trinity,* xiii; Petrie, *King Charles III of Spain,* 226.

15. Hilt, *Troubled Trinity,* 33, 60; Bergamini, *Spanish Bourbons,* 106.

16. Lovett, *Napoleon and the Birth of Modern Spain,* 1: 24; Hilt, *Troubled Trinity,* 104; Bergamini, *Spanish Bourbons,* 109.

17. Bergamini, *Spanish Bourbons,* 108.

18. Ibid., 106, 109.

19. Godoy's *Memoirs* quoted in Hilt, *Troubled Trinity,* 32–33.

20. Annette Kolodny, ed., "The Travel Diary of Elizabeth House Trist: Philadelphia to Natchez, 1783–84," in William L. Andrews, ed., *Journeys in New Worlds: Early American Women's Narratives* (Madison, Wis., 1990), 215.

21. Emily Foster, ed., *The Ohio Frontier: An Anthology of Early Writings* (Lexington, Ky., 1996), 79; "Diary of Elizabeth House Trist," 215.

22. John Filson, *Kentucke* (Wilmington, Del., 1784), and Timothy Flint, *Indian Wars of the West* (Cincinnati, 1823), quoted in Bernard W. Sheehan, "Paradise and the Noble Savage in Jeffersonian Thought," *WMQ,* 3d ser., 26 (1969): 333.

23. The leaders of Virginia's Loyal Land Company (one of several rival companies in the colony) were Dr. Walker, the mapmakers Peter Jefferson and Joshua Fry, and the Reverend James Maury, all from Albemarle County, along with John Lewis, from Staunton, and Edmund Pendleton, from Caroline County; Richard L. Morton, *Colonial Virginia* (Chapel Hill, 1960), 575–76; Malcolm J. Rohrbough, *The Trans-Appalachian Frontier: People, Societies, and Institutions, 1775–1850* (New York, 1978), 21–25. The percentage of slaves in Kentucky increased steadily from 16.9 percent in 1790, to 18.3 percent in 1800, 19.8 percent in 1810, and 22.5 percent in 1820, compared to the increase in the five southern Atlantic states from 35.3 percent in 1790 to 38.7 percent in 1820; Inter-university Consortium for Political and Social Research, Historical, Demographic, Economic, and Social Data: The United States, 1790–1970, at www.icpsr.umich.edu.

24. Lexington *Kentucky Gazette,* August 18, 1787, quoted in Rohrbough, *Trans-Appalachian Frontier,* 30.

25. Michael A. Bellesiles, *Arming America: The Origins of a National Gun Culture* (New York, 2000).

26. The combined population of the Apalache, Caddo, Chickasaw, Choctaw, Creek, and Tunica tribes in the Lower Mississippi area was about thirty thousand; Daniel H. Usner, Jr., *Indians, Settlers, and Slaves in a Frontier Exchange Economy: The Lower Mississippi Valley Before 1783* (Chapel Hill, 1992), 114–15n; David J. Weber, *The Spanish Frontier in North America* (New Haven, 1992), 274.

27. John G. Clark, *New Orleans, 1718–1812: An Economic History* (Baton Rouge, 1970), 212.

28. Lawrence Kinnaird, ed., *Spain in the Mississippi Valley, 1765–1794, Annual Report of the American Historical Association for the Year 1945* (Washington, D.C., 1946), 2: xviii, 125.

29. Clark, *New Orleans: An Economic History,* 213–14.

30. Daniel Clark to James Madison, September 8, 1803, *Territorial Papers,* 45; Josephe Xavier de Pontalba and Phineas Bond quoted in Arthur P. Whitaker, "The Commerce of Louisiana and the Floridas at the End of the Eighteenth Century," *HAHR* 8 (1928): 197n, 198n.

31. The late Julian P. Boyd presented Knox's tabulations in his "Threat of Disunion in the West," a chapter-length editorial note in *Jefferson Papers,* 19: 437.

32. Carlos de Grand-Pré to Governor Miró, April 14, 1790, in Kinnaird, ed., *Spain in the Mississippi Valley,* 3: 325.

33. Miró to Josef de Ezpeleta, January 28 and February 20, 1788, Spanish Despatches, Book 3, Legajo 1394, nos. 5 and 48.

34. Miró to Josef de Ezpeleta, February 20, 1788, Spanish Despatches.

35. Miró to Domingo Cabello, October 30, 1789, Spanish Despatches, Book 4, Legajo 1425, no. 36; Gerald M. Craig, *Upper Canada: The Formative Years, 1784–1841* (Toronto, 1963), 9–10.

36. Miró to Cabello, October 30, 1789, Spanish Despatches. Miró wrote that Fitzgerald entered the Mississippi by way of the St. Peter River (now the Minnesota River), which flows from the southwest to meet the Mississippi at Minneapolis; Timothy Flint, *A Condensed Geography and History of the Western States or the Mississippi Valley* (Cincinnati, 1828), 2: 438; I am grateful to Edward James Redmond, of the Map Division of the Library of Congress, for this information.

37. Herbert Eugene Bolton, "Defensive Spanish Expansion and the Significance of the Borderlands" (originally published in 1930), in John Francis Bannon, ed., *Bolton and the Spanish Borderlands* (Norman, Okla., 1964), 51.

38. Carondelet, Military Report on Louisiana and West Florida, November 24, 1794, in Robertson, *Louisiana,* 1: 297–98.

39. Joseph G. Dawson III, ed., *Louisiana Governors: From Iberville to Edwards* (Baton Rouge, 1990), 64–69; anonymous Spanish report quoted in Jack D. L. Holmes, "Some Economic Problems of Spanish Governors of Louisiana," *HAHR* 42 (1962): 537–38.

40. Carondelet, Military Report, in Robertson, *Louisiana,* 1: 298–99.

41. Ibid., 1: 298–99, 344–45; *Territorial Papers,* 33.

42. Jack D. L. Holmes, *Gayoso: The Life of a Spanish Governor in the Mississippi Valley, 1789–1799* (Baton Rouge, 1965), 4–5; Dawson, *Louisiana Governors,* 70–74. Both reports are published in Robertson, *Louisiana,* 1: 269–354.

43. Holmes, *Gayoso,* 4–10.

44. Fray Bailío Antonio Valdés to Carlos III, November 2, 1787, quoted in ibid., 10.

45. Floridablanca to Gardoqui, Aranjuez, May 24, 1788, quoted in Michael A. Otero, "The American Mission of Diego de Gardoqui, 1785–1789" (Ph.D. diss., University of California, Los Angeles, 1949), 224.

46. Holmes, *Gayoso,* 10–11, 30; Dawson, *Louisiana Governors,* 64–65.


CHAPTER SEVEN: QUESTIONS OF LOYALTY

1. Wilkinson's declaration of allegiance to Spain, August 22, 1787, translated in William R. Shepard, "Wilkinson and the Beginnings of the Spanish Conspiracy," *AHR* 9 (1903–1904): 497.

2. Esteban Miró to Antonio Valdés y Bazan, April 11, 1789, Archivo Histórico Nacional, Papeles de Estado, Legajo 3893A, translated in Shepard, "Wilkinson and the Beginnings of the Spanish Conspiracy," 491n.

3. James Wilkinson, *Memoirs of My Own Time* (3 vols., Philadelphia, 1816), 2: 114.

4. James Ripley Jacobs, *Tarnished Warrior: Major-General James Wilkinson* (New York, 1938), xii, 1–9.

5. Ibid., 9–65.

6. Humphrey Marshall, quoted in ibid., 71.

7. Samuel Flagg Bemis, *Pinckney's Treaty: America's Advantage from Europe's Distress, 1783–1800* (Baltimore, 1926; rev. ed., New Haven, 1960), 113; Patricia Watlington, *The Partisan Spirit: Kentucky Politics, 1779–1792* (New York, 1972), 103–4. I follow Watlington's enumeration of the Kentucky conventions.

8. Watlington, *Partisan Spirit,* 104; Bemis, *Pinckney's Treaty,* 113.

9. Bemis, *Pinckney's Treaty,* 114.

10. Watlington, *Partisan Spirit,* 38–39, 56–57, 118–19; Madison to Muter, January 7, 1787, *Madison Papers,* 9: 231; Sandra Gioia Treadway, ed., *Journals of the Council of State of Virginia,* vol. 5 (Richmond, 1982), 395.

11. Muter to Madison, February 20, 1787, *Madison Papers,* 9: 280; Watlington, *Partisan Spirit,* 56–57, 119–21, 130–31; James Wilkinson to James Hutchinson, June 20, 1785, in "Letters of General James Wilkinson, addressed to Dr. James Hutchinson, of Philadelphia," *Pennsylvania Magazine of History and Biography* 21 (1888): 57.

12. Wilkinson to Hutchinson, June 20, 1785, *Pennsylvania Magazine of History and Biography* 21 (1888): 56.

13. Arthur P. Whitaker, "James Wilkinson's First Descent to New Orleans in 1787," *HAHR* 8 (1928): 82–97.

14. Robert C. Anderson to the Governor of St. Louis, January 1, 1787, ibid., 94. Miró already knew about General (not Colonel) Thomas Green, whose letter extolling Clark's raid at Vincennes had been intercepted and forwarded to Gardoqui, who presented it to John Jay, who forwarded it to Congress, which immediately passed resolutions condemning these irresponsible acts; Bemis, *Pinckney's Treaty,* 117–18.

15. Wilkinson à son Excellance le Gouverneur de St. Louis, December 20, 1786, in Whitaker, "Wilkinson's First Descent," 93–94.

16. Humphrey Marshall, *The History of Kentucky. Exhibiting an Account of the Modern Discovery; Settlement; Progressive Improvement; Civil and Military Transactions; and the Present State of the Country* (2d ed., Frankfort, Ky., 1824), 271. Following Watlington's example, I, too, have edited Marshall's exuberant punctuation; Watlington, *Partisan Spirit,* 124.

17. Grand-Pré to Miró, June 18, 1787, Whitaker, "Wilkinson's First Descent," 95–96; Watlington, *Partisan Spirit,* 140; Jacobs, *Tarnished Warrior,* 77.

18. Watlington, *Partisan Spirit,* 140; Shepard, "Wilkinson and the Beginnings of the Spanish Conspiracy," 494 and n.; Whitaker, "Wilkinson's First Descent," 90. Some writers contend that Wilkinson was arrested upon his arrival in New Orleans, that he had previously corresponded with Miró, or that resident Americans had persuaded Miró not to confiscate Wilkinson's cargo. Whitaker convincingly refutes these statements and confirms Wilkinson's statement that he arrived in New Orleans as a "perfect stranger" (ibid., 83–84).

19. Translated in Shepard, "Wilkinson and the Beginnings of the Spanish Conspiracy," 496–97. Assiduously parsing the words of his oath and declaring it "a meaningless gesture" with "no allegation of fealty of Spain," Wilkinson's biographers protest too much; Jacobs, *Tarnished Warrior,* 81; Thomas Robson Hay and M. R. Werner, *The Admirable Trumpeter: A Biography of General James Wilkinson* (Garden City, N.Y., 1941), 87.

20. Shepard, "Wilkinson and the Beginnings of the Spanish Conspiracy," 505.

21. Ibid., 498.

22. Ibid., 499.

23. Ibid., 501–3.

24. Ibid., 503.

25. Ibid., 501, 505; Jacobs, *Tarnished Warrior,* 86.

26. Shepard, "Wilkinson and the Beginnings of the Spanish Conspiracy," 504n; Hay and Werner, *Admirable Trumpeter,* 88.

27. Shepard, "Wilkinson and the Beginnings of the Spanish Conspiracy," 505.

28. Ibid., 500.

29. Michael A. Otero, "The American Mission of Diego de Gardoqui, 1785–1789" (Ph.D. diss., University of California, Los Angeles, 1949), 224; Arthur Preston Whitaker, *The Spanish-American Frontier, 1783–1795: The*

*Westward Movement and the Spanish Retreat in the Mississippi Valley* (Lincoln, Neb., 1927), 101.

30. From Blountville and Sevierville, Tennessee, to New Madrid, Missouri, perhaps a dozen localities in the Mississippi watershed owe their existence to separatist schemes, colonization projects, or land companies led by William Blount, John Sevier, and James Wilkinson (for the three towns mentioned) as well as Pierre Wouves d'Arges, Bryan Bruin and his son Peter Bryan Bruin, William Butler, William Fitzgerald, Richard Henderson, Andrew Jackson, James Kennedy, Augustin Macarty, George Morgan, Mauricio Nowland, James O'Fallon, Peter Paulus, James Robertson, Daniel Smith, James White, and countless associates and investors—all jockeying for land, political advantage, financial support, and prospective settlers. The resulting historical literature is vast and often tangled, as in Thomas Perkins Abernethy's classic *Western Lands in the American Revolution* (New York, 1937). Of the older scholarship about individual entrepreneurs, Arthur P. Whitaker's "Spanish Intrigue in the Old Southwest: An Episode, 1788–89," *MVHR* 12 (1925–1926): 155–76, and Max Savelle's "The Founding of New Madrid, Missouri," *MVHR* 19 (1932–1933): 30–56, are instructive. Examples of more recent work include Andrew R. L. Cayton " 'Separate Interests' and the Nation-State: The Washington Administration and the Origins of Regionalism in the Trans-Appalachian West," *JAH* 79 (1992–1993): 39–67, and Peter J. Kastor " 'Equitable Rights and Privileges': Divided Loyalties in Washington County, Virginia, During the Franklin Separatist Crisis," *VMHB* 105 (1997): 193–226. Gilbert C. Din's "Immigration Policy of Governor Esteban Miró in Spanish Louisiana," *Southwestern Historical Quarterly* 73 (1969–1970): 155–75, is definitive on its subject, and Din's "Pierre Wouves d'Arges in North America: Spanish Commissioner, Adventurer, or French Spy?" *Louisiana Studies* 12 (1973): 354–75, dispels mysteries about the French adventurer whose colonization proposals encouraged Aranda and Floridablanca to shift their attitudes about immigration as a means to bolster Spanish control of the Louisiana borderlands.

31. Whitaker, *Spanish-American Frontier*, 101–2.

32. Ibid.

33. "Miró's Offer to Western Americans, April 20, 1789," in Lawrence Kinnaird, ed., *Spain in the Mississippi Valley, 1765–1794: Annual Report of the American Historical Association for the Year 1945* (Washington, D.C., 1946), 3: 269–71.

34. Caroline Maude Burson, *The Stewardship of Don Esteban Miró, 1782–1792: A Study of Louisiana Based Largely on the Documents in New Orleans* (New Orleans, 1940), 152–64; Patricia Watlington, *The Partisan Spirit: Kentucky Politics, 1779–1792* (New York, 1972), 133–87.

35. Esteban Miró to Luis de Las Casas, October 7, 1790, in Burson, *Stewardship of Don Esteban Miró*, 166; Jacobs, *Tarnished Warrior*, 88–109.

36. Miró to Antonio Valdés y Bazan, May 20, 1789, and Las Casas to the count of Campo de Alange, February 17, 1791, in Din, "Immigration Policy," 171, 173.

37. Jack D. L. Holmes, "Irish Priests in Spanish Natchez," *Journal of Mississippi History* 29 (1967): 169–80.

38. Ibid., 173–76.

39. Gayoso to Manuel Godoy, March 31, 1795, in ibid., 176–79; Holmes, *Gayoso: The Life of a Spanish Governor in the Mississippi Valley, 1789–1799* (Baton Rouge, 1965), 77–85. Miró's successor believed that "if disputes and quarrels over religious matters are not cut off at their roots or checked, they will have the most perverse and evil results"; Carondelet to Carlos Louis Boucher de Grand-Pré, July 26, 1795, ibid., 83.

## CHAPTER EIGHT: BANNERS OF BLOOD

1. Quoted in Schama, *Citizens*, 367–68.

2. "Modern History Sourcebook: 'Ça Ira,'" at www.fordham.edu/halsall/mod/caira.html.

3. Richard E. Greenleaf, "The Inquisition in Spanish Louisiana, 1762–1800," *New Mexico Historical Review* 50 (1975): 45–72; Charles Gayarré, *History of Louisiana* (2d ed., New Orleans, 1879), 3: 268–69; Glenn R. Conrad, ed., *Dictionary of Louisiana Biography* (New Orleans, 1988), 726–27; F. L. Gassler, "Père Antoine, Supreme Officer of the Holy Inquisition . . . in Louisiana," *Catholic Historical Review* 2 (1922): 59–63; Christina Vella, *Intimate Enemies: The Two Worlds of the Baroness de Pontalba* (Baton Rouge, 1997), 45.

4. Greenleaf, "Inquisition in Spanish Louisiana," 48–49; Gayarré, *History of Louisiana*, 3: 268–69. Forty-two compilations of the *Index Librorum Prohibitorum* appeared between 1559 and 1966 (http://www.fordham.edu/halsall/mod/indexlibrorum.html).

5. Greenleaf, "Inquisition in Spanish Louisiana," 48–49; Gayarré, *History of Louisiana*, 3: 268–69.

6. Ibid. (emphasis added); Sir Charles Petrie, *King Charles III of Spain: An Enlightened Despot* (New York and London, 1971), 112–35.

7. Gayarré, *History of Louisiana*, 3: 268–69.

8. Ibid.; Greenleaf, "Inquisition in Spanish Louisiana," 49–50.

9. Gayarré, *History of Louisiana*, 3: 268–69. Greenleaf, "Inquisition in Spanish Louisiana," 50.

10. Gayarré, *History of Louisiana*, 3: 268–69.

11. James Pitot, *Observations on the Colony of Louisiana from 1796 to 1802*, trans. Henry C. Pitot (Baton Rouge, 1979), 31; Manuel Gayoso de Lemos, "Political Condition of the Province of Louisiana," in Robertson, *Louisiana*, 1: 283.

12. Georges Lefebvre, *The French Revolution: From Its Origins to 1793* (New York, 1962), 99–101; Schama, *Citizens*, 281–83.

13. Schama, *Citizens*, 305.

14. Honoré-Gabriel Riqueti, comte de Mirabeau, quoted in Schama, *Citizens*, 305.

15. Schama, *Citizens,* 305–7; Lefebvre, *French Revolution to 1793,* 116–19.

16. Schama, *Citizens,* 385.

17. Ibid., 383–88; Lefebvre, *French Revolution to 1793,* 123–24.

18. Schama, *Citizens,* 389–406, 420.

19. Ibid., 389–406, 420, 619–24.

20. Ibid., 367–68, 422–25; Jean-Paul Rabaut Saint-Etienne, quoted in Edmund Burke, *Reflections on the Revolution in France* (London, 1790), ed. Thomas H. D. Mahoney (Indianapolis and New York, 1955), 196n; "Modern History Sourcebook: 'Ça Ira.'"

21. Burke, *Reflections on the Revolution in France,* 96–97; Stanley Elkins and Eric McKitrick, *The Age of Federalism* (New York, 1993), 303–73.

22. Schama, *Citizens,* 782–83, 804–5.

23. W. B. Allen, ed., *Works of Fisher Ames* (Indianapolis, 1983), 190; Dumas Malone, *Jefferson and the Ordeal of Liberty* (Boston, 1962), 48.

24. Gabriel H. Lovett, *Napoleon and the Birth of Modern Spain* (New York, 1965), 1: 17–18.

25. Ibid.

26. Samuel Flagg Bemis, *Pinckney's Treaty: America's Advantage from Europe's Distress, 1783–1800* (Baltimore, 1926; rev. ed., New Haven, 1960), 168–69; Douglas Hilt, *The Troubled Trinity: Godoy and the Spanish Monarchs* (Tuscaloosa, 1987), 44.

27. Lovett, *Napoleon and the Birth of Modern Spain,* 20–21; Hilt, *Troubled Trinity,* 44–45.

28. J. H. Bernardin de Saint Pierre, *Voyage to Isle de France, Isle de Bourbon, The Cape of Good Hope . . . with New Observations on Nature and Mankind by an Officer of the King* (Paris, 1773), quoted in Sidney W. Mintz, *Sweetness and Power: The Place of Sugar in Modern History* (New York, 1985), ii.

29. Carolyn E. Fick, *The Making of Haiti: The Saint Domingue Revolution from Below* (Knoxville, Tenn., 1990), 22–25; C. L. R. James, *The Black Jacobins: Toussaint L'Ouverture and the San Domingo Revolution* (2d ed., New York, 1963), 49–50. In 1789, St. Domingue provided 64 percent of the French export trade, 2.2 times the value of Britain's exports to its remaining colonies.

30. Ibid.; Robert Louis Stein, *The French Sugar Business in the Eighteenth Century* (Baton Rouge, 1988), 23–26.

31. Fick, *Making of Haiti,* 15–22.

32. John Lynch, "The Origins of Spanish American Independence," in Leslie Bethel, ed., *Cambridge History of Latin America,* vol. 3 (London and New York, 1984), 47.

33. James, *Black Jacobins,* 17; Fick, *Making of Haiti,* 34–39.

34. James, *Black Jacobins,* 12–13, 22–24; Martin Ros, *Night of Fire: The Black Napoleon and the Battle for Haiti,* trans. Karin Ford-Treep (New York, 1994), 14–15, 20–21.

35. Ros, *Night of Fire,* 2.

36. Carolyn E. Fick, "The Saint Domingue Slave Insurrection of 1791: A Socio-Political and Cultural Analysis," *Journal of Caribbean History* 25 (1991): 16–18; see also James, *Black Jacobins*, 18, 85.

37. Thomas Marc Fiehrer, "The Baron de Carondelet as Agent of Bourbon Reform: A Study of Spanish Colonial Administration in the Years of the French Revolution" (Ph.D. diss., Tulane University, 1977), 478–79.

38. Governor Miró to Luis de Las Casas, July 2 and August 28, 1791, Spanish Despatches, Book 5, Legajo 1440, nos. 204 and 240.

39. Fiehrer, "Baron de Carondelet," 478–79.

40. Ibid., 480–81; Alfred N. Hunt, *Haiti's Influence on Antebellum America: Slumbering Volcano in the Caribbean* (Baton Rouge, 1988), 26–27.

41. Fiehrer, "Baron de Carondelet," 481–82.

42. Lester D. Langley, *The Americas in the Age of Revolution, 1750–1850* (New Haven, 1996), 106–10.

43. Kimberly Hanger, *Bounded Lives, Bounded Places: Free Black Society in Colonial New Orleans, 1769–1803* (Durham, N.C., 1997), 154–62.

44. Fiehrer, "Baron de Carondelet," 480; Kimberly Hanger, "Conflicting Loyalties: The French Revolution and Free People of Color in Spanish New Orleans," *Louisiana History* 34 (1993): 25–33.

45. Hanger, "Conflicting Loyalties," 25–33.

46. Ibid. López and Declouet married in 1797, two years after she instituted ecclesiastical proceedings to prove her descent from Native Americans and have their eldest daughter's baptism record transferred from the nonwhite to the white register books in the diocesan archive; Hanger, *Bounded Lives, Bounded Places*, 93–94.

47. Paul LaChance, "The Politics of Fear: French Louisianians and the Slave Trade, 1786–1809," *Plantation Society in the Americas* 1: 2 (June 1979): 169; Hanger, *Bounded Lives, Bounded Places*, 150–51; Fick, *Making of Haiti*, 118–34.

48. Ulysses S. Ricard, Jr., "The Pointe Coupée Slave Conspiracy of 1791," *Proceedings of the International Congress of the French Colonial Historical Society* (in press; typescript at Amistad Research Center, Tulane University, New Orleans), 10, 13; Jack D. L. Holmes, "The Abortive Slave Revolt at Pointe Coupée, Louisiana, 1795," *Louisiana History* 11 (1970): 342. The decree was published in French and English and widely distributed throughout the Caribbean; Gwendolyn Midlo Hall, *Africans in Colonial Louisiana: The Development of Afro-Creole Culture in the Eighteenth Century* (Baton Rouge, 1992), 346.

49. Hall, *Africans in Colonial Louisiana*, 344–61. Influences of American and French revolutionary thought in Eastern Europe are summarized in Béla K. Király and Goergoe Barany, eds., *East Central European Perceptions of Early America* (Lisse, 1977).

50. Hall, *Africans in Colonial Louisiana*, 344–61.

51. Ibid.; Joseph de Pontalba to Jeanne Louise de Pontalba, March 27–30, 1796, quoted in LaChance, "Politics of Fear," 168.

52. Hall, *Africans in Colonial Louisiana,* 344; Holmes, "The Abortive Slave Revolt at Pointe Coupée," 343–62.

## CHAPTER NINE: A NEW ERA IN WORLD HISTORY

1. Quoted in Harry Ammon, *The Genet Mission* (New York, 1973), 86.

2. Lachaise to the Democratic Society of Lexington, Kentucky, May 9, 1794, Philip S. Foner, ed., *The Democratic-Republican Societies, 1790–1800: A Documentary Sourcebook of Constitutions, Declarations, Addresses, Resolutions, and Toasts* (Westport, Conn., 1976), 368.

3. Schama, *Citizens,* 639–40.

4. Ibid., 643; Ammon, *Genet Mission,* 20. Genet spelled his name without a circumflex accent on the second *e,* which gained currency among American writers about 1900; ibid., vii.

5. Ibid., 1–6.

6. Ibid., 6–9.

7. Ibid.

8. Ibid., 25–29. On the eve of Genet's appointment, the French plan was "to begin their attack at the mouth of the Mississippi, and to sweep along the bay [i.e., Gulf] of Mexico Southwardly, and . . . have no objections to our incorporating into our government the two Floridas"; Jefferson, "Notes on Conversations with William Stephen Smith . . . ," February 20, 1793, *Jefferson Papers,* 25: 244–45. Article 22 of the 1778 treaty stipulated that "it shall not be lawful for any foreign Privateers . . . who have Commissioners from any other Prince or State in enmity with either Nation to fit their Ships in the Ports of either one or the other of the aforesaid Parties." Stanley Elkins and Eric McKitrick, *The Age of Federalism* (New York, 1993), 819n.

9. Ammon, *Genet Mission,* 30–31.

10. Ibid., vii, 44–53; John Dawson to James Madison, May 13, 1793, *Madison Papers,* 15: 15.

11. Elkins and McKitrick, *Age of Federalism,* 354–57; Ammon, *Genet Mission,* 37–41; Jefferson to Monroe, June 4, 1793, *Jefferson Papers,* 26: 190.

12. "I wondered at first at this restriction," Jefferson noted, "but when E[dmund] R[andolph, Washington's attorney general,] afterwards communicated to me his conversation of the 24th I became satisfied it was a small sacrifice to the opinion of Hamilton"; Jefferson, "Notes on the Reception of Edmond Charles Genet," March 30, 1793; Jefferson to Madison, May 19, 1793, *Jefferson Papers,* 25: 469–70; 26: 62.

13. Jefferson, "Opinion on the Restoration of Prizes," May 16, 1793; Jefferson to Madison, May 19, 1793; *Jefferson Papers,* 26: 50–51, 61–62.

14. Jefferson to Madison, July 7, 1793, ibid., 26: 444.

15. Jefferson to William Carmichael and William Short, March 23, 1793; Jefferson, "Notes of . . . Conversations with Edmond Charles Genet," July 5, 1793, ibid., 25: 430–31, 26: 438; Dorchester quoted in Joanne B. Freeman, *Affairs of Honor: National Politics in the New Republic* (New Haven, 2001), 45.

16. Jefferson, "Notes of . . . Conversations with Edmond Charles Genet," July 5, 1793, *Jefferson Papers*, 26: 438.

17. Ibid.

18. Jefferson to Governor Isaac Shelby, June 28, 1793 (with revisions made in July), *Jefferson Papers*, 26: 393–96, 438–39; "American Philosophical Society's Subscription Agreement for André Michaux's Western Expedition," January 22, 1793, *Jefferson Papers*, 25: 81. Michaux's journal was published in the *Proceedings of the American Philosophical Society* 26 (1889). Michaux also carried letters of introduction to Clark and Shelby from Kentucky senator John Brown; Frederick Jackson Turner, ed., "Correspondence of George Rogers Clark and Edmond Genet," *Annual Report of the American Historical Association for the Year 1896* (Washington, D.C., 1897), 982–83.

19. James Alton James, *The Life of George Rogers Clark* (Chicago, 1928), 408–11, 418, 495; Jerome O. Steffen, *William Clark: Jeffersonian Man on the Frontier* (Norman, Okla., 1977), 15–30; Malcolm Everett Gardner, "The Projected Attack of George Rogers Clark and Citizen Genet Against Spanish Louisiana, 1793–1794" (M.A. thesis, University of Virginia, 1932).

20. Steffen, *William Clark*, 26–29; John E. Selby, *The Revolution in Virginia, 1775–1783* (Williamsburg, 1988), 222–24. Regardless of Clark's private difficulties with debt or alcohol, he was certainly as capable of organizing a successful expedition as Anthony Wayne, whose debts stemmed from his incompetence as a rice planter and whom Washington feared was "addicted to the bottle"; Andrew R. L. Cayton, " 'Noble Actors' upon 'the Theatre of Honour': Power and Civility in the Treaty of Greenville," in Andrew R. L. Cayton and Fredrika J. Teute, eds., *Contact Points: American Frontiers from the Mohawk Valley to the Mississippi, 1750–1830* (Chapel Hill, 1998), 249.

21. Ibid.

22. Louise Phelps Kellogg, ed., "Letter of Thomas Paine [to Dr. James O'Fallon, February 17], 1793," *AHR* 29 (1923–1924): 504. The letters written by Clark and O'Fallon later in 1792 are not known to be extant.

23. Kellogg, "Letter of Thomas Paine, 1793," 504.

24. Morris and Paine detested each other, but Morris invited Genet to dinner on December 28, 1792, and described him to Washington as a man "more of Genius than Ability and you will see in him at first Blush the Manners and Look of an Upstart." When Paine was imprisoned by Robespierre in December 1793 and seemed destined for the guillotine, Morris did little to help, observing that "if he is quiet in prison, he may have the good luck to be forgotten," but if not "the long suspended axe might fall on him"; Alexander DeConde, *Entangling Alliance: Politics and Diplomacy Under George Washington* (Durham, N.C., 1958), 330–36.

25. John Carl Parish, "The Intrigues of Doctor James O'Fallon," *MVHR* 17 (1930–1931): 259; Gardner, "Projected Attack of Clark and Genet," 17–19; see also unsigned fragment, February 3, 1793, and Clark to Genet, October 25, 1793, Turner, "Correspondence of Clark and Genet," 973, 1016.

26. Clark to Genet, February 5, 1793, Turner, "Correspondence of Clark and Genet," 970.

27. Ibid.

28. When not collecting botanical specimens and notes, as on his November–December 1793 trek from Danville to Philadelphia, Michaux averaged 23.2 miles a day. On this trip out to meet Clark, Michaux covered only 12.3 miles a day.

29. Richard Lowitt, "Activities of Citizen Genet in Kentucky, 1793–1794," *Filson Club Historical Quarterly* 22 (1948): 258–59.

30. Ibid.; Patricia Watlington, *The Partisan Spirit: Kentucky Politics, 1779–1792* (New York, 1972), 59. A few months later, after meeting with Lachaise, Logan changed his mind and offered to join Clark in the expedition against Louisiana; Logan to Clark, December 31, 1793, Turner, "Correspondence of Clark and Genet," 1026.

31. John Clark to James O'Fallon, May 28, 1792, Draper Manuscripts, 4 CC 172, State Historical Society of Wisconsin, Madison.

32. James O'Fallon to Fanny Clark O'Fallon, November 23, 1793, Draper Manuscripts, 2 M 47, ibid.

33. Ibid.

34. Ibid.; Cayton, "Treaty of Greenville," 235–69; see also Wayne to O'Fallon, September 16, 1793, Turner, "Correspondence of Clark and Genet," 1001.

35. James O'Fallon to Fanny O'Fallon, November 23, 1793, State Historical Society of Wisconsin; Gayoso to Carondelet, December 23, 1793, Turner, "Correspondence of Clark and Genet," 1031; Parish, "The Intrigues of Doctor James O'Fallon," 261.

36. James O'Fallon to Fanny O'Fallon, November 23, 1793; Freeman, *Affairs of Honor*, 172.

37. Foner, *Democratic-Republican Societies*, 364; Eugene Perry Link, *Democratic-Republican Societies, 1790–1800* (New York, 1942), 125–49; E. Merton Coulter, "The Efforts of the Democratic Societies of the West to Open the Navigation of the Mississippi," *MVHR* 11 (1924): 376–89; Albrecht Koschnik, "The Democratic Societies of Philadelphia and the Limits of the American Public Sphere, Circa 1793–1795," *WMQ* 3d ser. 63 (2001): 615–36.

38. Foner, *Democratic-Republican Societies*, 127, 361, 365.

39. Clark to Genet, October 3, 1793, Turner, "Correspondence of Clark and Genet," 1008; Gardner, "Projected Attack of Clark and Genet," 61–62; Link, *Democratic-Republican Societies*, 140.

40. Lowitt, "Activities of Citizen Genet in Kentucky," 259.

41. Jefferson to Morris, August 16, 1793, *Jefferson Papers*, 26: 697–711, quoted at 710.

42. Viar and Jaudenes to Jefferson, August 27, 1793, with enclosure, ibid., 26: 771–74; Carondelet to Godoy, October 25, 1793, Turner, "Correspondence of Clark and Genet," 1017.

43. Viar and Jaudenes to Carondelet, August 21, 1793, Turner, "Correspondence of Clark and Genet," 999–1000.

44. Jefferson to Viar and Jaudenes, August 29, 1793, *Jefferson Papers*, 26: 785–86.

45. Jefferson to Shelby, August 29, 1793, with enclosure, ibid., 26: 785–86.

46. Watlington, *Partisan Spirit*, 59–60, 223.

47. Patricia Watlington, "John Brown and the Spanish Conspiracy," *VMHB* 75 (1967): 52–68; Foner, *Democratic-Republican Societies*, 358–59, 363.

48. Shelby to Jefferson, October 5, 1793, *Jefferson Papers*, 27: 196; Shelby to Charles Depauw, November 28, 1793, Turner, "Correspondence of Clark and Genet," 1023.

49. Morris to Jefferson, February 13, 1793, *Jefferson Papers*, 25: 192; Clark to Michaux, October 3, 1793, Turner, "Correspondence of Clark and Genet," 1009.

50. Carondelet to Godoy, January 1, 1794, and enclosed extract of a letter from Gayoso to Carondelet, n.d.; Turner, "Correspondence of Clark and Genet," 1028–29.

51. Ibid.

52. Clark to Genet, February 5, October 3, 1793; Clark to Charles Depauw, January 5, 1794; Turner, "Correspondence of Clark and Genet," 970, 1008.

53. Jefferson's November 6, 1793, letter to Shelby was accompanied by a supporting letter from Knox dated November 9, ibid., 27: 312–13; Archibald Henderson, "Isaac Shelby and the Genet Mission," *MVHR* 6 (1920): 454–57.

54. Jefferson to Shelby, November 6, 1793, *Jefferson Papers*, 27: 312–13 (emphasis added); Henderson, "Shelby and the Genet Mission," 455–56.

55. Quoted in ibid., 463; Maude Howlett Woodfin, "Citizen Genet and His Mission" (Ph.D. diss., University of Chicago, 1928), 453–54.

56. Henderson, "Shelby and the Genet Mission," 466; Edward Cody Burnett, ed., "George Rogers Clark to Genet, [April 28], 1794," *AHR* 18 (1912–1913): 781.

57. Ibid.

58. Ibid.

59. Ibid.

## CHAPTER TEN: MR. PINCKNEY'S MISSION

1. Short to Secretary of State, January 16, 1795, in Samuel Flagg Bemis, *Pinckney's Treaty: America's Advantage from Europe's Distress, 1783–1800* (Baltimore, 1926; rev. ed., New Haven, 1960), 248–49n.

2. José Luis Sancho, *Royal Seat of La Granja de San Ildefonso and Riofrío* (Madrid, 1996), 13–15, 69–79; Bemis, *Pinckney's Treaty*, 204–6; Harry Ammon, *The Genet Mission* (New York, 1973), 171–72; Carondelet to Godoy, July 9, 1794, Frederick Jackson Turner, ed., "Correspondence of George Rogers Clark and Edmond Genet," *Annual Report of the American Historical Association for the Year 1896* (Washington, D.C., 1897), 1066; James Alton James, *The Life of*

*George Rogers Clark* (Chicago, 1928), 427; James Ripley Jacobs, *Tarnished Warrior: Major-General James Wilkinson* (New York, 1938), 272; Thomas Robson Hay and M. R. Werner, *The Admirable Trumpeter: A Biography of General James Wilkinson* (Garden City, N.Y., 1941), 141; Georges Lefebvre, *The French Revolution: From 1793 to 1799* (New York, 1964), 131–36; Schama, *Citizens*, 840–47; Stanley Elkins and Eric McKitrick, *The Age of Federalism* (New York, 1993), 375–449.

3. Minutes of the Spanish Council of State, July 7, 1794, in Bemis, *Pinckney's Treaty*, 204n.

4. Short to Thomas Pinckney, October 12, 1793, ibid., 191–92n.

5. Minutes of the Spanish Council of State, July 7, 1794, in Bemis, *Pinckney's Treaty*, 204n.

6. Douglas Hilt, *The Troubled Trinity: Godoy and the Spanish Monarchs* (Tuscaloosa, 1987), 40–43.

7. Minutes of the Spanish Council of State, July 7, 1794, in Bemis, *Pinckney's Treaty*, 205n.

8. Ibid., 205–6n.

9. Ibid., 207. Between July 1794 and the signing of Pinckney's Treaty in October 1795, Godoy regarded the prospect of Kentucky separatism as an alternative policy in the event of an alliance between Great Britain and the United States, instructing Jaudenes and Carondelet in February "to continue to assure [the inhabitants of Kentucky] of the good faith with which we proceed; and . . . [to] set up with the greatest secrecy direct negotiations with them, to hold them off until we can settle the question of the important points on which we are now treating with the [United] States. This will serve to keep them devoted to us in case the States do not accept the just propositions which we are making to them"; minutes of Godoy's reply ca. February 15, 1795, to Jaudenes's despatch no. 250; Godoy to Carondelet, February 21, 1795, ibid., 233.

10. Bemis, *Pinckney's Treaty*, 208–17. Bemis examined the document as it was deciphered in Jaudenes's office and found "a few uncertainties about certain minor parts of the instructions, but nothing that [one] cannot puzzle out easily and clearly"; ibid., 213n.

11. Ibid., 213–17.

12. Ibid., 212–13.

13. Jaudenes to Randolph, March 25, 1795, ibid., 212–13n.

14. Randolph to Short, April 5, 1795, ibid., 270n.

15. Jaudenes to Randolph, March 25, 1795, ibid., 212–13n; for the implications of the title, see ibid., 253–54.

16. Godoy to Jaudenes, May 9, 1794, and Jaudenes to Secretary of State Edmund Randolph, August 15, 1794, ibid., 208–9. Carmichael died in Madrid on February 9, 1795, ibid., 235.

17. Randolph to Pinckney, November 28, 1794, ibid., 252.

18. Short to Nicolaas and Jacob Van Staphorst and Nicholas Hubbard, October 1, 1794; Short to Secretary of State, January 16, 1795; Bemis, *Pinckney's Treaty*, 236n, 248–49n.

19. Pinckney to Randolph, June 23, 1794; Bemis, *Pinckney's Treaty*, 247–48n.

20. Bemis, *Pinckney's Treaty*, 251, 267; Thomas Jefferson to James Monroe, July 6, 1796, quoted in Harry Ammon, *James Monroe: The Quest for National Identity* (New York, 1971), 114.

21. Reasonable people can disagree about the extent of Godoy's knowledge of Jay's Treaty. In the first edition of *Pinckney's Treaty: America's Advantage from Europe's Distress, 1783–1800* (Baltimore, 1926), Samuel Flagg Bemis asserted that Godoy did not see the full text of Jay's Treaty until after the signing of Pinckney's Treaty. Soon thereafter, Arthur P. Whitaker contended that Godoy *was* familiar with the terms of Jay's Treaty in his *Spanish-American Frontier, 1763–1795: The Westward Movement and the Spanish Retreat in the Mississippi Valley* (Boston, 1927), 203–7, and in two supplementary journal articles ("New Light on the Treaty of San Lorenzo: An Essay in Historical Criticism," *MVHR* 15 [1929]: 435–54, and "Godoy's Knowledge of the Terms of Jay's Treaty," *AHR* 35 [1929–1930]: 804–10). Bemis answered Whitaker's objection persuasively in the second edition of *Pinckney's Treaty* (New Haven, 1960), 284–93. Their contention is not over what Godoy did, but whether his fears of British retaliation and an Anglo-American alliance were reasonable. If Godoy did not have the text of Jay's Treaty prior to signing with Pinckney (Bemis's view), Spain's virtual capitulation to American demands is more explicable. If Godoy knew that Jay's Treaty did not create an Anglo-American alliance (Whitaker's view), Spain's action was more foolhardy. Even if he had the full text of Jay's Treaty, however, Godoy could not have precluded the possibility of secret provisions hostile to Spain's interests. Godoy seems to have underestimated the American commitment to neutrality, but surely the fear of a future alliance between the United States and Great Britain came reasonably to a man who contemplated an alliance with France in connection with the Treaty of Basle and then in 1796 entered a fateful Franco-Spanish alliance by the secret Treaty of San Ildefonso.

22. Minutes of the Spanish Council of State, August 14, 1795, quoted in Bemis, *Pinckney's Treaty*, 274.

23. Pinckney to Short, October 25, 1795, quoted in ibid., 281n.

24. Ibid., 312.

25. Ibid.; Arthur Preston Whitaker, *The Mississippi Question, 1795–1803: A Study in Trade, Politics, and Diplomacy* (New York, 1934), 24, 301. See Appendix A for the entire text of Pinckney's Treaty.

26. *Kentucky Gazette*, March 26, 1796.


## Chapter Eleven: Affairs of Louisiana

1. Quoted in Spenser Wilkinson, *The Rise of General Bonaparte* (Oxford, 1930), 144.

2. "Essai sur les avantages à retirer [sic] de colonies nouvelles dans circonstances présentes," Sir Henry Lytton Bulwer, *Historical Characters: Talleyrand,*

*Cobbett, Mackintosh, Canning* (London, 1868), 1: 456. When published in Paris in 1799, Talleyrand's lecture was entitled *Essai sur les Avantages à Tirer de Colonies Nouvelles dans Circonstances Présentes;* J. F. Bernard, *Talleyrand: A Biography* (New York, 1973), 622.

3. Robert B. Asprey, *The Rise of Napoleon Bonaparte* (New York, 2000), 4–20.

4. Ibid., 13–20; Alan Schom, *Napoleon Bonaparte* (New York, 1997), 1–11; Wilkinson, *Rise of General Bonaparte*, 3–7.

5. Schom, *Napoleon Bonaparte*, 9–11.

6. Ibid., 11; Asprey, *Rise of Napoleon Bonaparte*, 27–28, 37, 40, 47.

7. Ibid., 32, 47.

8. Guillaume-Thomas, Abbé de Raynal, *Philosophical and Political History of the Settlements and Trade of the Europeans in the East and West Indies*, trans. J. O. Justamond (London, 1783), 5: 309–10; C. L. R. James, *The Black Jacobins: Toussaint L'Ouverture and the San Domingo Revolution* (2d ed., New York, 1963), 25; Martin Ros, *Night of Fire: The Black Napoleon and the Battle for Haiti*, trans. Karin Ford-Treep (New York, 1994), 63, 87.

9. Schom, *Napoleon Bonaparte*, 12–22.

10. Ibid., 22–27; Georges Lefebvre, *The French Revolution: From 1793 to 1799* (New York, 1964), 173.

11. Schom, *Napoleon Bonaparte*, 27–28; Evangeline Bruce, *Napoleon and Josephine: An Improbable Marriage* (New York, 1995), 140–49, 162–63.

12. Bruce, *Napoleon and Josephine*, 163.

13. Schom, *Napoleon Bonaparte*, 35.

14. Ibid., 200.

15. Ibid., 48; Asprey, *Rise of Napoleon Bonaparte*, 253.

16. The aptly named anarchist Gracchus Babeuf is quoted in Schom, *Napoleon Bonaparte*, 200.

17. Asprey, *Rise of Napoleon Bonaparte*, 325.

18. Schom, *Napoleon Bonaparte*, 203–4.

19. Asprey, *Rise of Napoleon Bonaparte*, 343; Schom, *Napoleon Bonaparte*, 235.

20. Asprey, *Rise of Napoleon Bonaparte*, 245, 247. Napoleon enjoyed the company of women in society and the boudoir, but avoided the influential salons that many politicians frequented.

21. J. F. Bernard, *Talleyrand: A Biography* (New York, 1973), 173; Lefebvre, *French Revolution: From 1793 to 1799*, 291–92. The modern Institut de France comprises five learned societies: L'Académie Française (founded in 1635 by Cardinal Richelieu to standardize the French language) with forty members; L'Académie des Inscriptions et Belles-Lettres (organized in 1663 for the study of antiquities, numismatics, and languages) with forty-five members; L'Académie des Sciences (created in 1666 to promote mathematics and physical sciences) with one hundred thirty members; L'Académie des Beaux-Arts (established in 1648 for the fine arts) with fifty members; and L'Académie des Sciences Morales et Politiques (founded with the Institut de France in 1795) with

fifty members in the fields of history and geography, law and jurisprudence, morals, philosophy, and political economy.

22. Bernard, *Talleyrand,* 173–77; Doina Harsanyi, "A Second Chance: Talleyrand's Approach to Power During the Directory," paper presented at the annual meeting of the Southern Historical Association, Birmingham, Ala., November 13, 1998. Talleyrand's lectures—"Essai sur les avantages à retirer [sic] de colonies nouvelles dans circonstances présentes" and "Mémoires sur les relations commerciales des Etats-Unis avec l'Angleterre"—are printed in Sir Henry Lytton Bulwer, *Historical Characters: Talleyrand, Cobbett, Mackintosh, Canning* (London, 1868), 1: 451–81, from the manuscripts at the Institut de France; I am indebted to Doina Harsanyi for this information.

23. Harsanyi, "A Second Chance," 7; Talleyrand's lectures in Bulwer, *Historical Characters,* 453.

24. Harsanyi, "A Second Chance," 6–7; Talleyrand's lectures in Bulwer, *Historical Characters,* 480–81.

25. Ibid., 456–57; Harsanyi, "A Second Chance," 8.

26. Talleyrand's lectures in Bulwer, *Historical Characters,* 461. Talleyrand mentioned three authorities by name in the two lectures: Machiavelli, Montesquieu, and Choiseul.

27. *Diplomatic Correspondence of the United States of America, from the Signing of the Definitive Treaty of Peace, 10th September, 1783, to the Adoption of the Constitution, March 4, 1789* (Washington, D.C., 1855), 1: 241; William Blount to Richard Caswell, January 28, 1787, *Letters of Delegates,* 24: 75.

28. Alexander DeConde, *This Affair of Louisiana* (New York, 1976), 76–78; E. Wilson Lyon, "Moustier's Memoir on Louisiana," *MVHR* 22 (1935–1936): 251–66; Lyon, *Louisiana in French Diplomacy, 1789–1804* (Norman, Okla., 1934), 60–66.

29. The discomfort occasioned by Moustier's odd behavior, offensive table manners, and dubious relationship with his sister-in-law and companion Madame de Bréhan are summarized in Dumas Malone, *Jefferson and the Rights of Man* (Boston, 1951), 197–98.

30. Lyon, "Moustier's Memoir," 253; DeConde, *This Affair of Louisiana,* 79–80.

31. Gilbert C. Din, " 'For Defense of Country and the Glory of Arms': Army Officers in Spanish Louisiana, 1766–1803," *LH* 43 (2002): 6.

32. DeConde, *This Affair of Louisiana,* 80–81.

33. Stuart Gerry Brown, ed., *The Autobiography of James Monroe* (Syracuse, 1959), 136–37.

34. *New York Herald* article reprinted in the *New Hampshire and Vermont Journal: Or the Farmer's Weekly Museum* of Walpole, New Hampshire, September 6, 1796, quoted in DeConde, *This Affair of Louisiana,* 81.

35. Pickering to King, February 15 and June 20, 1797, quoted in DeConde, *This Affair of Louisiana,* 84–85.

36. Carondelet, Military Report on Louisiana and West Florida, November 24, 1794, in Robertson, *Louisiana,* 1: 298–99; Abraham Steiner and Frederick

C. De Schweinitz, 1799, and *Knoxville Gazette,* May 22, 1795, and February 11, 1794, quoted in Charles H. Faulkner, " 'Here Are Frame Houses and Brick Chimneys': Knoxville, Tennessee, in the Late Eighteenth Century," in David Colin Crass, Steven D. Smith, Martha A. Zierden, and Richard D. Brooks, eds., *The Southern Colonial Backcountry: Interdisciplinary Perspectives on Frontier Communities* (Knoxville, 1998), 139, 142; Edward A. Chappell, "Housing a Nation: The Transformation of Living Standards in Early America," in Cary Carson, Ronald Hoffman, and Peter J. Albert, eds., *Of Consuming Interests: The Style of Life in the Eighteenth-Century* (Charlottesville, 1994), 167–232; Elizabeth A. Perkins, "The Consumer Frontier: Household Consumption in Early Kentucky," *JAH* 78 (1991–1992): 486–510.

37. Talleyrand's lectures in Bulwer, *Historical Characters,* 466–68, quotation at 474; François Michaux quoted in Perkins, "The Consumer Frontier," 499.

38. Lewis E. Atherton, *The Frontier Merchant in Mid-America* (Columbia, Mo., 1971), 82; Perkins, "The Consumer Frontier," 510. Sturdy Conestoga wagons originated in eastern Pennsylvania early in the eighteenth century, were generally drawn by six horses, and could carry almost eight tons of freight. The lighter prairie schooner was adapted from common farm wagons later in the nineteenth century and was usually pulled by two or four horses or oxen.

39. Perkins, "The Consumer Frontier," 493; John Wesley Hunt's wagon inventories for Mathias Vankirk, John Hack, William Graham, Elisha Phipps, and Minshal Williams, October 26–29, 1795, are among five boxes of uncalendared papers, 1784–1811, in the Hunt-Morgan Family Papers, 63 M 202, University of Kentucky, Lexington. I am grateful to archivist Claire McCann for bringing these papers to my attention.

40. Two-page dry goods inventory, ca. 1800, Hunt-Morgan Papers, University of Kentucky; François Michaux quoted in Perkins, "The Consumer Frontier," 502; export figures from the *Kentucky Gazette,* May 18, 1801, ibid., 507.

41. Invoice from the Pittsburgh Glass Works, July 14, 1800, invoice "No. 19" from Mathew Carey, May 22, 1795, Hunt-Morgan Papers; Mary Wollstonecraft, *A Vindication of the Rights of Woman; with Strictures on Political and Moral Subjects* (London, Dublin, and Boston, 1792), quoted Talleyrand's observation "that to see one half of the human race excluded by the other from all participation in government, was a political phænomenon that, according to abstract principles, it was impossible to explain."

42. James A. Ramage, *John Wesley Hunt: Pioneer Merchant, Manufacturer, and Financier* (Lexington, Ky., 1974), 41–55, 72–73; Charles P. Stanton, *Bluegrass Pioneers: A Chronicle of the Hunt and Morgan Families of Lexington, Kentucky* (2d ed., Brooklyn, N.Y., 1989), 6–15; Hunt-Morgan Papers, University of Kentucky, passim; John Wesley Hunt Papers, 1792–1849, Filson Club, Louisville, Kentucky.

43. Perkins, "The Consumer Frontier," 506; John G. Clark, *New Orleans, 1718–1812: An Economic History* (Baton Rouge, 1970), 213–14; Robertson, *Louisiana,* 298–99.

44. Bernard, *Talleyrand,* 177–227; Isser Woloch, *Napoleon and His Collaborators: The Making of a Dictatorship* (New York, 2001), 9–35.

45. George Rudé, *The Crowd in the French Revolution* (New York, 1959), 95–98; Sidney W. Mintz, *Sweetness and Power: The Place of Sugar in Modern History* (New York, 1985), 108–26.

46. Robert Louis Stein, *The French Sugar Business in the Eighteenth Century* (Baton Rouge, 1985), ix–x, 166–67.

47. Lyon, "Moustier's Memoir," 251–66; Lyon, *Louisiana in French Diplomacy,* 79–98.

48. Urquijo was chief minister from March 1798 through December 1800, when Manuel Godoy returned as the power behind the throne; Douglas Hilt, *The Troubled Trinity: Godoy and the Spanish Monarchs* (Tuscaloosa, 1987), 71–94, 112–18.

49. Urquijo to the marquis de Musquiz, June 22, 1800, quoted in Lyon, *Louisiana in French Diplomacy,* 104.

50. Lyon, *Louisiana in French Diplomacy,* 104–10.

51. Ibid., 107–9.

52. Schom, *Napoleon Bonaparte,* 303–32; Lyon, *Louisiana in French Diplomacy,* 108–11.

53. François Barbé-Marbois, *The History of Louisiana; Particularly of the Cession of That Colony to the United States of America,* reprint of the 1830 Philadelphia edition with an introduction by E. Wilson Lyon (Baton Rouge, 1977), 200.

## Chapter Twelve: The Embryo of a Tornado

1. John Stevens Cabot Abbott, *Napoleon at St. Helena; or, Interesting Anecdotes and Remarkable Conversations of the Emperor During the Five and a Half Years of His Captivity* (New York, 1855), 259, 592–93.

2. *State Papers and Correspondence,* 16.

3. William Vans Murray to John Quincy Adams, March 30, 1801, in Worthington C. Ford, ed., "Letters of William Vans Murray to John Quincy Adams, *Annual Report of the American Historical Association for the Year 1912* (Washington, D.C., 1914), 693; Peter P. Hill, *William Vans Murray, Federalist Diplomat: The Shaping of Peace with France, 1797–1801* (Syracuse, 1971).

4. Douglas Hilt, *The Troubled Trinity: Godoy and the Spanish Monarchs* (Tuscaloosa, 1987), 117–19.

5. E. Wilson Lyon, *Louisiana in French Diplomacy, 1789–1804* (Norman, Okla., 1934), 123–25.

6. Evangeline Bruce, *Napoleon and Josephine: An Improbable Marriage* (New York, 1995), 192, 345; Jean Savant, *Napoleon in His Time* (New York, 1958), 157–58; Desmond Seward, *Napoleon's Family* (London, 1986), 57–59.

7. Savant, *Napoleon in His Time,* 158; Alan Schom, *Napoleon Bonaparte* (New York, 1997), 342–43.

8. Alexander DeConde, *This Affair of Louisiana* (New York, 1976), 100; Martin Ros, *Night of Fire: The Black Napoleon and the Battle for Haiti*, trans. Karin Ford-Treep (New York, 1994), 156; Leclerc's instructions were dated October 31, 1801, Carl Ludwig Lokke, "The Leclerc Instructions," *Journal of Negro History* 10 (1925): 80–98; Jon Kukla, ed., *A Guide to the Papers of Pierre Clément Laussat, Napoleon's Prefect for the Colony of Louisiana, and of General Claude Perrin Victor* (New Orleans, 1993), 159–63. Estimates of the initial strength of Leclerc's forces vary; Robert L. Paquette, "Revolutionary Saint Domingue in the Making of Territorial Louisiana," in David Barry Gaspar and David Patrick Geggus, eds., *A Turbulent Time: The French Revolution and the Greater Caribbean* (Bloomington, Ind., 1997), 204–25.

9. Lokke, "Leclerc Instructions," 89; Tobias Lear to James Madison, February 12, 1802, *Madison Papers: State*, 1: 463.

10. Ros, *Night of Fire*, 162; C. L. R. James, *The Black Jacobins: Toussaint L'Ouverture and the San Domingo Revolution* (2d ed., New York, 1963), 284–88; Thomas O. Ott, *The Haitian Revolution, 1789–1804* (Knoxville, 1973).

11. Tobias Lear to James Madison, February 28, 1802 (*Madison Papers: State*, 2: 499–524), provides a day-by-day account of the arrival of Leclerc's expedition based on Lear's diary.

12. Ibid., 502–4.

13. Ibid., 504–6.

14. Lokke, "Leclerc Instructions," 92–93, 98.

15. Ibid., 94–95, 98.

16. Ibid., 95–98; J. Christopher Herold, *The Mind of Napoleon* (New York, 1955), 189; see also Napoleon's notes for a draft decree, April 27, 1802, in which his euphemisms for reinstituting slavery were "police regulations which will assign [unpropertied blacks] to landed proprietors as agricultural laborers . . . to prevent vagrancy and insubordination," and "laws and regulations to which the blacks were subject in 1789 shall remain in force"; ibid., 187–88.

17. James, *Black Jacobins*, 317–18.

18. Ibid., 323–24.

19. Ibid., 325–29.

20. Ibid., 333–35, 362–65; Ros, *Night of Fire*, 203–12.

21. James, *Black Jacobins*, 334.

22. Leclerc to Napoleon, August 6 and August 9, 1802, in James, *Black Jacobins*, 343–45; Ros, *Night of Fire*, 203.

23. Leclerc to the minister of marine, Denis Decrès, August 25, 1802, in James, *Black Jacobins*, 346; Lester D. Langley, *The Americas in the Age of Revolution, 1750–1850* (New Haven, 1996), 133.

24. James, *Black Jacobins*, 354–55.

25. Ibid., 355; Langley, *Americas in the Age of Revolution*, 131–35.

26. James, *Black Jacobins*, 360. Ros (*Night of Fire*, 50) and others confuse the son, Donatien Marie Joseph de Vimeur, vicomte de Rochambeau (1755–1813), and his father, Jean Baptiste Donatien de Vimeur, comte de

Rochambeau (1725–1807); see Jean Edmund Weelen, *Rochambeau: Father and Son: A Life of Maréchal de Rochambeau and the Journal of the Vicomte de Rochambeau* (New York, 1936).

27. Ros, *Night of Fire*, 192–97; James, *Black Jacobins*, 360–62, 369.

28. David Patrick Geggus, "Slavery, War, and Revolution in the Greater Caribbean, 1789–1815," in Gaspar and Geggus, eds., *A Turbulent Time*, 25.

29. David Humphreys to James Madison, March 23, 1801; Rufus King to James Madison, March 29, 1801; William Vans Murray to James Madison, May 7, 1801, *Madison Papers: State*, 1: 36, 55–56, 146 (emphasis in originals).

30. James Madison to Alexander Hamilton, May 26, to James Monroe, June 1, and to Charles Pinckney, June 9, 1801; Rufus King to James Madison, November 10, 1801, *Madison Papers: State*, 1: 228–29, 245, 274–75; 2: 254.

31. Rufus King to James Madison, *Madison Papers: State*, 1: 250–51.

32. Ronald D. Smith, "Napoleon and Louisiana: Failure of the Proposed Expedition to Occupy and Defend Louisiana, 1801–1803," *LH* 12 (1971): 22, 26. Smith misdates Napoleon's letter to Decrès; see Lyon, *Louisiana in French Diplomacy*, 131.

33. Smith, "Napoleon and Louisiana," 28; Kukla, *Laussat Papers*, 7–8, 24.

34. Lyon, *Louisiana in French Diplomacy*, 134–35; Kukla, *Laussat Papers*, 59; "Secret Instructions for the Captain-General of Louisiana," November 26, 1802, in Robertson, *Louisiana*, 369, 371.

35. Smith, "Napoleon and Louisiana," 31–40; Lyon, *Louisiana in French Diplomacy*, 137–44; Pierre Clément Laussat, *Memoirs of My Life*, trans. Sister Agnes-Josephine Pastwa, ed. Robert D. Bush (New Orleans, 1978), 3–4, 114–15; Kukla, *Laussat Papers*, 164. Delayed from December 1 to January 10 while waiting the arrival of the *Surveillant* into the natural harbor of Ile d'Aix, Laussat identified his city of departure variously as the seaport of La Rochelle and the fortified city of Rochefort, twenty miles to the south.

36. Rufus King to James Madison, October 31, 1801, *Madison Papers: State*, 2: 214.

37. Stanley Elkins and Eric McKitrick, *The Age of Federalism* (New York, 1993), 510, 643–90; Alexander DeConde, *The Quasi-War: The Politics and Diplomacy of the Undeclared War with France, 1797–1801* (New York, 1966); Jefferson's First Inaugural Address, quoted in Walter LaFeber, "Jefferson and American Foreign Policy," in Peter S. Onuf, ed., *Jeffersonian Legacies* (Charlottesville, 1993), 375.

38. Jefferson to Elbridge Gerry, June 21, 1797, quoted in LaFeber, "Jefferson and American Foreign Policy," 375; George Dangerfield, *Chancellor Robert R. Livingston of New York, 1746–1813* (New York, 1960), 304.

39. Thomas Jefferson to Pierre Samuel Du Pont de Nemours, April 25, 1802, Dumas Malone, ed., *Correspondence Between Thomas Jefferson and Pierre Samuel Du Pont de Nemours, 1798–1817* (Boston and New York, 1930), 46–48.

40. Ibid., 47–49, 52, 67.

41. Thomas Jefferson to Robert R. Livingston, April 18, 1802, *State Papers and Correspondence*, 15–16.

42. Ibid., 16–17.

43. Ibid., 17.

44. Ibid.

45. Ibid.

46. Ibid., 17–18.

47. Ibid., 18.

48. Du Pont to Jefferson, April 30, May 12, 1802, *Correspondence*, 60, 63.

49. Du Pont to Jefferson, May 12, October 4, 1802, *Correspondence*, 63, 69–70.

### CHAPTER THIRTEEN: SELLING A SHIP

1. George Cabot to Rufus King, July 1, 1803; Henry Cabot Lodge, ed., *Life and Letters of George Cabot* (Boston, 1878), 331.

2. *The Literary Magazine and American Register* 2, no. 13 (September 1804): 484.

3. George Dangerfield, *Chancellor Robert R. Livingston of New York, 1746–1813* (New York, 1960), 7–15.

4. Ibid., 44–48.

5. Robert R. Livingston, "Thoughts on the . . . Election of 1792," and letter of "Aristides," *New York Journal*, April 4, 1792, quoted in Dangerfield, *Livingston*, 253, 260.

6. Thomas Jefferson to Robert R. Livingston, December 14, 1800, and Louis André Pichon to Robert R. Livingston, April 2, 1801, quoted in Dangerfield, *Livingston*, 301, 305.

7. Dangerfield, *Livingston*, 50, 125, 188, 309.

8. Ibid., 309–11.

9. Ibid.

10. Ibid., 331–36; Livingston to Madison, December 13, 1801, *Madison Papers: State*, 2: 309.

11. Livingston to Madison, May 20, 1802, ibid., 232. The text of Livingston's "Whether it will be advantageous to France to take possession of Louisiana?" is printed in *State Papers and Correspondence*, 36–50.

12. Livingston, "Whether it will be advantageous to France to take possession of Louisiana?" 39, 45.

13. Ibid., 43–44.

14. Ibid., 46–47.

15. Robert R. Livingston to James Madison, August 10, 1802, *Madison Papers: State*, 3: 468.

16. Livingston to King, August 2, 1802, Edward Alexander Parsons, ed., *Original Letters of Robert R. Livingston, 1801–1803* (New Orleans, 1953), 99; Livingston to Jefferson, October 28, 1802, *State Papers and Correspondence*, 59.

17. Dangerfield, *Livingston*, 341–43.

18. Ibid., 342.

19. Ibid., 345.

20. Ibid.

21. Livingston to Madison, August 16, 1802, *Madison Papers: State,* 3: 491–92.

22. Livingston, "Whether it will be advantageous to France to take possession of Louisiana?" 48, 49. The Spanish denied to Americans living on the Tombigbee River (now in Alabama) the right to trade through Mobile and forced them to trade through New Orleans subject to duties of 6 percent or more; Daniel Clark to James Madison, June 22, 1802; *Madison Papers: State,* 3: 331.

23. Thomas Jefferson to Robert R. Livingston, April 18, 1802, *State Papers and Correspondence,* 17; Thomas Jefferson to Pierre Samuel Du Pont de Nemours, April 25, 1802, Dumas Malone, ed., *Correspondence Between Thomas Jefferson and Pierre Samuel Du Pont de Nemours, 1798–1817* (Boston and New York, 1930), 47; James Madison to Charles Pinckney, September 25, 1801; *Madison Papers: State,* 2: 131.

24. James Madison to Robert R. Livingston, January 18, 1803; *Madison Papers: State,* 4: 259; Robert R. Livingston to Thomas Jefferson, October 28, 1802, *State Papers and Correspondence,* 59; Dangerfield, *Livingston,* 342. In a massive biography that ably portrays James Monroe's perceptions of events he had not witnessed, Harry Ammon wrote that "it is quite probable that this offer, though it was rejected at the time, may have given currency to the idea that the United States might be willing to take all Louisiana"; Ammon, *James Monroe: The Quest for National Identity* (Charlottesville, 1971), 218.

25. Thomas Jefferson to Robert R. Livingston, April 18, 1802, *State Papers and Correspondence,* 16.

26. Jon Kukla, ed., *A Guide to the Papers of Pierre Clément Laussat, Napoleon's Prefect for the Colony of Louisiana, and of General Claude Perrin Victor* (New Orleans, 1993), 28. Morales's proclamation is printed in *State Papers and Correspondence,* 54–55. Alexander DeConde and others mistakenly date Morales's proclamation to October 18, the date of two letters informing James Madison of the proclamation; DeConde, *This Affair of Louisiana* (New York, 1976), 119; William E. Hulings to James Madison, October 18, 1802, *Madison Papers: State,* 4: 30; William C. C. Claiborne to James Madison, October 18, 1802, *State Papers and Correspondence,* 55. The editors of Madison's papers date their abstract of Claiborne's letter to October 29; *Madison Papers: State,* 4: 67.

27. Jack D. L. Holmes, "Dramatis Personae in Spanish Louisiana," *Louisiana Studies* 6 (1967): 155–61; Holmes, *Gayoso: The Life of a Spanish Governor in the Mississippi Valley, 1789–1799* (Baton Rouge, 1965), 218–22. "Roscoe R. Hill's catalogue of one section in the Archives of the Indies," Holmes noted, "devotes five columns just *listing the bundles* containing materials on the controversial Morales"; "Dramatis Personae," 161.

28. Pinckney's Treaty, Article 22; Daniel Clark to James Madison, March 8, 1803, *Madison Papers: State,* 4: 401.

29. *Guardian of Freedom* (Frankfort, Ky.), November 3, 10, December 1, 8,

1802; *Scioto Gazette* (Chillicothe, Ohio), December 18, 1802; microfilm, Library of Virginia, Richmond.

30. *Guardian of Freedom,* December 8, 1802; *Scioto Gazette,* December 18, 1802.

31. *Guardian of Freedom,* December 1, 1802; Daniel Clark to James Madison, March 8, 1803, *Madison Papers: State,* 4: 401–2.

32. James Madison to Charles Pinckney, November 27, 1802; Carlos Martínez Yrujo to James Madison, November 27, 1802, *Madison Papers: State,* 4: 146–49; *Guardian of Freedom,* February 2, 1803.

33. Madison to Pinckney, November 27, 1802, *Madison Papers: State,* 4: 147; Wilkinson to Brown, October 28, 1802, quoted in Stuart Seely Sprague, "Jefferson, Kentucky and the Closing of the Port of New Orleans, 1802–1803," *Register of the Kentucky Historical Society* 70 (1972): 312; James Morrison to Wilson Cary Nicholas [1802], ibid.; Barr to Breckinridge, January 4, 1803; ibid., 315. Chargé d'affaires Pichon reported the secretary of state's warning in a letter to Talleyrand dated November 28, 1802; *Madison Papers: State,* xxvi.

34. John Stratton to John Cropper, January 10, 1803, John Cropper Papers, Mss1c8835a, 276–83, Virginia Historical Society, Richmond; letter from Natchez, January 20, 1803, *Western Spy and Hamilton Gazette* (Cincinnati), February 23, 1803, quoted in Sprague, "Kentucky and the Closing of the Port," 314.

35. Edward Channing, *History of the United States* (New York, 1926), 4: 326–27; E. Wilson Lyon, "The Closing of the Port of New Orleans," *AHR* 37 (1931–1932): 280–83; "A Report to the King on the Closing of New Orleans," ibid., 284–89; A. P. Whitaker, "France and the American Deposit at New Orleans," *HAHR* 11 (1931): 485–502.

36. Lyon, "Closing of the Port," 282; "Secret Instructions for the Captain-General of Louisiana," November 26, 1802, in Robertson, *Louisiana,* 366; Whitaker, "France and the American Deposit," 498–501.

37. E. Wilson Lyon, *Louisiana in French Diplomacy, 1759–1804* (Norman, Okla., 1934), 194; DeConde, *This Affair of Louisiana,* 151.

38. Ibid., 153; Alan Schom, *Napoleon Bonaparte* (New York, 1997), 308–32.

39. Robert Livingston to President Jefferson, March 12, 1803, *State Papers and Correspondence,* 145; Livingston to Rufus King, March 15, 1803, *Original Letters of Robert R. Livingston,* 106; Henry Adams, *History of the United States of America During the Administrations of Thomas Jefferson* (New York, 1889); my citations are to the Library of America edition (New York, 1986), 314.

40. Carl Ludwig Lokke, "Secret Negotiations to Maintain the Peace of Amiens," *AHR* (1943–1944): 57–58.

41. Ibid., 58; John J. McCusker, *How Much Is That in Real Money? A Historical Price Index for Use as a Deflator of Money Values in the Economy of the United States* (Worcester, Mass., 1992), 321, 343, 350.

42. Dialogue is quoted from Adams, *History,* 324–28, and DeConde, *This Affair of Louisiana,* 165–66; both accounts are based upon Lucien Bonaparte's memoirs of the conversation.

43. W. F. Jackson Knight, trans., *The Aeneid* (London, 1956), 31; Danger-field, *Livingston*, 362.

44. Adams, *History*, 328; François Barbé-Marbois, *The History of Louisiana; Particularly of the Cession of That Colony to the United States of America* (Philadelphia, 1830; rpt., Baton Rouge, 1977), 263.

45. Schom, *Napoleon Bonaparte*, 310–13.

46. E. Wilson Lyon, *The Man Who Sold Louisiana: The Career of François Barbé-Marbois* (Norman, Okla., 1942), 3–71; William Peden, ed., *Notes on the State of Virginia* (Chapel Hill, 1954), xi–xv.

47. Lyon, *Man Who Sold Louisiana*, 72–117.

48. Barbé-Marbois, *History of Louisiana*, 263–64.

49. Ibid., 264.

50. Ibid., 264–66.

51. Ibid., 270–72.

52. Ibid., 274–75.

53. Ibid., 276.

54. Ibid.

## CHAPTER FOURTEEN:
### MIDNIGHT IN THE GARDEN OF RUE TRUDON

1. Robert R. Livingston to Rufus King, May 11, 1803, Edward Alexander Parsons, ed., *Original Letters of Robert R. Livingston, 1801–1803* (New Orleans, 1953), 123–24.

2. Alexander Hamilton to Charles Cotesworth Pinckney, December 29, 1802, in Joanne B. Freeman, ed., *Alexander Hamilton: Writings* (New York, 2001), 994; [Douglass Adair], "Hamilton on the Louisiana Purchase: A Newly Identified Editorial from the *New-York Evening Post*," *WMQ* 3d ser., 12 (1955): 269–71; Adair, *Fame and the Founding Fathers*, ed. Trevor Colbourn (New York, 1974), 260–85.

3. *New-York Evening Post*, February 8, 1803, Harold C. Syrett, ed., *Papers of Alexander Hamilton* (New York, 1979), 26: 83.

4. Ibid. Among the works of modern historians, I have found only one suggestion that conquest might have been preferable to purchase: "A military expedition," Forrest McDonald contends, "would have been far cheaper"; *Alexander Hamilton: A Biography* (New York, 1979), 358.

5. Thomas Jefferson to James Monroe, January 13, 1803, Merrill D. Peterson, ed., *Thomas Jefferson: Writings* (New York, 1984), 1111.

6. Thomas Jefferson to Meriwether Lewis, February 23, 1803; Carlos Martínez de Yrujo to Pedro Cevallos, December 2, 1802; Donald Jackson, ed., *Letters of the Lewis and Clark Expedition with Related Documents, 1783–1854* (2d ed., Urbana, Ill., 1978), 2–6 and passim.

7. Jefferson's Message to Congress, January 18, 1803; ibid., 10–13 and passim; Stephen A. Ambrose, *Undaunted Courage: Meriwether Lewis, Thomas Jef-*

*ferson, and the Opening of the American West* (New York, 1996); Jerome O. Steffen, *William Clark: Jeffersonian Man on the Frontier* (Norman, Okla., 1977).

8. William Coleman in the *New-York Evening Post,* February 8, 1803, quoted in Dumas Malone, *Jefferson the President: First Term, 1801–1805* (Boston, 1970), 277; Pichon to Talleyrand, December 22, 1803, quoted in Henry Adams, *History of the United States of America During the Administrations of Thomas Jefferson* (New York, 1889; Library of America edition, New York, 1986), 289.

9. Thomas Jefferson to James Monroe, January 10, 1803, Paul Leicester Ford, ed., *Works of Thomas Jefferson* (New York, 1905), 9: 416–17.

10. Ibid.

11. Adams, *History,* 291–92; Malone, *Jefferson the President: First Term,* 270–71; Harry Ammon, *James Monroe: The Quest for National Identity* (Charlottesville, 1971), 204.

12. David Holmes to Senator James Allen, January 12, 1803, Mss2 AL 548 b 2, Virginia Historical Society, Richmond; Howard P. Hildreth, "David Holmes," *Virginia Cavalcade* 16 (Spring 1967): 38–40.

13. Joanne B. Freeman, *Affairs of Honor: National Politics in the New Republic* (New Haven, 2001), 174–76; Stuart Gerry Brown, ed., *The Autobiography of James Monroe* (Syracuse, 1959), 156.

14. Thomas Jefferson to Robert R. Livingston, April 18, 1802, *State Papers and Correspondence,* 16–17.

15. Jefferson to Randolph, December 1, 1803, Jefferson Papers, 1st ser., Library of Congress, Washington, D.C., quoted in Jon Kukla, "Order and Chaos in Early America: Political and Social Stability in Pre-Restoration Virginia," *AHR* 90 (1985): 298.

16. James Monroe to Thomas Monteagle Bailey [i.e., Bayly], March 6, 1803, Mss2 M7576 a 18, Virginia Historical Society, Richmond; *Autobiography of James Monroe,* 154–56. Ammon follows Monroe's letter of April 9 in describing the voyage as "29 days from the Hook," but the entire voyage took thirty-one days; Ammon, *Monroe,* 207; James Monroe to James Madison, April 9, 1803, *Madison Papers: State,* 4: 497.

17. Ammon, *Monroe,* 207; *Autobiography of James Monroe,* 154–56. The first significant message conveyed by Chappe's optical telegraph was of a French victory against Austria on November 30, 1794.

18. Robert Livingston to James Monroe, April 10, 1803, quoted in Dangerfield, *Livingston,* 358. The quotation from this letter in Ammon, *Monroe,* 208, has six transcription errors.

19. *Autobiography of James Monroe,* 158. On April 15, 1803, Monroe vented his feelings in a private letter addressed to Madison but "not sent" (*State Papers and Correspondence,* 164–65; Ammon, Monroe, 617n30), although Monroe allowed John Mercer to make a copy (*Madison Papers: State,* 4: 522–23n3).

20. Lyon, *Louisiana in French Diplomacy,* 214; Dangerfield, *Livingston,* 358. The entire debate was published on June 1, 1803, in William Duane, *Mis-*

*sissippi Question: Report of a Debate in the Senate of the United States . . . on Certain Resolutions Concerning the Violation of the Right of Deposit in the Island of New Orleans* (Philadelphia, 1803). E. B. Williston, comp., *Eloquence of the United States* (Middleton, Conn., 1827) reprinted Ross's resolutions (2: 236), John Breckinridge's Republican substitute resolutions (2: 282), and major speeches by De Witt Clinton, James Ross, and Gouverneur Morris, February 23–25, 1803 (2: 236–319). The resolutions and debates were extensively reported in contemporary American newspapers as well.

21. Lowell H. Harrison, "John Breckinridge and the Acquisition of Louisiana," *Louisiana Studies* 7 (1968): 20–22; Duane, *Mississippi Question,* 34–35; Williston, *Eloquence of the United States,* 2: 282.

22. Speech of James Ross, February 24, 1803, in Duane, *Mississippi Question,* 97–98.

23. Ibid., 111; Lyon, *Louisiana in French Diplomacy,* 202–3.

24. Pichon to Talleyrand, February 18, 1803, Lyon, *Louisiana in French Diplomacy,* 202–3.

25. Talleyrand to Decrès, May 24, 1803, ibid., 203.

26. "Many years later," wrote E. Wilson Lyon in reference to Monroe's letter to the marquis de Lafayette on May 2, 1829, "Monroe contended that Napoleon's sudden action was due to the news of [Monroe's] arrival at Havre, but, if this were true, it is difficult to see why Bonaparte did not delay the whole matter until Monroe joined Livingston"; Lyon, *Louisiana in French Diplomacy,* 214n.

27. Dangerfield, *Livingston,* 361.

28. Quotations from this conversation are from Livingston's detailed letter to James Madison, April 11, 1803; *Madison Papers: State,* 4: 500–2.

29. Ibid., François Barbé-Marbois, *History of Louisiana; Particularly of the Cession of That Colony to the United States of America* (Philadelphia, 1830; rpt., Baton Rouge, 1977), 278.

30. Livingston to Madison, April 11, 1803; *Madison Papers: State,* 4: 500–2.

31. Ibid.

32. Ibid.

33. Ammon, *Monroe,* 212; Monroe to Madison, *Madison Papers: State,* 5: 297.

34. Dangerfield, *Livingston,* 376–80; Ammon, *Monroe,* 215–18; and *Madison Papers: State,* passim.

35. The events of April 12 and 13 are recounted in Livingston's famous letter to Madison, dated "Paris 13 April 1803 (Midnight)." The Historic New Orleans Collection displays the recipient's copy (19MSS132) in its History Galleries at 533 Royal Street. Quotations are from the definitive transcription in *Madison Papers: State,* 4: 511–15, except that Livingston's disconcerting capitalization of ordinary words beginning with *s* has been suppressed. Harry Ammon makes the case that "although it does not materially affect the sequence of events," Livingston penned this letter in the wee hours of April 14th, describing events that occurred on the 12th and 13th; Ammon, *Monroe,* 616n28. In the same note,

however, Ammon apparently conflates Livingston's two meetings with Talleyrand on the 11th and 12th into one on the 11th; ibid.

36. Livingston to Madison, midnight, April 13 [*sic,* 14], 1803, *Madison Papers: State,* 4: 512; Dangerfield, *Livingston,* 361, 363. Livingston's house stood near 72 rue Auber.

37. Livingston to Madison, midnight, April 13 [*sic,* 14], 1803; Monroe to Madison, September 17, 1803; *Madison Papers: State,* 4: 512, 5: 440.

38. Livingston to Madison, midnight, April 13 [*sic,* 14], 1803, *Madison Papers: State,* 4: 512.

39. Livingston to Madison, midnight, April 13 [*sic,* 14], 1803; Monroe to Madison, September 17, 1803; *Madison Papers: State,* 4: 512, 5: 440; Dangerfield, *Livingston,* 313.

40. Monroe to Madison, September 17, 1803; *Madison Papers: State,* 5: 440. This account of conversations on the evening of April 13 was written *after* adherents of Monroe and Livingston had begun squabbling in the newspapers over which minister had done more to bring about the Louisiana Purchase. John Mercer and Fulwar Skipwith were present at the dinner and walked home with Monroe. If Monroe's memory was accurate, on the walk home Skipwith made disparaging remarks about Livingston having "complained of his misfortune" in respect to Monroe's arrival just as the deal was coming together. The present narrative affords less credence to Monroe's report of Skipwith's alleged remarks than does Ammon, *Monroe,* 210–11, and none to the assertion that "a rupture" between Livingston and Monroe was imminent at that time. For his part, Livingston strove to keep Monroe in the loop, meeting with him the next morning to inform him "in substance what Mr. Marbois afterwards told me himself"; Monroe to Madison, April 19, 1803; Monroe to Madison, September 17, 1803, *Madison Papers: State,* 4: 538–39; 5: 440.

41. Livingston to Madison, midnight, April 13 [*sic,* 14], 1803, *Madison Papers: State,* 4: 512.

42. Livingston to Madison, midnight, April 13 [*sic,* 14], 1803, *Madison Papers: State,* 4: 513; Livingston's run-on sentence has been corrected by the insertion of a period after "treasury."

43. James Monroe to James Madison, April 15, 1803; *Madison Papers: State,* 4: 520–21.

44. Ibid; Ammon, *Monroe,* 212–13.

45. Barbé-Marbois, *History of Louisiana,* 280–81.

46. Ibid., 281.

47. Livingston to Madison, April 18, 1803, *Madison Papers: State,* 4: 525–26.

48. Ibid.

49. Photographs of Monroe's twelve-page journal of the treaty negotiations, April 27–ca. May 10, 1803, are reproduced in Worthington Chauncey Ford, ed., *Papers of James Monroe Listed in Chronological Order from the Original Manuscripts in the Library of Congress* (Washington, D.C., 1904). Ford's calendar has been supplanted by Daniel Preston, ed., *A Comprehensive Catalogue of the Correspondence and Papers of James Monroe* (Westport, Conn., 2001).

50. Monroe's journal, April 27–ca. May 10, 1803.

51. Ibid.

52. Ibid.

53. Appendix B: Louisiana Purchase Treaty, Article III.

54. Monroe's journal, April 27–ca. May 10, 1803.

55. Ibid; Barbé-Marbois, *History of Louisiana,* 312.

56. Barbé-Marbois, *History of Louisiana,* 310; Monroe's journal, April 27–ca. May 10, 1803.

57. The importance that Jefferson attached to these cabinet deliberations about Louisiana is apparent from the way he recorded them. For more than two years Jefferson kept close at hand a single sheet of paper, docketed "Louisiana," on which he recorded notes of nine cabinet meetings about the Mississippi crisis and the implications of the Louisiana Purchase during thirty months from May 1803 through November 1805. The document is found on Reel 29 of the Jefferson Papers at the Library of Congress, filed with undated material at the end of the chronological sequence of 1803 documents. I am indebted to Barbara Oberg, of the Papers of Thomas Jefferson at Princeton University, and Sandra Gioia Treadway, at the Library of Virginia, for assistance in locating this document after I discovered that Caryn Cossé Bell's otherwise valuable *Revolution, Romanticism, and the Afro-Creole Protest Tradition in Louisiana, 1718–1868* (Baton Rouge, 1997), 31n47, cites the wrong date. The attorney general attended only three of these nine meetings, but except for Madison's early departure from the meeting on July 16 and Robert Smith's absence on October 4, 1803, the other four cabinet secretaries all participated. The membership and operation of Jefferson's "executive council" is described in Dumas Malone, *Jefferson the President: First Term, 1801–1805* (Boston, 1970), 5–66, and more generally in James Sterling Young, *The Washington Community, 1800–1828* (New York, 1966), and Noble E. Cunningham, *The Process of Government Under Jefferson* (Princeton, 1978), 60–71.

58. Notes of cabinet meetings, May 7, 1803–November 19, 1805, Jefferson Papers, Library of Congress.

59. Ibid.


## Chapter Fifteen: An Immense Wilderness

1. Gates to Jefferson, July 7, 1803, Jefferson Papers, Library of Congress.

2. Calculator VII, *The Balance and Columbian Repository* (Hudson, New York), September 20, 1803, quoted in Victor Adolfo Arriaga Weiss, "Domestic Opposition to the Louisiana Purchase: Anti-Expansionism and Republican Thought" (Ph.D. diss., University of Virginia, 1993), 142.

3. *Boston Independent Chronicle,* June 30, 1803, quoted in Suzanne Van Meter, "A Noble Bargain: The Louisiana Purchase" (Ph.D. diss., Indiana University, 1977), 177. The three brief notices in the *New-York Evening Post* are quoted in [Douglass Adair], "Hamilton on the Louisiana Purchase: A Newly Identified Editorial from the *New-York Evening Post*," *WMQ,* 3d ser., 12 (1955):

273; Roy F. Nichols, "The Louisiana Purchase: Challenge and Stimulus to American Democracy," *LHQ* 38 (1955): 1–25.

4. King to Monroe and Livingston, May 7, [May 11,] 1803, Edward Alexander Parsons, ed., *Original Letters of Robert R. Livingston, 1801–1803* (New Orleans, 1953), 122–23; Hawkesbury to King, *State Papers and Correspondence,* 197; personal conversations with Robert V. Remini and Tim Pickles. Monroe and Livingston's letter of May 9 is misdated May 7 in *State Papers and Correspondence,* 183. For the cooperation between King and Livingston to avert a British expedition see Robert Ernst, *Rufus King: American Federalist* (Chapel Hill, 1968), 270–77, and Parsons, ed., *Original Letters of Robert R. Livingston,* passim.

5. King to Madison, May 16, 1803, and enclosures, *Madison Papers: State,* 5: 2–4; Van Meter, "A Noble Bargain," 177. King's July 2 letter to Madison from New York stated that "the Receipt of my dispatches will have apprized you of my arrival"; *Madison Papers: State,* 5: 140, and see King to Madison, July 8, 1803, ibid., 5: 151–52. Two weeks later Madison wrote a Virginia neighbor that "our official information, which is indirect by a letter from our Envoys to Mr. King, amounts only to what you see in the Newspapers"; Madison to Isaac Hite, July 16, 1803, ibid., 5: 187.

6. Jefferson to Thomas Mann Randolph, July 5, 1803, Jefferson Papers, Library of Congress; Van Meter, "A Noble Bargain," 177; *European Magazine,* July 1803.

7. Gates to Jefferson, July 7, 1803, David Campbell to Jefferson, October 23, 1803, Jefferson Papers, Library of Congress; Pichon to Talleyrand, July 7, 1803, Van Meter, "A Noble Bargain," 181–82.

8. John Smith to Jefferson, August 9 and August 30, 1803, Jefferson Papers, Library of Congress; Pichon to Talleyrand, July 7, 1803, Van Meter, "A Noble Bargain," 181–82.

9. James Madison to Daniel Clark, July 20, 1803, *Madison Papers: State,* 5: 202.

10. Livingston and Monroe to Madison, May 13, 1803, *Madison Papers: State,* 4: 601–2.

11. Ibid., 602.

12. Ibid., 602–3.

13. Notes of cabinet meetings, May 7, 1803–November 19, 1805, Jefferson Papers, Library of Congress.

14. Ibid.

15. Ibid.

16. Ibid; John Breckinridge to Thomas Jefferson, September 10, 1803, *Territorial Papers,* 47–48.

17. Pichon to Talleyrand, July 7, 1803, Van Meter, "A Noble Bargain," 181–82; George William Erving to James Madison, May 16, 1803, *Madison Papers: State,* 5: 7–8.

18. James Monroe to James Madison, May 14, 1803, ibid., 4: 611; Erving to Madison, August 31, 1801, ibid., 2: 38–40. Founded by Fisher Ames and other

Federalists associated with the old Essex Junto, the *Palladium* was intended as a national voice for the party of the "rich and wise and good." Its mission was to "whip Jacobins as a gentleman would a chimney-sweeper, at arm's length, and keeping aloof from the soot"; Winfred E. A. Bernhard, *Fisher Ames: Federalist and Statesman, 1758–1808* (Chapel Hill, 1965), 332–33; Fisher Ames to Jeremiah Smith, December 14, 1802, William B. Allen, ed., *Works of Fisher Ames* (rev. ed., Indianapolis, 1983), 1451. For Rufus King's political ambitions see Theodore Sedgwick to Alexander Hamilton, January 27, 1803, Harold C. Syrett, ed., *Papers of Alexander Hamilton* (New York, 1979), 26: 79–80; Ernst, *Rufus King*, 274–87.

19. Erving to Madison, May 16, 1803, *Madison Papers: State*, 5: 8.

20. Adair, "Hamilton on the Louisiana Purchase, [July 5, 1803,]" 273–74, 277.

21. Ibid., 274–75, 278.

22. Ibid., 276.

23. Ibid.

24. *Columbian Centinel*, July 3, 1803, quoted in Van Meter, "A Noble Bargain," 184–85. Ames's brother, an avid Republican, revealed the identity of Fabricius in his diary; Charles Warren, ed., *Jacobin and Junto, or Early American Politics as Viewed in the Diary of Dr. Nathaniel Ames, 1758–1822* (Cambridge, Mass., 1931), 162. In light of David Hackett Fischer's corrections in "The Myth of the Essex Junto," *WMQ*, 3d ser., 21 (1964): 191–235, it should be noted that Fisher Ames described himself "as one of the Essex Junto" in a letter to Jeremiah Smith, February 16, 1801; *Works of Fisher Ames*, 1408. Elisha P. Douglass, "Fisher Ames, Spokesman for New England Federalism," *Proceedings of the American Philosophical Society* 103 (1959): 693–715, is a good survey of Ames's career.

25. *Columbian Centinel*, July 3, 1803, quoted in Van Meter, "A Noble Bargain," 184–85.

26. Ames to Dwight, March 19, 1801; Ames to King, February 23, 1802; Ames to Christopher Gore, October 3, 1803; "The Dangers of American Liberty" (emphasis added); *Works of Fisher Ames*, 1409, 1427, 130, 1463, 160.

27. "The Republican X," August 30, 1804; "Monitor," April 17, 1804; *Works of Fisher Ames*, 263, 266, 268, 225; Kevin M. Gannon, "Escaping 'Mr. Jefferson's Plan of Destruction': New England Federalists and the Idea of a Northern Confederacy, 1803–1804," *Journal of the Early Republic* 21 (2001): 423–24. Based on the census of 1790, Essex attorney Nathan Dane attributed thirteen of the south's forty-four seats in Congress (and the same number of electoral votes) to the representation of slaves under the three-fifths clause; Andrew Jay Johnson III, "The Life and Constitutional Thought of Nathan Dane" (Ph.D. diss., Indiana University, 1964), 81.

28. Ames to Thomas Dwight, October 31, 1803; *Works of Fisher Ames*, 1468–69; Abraham Ellery to Alexander Hamilton, October 25, 1803, Syrett, ed., *Hamilton Papers*, 26: 166–67; Josiah Quincy to Oliver Wolcott, September 5, 1803, Robert A. McCaughey, *Josiah Quincy, 1772–1864: The Last Federalist*

(Cambridge, Mass., 1974), 30–31; Samuel Taggart, An Oration Delivered at Conway, July 4, 1804 (Northampton, Mass., 1804), 7–8, quoted in James M. Banner, Jr., *To the Hartford Convention: The Federalists and the Origins of Party Politics in Massachusetts, 1789–1815* (New York, 1970), 111.

29. Higginson to Pickering, November 22, 1803, J. Franklin Jameson, ed., "Letters of Stephen Higginson, 1783–1804," *Annual Report of the American Historical Association for the Year 1896* (Washington, D.C., 1897), 1: 837.

30. Johnson, "Life and Constitutional Thought of Nathan Dane," 85; Richard E. Welch, Jr., *Theodore Sedgwick, Federalist: A Political Portrait* (Middletown, Conn., 1965), 242–43; Alexander Hamilton to Theodore Sedgwick, July 10, 1804, in Joanne B. Freeman, ed., *Alexander Hamilton: Writings* (New York, 2001), 1022.

31. Thomas Jefferson to Martin Van Buren, June 29, 1824; I am indebted to John P. Kaminski for a transcript of this letter in which Jefferson wrote "that for thirty years past, [Pickering] has been industriously collecting materials for vituperating the characters he had marked for his hatred."

32. Notebook, 1827 (Pickering Papers, Massachusetts Historical Society, 1: 216); Pickering to Fisher Ames, March 11, 1806; Pickering to James McHenry, January 5, 1811; and Pickering to James McHenry, December 29, 1808; all quoted in Edward Hake Phillips, "Timothy Pickering's 'Portrait' of Thomas Jefferson," *Essex Institute Historical Collections* 92 (1958): 309.

33. Gannon, "Escaping 'Mr. Jefferson's Plan,' " 434. Throughout the first quarter of the nineteenth century, four out of five members of Congress lived in boardinghouses occupied *only* by colleagues from their state or region. Men who lived and dined together overwhelmingly voted together. James Sterling Young's study of roll-call votes revealed that congressmen living in the same boardinghouse voted either unanimously or with one dissent three times out of four (74.2 percent) and senators four times out of five (83.3 percent); Young, *Washington Community, 1800–1828*, 101–5.

34. Pickering to Richard Peters, December 24, 1803; Pickering to George Cabot, January 29, 1804; Henry Adams, *Documents Relating to New-England Federalism, 1800–1815* (Boston, 1905), 338–42.

35. Everett Somerville Brown, ed., *William Plumer's Memorandum of Proceedings in the United States Senate, 1803–1807* (New York, 1923), 6–9; Lynn W. Turner, *William Plumer of New Hampshire, 1759–1850* (Chapel Hill, 1962), 133–50, and Plumer to Bradbury Cilley, January 15, 1804, quoted 138.

36. Tapping Reeve to Uriah Tracy, February 7, 1804, Adams, *Documents Relating to New-England Federalism*, 342–43; Mary-Jo Kline and Joanne Wood Ryan et al., eds., *Political Correspondence and Public Papers of Aaron Burr* (Princeton, 1983), lx–lxi; Gannon, "Escaping 'Mr. Jefferson's Plan,' " 437.

37. Roger Griswold to Oliver Wolcott, March 11, 1804; Adams, *Documents Relating to New-England Federalism*, 355–58.

38. *Plumer's Memorandum*, 517–18; Gannon, "Escaping 'Mr. Jefferson's Plan,' " 438–39; Milton Lomask, *Aaron Burr: The Years from Princeton to Vice President, 1756–1805* (New York, 1979), 336–42. For evidence that the sepa-

ratists' dealings with Burr were known to the likes of Hamilton and King, see Rufus King's memorandum of the April 4 meeting between Burr and Griswold, dated April 5 and based on King's conversations with Griswold, Wolcott, or both; Kline and Wood, *Papers of Aaron Burr*, 862–65.

39. Gannon, "Escaping 'Mr. Jefferson's Plan,' " 440; William Keteltas to Aaron Burr, February 27, 1804, Kline and Wood, *Papers of Aaron Burr*, 844–46; Syrett, ed., *Hamilton Papers*, 26: 187–90.

40. *New York City Commercial Advertiser*, April 14, 1804, quoted in Kline and Wood, *Papers of Aaron Burr*, 842; Thomas Fleming, *Duel: Alexander Hamilton, Aaron Burr, and the Future of America* (New York, 1999), 231–33.

41. Lomask, *Aaron Burr, 1756–1805*, 343; Gannon, "Escaping 'Mr. Jefferson's Plan,' " 440; James Cheetham, in the *American Citizen*, May 5, 1804, quoted in Fleming, *Duel*, 253.

42. Fleming, *Duel*, 231–33, quoted from documents printed in Harold C. Syrett and Jean G. Cooke, eds., *Interview in Weehawken: The Burr-Hamilton Duel, As Told in the Original Documents* (Middletown, Conn., 1960), 48; Lomask, *Aaron Burr, 1756–1805*, 343–48.

43. Fleming, *Duel*, 283–99; "It is not to be denied," Hamilton had written in a note not found until after his death, "that my animadversions on the political principles, character and views of Col. Burr have been extremely severe, and on several occasions I, in common with many others, have made very unfavourable criticisms on particular instances of the private conduct of this gentleman"; Lomask, *Aaron Burr, 1756–1805*, 352–53.

44. Fleming, *Duel*, 301–17; Joanne B. Freeman, *Affairs of Honor: National Politics in the New Republic* (New Haven, 2001), 159–98.

45. Fleming, *Duel*, 301–17; Alexander Hamilton to Theodore Sedgwick, July 10, 1804, in Freeman, ed., *Alexander Hamilton: Writings*, 1022.

46. Banner, *To the Hartford Convention*, 353–56; Charles Raymond Brown, *The Northern Confederacy According to the Plans of the "Essex Junto," 1796–1814* (Princeton, 1915); John Quincy Adams quoted in Gannon, "Escaping 'Mr. Jefferson's Plan.' "

47. Timothy Pickering to John Lowell, January 23 and January 24, 1815, in Adams, *Documents Relating to New-England Federalism*, 423–26.

48. Turner, *William Plumer*, 111–12; Jefferson to Dickinson, August 9, 1803; Jefferson to Breckinridge, August 12, 1803, Paul Leicester Ford, ed., *The Works of Thomas Jefferson* (New York, 1905), 10: 7, 29.

49. The treaty and Jefferson's attempts to draft a suitable amendment are printed in my Appendixes B and D.

50. "Theramanes," II and V, *Columbian Centinel and Massachusetts Federalist*, November 13 and 23, 1803; "American," *New-York Evening Post*, December 24, 1803; and "Incredulis," *New England Repertory*, July 16, 1803; quoted in Weiss, "Domestic Opposition to the Louisiana Purchase," 144–48; *Columbian Centinel and Massachusetts Federalist*, November 12, 1803, quoted in Mary Isabelle Deen, "Public Response to the Louisiana Purchase: A Survey

of American Press and Pamphlets, 1801–1804 (M.A. thesis, University of Virginia, 1972), 17.

51. Bernard W. Sheehan, *Seeds of Extinction: Jeffersonian Philanthropy and the American Indian* (Chapel Hill, 1973), 243–50.

52. Jefferson to Indian agent Benjamin Hawkins, August 13, 1786; Jefferson to Claiborne, May 24, 1803; Jefferson to Harrison, February 27, 1803, quoted in Christian B. Keller, "Philanthropy Betrayed: Thomas Jefferson, the Louisiana Purchase, and the Origins of Federal Indian Removal Policy," *Proceedings of the American Philosophical Society* 144 (2000): 39, 58.

53. Draft amendment, Appendix D; Jefferson to Gates, July 11, 1803; Jefferson to Dickinson, August 9, 1803; Ford, ed., *Works of Thomas Jefferson*, 10: 12–14, 29. Jefferson described the same plan to Kentucky senator John Breckinridge on August 12, 1803; ibid., 7; Keller, "Philanthropy Betrayed," 59–60.

54. Jefferson to William Henry Harrison, February 27, 1803, Keller, "Philanthropy Betrayed," 39–40, 60.

55. Address to the Chiefs of the Choctaw Indians, October 17, 1820, Harold D. Moser et al., eds., *Papers of Andrew Jackson*, vol. 4, *1816–1820* (Knoxville, 1994), 394; Keller, "Philanthropy Betrayed," 66. For the aftermath of Jefferson's policy shift see David S. Heidler and Jeanne T. Heidler, *Old Hickory's War: Andrew Jackson and the Quest for Empire* (Mechanicsburg, Penn., 1996) and Robert V. Remini, *Andrew Jackson and His Indian Wars* (New York, 2001).

56. Livingston to Madison, June 3, 1803, *Madison Papers: State*, 5: 52–53.

57. Livingston to Jefferson, June 2, 1803, Jefferson Papers, Library of Congress; Monroe to Madison, June 3, 1803; and Livingston to Madison, June 25, 1803, *Madison Papers: State*, 5: 54n1, 55, 120.

58. Harry Ammon, *James Monroe: The Quest for National Identity* (Charlottesville, 1971), 221; Monroe to Madison, August 15, August 31, 1803, *Madison Papers: State*, 5: 310–11, 363–67; Stuart Gerry Brown, ed., *The Autobiography of James Monroe* (Syracuse, 1959), 187–92; Philip Ziegler, *The Sixth Great Power: A History of One of the Greatest of All Banking Families, the House of Barings, 1762–1929* (New York, 1988), 70–73.

59. Jefferson to Gates, July 11, 1803; Ford, ed., *Works of Thomas Jefferson*, 10: 13.

60. Jefferson to Breckinridge, Jefferson to Madison, and Jefferson to Thomas Paine, August 18, 1803; Jefferson to Lincoln, August 30, 1803, Ford, ed., *Works of Thomas Jefferson*, 10: 7–10.

61. Jefferson to Nicholas, September 7, 1803, ibid., 10–11.

62. John Rutledge, Jr., to Harrison Grey Otis, October 1, 1803, quoted in Alexander DeConde, *This Affair of Louisiana* (New York, 1976), 186; R. Earl McClendon, "Origin of the Two-Thirds Rule in Senate Action upon Treaties," *AHR* 36 (1930–1931): 768–72.

63. *Plumer's Memorandum*, 1–14, quoted at 13; Jon Kukla, ed., *A Guide to*

*the Papers of Pierre Clément Laussat, Napoleon's Prefect for the Colony of Louisiana, and of General Claude Perrin Victor* (New Orleans, 1993), 58.

64. John Rutledge, Jr., to Harrison Grey Otis, October 1, 1803, quoted in DeConde, *This Affair of Louisiana,* 186.

65. These arguments are recorded in the *Debates and Proceedings in the [Eighth] Congress of the United States* (Washington, D.C., 1852) and sharply depicted in the chapters on the Louisiana debate and legislation in Henry Adams, *History of the United States of America During the Administrations of Thomas Jefferson* (New York, 1889), Library of America edition (New York, 1986), 366–92. These and other early congressional debates are available on-line through the American Memory project of the Library of Congress at http://memory.loc.gov/ammem/amlaw/lawhome.html.

66. Caesar A. Rodney quoted in Adams, *History,* 371–72; Jefferson to Wilson Cary Nicholas, September 7, 1803; Ford, ed., *Works of Thomas Jefferson,* 10: 10–11; Jefferson to John Breckinridge, August 12, 1803, ibid., 10: 7.

67. Louisiana Purchase Treaty, see Appendix B; Senator Samuel White of Delaware, November 3, 1803, *Debates and Proceedings in the [Eighth] Congress,* 33.

68. Senator Uriah Tracy of Massachusetts, November 3, 1803, *Debates and Proceedings in the [Eighth] Congress,* 58; Adams, *History,* 370–75; Gouverneur Morris to Henry W. Livingston, December 4, 1803, quoted in DeConde, *This Affair of Louisiana,* 210.

69. Merchant, *Gazette of the United States,* November 8, 1803, quoted in Weiss, "Domestic Opposition to the Louisiana Purchase," 147; George F. Kennan, *American Diplomacy, 1900–1950* (New York, 1951), 21–22, quoted in Robert L. Beisner, *Twelve Against Empire: The Anti-Imperialists, 1898–1900* (New York, 1968), 234.

70. Jefferson to General George Rogers Clark, December 25, 1780; H. R. McIlwaine, ed., *Official Letters of the Governors of the State of Virginia,* vol. 2: *The Letters of Thomas Jefferson* (Richmond, 1928), 253; Jefferson to Archibald Stuart, January 25, 1786, *Jefferson Papers,* 9: 217–19.

## CHAPTER SIXTEEN:
## FLUCTUATIONS OF THE POLITICAL THERMOMETER

1. Jefferson to Randolph, December 1, 1803, Jefferson Papers, Library of Congress, Washington, D.C., quoted in Jon Kukla, "Order and Chaos in Early America: Political and Social Stability in Pre-Restoration Virginia," *AHR* 90 (1985): 298.

2. Pierre Clément Laussat, *Memoirs of My Life to My Son During the Years 1803 and After, Which I Spent in Public Service in Louisiana as Commissioner of the French Government for the Retrocession to France of That Colony and for Its Transfer to the United States,* trans. Sister Agnès-Josephine Pastwa (Baton Rouge, 1978), 36.

3. Jefferson to De Witt Clinton, December 2, 1803; Ford, ed., *Works of Thomas Jefferson,* 10: 55.

4. Jefferson's comparison of slaves and Louisianans with "children" announces profound similarities between this debate and subsequent American arguments about emancipation and Reconstruction policies: "Men probably of any color, but of this color we know, brought from their infancy without necessity for thought or forecast," he wrote to Edward Coles on August 25, 1814, "are by their habits rendered as incapable as children of taking care of themselves, and . . . their amalgamation with the other color produces a degradation to which no lover of his country, no lover of excellence in the human character can innocently consent"; Merrill D. Peterson, ed., *Thomas Jefferson: Writings* (New York, 1984), 1345. Jefferson's attitude toward free people of color is discussed in my epilogue.

5. Jefferson to De Witt Clinton, December 2, 1803; Ford, ed., *Works of Thomas Jefferson,* 10: 55; Jefferson to Randolph, December 1, 1803, Library of Congress.

6. Thomas Jefferson to Albert Gallatin, November 9, 1803, *Territorial Papers,* 100–1. The administration relied upon the principle established by Sir James Mansfield's decision in *Campbell v. Hall* (1774) regarding the conquered province of Grenada that "the laws of a conquered country continue in force until they are altered by the conqueror"; see Clarence E. Carter's explanation in ibid., 90n10. Mark F. Fernandez's "Louisiana Legal History: Past, Present, and Future," in Warren M. Billings and Mark F. Fernandez, eds., *A Law unto Itself? Essays in the New Louisiana Legal History* (Baton Rouge, 2001), 1–22, ably describes recent scholarship challenging the legal historiography that culminated in George Dargo's *Jefferson's Louisiana: Politics and the Clash of Legal Traditions* (Cambridge, Mass., 1975).

7. William Eustis and George Washington Campbell, February 28, 1804, *Debates and Proceedings in the [Eighth] Congress,* 1058, 1064; Everett Somerville Brown, ed., *William Plumer's Memorandum of Proceedings in the United States Senate, 1803–1807* (New York, 1923), 145; Henry Adams, *History of the United States of America During the Administrations of Thomas Jefferson* (New York, 1889), Library of America edition (New York, 1986), 380–89; Alexander DeConde, *This Affair of Louisiana* (New York, 1976), 210–13; David A. Carson, "Blank Paper of the Constitution: The Louisiana Purchase Debates," *The Historian* 54 (1992): 477–90. The act enabling the president to take possession of Louisiana vested "all the military, civil, and judicial powers . . . in such person and persons . . . as the President of the United States shall direct for maintaining and protecting the inhabitants of Louisiana in the free enjoyment of their liberty, property and religion"; *Territorial Papers,* 89–90.

8. Jefferson to Madison, July 31, 1803, *Madison Papers: State,* 5: 255.

9. Thomas Jefferson to William C. C. Claiborne, July 17 and July 18, 1803; James Madison to Claiborne, October 31, 1803; Commission to Claiborne and James Wilkinson, October 31, 1803; Jefferson to Claiborne, August 30, 1804;

Commission to Claiborne, January 17, 1806; *Territorial Papers*, 3–5, 91–95, 281–84, 571; Jared William Bradley, ed., *Interim Appointment: W. C. C. Claiborne Letter Book, 1804–1805* (Baton Rouge, 2002), passim.

10. Laussat, *Memoirs of My Life*, 11, 17–18, 117n21, 118n25.

11. Ibid., 56–57.

12. Réponses sur La Louisiane, Laussat Papers, Historic New Orleans Collection, quoted in Laussat, *Memoirs of My Life*, 119n31; Kukla, *Laussat Papers*, 110. New Orleans today has many fine bookstores and libraries, but in other respects *plus ça change, plus c'est la même chose.*

13. Laussat, *Memoirs of My Life*, 36, 57; Kukla, *Laussat Papers*, 56–63, 70–77. Lacking directives from France, Laussat declined several urgent requests from General Rochambeau for money for St. Domingue, ibid., 74.

14. Laussat, *Memoirs of My Life*, 94–96.

15. Ibid., 78.

16. Ibid., 78–79; Laussat to Denis Decrès, July 18, 1803, Robertson, *Louisiana*, 2: 41–43.

17. Laussat, *Memoirs of My Life*, 79–81.

18. Ibid., 75; William C. C. Claiborne to James Madison, December 27, 1803, Dunbar Rowland, ed., *Official Letter Books of W. C. C. Claiborne, 1801–1816* (Jackson, Miss., 1917), 1: 313; Christina Vella, *Intimate Enemies: The Two Worlds of the Baroness de Pontalba* (Baton Rouge, 1997), 23–27; Gilbert C. Din and John E. Harkins, *The New Orleans Cabildo: Colonial Louisiana's First City Government, 1769–1803* (Baton Rouge, 1996), 297–301. Claiborne revised his opinion of Laussat's reforms in a letter to Jefferson on November 25, 1804, *Territorial Papers*, 338–40.

19. Laussat, *Memoirs of My Life*, 77–78.

20. Claiborne to Jefferson, December 8, 1803, *Territorial Papers*, 135; Judith Kelleher Schafer, *Slavery, the Civil Law, and the Supreme Court of Louisiana* (Baton Rouge, 1994), 1–3, 80.

21. Notes of cabinet meetings, May 7, 1803–November 19, 1805, Jefferson Papers, Library of Congress; Claiborne to Jefferson, December 8, 1803, *Territorial Papers*, 135–36.

22. Daniel Clark to William C. C. Claiborne and James Wilkinson, December 12, 1803, *Territorial Papers*, 137. By early January similar rumors had reached Louis André Pichon, who recommended that Laussat send the prisoners to Europe. A ship carrying some French surgeons and officers from St. Domingue did land at New Orleans in January, but Laussat's papers offer no further information about the troops aboard the three Danish ships; Kukla, *Laussat Papers*, 116–17.

23. Claiborne to Madison, "Camp near New-Orleans," December 17, 1803, *Territorial Papers*, 138; Kukla, *Laussat Papers*, 103–4.

24. Laussat, *Memoirs of My Life*, 88–89.

25. Laussat's word *domination* may be translated as "power," "dominion," or "domination." Sister Agnès-Josephine Pastwa chose the third (ibid., 89); I have substituted the second.

26. Ibid., 88–89; Wilkinson to Madison, December 20, 1803; *Territorial Papers,* 138–39; James Ripley Jacobs, *Tarnished Warrior: Major-General James Wilkinson* (New York, 1938), 205–6.

27. Postscript, "1 oClock of the Morning," December 21, 1803; Wilkinson to Secretary of War Henry Dearborn, January 11, 1804, *Territorial Papers,* 139, 159–60; see also Claiborne to Madison, April 14, 1804, ibid., 221.

28. Claiborne to Madison, December 27, 1803, Rowland, ed., *Official Letters,* 1: 314; Kimberly S. Hanger, *Bounded Lives, Bounded Places: Free Black Society in Colonial New Orleans, 1769–1803* (Durham, N.C., 1997), 109–35, 171–75.

29. Claiborne to Madison, December 27, 1803, Rowland, ed., *Official Letters,* 1: 314.

30. Wilkinson to Dearborn, January 11, 1804, *Territorial Papers,* 160.

31. Address from the Free People of Color, January [16,] 1804; ibid., 174–75; Claiborne to Madison, January 17, 1804, Rowland, ed., *Official Letters,* 1: 339–41.

32. Kimberly S. Hanger, "Conflicting Loyalties: The French Revolution and Free People of Color in Spanish New Orleans," *LH* 34 (1993): 25–33.

33. Benjamin Morgan to Chandler Price, August 7, 1803, *Territorial Papers,* 7 (dashes inserted for clarity); Claiborne to Madison, December 27, 1803, Rowland, ed., *Official Letters,* 1: 314.

34. Ellen Holmes Pearson, "Imperfect Equality: The Legal Status of Free People of Color in New Orleans, 1803–1860," in Warren M. Billings and Mark F. Fernandez, eds., *A Law unto Itself? Essays in the New Louisiana Legal History* (Baton Rouge, 2001), 191–210; Caryn Cossé Bell, *Revolution, Romanticism, and the Afro-Creole Protest Tradition in Louisiana, 1718–1868* (Baton Rouge, 1997), 29–40.

35. Hanger, *Bounded Lives, Bounded Places,* 163–67; Bell, *Revolution, Romanticism, and the Afro-Creole Protest Tradition,* 35–48.

36. Senator Samuel White of Delaware, November 3, 1803, *Debates and Proceedings in the [Eighth] Congress of the United States* (Washington, D.C., 1852), 33; Calculator VII, *The Balance and Columbian Repository,* September 20, 1803; Fabricius III, *Columbian Centinel and Massachusetts Federalist,* July 16, 1803; Theramanes V, ibid., November 23, 1803; Victor Adolfo Arriaga Weiss, "Domestic Opposition to the Louisiana Purchase: Anti-Expansionism and Republican Thought" (Ph.D. diss., University of Virginia, 1993), 125, 142, 152; Fisher Ames to Christopher Gore, October 3, 1803; Ames to Thomas Dwight, October 31, 1803; William B. Allen, ed., *Works of Fisher Ames* (rev. ed., Indianapolis, 1983), 1463, 1468–69.

37. The Vieux Carré Survey at the Historic New Orleans Collection lists no establishment called *The House of the* Rising Sun—but it does list a Rising Sun tavern on Conti Street, just around the corner from the Williams Research Center.

38. Arnold R. Hirsch and Joseph Logsdon, eds., *Creole New Orleans: Race and Americanization* (Baton Rouge, 1992); Hanger, *Bounded Lives, Bounded*

*Places,* 22; Bell, *Revolution, Romanticism, and the Afro-Creole Protest Tradition,* 11, 78.

39. Benjamin H. B. Latrobe, *Impressions Respecting New Orleans by Benjamin Henry Boneval Latrobe: Diary and Sketches, 1818–1820,* ed. Samuel Wilson, Jr. (New York, 1951), 18.

40. Michaux and Genet are treated in Chapter 9. The antecedents of the Lewis and Clark expedition are documented in the expanded second edition of Donald Jackson, ed., *Letters of the Lewis and Clark Expedition, with Related Documents, 1783–1854* (2d ed., Urbana, Ill., 1978), 654–75; Stephen A. Ambrose, *Undaunted Courage: Meriwether Lewis, Thomas Jefferson, and the Opening of the American West* (New York, 1996), 138–39.

41. Fisher Ames to Christopher Gore, October 3, 1803, *Works of Fisher Ames,* 1463; Fabricius III, *Columbian Centinel and Massachusetts Federalist,* July 16, 1803; Weiss, "Domestic Opposition to the Louisiana Purchase," 142; Denis Decrès to General Claude Perrin Victor, November 26, 1802, quoted in Adams, *History,* 306.

42. Robert Livingston to James Madison, May 20, *1803; Madison Papers: State,* 5: 19.

43. Lyon, *Louisiana in French Diplomacy,* 104–10; Philip Coolidge Brooks, *Diplomacy and the Borderlands: The Adams-Onís Treaty of 1819* (Berkeley, 1939), 5.

44. James Madison to Charles Pinckney, October 13, 1803, *Madison Papers: State,* 5: 511–13 and passim.

45. Douglas Hilt, *The Troubled Trinity: Godoy and the Spanish Monarchs* (Tuscaloosa, 1987), 168; Alan Schom, *Napoleon Bonaparte* (New York, 1997), 453–72.

46. Hilt, *Troubled Trinity,* 166.

47. Schom, *Napoleon Bonaparte,* 466; David Gates, *The Spanish Ulcer: A History of the Peninsular War* (London, 1985). The future Ferdinand VII and his younger brothers spent four years of exile at Talleyrand's Valençay estate before he returned to the Spanish throne in 1814; J. F. Bernard, *Talleyrand: A Biography* (New York, 1973), 285–89.

48. Bernard, *Talleyrand,* 278–96; Gates, *Spanish Ulcer.*

49. Brooks, *Adams-Onís Treaty,* 13–14.

50. Jefferson to Madison, November 26, 1809, quoted in ibid., 16. Brooks noted that Jefferson's letter confused the 1808 dispute between Carlos and Ferdinand with the 1809 contest between Joseph Bonaparte and the Junta; ibid., 27n26.

51. Hubert B. Fuller, *The Purchase of Florida: Its History and Diplomacy* (Cleveland, 1906), 217, 225, and Luis de Onís to Carlos Martínez de Yrujo, February 22, 1819, quoted in Brooks, *Adams-Onís Treaty,* 57, 164, 184–91.

52. Both the Adams-Onís Treaty and the John Melish map of 1818 are printed in ibid., 205–14, 216–19.

53. *National Register,* February 27, 1819, quoted ibid., 171. Jed Han-

delsman Shugerman, "The Louisiana Purchase and South Carolina's Reopening of the Slave Trade in 1803," *Jounral of the Early Republic* 22 (2000): 263–90.

## EPILOGUE: A VARIOUS GABBLE OF TONGUES

1. Benjamin H. B. Latrobe, *Impressions Respecting New Orleans by Benjamin Henry Boneval Latrobe: Diary and Sketches, 1818–1820*, ed. Samuel Wilson, Jr. (New York, 1951), 18–19.

2. *Aurora General Advertiser*, May 12, 1804, quoted in Isaac Newton Phelps, *The Iconography of Manhattan Island, 1498–1909* (5 vols., New York, 1915–1928), 5: 1422.

3. Ibid.

4. David Ramsay, *An Oration on the Cession of Louisiana to the United States delivered on the 12th May, 1804, in St. Michael's Church, Charleston, South-Carolina* (Charleston, 1804); Abraham Bishop, *Oration, in honor of the Election of President Jefferson, and the Peaceable acquisition of Louisiana, delivered at the National Festival, in Hartford, on the 11th of May, 1804* (New Haven, 1804); Samuel Brazer, Jr., *Address pronounced at Worcester, on May 12th, 1804, in Commemoration of the Cession of Louisiana to the United States* (Worcester, Mass., 1804); Chapman Johnson, *An Oration, on the late Treaty with France by which Louisiana was acquired, delivered in Staunton on the third of March, 1804* (Staunton, Va., 1804); David Augustus Leonard, *An Oration delivered at Raynham, Massachusetts, Friday, May 11th, 1804, on the late Acquisition of Louisiana at the unanimous request of the Republican citizens of the County of Bristol* (Newport, R. I., 1804); W. M. P., *A Poem on the Acquisition of Louisiana respectfully dedicated to the committee appointed for the celebration of that great event in this city* (Charleston, 1804).

5. Ramsay, *Oration on the Cession of Louisiana*, 4.

6. Bernard DeVoto, "Celebrating 150 Years of the Louisiana Purchase," *Collier's* (March 21, 1953): 44–47. The official estimate of the original area of the Louisiana Purchase in 1803 is 909,130 square miles; E. M. Douglas, comp., *Area of the United States in 1783; Area of the Louisiana Purchase of 1803; Area of the Territories and States Formed Since 1783* (Washington, D.C., 1930), 1–2. According to the U.S. Department of Commerce, the final boundaries drawn in 1818–1819 enclosed an area of 827,192 square miles; *Historical Statistics of the United States* (Washington, D.C., 1975), 428 table J1–2.

7. "From the Trenton *True American*," August 6, 1803, reprinted in the *Maryland Gazette*, September 15, 1803.

8. Suzanne R. Van Meter, "A Noble Bargain: The Louisiana Purchase" (Ph.D. diss., Indiana University, 1977), 253.

9. [Julien Poydras], "Private and Commercial Correspondence" (typescript, Historical Center, Louisiana State Museum, New Orleans), 5, 52, 53–54, 65–74, 83, 101.

10. Thomas Jefferson to Edward Coles, August 25, 1814, in Merrill D. Peterson, ed., *Thomas Jefferson: Writings* (New York, 1984), 1345.

11. Paul F. LaChance, "The 1809 Immigration of Saint-Domingue Refugees to New Orleans: Reception, Integration and Impact," *Louisiana History* 29 (1988): 109–41; Joseph G. Tregle, Jr., *Louisiana in the Age of Jackson: A Clash of Cultures and Personalities* (Baton Rouge, 1999).

12. Latrobe, *Impressions Respecting New Orleans,* 18–19.

## APPENDIX A

From Hunter Miller, *Treaties and Other International Acts of the United States of America,* vol. 2 (Washington, D.C., 1931), 318–48.

1. For the work of these boundary commissioners see John C. Van Horne, "Andrew Ellicott's Mission to Natchez (1796–1798)," *Journal of Mississippi History* 45 (1983): 160–85.

## APPENDIX B

From Miller, *Treaties,* 2: 498–511.

## APPENDIX C

From Miller, *Treaties,* 2: 512–15, 516–28.

## APPENDIX D

1. Paul Leicester Ford, ed., *Works of Thomas Jefferson,* vol. 10 (New York, 1905), 3–12.

2. *Madison Papers: State,* 5: 156.

3. Ford, ed., *Works of Thomas Jefferson,* 10: 4–5n.

4. Ibid., 3–8.

5. *Madison Papers: State,* 5: 340–41.

# Acknowledgments

On January 11, 1997, I was sitting next to Arthur Schlesinger, Jr., on the stage of Le Petit Théâtre du Vieux Carré at a conference honoring the late Bernard DeVoto. As we talked while waiting for the panel to begin, I mentioned that I had been looking for a book about the Louisiana Purchase, had not yet found what I wanted, and was toying with the idea of writing it. "That," Professor Schlesinger said, "would be a good reason for you to write that book." A year later, getting ready for a black-tie New Year's Eve party on the Gulf Coast, I mentioned my conversation with Professor Schlesinger after regaling my friend Robin Moyer with tales of Carlos IV, Maria Luisa, and Manuel Godoy. Robin pulled a twenty from his wallet and said, "I want the first copy of your book." As I accepted his offer I also yielded to Professor Schlesinger's advice. *A Wilderness So Immense* became the book I had been looking for.

That spring, John M. Barry, whose *Rising Tide* had captivated me, graciously commended me to his literary agent—the Sagalyn Agency—where Dan Kois welcomed my phone call. He, Ethan Kline, and Raphael Sagalyn helped me fashion my ideas into a decent proposal. Jane Garrett at Knopf offered a contract, and I began work in earnest—always grateful for her enthusiastic support. Early in 1999 Susan Larson, Patricia Brady, and Sandra Gioia Treadway read my earliest draft chapters and offered their encouragement. To these fine people I am deeply indebted, both for their initial confidence and their subsequent counsel and support.

I am grateful to the Virginia Historical Society for a Mellon Fellowship and the Thomas Jefferson Memorial Foundation for a research fellowship at the International Center for Thomas Jefferson Studies as the book took shape. On a meandering research trip through the Cumberland Gap into Kentucky and Tennessee and then along the Natchez Trace back to the Mississippi River, I benefited from the advice of many librarians, archivists, and curators—especially at the Kentucky Historical Society, the Filson Club, and the Special Collections Department of the University of Kentucky (where Claire McCann led me to the Hunt-Morgan Family Papers). Back in New Orleans, I relied heavily on the collections of the Howard Tilton Library at Tulane and the library holdings (and access to JSTOR) at Loyola University—as well as the Williams Research Center of the Historic New Orleans Collection, the Earl K. Long Library at the University of New Orleans, and the Historical Center of the Louisiana State Museum. After returning to Virginia early in 2000, I became dependent again (both in person and online) upon the Library of Congress, the Alderman Library at the University of Virginia, and especially the Library of Virginia.

Invitations to speak about the Louisiana Purchase at Carthage College, Virginia Tech, the Louisiana State Museum, James Madison University, the Louisiana Association of Museums, the Jefferson Memorial at St. Louis, the University of New Orleans, McNeese State University, and Metairie Park Country Day School—and a paper presented at the Organization of American Historians meeting in St. Louis—afforded me valuable opportunities to test and polish some of the reflections in the epilogue. To all those audiences I am grateful, but especially to those listeners who asked challenging questions.

In the Manuscripts Department of the Library of Congress, Staley Hitchcock and Paul H. Smith, now retired, rummaged their editorial files to help me comprehend the Jay-Gardoqui negotiations, and I am also indebted to Edward James Redmond in the Map Division. Christina Vella offered keen advice on Spanish Louisiana and its historiography, and Gary J. Mannina lent his sharp eye to French details. Lucia C. Stanton and Susan R. Stein graciously responded to questions about Jefferson in Paris and at Monticello, and Diane Swann-Wright's yuletide hospitality was memorable. John P. Kaminski was generous with his unrivaled insights about the Founders and their world, and Barbara J. Oberg helped locate an elusive document in Jefferson's papers at the Library of Congress. Patricia Brady confirmed the translations of some critical documents from the Archivo Históric Nacional. A. Lee Levert tracked down a map that had eluded my grasp, and Warren M. Billings and Mark F. Fernandez guided me past the shoals of Louisiana legal history. Long before reading chapters of my book, Jason Berry in New Orleans, W. W. Abbot in Charlottesville, and James F. Sefcik at the Louisiana State Museum sustained me with their friendship and support. Death claimed both Nelson Peter Ross, my undergraduate mentor, and Donald Haynes, former state librarian of Virginia and director of the Virginia Historical Society, years before I began work on the Louisiana Purchase, but I hope my pages reflect the standards of clarity and precision I learned from them. Close readings by Amy Kukla and Sandra Gioia Treadway—and the skills of Jane Garrett, Sophie Fels, and Rita Madrigal—helped me in that quest.

Amy, Jennifer, and Elizabeth have learned to appreciate their dad and his writing, and to recognize the love that is sometimes hidden beneath his words. For my parents and family, however, mere words are truly inadequate.

# Index

## A NOTE ABOUT THE AUTHOR

A native of small-town Wisconsin, Jon Kukla accepted his B.A. from Carthage College (1970) and his M.A. (1971) and Ph.D. (1980) from the University of Toronto. In Richmond, Virginia, from 1973 through 1990, he directed historical research and publishing at the Library of Virginia and dabbled in documentary editing, historic preservation, archaeology, and public history. He spent the next decade in the French Quarter, as director of the Historic New Orleans Collection from 1992 to 1998, adding museum exhibits, television, and historic building renovation to his bag of tricks. He returned to the Old Dominion in 2000 as director of the Patrick Henry Memorial Foundation. His books, articles, and reviews include "Order and Chaos in Early America" in the *American Historical Review* (1985) and *The Bill of Rights: A Lively Heritage* (1987). Mr. Kukla currently resides at Red Hill plantation, a few hundred yards from Patrick Henry's grave, with his cat, Talleyrand, and Jennifer's rabbit.

## A NOTE ON THE TYPE

This book was set in Caledonia, a face designed by William Addison Dwiggins (1880–1956) for the Mergenthaler Linotype Company in 1939. It belongs to the family of types referred to by printers as "modern," a term used to mark the change in type styles that occurred around 1800. Caledonia was inspired by the Scotch types cast by the Glasgow type-founders Alexander Wilson & Sons circa 1833. However, there is a calligraphic quality about Caledonia that is completely lacking in the Wilson types.

Dwiggins referred to an even earlier typeface for this "liveliness of action"—one cut around 1790 by William Martin for the printer William Bulmer. Caledonia has more weight than the Martin letters, and the bottom finishing strokes of the letters are cut straight across, without brackets, to make sharp angles with the upright stems, thus giving a modern-face appearance.

W. A. Dwiggins began his association with the Mergenthaler Linotype Company in 1929, and over the next twenty-seven years he designed a number of book types, the most interesting of which are Metro, Electra, Caledonia, Eldorado, and Falcon.

COMPOSED BY NORTH MARKET STREET GRAPHICS, LANCASTER, PENNSYLVANIA

PRINTED AND BOUND BY BERRYVILLE GRAPHICS, BERRYVILLE, VIRGINIA

DESIGNED BY ROBERT C. OLSSON